P9-CES-639

THE TEACHER'S TOOLBOX FOR DIFFERENTIATING INSTRUCTION

700 Strategies, Tips, Tools and Techniques

by

Linda Tilton

with illustrations by Dana Hanson

Covington Cove Publications
Shorewood, Minnesota

THE TEACHER'S TOOLBOX FOR DIFFERENTIATING INSTRUCTION © copyright 2003 by Linda Tilton. All rights reserved. With the exception of pages indicated as "reproducible," no part of this book may be reproduced in any form whatsoever, by photography or xerography or by any other means, by broadcast or transmission, by translation into any kind of language, nor by recording electronically or otherwise, without permission in writing from the author, except by a reviewer, who may quote brief passages in critical articles or reviews. Reproducible pages may be photocopied for classroom use only; all other restraints on reproduction and distribution as described above remain in effect.

ISBN 0-9653529-7-8

Library of Congress Catalog Number: 2002114903

Cover and interior design by Mori Studio

Printed in the United States of America

First Printing: January 2003

07 06 05 04 03   6 5 4 3 2 1

to order, or to contact Linda Tilton for staff development:
Covington Cove Publications
5620 Covington Road
Shorewood, Minnesota 55331
1-888-LEARN-11
www.LindaTilton.com
e-mail: lindtilton@aol.com

To Louis, Brian, Sean, Christopher and Annemarie

I love you to the moon and back . . .

ACKNOWLEDGMENTS

To all of the dedicated teachers who have modeled, shared and taught me so many ideas to help students succeed, thank you. You have inspired me with your insight, your enthusiasm and your love of education.

I feel tremendous gratitude to the following individuals who, in addition to my husband and children, have helped me in so many ways:

Dana Hanson for sharing her extraordinary talent through her whimsical artwork;

Jack Caravela at Mori Studio for his considerable expertise in book design;

Milt Adams at Beaver's Pond Press for his knowledge and guidance as a mentor;

Robert and Dorothy Kollitz, my parents, for their encouragement and support;

Jayne Buscho, author of *Pig Tales and Humpback Whales* for "Peculiar Primitive Platypus;" and

Robert Ricken, author of *Love Me When I'm Most Unlovable* for his poem about everyone's favorite teacher.

"There are two ways to live your life. One is though nothing is a miracle. The other is as though everything is a miracle."

–Albert Einstein

LETTER FROM THE AUTHOR

Writing *The Teacher's Toolbox for Differentiating Instruction* was an absolute joy! It truly is a culmination of over 30 years in the field of education.

During my career, I have been an English teacher at the middle and high school levels, a reading teacher, and a special educator at all grade levels. My current role in staff development takes me into schools and classrooms all over the country where I have the privilege of meeting thousands of dedicated teachers.

Every idea suggested in *The Teacher's Toolbox for Differentiating Instruction* comes from real classrooms in the real world. Every idea is teacher-tested! Every strategy is one that I have used successfully with my own students or is one that another teacher has suggested and has enthusiastically endorsed. These are ideas that work.

In selecting strategies to include, I used the following criteria.

The strategy, tip, tool or technique must be:

- Useful in differentiating instruction for all learners
- Highly practical for the general classroom
- Results-driven
- Focused on improving learning and achievement
- Attuned to student readiness, level, and learning style
- Simple to implement
- Inexpensive and cost effective
- Teacher-tested with a proven track record
- Time-efficient for the teacher
- Applicable for both general education and special education teachers
- Effective in recognizing and celebrating individual differences

My hope is that you will use these strategies, tips, tools and techniques to enhance your existing curriculum. Make the resource come alive. Write notes in the margins. Copy the reproducible pages. Highlight and star your favorite "keepers." Change and adapt these ideas to suit your content and grade level. Pick and choose strategies that will move your students to the next level. Most of all, enjoy your students and enjoy teaching.

Thank you for the countless ways you make a difference in the lives of children. Everyone says, "Teachers change lives!" Never doubt that you do.

–Linda Tilton

LIST OF CHAPTERS

TABLE OF CONTENTS

The Teacher's Toolbox for Differentiating Instruction © Linda Tilton 1-888-LEARN-11

LIST OF REPRODUCIBLE PAGES

INTRODUCTION

There is always one moment in childhood when the door opens and lets the future in.

–Graham Greene

Welcome to a celebration of practical ideas for today's classroom! The purpose is to provide you with highly effective strategies, tips, tools and techniques to use in teaching your own content in a variety of ways. Weave these ideas into the fabric of your curriculum as you differentiate instruction for all learners.

Each year, each semester, new students bring different needs to the classroom. Students do not all learn in the same way. As the analogy goes, we cannot simply alter the same suit of clothes. One suit will not fit everybody. We can use the same fabric but how we style it, shape it, cut it and structure it will become the framework of a challenging and rigorous curriculum.

The strategies suggested in *The Teacher's Toolbox for Differentiating Instruction* are not meant to supplant your curriculum or add new concepts. Instead, these strategies can help you personalize your existing content by offering a variety of options, choices and tools to reach two key goals of high standards and high expectations for all students.

An underlying concept throughout this resource focuses on *keeping the content but changing the delivery*. Our role as educators is to continually try proven, practical approaches with each student until we discover what works. Students may learn in different ways, but *all students can learn*.

HOW TO USE THIS BOOK

It is designed for all school staff grades K–12.

- New teachers will find hundreds of ideas all in one place.

- Experienced teachers will discover fresh ideas to add to their repertoire of teaching techniques.

- Both general education teachers and special education staff will find highly effective strategies, tips, tools and techniques to use in a variety of classroom settings including the co-taught classroom.

- Paraprofessionals will find concrete ideas to help them as they support students every day in the classroom.

- Administrators will find specific suggestions for encouraging excellence by providing the support needed for teachers and students to do their best.
- Parents will also find practical strategies to help their children at home with organizational skills, tools for review and strategies to reinforce learning.

THE LIST OF CHAPTERS AND TABLE OF CONTENTS

The List of Chapters provides a thumbnail description of content for each chapter. The Table of Contents that follows is extensive, detailed and easy to use. It is organized so that all of the strategies on one topic will be at your fingertips, ready for quick reference. You will find:

- 13 chapters divided by topics
- categories within each chapter
- subheadings listing major strategies, tips, tools and techniques
- approximate grade levels for use

Chapters 1 through 11 focus on effective practices specifically for students. These are ideas to *take back and use immediately* within the framework of your curriculum. The last two chapters focus on teachers and administrators working together for student success. Chapter 12 highlights strategies for collaborating and co-teaching effectively. Chapter 13 describes how administrative support can provide what teachers want and need to help students succeed.

For All Students

The strategies suggested apply to a wide range of students because our classrooms today are filled with students at all levels. We have students with identified special needs, students "falling through the cracks," high-potential students, students on 504 Plans, and students in the middle. Everyone counts. As teachers, we must accept our students as they are and move them forward in the learning process.

For All Grade Levels

Strategies are included for all grade levels. Next to each tip, tool or technique is the general level of application. It is approximate. Many strategies can be easily adapted for a broad range of levels. You may discover that an idea listed for students in the lower grades may work very well for older students in a different context.

Across Content Areas

The strategies also apply across content areas. As you think about a specific strategy, consider how it could be used in a variety of subject areas. The strategy itself may illustrate a general concept such as the value of "hands-on" learning. Consider how kinesthetic learners in your classroom could benefit from the same focus.

Large Group, Small Group and Individual Use

You will find ideas that fit a range of classroom configurations. Some ideas can be used with the whole class. Others lend themselves to group work within the class or individual use.

FEATURES TO HELP YOU

Reproducible Pages

40 pages are designed for you to copy and use with your students immediately. The icon showing two overlapping pages like this indicates pages that can be reproduced.

☞ Practical Pointers:

These indicate "How To" tips in using the strategy effectively. A hand and dots indicate these.

O⸗ KEY IDEAS

These are critical thoughts focusing on why the concept is important for your students. A key in a gray box indicates a Key Idea.

Single-Column Format

Strategies follow one after the other in a single column format to make it easy to flag favorites or write notes in the margins.

PICK AND CHOOSE! CHANGE AND ADAPT!

Frequently during staff development, a teacher will come up to me and say, "When you suggested that idea, I starting thinking that I would use it with my students but I might try it this way." Then I would hear an excellent adaptation that would be ideal for that teacher in that classroom.

No single strategy will work for every single student, every time, in every situation. No one strategy is intended to be used at the exclusion of many other strategies. Just as we have all kinds of students, we need all kinds of ideas. Have fun with these strategies. Be creative. Adjust them for your students in your classroom.

The process of differentiating instruction recognizes that the sky is *not* the limit for our students. Key concepts, critical vocabulary, outcomes and results need to be established and determined first. Then how students demonstrate what they need to know and do can be accomplished in a variety of ways. *The Teacher's Toolbox for Differentiating Instruction* provides over 700 strategies to accomplish that goal.

I wanted to thank you,

   visit you,

   write you,

      and show you my appreciation

      for the rest of my life.

As years passed I realized

      you'd know that I love you,

      and can find my own way

         because of you.

But . . . I'll always remember

   my favorite teacher.

Everyone does.

   —Robert Ricken

From *Love Me When I'm Most Unlovable—The Middle School Years.* Used by permission of Robert Ricken. For information concerning the National Association of Secondary School Principals (NASSP) services and/or programs, please call (703) 860-0200 or visit www.principals.org

TAMING THE PAPER MONSTER

Research shows that the average person spends 150 hours each year looking for misplaced items . . .

—Barbara Hemphill, Time Management Expert

FIRST THINGS FIRST! GETTING STUDENTS ORGANIZED!

How many of you have disorganized students? Whether you are teaching first grade, eighth grade English or tenth grade biology, you face students who do not finish work, do not get projects in on time, can't find things, can't remember, left it at home, left it on the bus or threw it out by mistake. I could go on and on—so could you!

A critical component of school success lies in organizational skills. The late Erma Bombeck loved to accuse the washing machine of eating socks. At school socks may not be a problem but how many of you have come into contact with homework-eating backpacks? Students' lockers can be an even bigger culprit.

One parent of a middle school son told me that her family began missing jackets. A variety of jackets were unaccounted for and no one seemed to know what happened to them. When her high school son received a bill for his missing soccer team jacket, the whole family was in an uproar. Finally, she accompanied her seventh grade son to his locker after school one day. What do you think they found? The question is *how many* jackets do you think they found? There were *six*—count them—*six jackets piled in the bottom of the locker.* Yes, the soccer jacket was there too.

The explanation was simple. A reasonable guess might be that the weather was cool in the morning and warmer in the afternoon. The real reason was that Michael was afraid that he might miss the bus after school. In his hurry, he often bypassed his locker and his jacket. Of course, the next chilly morning, he had to find a replacement jacket.

The solution was simple. Michael needed to learn how to organize his materials so that he could leave his last class with enough time to stop at the locker and still make the bus.

If the average person spends about 150 hours each year looking for lost items and papers, think about some of our students. Can you even imagine how many hours each school year some students devote to searching for assignments, books, notes, clothing and other items? Can you imagine how many of these searches are fruitless? It boggles the mind. If those 150 hours could be spent *learning* rather than *looking*, our students would be far ahead academically. The ability to organize is a life skill. If organizational skills are easy for you, count yourself lucky. Many of us as adults might describe ourselves as a work in progress! How many of us have boxes of family photos, for example, that we have been planning to arrange in albums? The planning process has been in the works for years! I speak from experience here.

Like photo albums, baby books are another case in point. My four children's baby books never went much beyond the footprint and a lock of hair from "Baby's First Haircut." I do have boxes, though, filled with school papers and projects. I have even purchased four large scrapbooks that I hope to fill soon . . .

How many of us have junk drawers where we have placed things "just for now"? How many of us cannot find things that we stashed somewhere "in case we would ever need them . . ." How many of us use a desk as a landing place but find it too crowded to use as a work space? If you can relate, you probably have a great deal of empathy for some of our students.

Just as strong organization skills are "natural" for some adults and are more difficult for others, the same is true for our students. Let's get our students organized! They need help. They need ideas that work. They need models to follow. They need simple, workable, sensible solutions to tame the Paper Monster. I have a dream and that dream is that in any classroom on any day, every paper has a home. In my dream, there are no loose papers!

O⌐ᴈ KEY IDEA

The most important rule of paper organization is "No loose papers!"

Loose papers confuse, distract and overwhelm the student. When it comes to papers and materials, there are three key words to teach our students: Organize! Organize! Organize! In "Taming the Paper Monster," I've listed dozens of strategies, tips, tools, and techniques to help students manage, reduce, and organize papers. These ideas can be adapted for a variety of grade levels and subject areas. You will find ideas in nine different categories that follow spanning everything from where to put paper, how to file it, how to manage work-space to organizing a locker. Pick and choose. See which ideas appeal to you and your students!

- Places for Papers
- Assignment Systems
- Filing Techniques
- Save a Tree
- Calendar Tools
- Communication Tools
- Workspace Tips
- Paper at Home
- Locker Logistics

The Teacher's Toolbox for Differentiating Instruction © Linda Tilton 1-888-LEARN-11

PLACES FOR PAPERS

Accordion File

Grades 4–12

The first one, the accordion file, is an excellent tool for all grade levels but is especially applicable for middle and high school students. Sturdy plastic expandable files are available at discount and office supply stores. They come with a variety of divisions. For middle and high school, six pockets are handy. Every pocket has a class name on top so that every paper has a "home." The concept is simple and easy to implement. My own daughter who is a junior in high school finally adopted the accordion file approach and loves it.

Think about math. Every math paper, worksheet, assignment list, review page, *anything related to math* goes into that math pocket. Retrieval is easy later when students know where to look.

☞ **The Practical Pointer:**

Look for the plastic accordion files that have pockets in front to hold compact disks and floppy disks. Encourage students to label pockets in the same order as the student attends class during the day.

While the accordion file can be an effective organizer for the whole class, an individual student can use it without teacher input and follow-through. Some students may need guidance periodically in deciding what to keep, what to throw out, when and where to store papers that will be needed later. Remind them that expanding the accordion beyond capacity defeats the purpose.

One parent told me that her children, both of whom had significant learning disabilities, found this tool to be the single most effective organizational strategy in high school. Both successfully managed their secondary classes by always carrying their accordion files with them wherever they went.

☞ **The Practical Pointer for Parents:**

The accordion file with twelve pockets makes an excellent storage container for parents to create a *school file* for each child in the family. It becomes the place to save report cards, portfolio summaries, awards and standardized test scores for each grade from first through high school graduation.

KEY IDEA

I have discovered that students will be more inclined to use an accordion file when they see a parent using one for any purpose.

Three-Ring Binder

Grades 3–12

In addition to the accordion folder, another option for managing papers is the three-ring binder. There are many different ways to organize a binder depending on its use. One teacher may require it for just one subject, dividing sections into categories such as vocabulary, notes, study guides, key points and review.

It can also be used very effectively for all subject areas with one section per class. What is described here in this section is a composite of several approaches. In my own classroom experience and in many other classrooms where I have visited, I have found that the three-ring binder works best when it contains four components:

- sections
- dividers with pockets
- a plastic pouch
- calendar

SECTIONS

Like the accordion file, there is a separate section for each class. Blank paper, lined paper or graph paper is stored as needed in each section. The three-ring notebook has the clear advantage of securely binding each page in each section. All handouts, worksheets and study guides do need to be three-hole punched. I have had students stash papers from every class in the *front* of the three-ring binder because they didn't have time to punch the holes. Using prepunched paper for materials saves a lot of class time and aggravation. Sometimes the biggest problem is the noise created by 25–30 students punching holes in papers, and then snapping the binder open and closed during class. In fact, this noise was enough for one teacher to give up on the idea. Don't give up too soon.

☞ **The Practical Pointer:**
Set limits and specify when binders can be opened and closed.

DIVIDERS WITH POCKETS

Section dividers with pockets on both sides prevent loose papers. The front pocket has one purpose and one purpose only: *Papers to be turned in go here.* Class notes, study guides and handouts *do not* belong here *ever.* These materials are three-hole punched and are added to the content section.

The other side of the section divider also has a clear purpose: *The weekly syllabus goes here.* (See **Peek-at-the-Week** in the following section.) Only the current the syllabus belongs in this pocket.

With this very simple system, students always have the assignment calendar for the week and they know where it is. They also know where to put and retrieve homework, making it accessible and ready at the beginning of class. One social studies teacher commented that this system made a noticeable difference for his students both in knowing what was expected as well as getting assignments completed and turned in on time.

A PLASTIC POUCH

The three-ring binder typically allows space for the plastic pencil pouch that is also three-hole punched. Many are large enough to hold a calculator, markers, a highlighter, protractor, pens and pencils. "I forgot a pencil!" becomes a less frequent problem when the pouch is attached in the notebook. Students can tape a small list to the plastic pouch listing all the tools that they need. They can get in the habit of taking frequent inventory.

CALENDAR

The calendar doubles as the assignment notebook and is also three-hole punched. This is located in the front of the binder just behind the plastic pouch. (See **The Assignment Notebook** and **N-A-T** strategies described later in this chapter.)

☞ **The Practical Pointer:**
Students respond best when they learn that "This is the way we do things in this school or department or grade level."

⚷ KEY IDEA

When implementation is broad, compliance is best.

When this is a school-wide system or department-wide requirement or grade level approach, it is easier to manage. Students see other students carrying binders and are reminded to make sure they have theirs. However, I have used the three-ring notebook effectively on an individual basis when it was not a school-wide practice.

To make this paper management system work on a large scale takes true commitment from teachers. It should be noted that the three-ring binder requires some effort and a willingness to stick with it while students adjust to the process. It is essential that all teachers involved insist that their students bring their binders to class daily and use them.

It also takes some effort to maintain the system on an ongoing basis by allowing time occasionally to teach students how to sort through old materials. This is not different from using the accordion file. Periodically, some materials can be removed and filed elsewhere for later review while other materials can be discarded. Many students need assistance differentiating between the two.

O—⟁ KEY IDEA

Ultimately, the best organizational system for any student is the one that the student will actually use. Both the three-ring binder and the accordion file mentioned previously help students organize their materials. One is not better than the other; they are simply different. A combination of both tools is still another option.

Students need to see the value of consistently using a system that will help them store and find materials. Once they experience success and discover that being organized can make life easier, students are enthusiastic.

Four-Pocket Folders

Grades 2–12

For years, I used the most basic two-pocket folder system with elementary students to mange the paper flow. The left pocket held study guides and worksheets labeled *DO*. When finished, completed materials were transferred to the right hand pocket marked *DONE*. Completed papers were then turned in. This worked fairly well for many students.

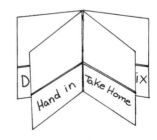

While I was visiting a classroom, I noticed that a teacher had improved the system. Each student had two pocket folders that had been stapled together in the crease with a saddle stapler. This created *four* pockets. In the ongoing goal of eliminating loose papers, this teacher discovered that the extra pockets served two needs.

- Where could students put materials that were finished but needed CORRECTIONS?

- Where could students place materials that were ready to TAKE HOME?

The four-pocket folder was born! Every paper had a "home" at last. The four pockets were labeled:

Do

Fix

Turn In

Take Home

I liked the concept and applied the same principle to creative writing folders used by middle school and high school students. The four pockets were labeled:

Writing Ideas

Rough Draft

Final Copy

Hand In

No loose papers! Success!

In and Out Folders

Grades 1–5

Two manila folders with the sides taped closed and the top open make excellent tools for holding paper. Tape one folder vertically to each side of the desk. The folder hanging downward from the right side has a large sign that says "IN" and the folder taped to the left says "OUT."

When a student receives a new study guide, worksheet or has work in progress, it is stored in the IN folder. Work that is completed and is ready to turn in, it goes into the OUT folder. There is a sense of accomplishment as the student moves work from IN to OUT, and the stored folders are out of the way of the workspace.

ASSIGNMENT SYSTEMS

Assignment Notebook

Grades K-12

Many schools initiate the concept of the assignment notebook or planner with students as early as kindergarten. Commercial assignment notebooks are frequently designated by three different grade groupings: grades K–2, grades 3–8 and grades 9–12. Look at several to see which one most closely meets the needs of your students. Some companies that sell planners will create a calendar specifically for your school listing your activities, conference days, sports and other events. For middle school students, look for planners that include extras such as hall passes, a limited number of "No Homework" tickets, useful study tips and reference tools including multiplication grids.

Many planners provide a space each day for parent signature and comments. In many schools, planners truly become the communication vehicle between home and school.

☞ **The Practical Pointer:**
Require students to carry their planners to every class, whether or not they think that they will "need them." They will have their planners and learn to rely on them.

N-A-T

Grades 4–12

There is a difference between *owning* an assignment notebook and *using* it effectively or even using it at all! Even with instruction, some students struggle with daily use. As a parent of four children who are now in high school and college, I remember a common scenario involving assignment notebooks that occurred at our house more than once. It would be homework time and one child would announce, "I can't do my math!" "And why not?" I would inquire.

Now, what would you guess was the most common reason I heard for this sad tale of woe? Why would a child who *has* an assignment notebook, *uses* an assignment notebook, *understands* the math most of the time, still *not* be able to do the math homework? You guessed it.

"I forgot my book!"

Does that sound familiar? The only solution on a night like that was to borrow a book from a neighbor.

There is, though, a simple solution to teach your students today and avoid this common problem. Along the way, my oldest son's social studies teacher taught him the **N-A-T** strategy. He taught me and I've passed it on to so many teachers because it works.

The **N-A-T** acronym teaches students how to record assignments in their planners a useful way. The **N-A-T** strategy is simple.

- **N** stands for **Need.** The first thing to write at the top of the assignment notebook in the space for each class is what is needed at home: math book, green folder, study guide or yellow notebook, for example.

- **A** refers to the **Assignment.** In short, simple terms, what is the task? State the assignment. It may be:

  Read pp. 56–60, or

  Do problems 1–7 on p. 34, or

  Answer study guide questions 1–10

Students need tips on how to be brief but include all the needed information.

- **T** is the **Turn in** date. When is this assignment due to be turned in, completed or assessed?

  Turn in tomorrow

  Turn in Jan 21

  Turn in Friday, March 10

This helps students in planning how to manage time and coordinate assignments from other classes.

The payoff: Standing at the locker at the end of the day, the student can quickly check the assignment notebook to see what to bring home, what to do and when.

☞ **The Practical Pointer:**

As a motivator, encourage the student to *highlight the box in green* when the assignment has been completed. The assignment is still legible if the student needs to refer to it later. Then, at the end of the week, any incomplete assignments are *highlighted in yellow* as a reminder.

⊶ KEY IDEA

It takes 21 days of doing something consistently to form a habit. Parent and teacher support are essential to implement the N-A-T strategy. It is well worth the effort.

Subject _____

N̶o̶:

A:

t:

Subject _____

N̶o̶:

A:

t:

Subject _____

N̶o̶:

A:

t:

Subject _____

N̶o̶:

A:

t:

Subject _____

N̶o̶:

A:

t:

Subject _____

N̶o̶:

A:

t:

Subject _____

N̶o̶:

A:

t:

Subject _____

N̶o̶:

A:

t:

The Teacher's Toolbox for Differentiating Instruction © Linda Tilton 1-888-LEARN-11

FILING TECHNIQUES

File Drawer at Home

Grades 6–12

At the end of a unit of study, the immediate use for study guides and notes may be finished but chances are that these materials will be needed later for a final exam or standardized test. Students need a simple system to store class notes, study guides, vocabulary cards and other information from each unit. A file drawer at home can be as simple as a cardboard box labeled "Math First Quarter" or "Social Studies Unit One: The Thirteen Colonies."

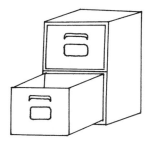

Hanging folders are inexpensive and can be used to separate materials by courses. The actual folders come in a rainbow of colors and are helpful in identifying different topics.

While a cardboard box is adequate for the purpose, a two-drawer metal file cabinet is a worthwhile investment that can be used throughout middle school and high school to hold materials from all classes. Two good sources for reasonably priced "used" file cabinets are garage sales and office supply stores.

Classroom Files

Grades 6–12

A possible alternative to home storage is filing student notes in the classroom itself. When space allows, some teachers provide designated file drawers where all students can keep notes from completed units to retrieve later for year-end review and assessments.

KEY IDEA

Information becomes outdated very quickly. Papers and notes must be current to be useful. Always ask the questions: How long should these papers and notes be stored? Will they be needed again? When?

It is interesting that in many offices there is a rule of thumb about items stored in filing cabinets. Fully 80 percent of what is filed will never be looked at again. As teachers, we can help our students decide what needs to be saved, where to put it, and how to label it so that they will be able to retrieve it when they need it.

Color-Code It!

Grades 6–12

When filing student notes in the classroom, a classwide color-coding storage system can be implemented. For example, all folders from Unit One are highlighted in yellow along the edge. Subsequent units can be color-coded simply by marking the tab with different colors. When students need to refer to notes from previous chapters, the notes are easy to find.

Cereal Box Portfolio

Grades K-4

An inexpensive and effective tool for storing portfolio papers is this idea that I observed in a fourth grade classroom. Each student brought a school picture or other personal photo and an empty cereal box. The cereal box lid was removed and the photo was glued onto the narrow side of the box.

This created a three-inch wide "folder" to store selected papers for a portfolio. The row of boxes fit easily on a classroom shelf, narrow side out. When students selected a "Keeper" for their personal portfolio, they tilted their box forward and slipped it inside. Students also liked selecting a photo to personalize their box. Materials for the portfolio stayed neat and were easy to sort later.

The Idea Grabber

Grade 4–12

How often do you think of an idea in the midst of doing something else? Do you ever have a brilliant brainstorm in the middle of the night? Do you find yourself scribbling a wonderful idea on the newspaper or corner of an advertisement? The thoughts may be worth saving but the paper trail is often hard to follow.

Students experience the same problem. A simple solution is to encourage them to keep a single, small notebook to record these thoughts and ideas. A question about an assignment, a reminder about an activity after school, an idea for a short story and other fleeting thoughts can be jotted down in one place. I save small pads of paper from hotel rooms and businesses for this purpose. The size is handy and when the pages are used up and I have dealt with the information, I just start a new one.

During class, the **Idea Grabber** can be close at hand on the corner of the desk. It can travel in a backpack and be kept on the table as the student does homework. The purpose of the **Idea Grabber** is to reduce loose paper and the frustration of lost information. A more detailed version might include sections for quick reference, such as writing ideas, phone numbers and birthdays. Sticky notes and Hefty Tabs™ make handy dividers.

This is different from the assignment notebook. As the name suggests, it is a spot to grab and write a fleeting idea in a place where it can be located later.

SAVE A TREE

Download Now

Grades 6–12

The volume of paper that students deal with every day can be reduced by increased use of the computer. More and more teachers are providing homework assignments, class notes and chapter outlines via e-mail attachments that students may or may not choose to download. In some situations, it is enough to study the content on the computer monitor and save it. Students can be selective in the material that they download and make hard copies of only what is needed.

PDA

Grades 9–12

As the cost of the palm-sized computer organizer decreases, more and more students will also have this option to manage and reduce paper. Some relatively inexpensive models are adequate for the organizational needs of students. Using a calendar, receiving reminder notices of due dates, taking class notes, receiving and sending text messages on the PDA all help to tame the Paper Monster.

CALENDAR TOOLS

Peek at the Week

Grades K-12

All students and parents benefit from receiving a weekly syllabus or "Peek at the Week." Adjusted for each grade level, it lists all assignments, library days, due dates for projects, field trip information and notices about saving lids from orange juice cans. It is not a lesson plan. Changes can always be made as needed.

☞ **The Practical Pointer:**
When each student receives *two* copies of the "Peek at the Week," one can be posted on the refrigerator at home and a second can be kept at school. Some middle and high

school students find it helpful to post one copy on the inside of their lockers. Needless to say, it may be wise to make a few extra copies. Students with organizational difficulties may need a third one by Wednesday . . .

The Family Calendar

Grades K-12

Teachers may want to pass this suggestion along to parents as another way to reduce paper and help our students become better organized. Eliminate paper calendars for each individual at home in favor of one large erasable monthly calendar for the whole family. Each person has a dry erase marker in a different color to color-code activities. Placed on the wall in a high traffic area, it is easy for both children and parents to see at a glance what is happening each day.

☞ **The Practical Pointer:**

Every Sunday night, the family can meet *briefly* around the kitchen table to look at the calendar and talk about the new week. Any conflicting activities or changes to the calendar can be made. These few minutes can make the week go much more smoothly.

Web Site Calendars

Grades K-12

In many schools, the Web site calendar is becoming an essential vehicle in improving communication between home and school. A large number of school districts now have district-wide Web sites with home pages for each teacher. Important dates and activities are listed and updated weekly.

This can greatly reduce the quantity of paper messages generated by schools. In education, we are a long way from becoming paperless, but some businesses are at that point. One small-business owner commented to me, "We do not have a pencil in our office. We don't need one. We don't use paper. Everything is on the computer." There is no Paper Monster in the vicinity!

O─ KEY IDEA

If your school district has not surveyed parents recently about accessibility to the Web, it would be helpful to do so. The information gained from a brief survey would enable the district to study the possibility of increasing communication to parents through the Internet. When

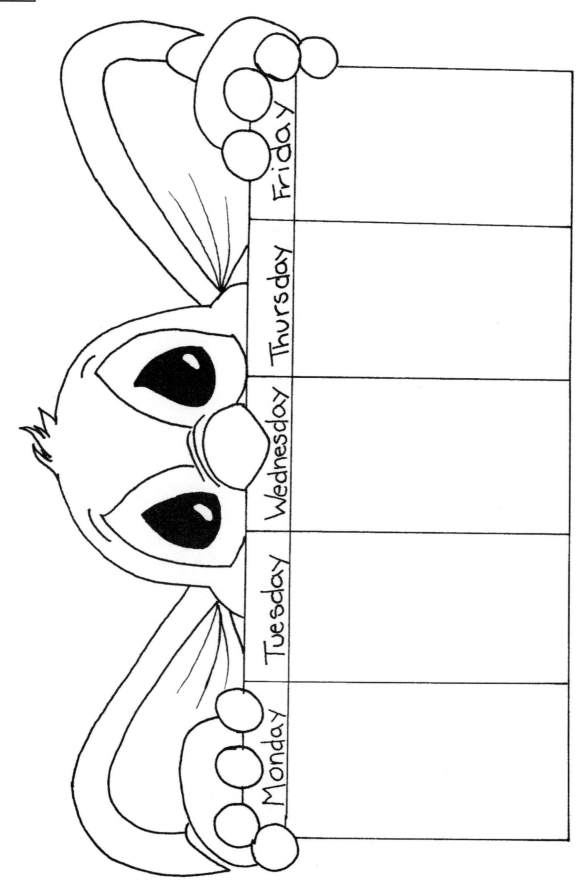

combining access to the Internet both at home and in the workplace, there may be a very high percentage of parents who could be reached electronically. It is fast, direct and could reduce the need for paper. However, you will need to provide information by U.S. mail or handout to those parents who need or prefer that option.

COMMUNICATION TOOLS

The Monday Envelope or The Friday Folder

Grades K-6

Too often at the elementary level, communication from school to home and back again is in the form of a paper trail that is sporadic and confusing. The Paper Monster rears its head almost daily. Flyers for community events, information on parent conferences, permission slips for field trips, work-sheets and homework all create a steady stream of papers. Many end up scrunched in a backpack, lost in a desk and, ultimately, miss the destination at either end.

An effective strategy to eliminate the daily paper flow is to use just one weekly vehicle that carries all papers from school to home and back. Parents know ahead of time when to expect and watch for this envelope or folder. Parents depend it for all routine communication, returned papers, and, when necessary, materials that require a parent signature.

Each student has a personal "mailbox" where papers are collected throughout the week. These papers will go into the envelope or folder. Volunteers or students themselves can create an assembly line for filling the folders on the designated day. The **Peek at the Week**, described earlier in this chapter, completes the packet.

☞ **The Practical Pointer:**
Whether Monday or Friday is selected, consistently send all informational materials and returned classwork home on this same day. To simplify the management end, every student is given an individual number in the classroom. This number is useful in many ways and is especially helpful in using a filing system for the Monday Envelopes or Friday Folders when they are returned. Storage is by number in a cardboard box. Any gap in sequence easily identifies a missing envelope or folder.

Which day works best for this communication vehicle? There are advantages to both. As long as it is consistent, either day can work. The Monday Envelope, as the name suggests, goes out every Monday and is returned to school every Tuesday. The Friday Folder is the same concept on Friday with the return on the following Monday. Both systems operate virtually the same way.

Monday has a distinct advantage in that students and parents are already engaged in a new week. Teachers report that on Monday everyone is more in tune with what will occur during the next several days. Compared to Friday, Monday can be a calmer night at home. The school routine is in place. Parents may have more time to look over papers and read flyers. Since field trip forms and other forms requiring a parent signature are due back the very next day, teachers report high compliance on Mondays. Information on large projects can be provided a week ahead, if necessary.

On the other hand, using Friday has the advantage of providing more time for next week's project, more time to study a new spelling list and more time to pick up any supplies needed for the social studies diorama.

The biggest disadvantage of the Friday Folder is that by then many students and parents say "Whew!" and park the backpack until Sunday night. By then, parents often have less time to read papers and flyers or pick up tag board at the discount store. In some families, Fridays can also be a day of transition. A child may leave the home of one parent to spend the weekend with the other parent. Materials, books and papers can be left behind or misplaced during the move.

O—⊼ KEY IDEA

Teachers like the weekly folder and parents rely on it. Communication improves dramatically and the Paper Monster ceases its roar. It is easy to implement schoolwide. In fact, compliance is best when it is part of the elementary school climate. Everyone understands, "This is the way we do things here at Clear Springs School." Whatever appeals to you, keep it simple and be consistent.

In my own children's elementary school, the Monday Folder was the routine throughout K–6 every Monday, every year, every grade level. As a parent of more than one child at that school, it was a system that was much appreciated.

This strategy also lends itself to including a *Tip of the Week* in reading or math for parents to use in helping their children at home.

In either case, the procedure for the Monday Envelope or Friday Folder is to return it the following school day. As a reward, some teachers stamp the date on the outside of the envelope or folder. Other teachers may put a small sticker on the outside. In some classrooms, the teacher does not handle the return; students simply file their folders in the designated location.

 ☞ **The Practical Pointer:**

To further tame the Paper Monster on the home front and save paper, flyers about community events and school functions are disseminated *only through the oldest child* in the family attending that school. At the beginning of the school year, teachers place an asterisk on the class list next to the name of the oldest child.

Raising the Flag

Grades K-4

How often have field trip permission slips, assessment information and other important pieces of communication grown old in a backpack while a parent was unaware that they were there?

Here is a quick and simple solution for school-to-home communication that I observed in an elementary classroom. The teacher used a bright piece of ribbon, approximately six inches long that was stapled to important piece of paper. On the end of the ribbon was a small triangular paper flag that students cut from a scrap of construction paper and stapled to the ribbon.

At the end of the day, the paper was positioned in the backpack so that the colorful flag and ribbon stuck out. At home, seeing the flag hanging from the backpack reminded both the student and parent: *Read This Tonight!*

Paperless Reminder

Grades K-5

Have a **Reminder!** stamp made at your local business store. To remind students to bring, to do, to tell, to study, to remember anything at all, just stamp their hands with the ink stamp. They are sure to notice some time that night at home and follow through.

Daily Announcements

Grades K-12

Some schools are controlling the Paper Monster and improving communication at the same time by offering parents an important e-mail option. Parents can receive an e-mail version of the same Daily Announcements that are read to students over the public address system at school. The e-mail is further tailored by grade level so that parents receive only those announcements that are applicable to their children's grade levels.

☞ **The Practical Pointer:**

Some parents elect to receive this information at work so they have the information before arriving at home.

 KEY IDEA

E-mail at the workplace can be the fastest means of reaching many parents in the event of any emergency including school closings due to severe weather.

Paper Clip Tip

Grades K-5

Another tool to tease the memory is a paper clip. Ask any student who wants a quick reminder to stick a clip on a collar, a sleeve or pocket. Students will notice the paper clip at home and it acts like the old string around a finger. Mention this tool to parents so that they will also watch for the paper clip and ask about it.

WORKSPACE TIPS

Clear the Workspace

Grades 1–12

Think now about the student's workspace at school or at home. Only what student is working on *at that time* should be visible. Anything else distracts. Encourage the student to remove books and papers from other subjects not related to the immediate task. Put materials that are not needed under the desk or on a shelf.

At home, if a student is doing homework at the kitchen table, move everything else to the far side or, if possible, clear the table completely. Reducing clutter reduces stress making the immediate task seem more manageable. It also gives the student a feeling of being in control of the task at hand rather than being overwhelmed by too much at once.

Thinking Outside the Desk!

Grades K-6

Just as some families outgrow their homes and need an addition, there are always a few elementary students who need an addition to their desks to manage the Paper Monster! I have encouraged some students who struggle with paper management to use a cardboard box such as a shoebox to contain overflow from the desk. It is stored in a designated location in a nearby bookcase. Reducing what is kept in the desk makes neatness manageable and materials easier to locate.

Bucket Brigade

Grades 1–5

"What are those ice cream pails doing hanging under every chair?" ask visitors in one Minnesota elementary school. The response is often an invitation to look inside. Students store anything that may not fit easily in their desks. This might include books that they are reading, lunches, folders or loose papers.

One teacher commented, "It is an inexpensive way to use space that is close, convenient and often unused. Each student's bucket will resemble the inside of the desk. Some will be well organized in the extended space and others will be, in a word, messy.

☞ **The Practical Pointer:**
Designate a day each month to take a few minutes to empty the buckets to keep them from overflowing with lost papers and overdue library books.

Becoming Pile Free

Grades 6–12

Teach students to know "where it goes" and put it there. Encourage them to avoid the "pile" syndrome of papers stacking up with nowhere to go. Piles of papers can be an indicator that the Paper Monster is taking over. Have you ever had so many different piles on your own desk as a teacher that you felt immobilized? For our students, the biggest problem is that papers tend to get lost in piles. You know the old saying about not seeing the forest for the trees . . .

Touch It Once

Grades 6–12

Another tip for avoiding piles of papers everywhere is to teach students a basic rule of organization—touch it once. A literal interpretation is not realistic when we are talking about homework and class assignments.

I tell students that when a material such as a study guide is handed out during class, "Touch this *once* now as you put it where it belongs. The next time you touch it is the time you are *working on it*. Avoid shuffling it around in your locker or in your backpack. Your *final touch* is when you are handing it in!"

AT HOME

Bulletin Board

Grades 4–12

A way to tame the Paper Monster at home is the traditional corkboard bulletin board. Where does the student post date-due slips from the library, notices about events, field trip reminders, important receipts and other must-save flyers? A bulletin board, located in prominent place, is one of the simplest paper management tools.

The bulletin board is the *one* designated place to keep these items. To make this work effectively, it is necessary to review the bulletin board periodically for anything that is outdated, finished, or no longer needed. The key is to keep what is posted to a minimum. Get rid of the old news so that the current information is highly visible.

White Board Messaging

Grades K-12

Small erasable white boards have many uses both in the classroom and at home. At home, small white boards can be an organizational tool to reduce paper messages and reminders. Help students establish the habit of making a list on the white board at night of things to remember the next morning before leaving for school.

> Remember gym shoes!
>
> Field trip money $4.00

I keep an erasable white board on the kitchen counter at home for family messages. The recipient just wipes off a message after reading it. All family messages are located in one place, written on the white board. Everyone knows where to look. Before we began this approach, messages were often written on the backs of envelopes or on whatever was handy. Several got lost. We switched to the white board approach several years ago. What a difference! I am no longer finding old phone messages on scraps of paper. It is a simple system and it works!

Individual Chalkboards

Grades K–5

Similar to the white board, a small chalkboard reduces paper. It can be used for messages but it is also an alternative to paper and pencil for reinforcing math facts, vocabulary words and spelling. Easily transportable, chalkboards can go along in the car for added practice time on the way to soccer or while waiting for a sibling to finish piano lessons.

Pack It the Night Before

Grades K–12

Loading the backpack the night before can solve one of the biggest problems in managing homework at home. When the study guide is finished, in it goes. When the questions are answered or the math problems are completed, in they go. Put papers and materials away and zip the backpack closed at night.

A student council group learned this tip the hard way at our house. They had put the finishing touches on their project promoting seatbelt use. At ten o'clock that night, everything was finished except to develop the role of 36 pictures taken of students driving into the school parking lot. The disposable camera was left on the chair nearby. The next morning, the camera was found under a bed disposed of by good old Dylan, the dog. As a teacher, I never wanted to believe the age-old excuse, "The dog ate my homework . . ."

The Collection Point

Grades K–12

Families can designate one place as a collection point for anything going out of the house. It may be that the counter by the back door is where everyone puts notes to be signed, library books, rented videos, backpacks, hockey skates to be sharpened, anything to go out the next morning. It saves stress when collected items are already gathered to be picked up on the way to work or school.

When mornings at home go smoothly, students are more likely to arrive at school on time with materials in hand, ready to learn.

LOCKER LOGISTICS

Locker Organization

Grades 5–12

Ideas for managing paper would not be complete without ideas for organizing the locker, that cave where the Paper Monster appears to devour assignments! Some lockers resemble one large loose-leaf binder that has popped open. Papers and books are everywhere, mixed in with gym shoes and clothing. The door can be closed only with one gigantic slam.

In helping a student learn how to organize a locker, I begin by asking questions. The first several center on the frequency factor.

- How many times each day do you go to your locker?

- Do you go once in the morning and pick up materials for all your morning classes?

- Do you stop again at lunchtime and pick up materials for the afternoon?

- Do you stop again before going home?

- On the other hand, do you stop several times during the day between classes?

- Once you get to class, how often do you discover that you brought the wrong materials?

The All-Day Locker

Grades 5–12

The answers are very revealing and can help a student organize a locker. For starters, a system of color-coding materials offers tremendous help.

For the student who stops once in the morning and once after lunch, a two-color system may work best. Select one color for all morning classes and another for the afternoon. For example, all folders and book covers for morning classes might be green. Afternoon folders and books might be red. Stopping at the locker early in the morning is simplified because the student grabs everything in green. The chances of arriving at morning classes with the wrong materials are reduced.

I used this two-color approach with several students who often brought the wrong book or folder to class. When they adopted this simple system, these students always had their materials.

Schoolwide Color-Coding

Grades 5–12

For students who make several trips to their lockers between classes, a multicolor system may work better. In some schools, the faculty unilaterally decides on a color for each subject. Blue may be the required color for math. Students see that everyone arriving for class has blue materials and it is a reminder to bring the same. All math materials are stored in the blue folder just as all social studies work may be stored in yellow.

☞ **The Practical Pointer:**
Most schools send parents a list of school supplies during the summer. Send the information on folders early in the summer or at the end of the previous school year. Most discount stores have their best prices on folders immediately after the Fourth of July.

Top to Bottom Lockers

Grades 5–12

In addition to organizing lockers by color-coding to manage papers and assist with organization, another approach is to organize a locker top to bottom. Many students purchase locker organizers that divide the locker into three shelves: top, middle and bottom. Materials for morning classes go in the bottom shelf; midday classes are located on the middle shelf and afternoon class materials are stored on the top shelf. In colder climates, students will need a shelving system that allows space for jackets.

☞ **The Practical Pointer:**
Many middle school students, in particular, do not recognize the need to organize their lockers. They do not think about it. When asked, they do not know how to begin. It is well worth some class time to offer some suggestions and enlist ideas from students asking the question: What works for you?

The Top Shelf

Grades 5–12

A locker strategy that works for some students is to designate that top shelf as a space for materials that will go home that night. Throughout the day, as a student opens and closes the locker, that student puts anything to go home that day on the top shelf. By the end of the day, everything to go home has already been collected in one spot. When racing to the bus or parking lot after school, the student can grab and go!

Spine In and Spine Out

Grades 5–12

Still another teacher told me that she advises her students to use the spine of a textbook as a signal. Place it in the locker *spine facing out* if it needs to go *home* that night; a text with the spine facing in is not needed for homework.

One student surprised me by telling me that he had never used his locker once during his freshman year at his high school of over 3500 students. He carried all his books with him every day the entire year and never wore a coat. This was especially perplexing because he lived in a cold climate. I asked him why. Surely his books weighed over 40 pounds!

You may have already guessed the reason. He told me that he had been absent the day locker assignments were given. He said that he didn't know where to go, or whom to ask and felt embarrassed. It was easier, he thought, to manage on his own.

☞ **The Practical Pointer:**
Some students will not ask for help even when it is available. In a very large high school, student mentors could be more approachable than adults for learning the ropes.

SUMMARY

When I received a message that Mr. Matthison had called, I was not at all alarmed. He was my nephew's middle school math teacher at the time and I was tutoring Michael weekly.

When I returned the call, however, I was more than a little surprised to discover that Michael had a failing average. Was I aware of that? It seems that the last 12 homework assignments were missing.

I had been coasting along assuming that everything was going well. We had gone over his math assignments and he had assured me that he brought his book home regularly. Michael spent time on his homework and had become a good student. To say that I was surprised was an understatement. Twelve assignments! How could that be!

I was waiting when Michael arrived for tutoring after school that day. We had something to discuss. He was adamant that every assignment was finished and he was going to turn them in. He wasn't sure where they were but he knew that he had them.

After some searching, sure enough, Michael found every one. Some were folded in the math book, a few were in his backpack and the rest were in his math notebook. If anything, he seemed irritated about the fuss. After all, he had done the work.

Michael met with his teacher and received reduced credit for his late assignments. Doing the assignment was a very important step, as Mr. Matthison explained, but getting that paper from Point A to Point B *on time* was equally important. The lower grade that trimester was a difficult lesson.

This chapter has included strategies, tips, tools and techniques to help Michael and all of our students tame the Paper Monster.

While these ideas are not the only ways to manage paper and materials, they may act as a starting point. Pick and choose. Suggest strategies to your students. Mention a few to parents. Model techniques that appeal to you as an adult. There will be fewer frantic pleas of *"Can you help me find my . . . ?" "Has anybody seen my . . . ?" "Did someone take my . . . ?"*

Instead, our dream of *No loose papers* just might come true! We will hear our students say with confidence, *"Oh, I can get that. I know just where I put it!"*

O─ᵏ KEY IDEA

Routines and procedures are the tools and training that make paper organization work. These strategies can help our students redirect their energies to their quest for knowledge instead of a search for lost assignments. Students need to know that this is how we do it. "This is where we put materials. This is why we do it this way. This can help you succeed."

☞ **The Practical Pointer:**
Experts on organization of paperwork agree that clutter increases stress. Many of our students feel overwhelmed and stressed much of the time. Taming the Paper Monster can be a great stress reducer.

It is interesting to note that the word "stressed" has the same letters as the word "desserts," just in a different order. Which would you rather have? Perhaps we can entice our students to discover that effective paper organization will help them feel more relaxed and reward them with a class celebration, complete with "desserts!"

"A teacher is the child's third parent."

—*Hyman Maxwell Berston*

2

ACCOUNTABILITY, RESPONSIBILITY, RESULTS

When people are put to the test, they step up to the plate.

–Dr. Jeri Nielsen *in* Ice Bound

Teachers no longer need to be the sage on the stage.
They need to be the guide on the side that brings out thinking.

–Barb Stoflet, Minnesota Teacher of the Year

How many of you have students who are too dependent on you? Our focus as educators is to help our students become independent, lifelong learners. Doing more "on their own" is a challenge for many of our students. As the 2002 Minnesota Teacher of the Year suggests, we must become the "guide on the side" by encouraging, directing and differentiating instruction for every learner we have in the classroom.

Several teachers, though, have commented to me that now more than ever students are coming to school unprepared for independent work. The concern is evident at all grade levels. One of the most consistent difficulties reported is that when a student gets "stuck," that student sits passively and waits for the teacher to notice.

*The only place where **success** precedes **work** is in the dictionary.*

–Unknown

"Katie will sit there for 20 minutes and not go on to the next one," remarked second grade teacher Latoya Baines. "She will wait until I walk over to her table and help her. How can I help my students learn to work independently? I want Katie to skip the one that is too difficult and try the next one. I have 25 students. If I am helping someone else, they need to take the initiative in asking partners for help."

English teacher John Earlandson added, "We do not have time to stand over students at the high school level. We have too many students who could do the work but need adults to hold their hands. How can we get them to do it on their own?"

Sound familiar? Ninth grade math teacher Ken Seiberlich offers to help his students by phone every school night from 7 P.M. until 8 P.M. He teaches five math classes a day and provides all of his students with his personal phone number to call for evening math help. Mr. Seiberlich told me about a student named Ira who called him one night for help.

He helped Ira work through five problems. By then, Mr. Seiberlich was quite sure that Ira could manage the rest successfully on his own. But when Ira arrived for class the next day, how many math problems do you think that Ira had completed? You are right if you guessed *five*. Exactly five. The completed problems were the same five that Mr. Seiberlich and Ira did together over the phone. It is not that Ira *couldn't* do the work; he simply *didn't*.

DIFFERENTIATE BETWEEN "CAN'T DO" AND "WON'T DO"

As teachers and parents, we are faced with determining how much help is needed in any task. There is a difference between "can't do" and the several variations of "won't do," "would rather not do," "would like to let someone else do it," or, simply, "later." When a child truly cannot do the task, we accommodate and modify *to the extent needed*. That is part of good teaching. Sometimes, though, "can't do" is really a matter of learning strategies that turn into "can do."

O—⚷ KEY IDEA

The first step is to take a good look at the assignment. Students need to be able to do the work successfully 80 percent of the time. This is critical for achievement. "Can't do" is a problem that needs to be addressed differently from "won't do."

When the real issue is "won't do," or "won't do unless the teacher is right next to me," the problem is lack of independence. This is a recurring theme in my consultation with teachers. How to encourage students to do more on their own is a major concern. A starting point is to recognize whether or not we, as teachers and parents, may be inadvertently fostering the dependence. A case in point occurred recently. I was observing a high school social studies class.

As class began, I quietly found an empty seat in the back of the classroom. As soon as the bell rang, the teacher picked up her grade book and began moving about the room checking in with students who were missing assignments, quizzes or projects. She stopped near a student to remind him, "Your questions from Chapter Ten are missing. Can you have those in by tomorrow?"

Then on to another, admonishing, "You owe me your vocabulary sheet! That is now three days late!" In another part of the room I heard her schedule a make-up quiz. Next I watched her as she handed still another student an additional copy of a graphic organizer. This process took several minutes.

My question for you, as a teacher, is this: How many individuals were hard at work in that classroom during this time? That would be just *one,* the teacher. All of the students were chatting with each other and it would be a fair guess to assume that much of the conversation was not about course content. The students did not seem to share the same concern about the gaps in the grade book did as their teacher.

O⇥ KEY IDEA

When there is a missing assignment and there are two individuals involved, surely one concerned person should be the student. Sometimes our assistance leads students to a feeling of helplessness and a belief that they cannot learn on their own.

As the teacher continued to remind individuals of missing assignments, the young man sitting in front of me turned around and asked me, "So, who are you?"

"I'm Mrs. Tilton. I'm just visiting your classroom," I responded.

He paused and asked, "So, what are you writing about us?"

I explained that I wasn't really writing anything about *them,* but I did have a few *ideas.* Normally during an observation, I would just sit quietly in the back. Since everyone else was talking, I felt comfortable having a conversation, too.

I had some questions for him this time. "Does your teacher do this fairly often? Does she take class time to follow up on missing assignments?"

"Oh, yes," he said, "She really kicks butt!"

"Well, I was just wondering," I told him. "I was thinking about that bulletin board over there. Do you suppose that she could give each of you an individual number, then post missing assignments by number on that bulletin board?"

He nodded slightly.

"Could she also put extra copies of the graphic organizer, the study guide and other extra papers on that table over there?"

He nodded again.

"Could she put a calendar there indicating dates to sign up for a make-up quiz?"

He thought she could . . .

"Then do you suppose," I added, "that you could go over there, check on missing assignments and handle it on your own?"

He thought he could . . .

There were three problems with this scenario:

1. The teacher was doing all the work.
2. The teacher was doing all the work.
3. The teacher was doing all the work.

The teacher had the best of intentions. Despite this, students ended up being more dependent on the teacher than was necessary. Independent learning is not about fostering dependency on the teacher.

Many of us have done the same thing; I know that I have. We also have had good intentions. The unfortunate message, though, when we hover over students is that students cannot do it on their own. The truth is *they can*. They can *if* we teach them the skills they need to do it.

> *"The most valuable ability is the ability to recognize ability."*
>
> –Harvey Mackay

O─ KEY IDEA

Students need to recognize their own ability and learn effective strategies to succeed on their own. They need us, as teachers, to believe in them and expect results.

It is all about shifting educational responsibility to students by giving them models, tools, tips and strategies to become independent learners. Without question, help should be provided for any student who needs it on an *as needed basis*. Even when a student has identified special needs, independence is still the goal. Adaptations and modifications should be used to meet a demonstrated need. Providing more help than is truly necessary is a disservice to the students we serve.

O─ KEY IDEA

If we are going to promote high expectations and high standards for all students, we must make students accountable for their learning. Our message to students can be, "Put yourself in charge. We'll teach you the skills. Now do it."

Students must *own* the learning process. As students learn skills for independent learning, they will discover that both retention and assessment scores will improve. No single strategy is a solution for everyone. We must provide a variety of opportunities for success as we differentiate instruction in our classrooms.

To that end, a variety of strategies, tips, tools, and techniques are included in "Accountability, Responsibility, Results." See which ideas appeal to you. Change and adapt the strategies to fit your students and your curriculum. One idea may trigger a different approach or jog your memory by reminding you of a successful technique that you have used in the past.

Note that some of the strategies are designed to be used individually, while others work well in small groups or with the whole class. Some are strategies that have withstood the test of time while others offer a new slant or a fresh approach.

For ease of use, the chapter is divided into seven categories that encourage all students to do more on their own.

- Ready to Learn
- Being Accountable
- Tools of the Trade
- Managing Assignments
- Self-Checking Tools and Tips
- Strategies for Results
- Healthy Choices

READY TO LEARN

Ninety percent of success is showing up.

–Woody Allen

The Wake-Up Call

Grades K–12

Arriving at school on time and ready to learn is the most basic starting point of independent learning. The simplest way to teach students to arrive on time is to encourage the use of an alarm clock as part of daily life. While this may seem too obvious to mention, it

is essential. Most of us as adults depend on the alarm clock to get up and get to work on time. Setting an alarm is a habit that we need to instill early. Even very young children can be taught to set the alarm each school night and get up on time.

While I am not diminishing the role of parents before school in the morning, I am suggesting that too often well-meaning parents make wake-up time their responsibility instead of the child's. I also mention this because of comments made by managers of businesses that hire many young people. One manager told me that he had just hired a young man for a job that would begin at 7 A.M. the next morning. Without batting an eye, the young man asked his new employer for a wake-up call. True story.

Still another employer told me that she had to fire an employee who was late for work repeatedly despite several warnings. The employee's response was indignant and defensive, "With traffic today, you can't be expected to be on time."

In a final example, an employer told me that she fired a salesperson who rarely got reports in on time. Despite training and several suggestions about how to manage the paperwork, the employee continued to cite his attention deficit disorder as the problem. No one disputed that he had ADD, but he was not excused from learning strategies for turning in his reports finished and on time.

⚷ KEY IDEA

When we expect and insist that our students do more on their own, we are training our students to succeed both in the classroom and in the workplace.

Ten Free Minutes

Grades K–12

As the saying goes, everyone has the same 24 hours each day. We all have the same 1,440 minutes adding up to 10,080 minutes in a week. No one can make time go faster and no one can slow it down. Time is the constant. High school students may tell you that, as far as their sleep is concerned, every minute counts. However, setting the alarm just ten minutes earlier adds ten free minutes to their morning and can make the day go more smoothly.

These free minutes will take the rush out of a morning, allow a quick review before an assessment, may be just enough time to get help from a teacher before school or visit with friends at a locker.

The Scarecrow

Grades K–12

Another simple technique to help students get to school on time is to encourage them to lay out their clothes the night before. Younger children may want to make a "scarecrow" of everything that they will wear the next day from socks and underwear to sweater and pants.

Middle and high school students would scoff at such a literal approach. They would discover, though, that deciding what to wear and *actually putting everything together* the night before would eliminate a frantic search in the morning through the laundry, under the bed or in a sibling's closet. It could mean the difference between a feeling of playing catch-up all day long or being in control of the day.

Wear a Wristwatch

Grades 1–12

The best place to find a helping hand is at the end of your arm . . .

–Old adage

Part of becoming an independent learner is being accountable for time. Encourage students from first grade on through high school to wear an inexpensive wristwatch and learn to depend on it.

Common features like alarms would be annoying if used in the classroom but can be helpful at home while doing homework. A student can allocate a certain amount of time for an assignment. Setting the alarm motivates the student to stay on task and it signals when it is time to change to another subject.

High Five Reminder

Grades K–5

Encourage students to give themselves an enthusiastic **High Five** just before leaving for school in the morning. It serves as a kinesthetic reminder to check that they have everything they need for the day. Students may ask themselves, "Do I have the 3 B's, the L and the N?" They are checking for:

- Backpack
- Bag lunch

- Books
- Library books. Is it Library Day?
- Notes to be signed. Did I bring anything home to be signed?

Your students may have different items to check. Adjust the strategy to fit their needs.

Refrigerator Picture

Grades K–3

In lieu of the **High Five** as a morning reminder, some young children respond well to checking a picture of a creature taped to the refrigerator. The creature has all the tools for the day and is "good to go!" It creates a strong visual reminder. Note that the reproducible can be changed depending on the unit, time of year, or special events.

Skip a Final

Grades 9–12

Regular attendance is a critical part of independent learning and helping our students become accountable for results. Attendance at my own daughter's high school has improved dramatically in the last five years since **Skip a Final** was implemented as a schoolwide policy. It is a simple plan with positive results. Ask any teacher who has been on the faculty longer than five years to name one of best strategies for improved attendance and improved learning. **Skip a Final** will be at the top. Students also give it an enthusiastic "thumbs up."

How It Works:

Students who have no more than a total of four *excused* absences, counting all class periods in all courses during one semester, may choose to skip one final exam of their choice. There are some additional conditions that must be met. The option is open to any student who has *no unexcused absences* in any class and at least a "C" average in the **Skip a Final** course. Note that three tardies count as an unexcused absence and disqualify a student.

Students know from the Student Handbook that the total of four excused absences from all classes means exactly that: four class periods. Total. Count them. It is very easy to monitor. The only exception is a school-sponsored event, such as a field trip, band concert, or athletic activity involving a specific student. Illness, orthodontia, doctor appointments, and funerals all count against the four class periods.

Despite cries of "Foul!" by some parents about funerals and doctor appointments, there are no exceptions. **Skip a Final** is an earned *privilege* for not missing more than four excused classes; it is not an *entitlement*. One student pleaded with her mother, a speech pathologist by training, to tighten her braces a week before the end of the semester rather than miss school time to go the orthodontist. The message sent is clear. Be there and be on time.

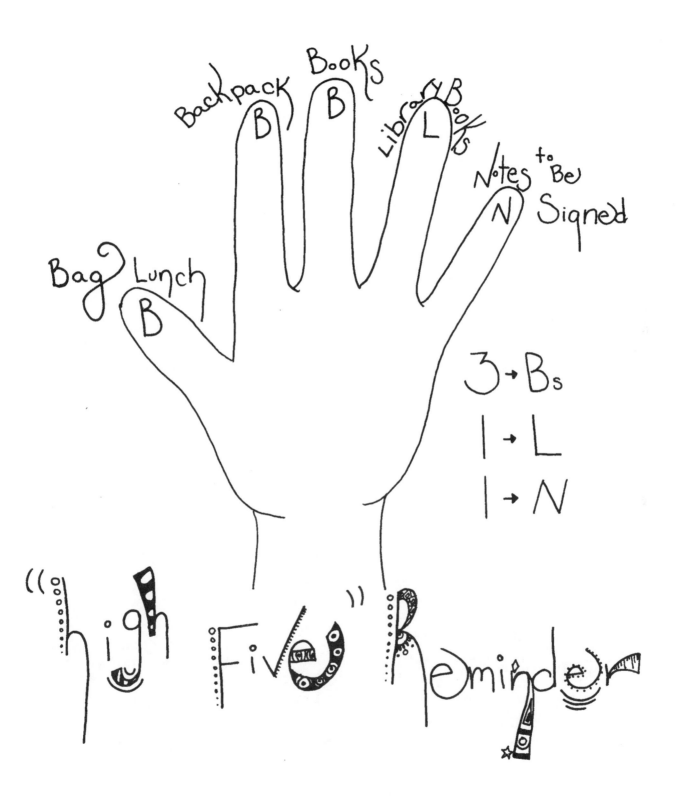

Backpack
B

Books
B

Library Books
L

Notes to Be Signed
N

Bag Lunch
B

3 → Bs
1 → L
1 → N

"high Five" Reminder

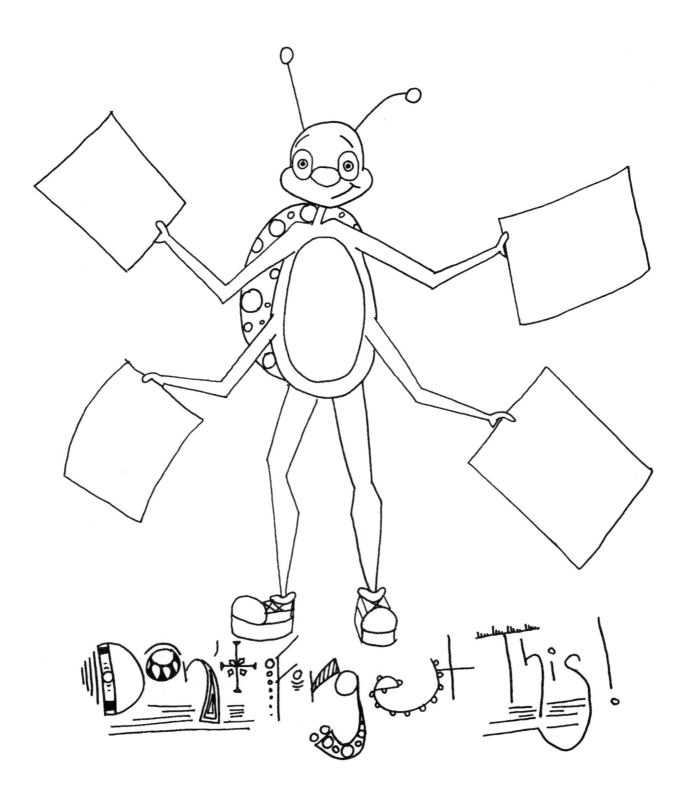

Grading is based on daily work with the points from the final omitted. Some students plan ahead and depend on **Skip a Final** to raise their grade in a challenging course. One student told me that *all* her grades were higher because she skipped her difficult French final every year, devoting the time instead to studying for math and science.

O⚬ᵣ KEY IDEA

As one science teacher lamented, "We can't teach them if they are not here." Part of independent learning is instilling in students an understanding of what is expected. Come to school every day, on time, ready to learn. As parents and teachers, we can work together to promote the same clear message, "School is your job. School comes first."

A business leader who works with many young adults said to me, "We'll train them on the job. You teach the basics. Most of all, teach them to show up every day, on time with a good attitude. We'll take it from there."

BEING ACCOUNTABLE

Goal Setting

Grades 4–12

No, I can't say I was ever lost, but I was bewildered once for three days.

–Daniel Boone's response when asked if he was ever lost in the woods

Goals help everyone map out a destination that is attainable. Setting goals is an important learning strategy that we can teach our students. We want them to see the results, the endpoint that we are working toward. During the process, goals provide the direction where we focus our efforts. Most of us would agree that written goals are powerful.

Research shows that writing down what you want to have happen in your life gives you a much greater chance of having your goals come true compared to somebody who doesn't write down her goals.

–Martha Beck, Ph.D.

I encourage secondary students to write three goals that they hope to accomplish in the class. To do this, students need to know *our objectives* and the *final product* that we as teachers have in mind as we shape our lessons, activities and assessment.

Without goals, our students can be a lot like Daniel Boone wandering about the continent. Unfortunately, our students may not be quite as lucky in finding the way to a positive outcome.

Avoiding Assignment Abandonment

Grades 4–12

I had a conversation recently with a businesswoman who oversees personnel in 250 retail stores. We were discussing the need for commitment in any aspect of life whether it is finishing an assignment in school or being a reliable employee every day at work. A common problem she faces with her employees, whom she described as mostly between the ages of 20 and 30, is "job abandonment." I had never heard the term.

When she started her job five years ago, she hadn't either. Now she deals with it daily. It refers to the employee who leaves for lunch and never returns or the employee who does not report for work without notifying anyone. Before she was hired, the old policy gave an employee three consecutive days of job abandonment before termination. She immediately changed the policy by reducing it to two.

If an employee simply did not show up for two consecutive days or left and did not return, the employee was officially fired. In many cases, she explained, the employees had no intention of ever returning. They simply quit by leaving or not arriving without informing a supervisor.

ASSIGNMENT ABANDONMENT

In the classroom, we often face the same issue that we might call **Assignment Abandonment**. Students begin an assignment and quit. Unlike the employer who fired the individual after two consecutive days of job abandonment, teachers cannot "fire" students who accumulate weeks' worth of missing assignments. The grade book displays a row of empty boxes. The pattern can develop quickly and it can be a very difficult cycle to break.

COLLECT IT

How can you turn that around? A strategy that worked for some of my students was to collect partially completed work when it was due. If a student had finished *half* of the study guide and it was due at the end of the class period, I collected it. If the student wanted to finish it at home, the student received another copy to take home. It helped some students realize that "due" meant "due."

Sometimes this added just enough incentive to encourage the student to finish the task and get credit for the whole assignment. I tried to help the student see that it made sense to complete the work. "You've done this much. I'll collect that now. It's due. You have already invested some time and effort. Why not do the rest and get credit?"

Homework Counts

Grades 5–12

Students are accountable when they know that homework counts. A second strategy that reduces abandoned assignments is making it a policy to grade homework. Many teachers view homework as a way for a student to reinforce learning and offer it as a choice. Some students need a nudge to get the message that homework is not an option; it is a commitment.

Call Home and Leave Yourself a Message

Grades 4–12

This quick tip works for students and adults alike. Have you ever called home from school and left yourself a message? Perhaps it would be a reminder about a phone call, an appointment or to bring something from home the next morning.

"Put a note on the mirror about my dental appointment, Tuesday, 4:00."

"Remember to pick up tag board for the social studies project."

"Bring the article for Brittany."

Students can do the same thing. Many students have cell phones that must be turned off during the day. They can call from another phone or be allowed to leave a text message as a reminder of something from early in the day that may otherwise have been forgotten. It works!

E-Mail Yourself

Grades 4–12

Another option is to suggest that students send themselves an e-mail to read at home that night. Almost all students check their e-mail daily. I use this strategy myself. Not only is it helpful to e-mail my own messages and reminders, I have also sent e-mail to family members living in the same house. It is a simple way to wish a child good luck on a test, send an affectionate note, or remind a family member about an upcoming event or appointment.

Back It Up

Grades 6–12

I have worked with several students who "lost" assignments on the computer because they forgot to make a back-up copy. Sometimes after backing it up on a disk, the material was still lost, due to using a bad disk. Remind students to back up all important computer work on *two disks*. This extra step can save a lot of aggravation.

The Human Billboard

Grades K–12

Students always notice when the teacher becomes a **Human Billboard.** It is a very simple strategy with lots of impact. Use a plastic page protector and punch two holes near the top opening. Make sure that you leave enough room at the top to slide in a sheet of paper. Tie a light cord through the holes, long enough to fit comfortably over your shoulders and fit over your head. You can insert any information that you want your students to notice during class or during the day. Just wear your message. They will not miss this strong visual cue!

> **Spelling test tomorrow**
>
> **Note book check on Thursday**
>
> **Signed grade slips earn five points**
>
> **Smile!!**

It can also be used to hold a picture of an activity that you will be doing later. For younger students, you may want to insert a book that you will be reading or a picture of a game for Game Day. To help students keep track of the rotating schedule for related arts classes, you might insert a picture depicting the class for that day such as a paintbrush for art, a musical note for music, a ball for physical education, or a keyboard for computer.

Name Badge

Grades 1–12

If the page protector seems just a bit over the top for you, consider wearing a plastic name badge, the type that you usually receive at conferences. Don't throw it away at the end of the conference. Put it to use. You can *wear* your message and it will be small and subtle. Students will see it and the follow through is up to them!

Red, Yellow, Green

Grades K–5

Another way to wear your message is to color-code it. Cue students when it is time to listen or time to talk by wearing colors hung on cards around your neck.

> The red card signals, *"Listen to me."*
>
> The green card signals, *"You can talk."*

The yellow card signals, *"Talk quietly to your partner."*

If you are wearing green and the noise level is too high, switch to yellow and walk around the room. Students will see the signal and adjust the volume.

 The Practical Pointer:
Discount stores sell inexpensive stoplights with the three colors. Use a switch to change from green to yellow if the noise level is getting too loud.

"Do Over!"
Grades 4–12

A quick tip with a big payoff is **"Do Over!"** While I was observing a middle school English class, teacher Meredith Kaplan called on a student. I strained to hear the response but could hear only part of it. Being able to hear student responses is a problem in many classrooms. Evidently students sitting around me were having the same problem because several students began to call out, **"Do over!"**

The student who was speaking turned and repeated the response, only louder this time. Ms. Kaplan explained to me later that the class had agreed together that when a response was inaudible, anyone could say, **"Do over!"** The class also agreed with Ms. Kaplan that saying **"Do over!"** once was enough. The speaker did not need to be bombarded with a chorus of 15 "Do over!" comments to get the picture.

Sometimes it was the teacher's comment that students could not hear, she added, and she was the one who needed to turn up the volume. **"Do Over!"** was another way that students could take charge of their learning.

 The Practical Pointer:
Too often the teacher may not realize that several students have missed an inaudible response and go right on. Sometimes the problem is exacerbated by noise from a fan or a heater. Students sitting near the source of extraneous noise may be missing part of the class. It can be helpful to take a noise inventory in different parts of the classroom. (See the section on using a microphone in "Creature Comforts" for more ideas.)

Celebrating Diversity
Grades 4–12

"Do over!" can become an opportunity to celebrate the foreign languages of students in your own school district. The Minneapolis public school system near my home has students who speak 80 different primary languages. I encourage teachers to learn "Repeat" in many different languages and incorporate the foreign words daily in class for this purpose. You may wish to use a map to teach students where the languages come from as students practice their new words for "Repeat."

TOOLS OF THE TRADE

Eliminate Time Wasters

Grades 6–12

Encourage students to keep a log of how they spend their study time in a week. Ask them to circle "time wasters" that form a pattern. Is it time spent on the phone? TV? Figuring out where to begin? Computer games? E-mail? The Internet? Recognizing where the time goes and eliminating or managing the culprits will enable students to focus on homework. Students will end up with more time to do what they like afterward.

Know Thyself

Grades 4–12

By fourth grade, students can begin to recognize the best and worst work times for their own body clocks. Is it best to do homework right after school? Does it work better to take a break and begin homework later? By high school age, most students know whether they are "morning people" or "night owls." We do not want students to schedule every minute of the their day but it helps to block out homework times that work best for them. One tip that almost always works in any time frame is to schedule the more difficult tasks first.

Stock the Top Ten

Grades 4–12

Students can save time doing homework by stocking up on basic study tools to keep at home. Collect supplies in a cardboard box. The container need not be elaborate, just convenient and available.

1. *paper:* including lined, blank, graph, and construction paper
2. *note cards:* different sizes and colors
3. *highlighters:* broad and narrow tipped
4. *highlighting tape:* at least three colors to color-code texts
5. *markers:* wide and narrow in multicolor sets
6. *sticky notes:* a variety of sizes and colors
7. *writing utensils:* pens, #2 pencils, colored pencils, crayons
8. *liquid "white-out"*
9. *assembling tools:* stapler, staples, tape and paper clips
10. *math tools:* as needed, including calculator, protractor and compass

Ready References

Grades 5–12

Though many students use basic reference tools, such as an encyclopedia, on the computer, it is still helpful to keep these three in book form at home near the designated study area.

1. dictionary

2. thesaurus

3. atlas

Some Assembly Required

Grades 2–12

A tip for both students and their parents is to assemble a **Project Box** to keep in a closet at home. Collect a wide range of typical supplies for projects such as old magazines, craft sticks, scissors, tape, foil stars, cutouts for letters, glitter, glue sticks, yarn, watercolor paints and templates for shapes. Tuck a few large white oak tag poster boards behind the coats and avoid last minute trips to the discount store.

☞ **The Practical Pointer:**

Watch for some of these items to be sale-priced during the summer. There will undoubtedly be hands-on projects at every grade level during the year and it is almost always less expensive to work with what is already available.

Start Here!

Grades 4–12

The first step is always the hardest . . .

Whenever students are working on a long-range project or a lengthy assignment, a common problem is often getting started again the next day or after a break. Valuable time is lost and procrastination sets in when a student wonders, "Where did I leave off? Where do I begin?"

A simple solution is to leave a **Start Here** note. Before ending a work session, the student writes a short note indicating where to begin. For example, the note might say:

Begin with an outline of pages 60–65.

    I. Causes of the Civil War

        A. ————

        B. ————

or

> Make vocabulary cards for the next five words on the list.

It is especially helpful to provide a quick head start by actually writing the first sentence of a new section or doing the first problem of an assignment. It can take just a few minutes to actually begin the task. Remind students to flag the page with a sticky note. When it is time to continue working, the student knows just where to continue.

MANAGING ASSIGNMENTS

A schedule defends from chaos and whim. It is a net for catching days . . .

–Annie Dillard

The DO-DUE Board!

Grades 3–12

Don't let the name throw you. A teacher shared this idea with me and was very enthusiastic about the results. Some of our students confuse *Do* and *Due*. The first *Do* is, of course, what has to be completed in order to have it finished by the *Due* date.

The **Do-Due Board** can be adapted to a wide variety of grade levels and subject areas. It demonstrates how to divide a task into manageable steps. It helps a student plan what to do each day from the day the assignment is given to completion on the due date.

The teacher explained that she used a large white dry-erase board divided into squares for days of the week. Laminating white oak tag board is another inexpensive option.

FROM DO TO DUE

Located on the wall in the classroom, the **Do-Due Board** can illustrate, for example, how a secondary student might see a long-range assignment as a series of short-term tasks. Too often, a long-range due date can quickly become overwhelming. How many of you know students who have good intentions but end up frantically trying to do it all the night before? That far away due date becomes never-never land.

MANAGING TIME

Each day, a progressive step is listed on the board. It is a realistic model to follow in determining what needs to be completed. It is often not the assignment itself that gets students into trouble, it is the inability to organize the task and manage time. Part of helping our students do more on their own equips them with the skills expected of them in both post-secondary settings and the workplace.

TRAINING FOR LIFE

It is a fact that it takes a long time to succeed in life,
and I think that two to five years should be enough.

–College student on career goals

Any of you who have taken your own children to college to begin freshman year have probably had an experience similar to my own during Parent Orientation. At two different schools, the university deans emphasized that the students had the ability to do the work or they would not have been admitted. One dean went so far as to say, "The admissions office never makes a mistake."

What both deans added was very telling. They each commented that freshmen need good management and planning skills. The volume of work and the pace of learning require these skills. One dean added a strong warning to parents and students, "Don't expect an extension on assignments. We do not reward poor planning." Certainly the same could be said of the workplace.

O—⫯ KEY IDEA

Some students may need extended time due to a disability. The majority of our middle and high school students, however, need to learn the skills necessary to meet a due date on time. In a nutshell, they need to learn how to divide any large task into bite-sized pieces to make it manageable and to complete it on time. We can teach students how to make the critical connection between planning and due dates.

At the elementary level, the **Do-Due Board** is applicable as well. It can be used to teach spelling test preparation, for example. The 15 spelling words may be given on Monday in anticipation of Friday's test. **The Do-Due Board** suggests learning five words on Monday, five more on Tuesday, the five last words on Wednesday with time to review on Thursday. The students will then be ready for the test on the due date, Friday.

☞ **The Practical Pointer:**
Start small. Demonstrate the concept of the **Do-Due Board** using two-day or three-day assignments. The model is a practical strategy for achieving success in nearly any project. Students can be encouraged to use this same strategy successfully at home. A

seemingly overwhelming task like cleaning a bedroom becomes manageable in small steps. Focus on one drawer, one shelf, or one corner of the room at a time.

O—x KEY IDEA

In all of our schools there is a "hidden curriculum." It simply means that there are assumed skills at certain grade levels. These assumed skills are critical to school success but may not always be taught directly. It is often assumed that by middle and high school, for example, students already know how to plan their time, how to organize tasks, and how to break longer assignments down into manageable pieces.

Sometimes there is an expectation that a skill was taught last year and that everyone should know it. We sometimes assume that our students have skills when in fact they do not. The reality is that a large number of our students need to be shown how to study and how to organize their time using models that are realistic and workable. Once students acquire the skills, success follows.

Cross That Off Your List!

Grades 6–12

A practical way to help students become accountable is to teach them to make lists. Many of us, as adults, rely of the proverbial **To Do List** to get through each day. Are you a list maker? I'm such a list maker that if I do something that was not on the list, I add it just so that I can cross it off. In fact, last weekend, I was making my usual Saturday loop of grocery store, post office, and bank as listed on a sticky note. I stopped at the drycleaners on my way home even though it wasn't on the list.

At home, I found myself standing next to the wastebasket adding "drycleaner" and crossing it off before throwing the list into the trash. I felt great! I probably should not admit that. However, there is a certain personal satisfaction and reward in seeing what has been accomplished. Completing a task and crossing it off the list later is a way of giving ourselves a small gift.

O━ᴈ KEY IDEA

A list helps good intentions become a reality. It also helps students create a big picture that can be arranged by priority. Having a plan instills confidence and a positive attitude.

Task and Time Priorities

Grades 6–12

> *Opportunity is missed by most people because it is dressed in overalls and looks like work.*
>
> –*Thomas Alva Edison*

Recognizing that everything on a **To Do List** is not of equal importance is a crucial step for students. The same amount of time cannot be allotted to everything or there will be no end in sight. Middle and high school students can be encouraged to prioritize their lists so that the most important and most difficult tasks are completed first. Many secondary students pack each day with classes, extracurricular activities, friends, volunteer work, jobs and family.

Unless we teach them to determine for themselves what really must be completed on a given day and what could be eliminated, reduced or delayed, these students can feel continuously overloaded. Of course, there is a difference between procrastination and priorities. It reminds me of a saying posted in a math teacher's classroom:

> *Work now. Get it done!*
>
> *Play later. It's more fun!*

The basis of any time management strategy is to assign values of A, B, or C to each task. Students determine which tasks are "A" value and need to be completed today. "B" tasks are next in importance and may need some time allocated today but do not need to be finished. "C" tasks are those that can be placed on the backburner for today and worked on, only if time permits. Those C tasks will eventually be moved to the B list and finally to the A priority list. By then, though, all the other A's will have been accomplished.

O—ʑ KEY IDEA

Teach students to avoid the "hummingbird syndrome" of flitting from one task to another. Whether or not we specifically label tasks A, B or C, adults learn to operate on some type of priority system to function effectively.

LIVING BY THE A, B, C'S

A good friend from out of town happened to be a weekend guest in my home recently. She was describing how much more time she has now that she has applied the A, B and C approach to every aspect of her life.

Space is one category that she prioritizes. I had never really looked at office or kitchen storage in terms of A or B or C space. She had. In just an hour over coffee, she rearranged my small kitchen. I learned that my all-purpose junk drawer was taking up top priority A space. We quickly moved the contents to less convenient but adequate C space.

"Linda," Kathy assured me, "You have plenty of storage space in this kitchen. You just have to figure out A storage, B storage and C storage. Arrange everything according to priority and usage." She was right. I moved the kabob skewers out of the top drawer and sent the old tile samples to the basement.

There were a few protests from the Tilton family who felt a little disorientated when I told them that the cereal had been upgraded to A space. We actually function better now in the new arrangement and cooking takes less time. Only one item, the peanut butter, has been moved back to its original spot.

The "I Did It!" List

Grades 6–12

A different slant to making lists is to approach it from the other direction. The **"I Did It!"** list encourages students to celebrate what they *have* accomplished in a day. Before going to bed at night, students take a few minutes to think about what was finished that day, record it and feel successful.

Perhaps not everything on the **To Do List** was crossed off, but several important tasks were completed or at least moved forward. That piece of paper is really a list of goals. Sometimes students and adults as well make lists that are insurmountable and unattainable. This can be discouraging, particularly for anyone who ends up saying, "I just can't do it all! I haven't gotten anything done."

The purpose of the **"I Did It!"** List is to step back and take satisfied, deep breath and say, "A-a-ah . . . Today was a good day! Now that I look at it, I accomplished a lot."

⊶ KEY IDEA

The "Don't Do It List" is still another option. Record things that you should not be doing at all. Either these are things that do not need to be done or, from an adult perspective, could be delegated to someone else.

SELF-CHECKING TOOLS AND TIPS

Removable Labels

Grades K–12

Some students need immediate reinforcement and attention when completing written materials such as study guides or review sheets. Our goal is to help students do more on their own without hovering over them ready to provide continuous assistance.

Removable labels serve the purpose by making any study guide, math worksheet or quiz "self-checking." Make a copy of the answer key, and then cover the answers with individual, removable labels. The student can write a response directly on the label and immediately peel it off to find the correct response beneath.

Feedback is immediate and the student can move on to the next one without consulting the teacher. The removable labels are effective review tools for students at all grade levels. While using them on a classwide basis would not be practical or necessary, these tools work very well on a small scale.

Parents may also find this tool valuable in encouraging independence during homework time. When the child is reviewing math facts or spelling words, a parent can first write the facts or spelling words on paper and cover the words with the blank removable labels. The child can practice independently and immediately check for accuracy. This will eliminate the constant question, "Is this right?"

☞ **The Practical Pointer:**
Removable labels can be purchased in any business supply store in a variety of sizes. Be sure to find the word "removable" on the package or they will be permanent.

Red Report Cover

Grades 2–5

A study guide becomes self-checking by using a red report cover. The answers are written on the study guide ahead of time *in red marker* and then the page is placed inside the red report cover. The questions will be visible through the red cover but the answers will not. Working independently, the student will be able to read each question, formulate an answer and then slide the page up just enough to expose the answer above the plastic. It is a quick way to review content independently and for the student to see which questions need more emphasis.

High School Flash Cards

Grades 9–12

A tried and true strategy for self-checking and increasing independent learning is the use of traditional flash cards. Some of my high school students made the incorrect assumption that flash cards were for elementary students only. In fact, using flash cards at all grade levels can be one of the most efficient ways to learn factual content. Vocabulary meanings, science concepts and historical data are just some of the types of rote information that can be learned quickly on basic flash cards.

As educators, even though our emphasis is on higher-level thinking, there is still a need to assimilate a high volume of factual information. Flash cards are simple, easy to make and lend themselves to brief study sessions.

Learning on a Ring

Grades K–12

Key rings are a simple but very effective way to manage flash cards. They are frequently available at no charge as advertising from a wide variety of businesses. Secondary students can attach vocabulary cards or important facts from each unit on separate rings. When it is time to study for final exams or for standardized assessments, it is easy to flip through the ring and remove the items that they already know, thus allowing them to concentrate on the more difficult ones. Cards on a ring make periodic review fast and efficient. The rings can be stored in a shoebox or desk drawer at home.

Key rings also work well with primary students as a strategy to hold colors samples, shapes and spelling words. During the September staff development session at a school one year, I had suggested placing spelling words on a ring. New words could be written on note cards each week, a hole punched in the corner, and the note cards attached to a key ring.

Students could easily carry their key rings to and from school. As students learned their spelling words, those words could be removed from the ring until all words could be spelled with confidence.

When I went back to the same school for a follow-up meeting in December, I learned that the entire building had adopted this simple concept. "Spelling-on-a-ring" had become the rage! Students had key rings hanging from their backpacks and were trading key rings at recess! They especially liked the key rings with an expandable cord that fit on a wrist.

Alternatives to typical key rings can also be used to hold flash cards and spelling words. Shower rod rings, metal hoops for holding papers together, large safety pins *taped closed*, pipe cleaners and decorative ribbon work well, too.

 The Practical Pointer:

When I speak to parent groups, I frequently suggest using key rings for "glove compartment learning." Place math facts, colors, shapes and vocabulary cards on note cards and attach them to key rings. Store them in the glove compartment in the car. Reviewing on the run becomes much more manageable when time spent waiting for a sibling becomes "the teachable moment."

Dialogue in Color
Grades 3–6

Here is a simple technique to help students who struggle with writing dialogue and understanding when to indent for a new speaker. After students have written the dialogue, ask them to go back and, using as many different colored markers as there are speakers, highlight each time a new speaker begins.

A change in color indicates a need to indent. This self-checking technique has helped many of my students follow the rule for indenting dialogue. When they are satisfied with their writing, the final copy is completed without color.

Happy Face Dialogue
Grades 3–6

Another quick tip for writing dialogue is to encourage students to draw a **Happy Face Smile** underneath quotation marks at the beginning and end of a direct quotation. The quotation marks form the eyes and students have a clear reminder that a person is speaking.

Construction Paper Paragraph
Grades 3–5

Before writing a paragraph, many students benefit from making a construction paper model of a paragraph as a reminder of how to structure it. Each student receives a long, business envelope. Inside are strips of construction paper in four colors and sizes that students will arrange on their desks.

The green strip is the longest and is labeled *Topic Sentence*. The student lays this strip at the top of the desk.

Beneath the green strip on the desk will be two shorter red strips, labeled *Details*. These are arranged vertically with space left between.

The four yellow strips are shorter still and are each labeled *Supporting Details*. Students place two beneath each red strip.

Finally, an orange strip is removed from the envelope. It is almost as large as the green topic sentence strip and is labeled *Closing Sentence*.

> *Topic Sentence*
>
> > *Detail*
> >
> > > *Supporting Detail*
> > >
> > > *Supporting Detail*
> >
> > *Detail*
> >
> > > *Supporting Detail*
> > >
> > > *Supporting Detail*
>
> *Closing Sentence*

The technique creates a model that remains on the desk as the student writes. It becomes a self-checking tool for the student who can see very clearly the relationships among all of the elements in a typical paragraph. Once the actual paragraph is completed, the student can check to see if there is a "match."

Sentence-by-Sentence

Grades 3–12

What did we do before sticky notes? Sticky notes can be used in a 1001 ways! For our purposes here, let me suggest using them as a writing tool. Some students have difficulty writing a paragraph. These students will frequently start over again and again, not feeling satisfied.

Rather than creating a paper jungle, teach the student to write each sentence on a sticky note and then arrange the notes to form the paragraph. Encourage the student to read it over. Any single sentence can be changed easily by rewriting it on a new sticky note. When the paragraph is ready, it can be written once on paper.

UP Your Paragraph

Grades 1–5

This quick tip reminds students to check that every sentence begins in **Upper case** and ends with **Punctuation.** UP your paragraph! Before a paper is turned in, partners check each other's paragraph for the UP cue.

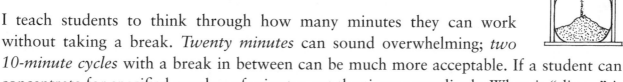

STRATEGIES FOR RESULTS

If you cut too many corners, you'll go around in circles!

—Wise Proverb

Manageable Segments

Grades K–12

Setting manageable time limits works well for all grade levels. I have used both kitchen timers and three-minute egg timers depending on the purpose. Even very young children can stay seated until an egg timer has run out. It is an easy visual cue. For older students doing homework, setting the timer on the stove or microwave at home can be highly motivating.

I teach students to think through how many minutes they can work without taking a break. *Twenty minutes* can sound overwhelming; *two 10-minute cycles* with a break in between can be much more acceptable. If a student can concentrate for specified number of minutes, set the timer accordingly. When it "dings," it is time to stretch or change activities.

☞ **The Practical Pointer:**
The use of a timer should never add pressure. The purpose is to teach time management skills by setting goals and rewarding success.

Sleep on It!

Grades 3–12

You may remember this quick idea from your own school experience. Whether it was a challenging multiplication fact, a difficult spelling word or information from your social studies class, you may remember being told to *sleep on it.* This simple technique worked then and it works today.

I encourage students to write that troublesome spelling word, for example, on a note card. Look at it just before bed and tuck it under the pillow. Look at it again the first thing in the morning. Say it aloud. Chances are that recall will be much better.

☞ **The Practical Pointer:**

Encourage your students to *see it, say it,* and *write it* for success!

Permanent Posters

Grades 3–6

Create permanent posters that provide key information and steps in completing a story problem in math or developing computer skills. Hang them on the wall so that students can use them independently or check the posters first before going to the teacher for help.

Playground Maps

Grades 1–5

At the elementary level, the playground offers a learning opportunity for geography. Enlist community volunteers to paint a map of the United States. A world map can depict the continents. During recess and also during a class trip outdoors, students can play on top of the world and learn locations at the same time.

Desktop Maps

Grades 2–12

A quick tip to improve knowledge of geography is to laminate maps onto the corner of every desk. Choose a U.S. map that is just large enough to outline the 50 states and star the general location of each capital. Many students need to review the location of specific states.

My home state of Minnesota is often associated with the Mall of America. That may be what put the state "on the map" for many people. Where Minnesota is actually located, however, is often unclear, even to some adults. Everyone knows that Minnesota is in the Midwest but beyond that, many people have only a vague idea.

The desk map strategy quickly closes the geography gap. Only seconds of class time each day are needed to mention a current news item and locate the state on individual maps. The event becomes more meaningful to students and, by the end of the year; everyone will have a better grasp of U.S. geography.

The same can be done with a small world map. Students can locate continents and general areas of the globe as part of discussion of current events. However, many secondary social studies teachers comment that they lack current world maps making it difficult to help students understand the impact of events in the world.

The Practical Pointer:

Sometimes the Internet is the best tool for acquiring current maps. Students need to see a location to create a strong visual picture.

Footprint Path

Grades K–3

Footprints made from construction paper and laminated to the floor create a path for younger students to follow in lining up to leave the room, traveling to the media center, or going to the computer lab. This practical strategy encourages independence and saves the teacher from repeating over and over where to stand and where to go.

 The Practical Pointer:

Color-code footprints to common locations so that students know to "Walk this way . . ." to the cafeteria, computer lab, gym and office.

Example Included

Grades 2–12

To encourage all students to do more on their own, one of the simplest techniques is to provide an example. When trying something new, adults wonder, "Is this the way it's supposed to look?" Students also benefit from a model. It may seem obvious but many materials do not provide an example to follow. It is one of the simplest ways to save time for both the teacher who is answering questions and the student who can get right to work.

At Your Own Pace

Grades 1–12

There is more to life than increasing its speed.

–Mohandas Gandhi

Timed tests and activities can be a motivator for some students. Timing math facts, in particular, is still a common practice at the elementary level. "See how many you can finish in one minute [or three minutes or five minutes]," may be the directive.

Timed activities are not motivating for everyone, however. We need to guard against the *faster is better* approach. Some students simply work more slowly and we need to recognize that. Other students, though, are motivated to "beat the clock" and can focus on a task better with a specific time limit. For the student who processes at a slower rate but who is still able to calculate the answer, timing is both discouraging and irrelevant. Is faster better? One of the goals of helping students work independently is to help them understand their own pace and learning style.

KEY IDEA

As adults, we accept that fact that not everyone works at the same pace. As long as the job gets done in a reasonable amount of time, there is usually leeway for personal style. Our students need the same consideration. One of the advantages of differentiating instruction in the classroom is that we can offer options that will fit every learning style and pace.

A Hat Trick

Grades K–12

The **Hat Trick** provides visual cues to alert students that it is time to work in groups, work independently or listen to directions. When the teacher puts on the old-fashioned top hat, students know that it is time to listen because the teacher is giving directions. A baseball cap indicates teamwork and students know that they will be working in groups. A blaze-orange hunting cap can indicate quiet time for individual projects.

One high school teacher simplified the idea even further. She wore just one hat and that was only when she was giving directions. She described her garage sale headgear as a large, attention-getting contraption that, like the directions, could not be missed!

Some teachers liked the concept but were a bit concerned about walking around with "hat head" all day. I suggested that they opt for a variety of headbands with hearts, antennae or antlers as ways of indicating the type of activity.

One teacher thought that wearing antlers could send a different sort of message each day. When the antlers were in the usual upright position, all was well. If those antlers were tilted forward like a charging bull, that would be a pretty good indicator to students that this day had not gotten off to the best start . . .

Absentee Buddies

Grades 6–12

Too often, when a student has been absent and returns to school, the student depends on the teacher for makeup work, information on tests, quizzes and handouts. The few minutes between classes at the middle and high school levels make this extremely difficult for most teachers. This occurs at the same time that the teacher is trying to provide extra help for students who need it.

Absentee Buddies is a simple strategy that shifts responsibility to students who were absent by first relying on peers for materials that they may have missed. Then, if needed, students could seek the teacher's help.

How It Works:

The first day of class everyone selects an **Absentee Buddy.** They exchange phone numbers and e-mail addresses. Each student receives a two-pocket folder. Name and class number are listed in marker on the top. The class number simplifies numerical filing. A box for each class period holds students' folders that are color-coded by section and numbered from 1 to 30.

When students arrive for class each day, one student takes attendance and calls "Buddies!" Students check to make sure that their buddy is present. If not, the partner goes to the box for that hour and retrieves the buddy's folder.

During the class period, the partner manages the folder for the absent buddy. If the weekly syllabus is distributed, the partner takes two to keep and puts the other two into the buddy's folder. If there are class notes, the partner goes to the shelf and picks up the carbonless copy paper and takes notes. At the end of class, the partner removes the white copy and places it in the buddy's folder, keeping the other copy. Afterward, the folder is placed back in the class box.

When the **Absent Buddy** returns, the individual goes directly to the box, retrieves the folder and finds makeup work, notes and any handouts already assembled. The procedure is easily understood by everyone and does not require teacher management.

If there are questions, the partner is the first person to ask. If there are still questions, it is time to go to the teacher.

HEALTHY CHOICES

A final strategy for students as part of "Accountability, Responsibility, Results" is: Eat breakfast. Numerous studies show that students who eat a healthy breakfast every day do better in school. Most students are aware of the connection between good nutrition and good grades but, unfortunately, start the day on an empty stomach, or worse, on poor food choices.

The same can said for a healthy lunch. During a recent school visit, I was observing high school classes during the middle of the day. It was a large school that started at 7:20 in the morning with five lunch periods spanning over two and a half hours. Some students left home early in the morning but did not eat lunch until afternoon. Teachers were sympathetic to hungry students. Eating in class was up to the discretion of the teacher.

In the classes that I visited, most teachers allowed food and many students took full advantage. The choice of food was what caught my attention. Several students were drinking 16-

ounce cola drinks and were eating the three C's: chips, candy, or cookies. Not one student in the three classes I visited brought any fruit, juice or milk. Everyone who chose to eat was consuming junk food and soft drinks.

The menu would not surprise most teachers. However, the impact of these food choices on learning cannot be ignored. A goal in your school might be for every teacher to promote the benefits of good nutrition, some of which are increased ability to concentrate and retain information.

☞ **The Practical Pointer:**
In fact, many school districts, and yours may be included, depend on the income from vending machines to add much needed revenue to support several school programs. What is sold in vending machines and when they are open to students, however, can be negotiated. When only healthy choices are offered, it is more likely that students will choose these foods.

SUMMARY

"Accountability, Responsibility, Results" is filled with "take back and use strategies" that can help many of our students experience greater success in school. It is all about "raising the bar" and expecting more in order to achieve more. We want all of our students to rise to the challenge and exceed their own expectations. The strategies suggested are not designed to lower expectations in any way. The focus is on personal accountability. We want our students to do more on their own and not be satisfied with anything less than 100 percent effort.

As we differentiate instruction, we personalize education by establishing overall goals and objectives but offer choices for students within that framework. We know that different kinds of learners need different kinds of strategies to develop competency and independence. The ultimate goal is to help students discover how they learn best, what motivates them, and how to manage tasks so that timelines are met. Success breeds success.

Show the child the road but expect the child
to reach his destination on his own.

–Haim Ginott

3

THE ALTERNATE ROUTE

It doesn't matter how you get there. There are so many roads that lead to the same end!

–College student with a learning disability

I like nonsense, it wakes up the brain cells. Fantasy is a necessary ingredient in living, it's a way of looking at life through the wrong end of a telescope.

–Theodor Seuss Geisel (Dr. Seuss)

Creativity is an essential part of good teaching, and as Dr. Seuss suggests, at times we need to try such a variety of approaches that we may in fact feel like we are looking through the wrong end a telescope. If that is what leads us to what sparks our students' interest, it may just work!

Just as we have many different students who learn in many different ways, there are many different routes to success. Every day in the classroom we help students compensate for personal challenges by using a variety of approaches while searching for one that clicks for each individual. We are constantly looking for practical solutions that enable each student to reach a goal.

Sometimes the solutions are small changes that make an enormous difference. Sometimes the solutions require significant changes for a particular student with special needs. Often the solution involves asking ourselves the question: This is the goal, how can I help this student achieve it?

We look for alternate routes in our daily lives outside of school as well. I was thinking about this the other day when I met my neighbor, Krista, and her five-year-old son, Sam, walking their dog, Skipper. Sam was determined to hold the leash but he was no match for the 60-pound golden retriever when a squirrel scampered by.

Krista solved the problem by giving Sam his own leash, but she also attached a second leash to Skipper's collar for herself. Skipper got his walk, Sam held the leash, and Mom was there, just in case. The solution was simple, but effective.

The focus of "The Alternate Route" is to provide simple but effective solutions for the classroom. As educators, we recognize that all students can learn but not always in the same way. Students may arrive at the same outcome using a variety of strategies, tools and techniques. Sometimes expectations have to be adjusted or goals adapted for particular students. There are difficulties that some of our students will never outgrow. These students need a boost to help them attain the highest standards and goals possible. The compensating strategies that they are learning may become the tools they use for a lifetime.

Among our students who face challenge are those who have identified special needs such as learning disabilities. These students comprise the single largest group receiving special education services. Other students who face challenges include those who may be diagnosed with attention deficit disorder or any of a myriad of disorders that make functioning in school difficult at best.

Still many other struggling students do not qualify for a particular program and do not have any type of "label." These students may also experience significant difficulties in our schools. It is these students who ultimately fall through the cracks.

When we talk to students in language that they can understand, show them how to use a variety of practical strategies, and expect them to be accountable for using compensating tools, we help them achieve high expectations.

The goal of "The Alternate Route" is to offer a wide range of strategies, tips, tools and techniques to help our students succeed despite the obstacles they face. On a fill-in-the-blank test, for example, a student with a memory deficit may be unable to *recall* specific terms but is able to *recognize* the correct answer among choices provided. A simple strategy described in this chapter suggests providing the terms on peel-off labels. It is the student's responsibility, then, to peel off the labels and attach the correct term next to the number.

In another example from the chapter, a student may have difficulty holding a pencil. One compensating technique is rolling a small piece of nonskid foam fabric around the pencil. It is a quick, on-the-spot tool that may be all that is needed to assist the student. After the teacher has provided the demonstration and it has been determined that the tool is appropriate for the student, the responsibility to *use it* belongs to the student.

STUDENT ACCOUNTABILITY

A concern that is sometimes expressed by teachers in my seminars is that the adults surrounding a child may be jumping through hoops to provide compensating strategies to help a student succeed. Teachers work hard at school and parents may also be jumping through similar hoops at home, also eager for the student to be successful. Some teachers see a problem when the only person *not in motion* is the student.

⊶ KEY IDEA

The student is the key player in making all of this work. The student must want to be part of the success. The obstacles are real and some are daunting. There are, though, many realistic ways to help a student compensate by working around those difficulties.

I am reminded of a telephone call that I received from a good friend not long ago. Her teenage son, Juan, was having trouble getting assignments in on time or at all. He had heard that some of his friends had attention deficit disorder and seemed to receive, as he put it, "extra privileges." He told his mother that he might also have attention deficit disorder and should not have to have his assignments in on time either.

The mother did not think attention deficit was the problem since it seemed to have surfaced coincidentally just as his social life was taking center stage. I told his mother that attention deficit disorder was a medical diagnosis and I was not qualified to diagnose it. That would require an extensive evaluation by a physician who was well versed in that specific area.

However, Juan needed to understand that should it be determined that he *did* have attention deficit disorder, it would not provide an excuse for not doing assignments. It would mean that he would need to learn some skills that would help him complete his assignments on time. He would need to learn how to work around it. Sometimes, but not always, specific accommodations would be needed but that would be determined after careful consideration of the individual situation.

⚷ KEY IDEA

A "label" is not an excuse. A diagnosis of attention deficit disorder does not exempt a student from a task. It would require that the student would learn specific skills to be successful.

In the meantime, I wondered aloud if this young man could benefit from general organizational strategies and study tips that would help any student manage a busy high school schedule.

The strategies suggested in "The Alternate Route" are practical, low-cost and time-efficient for both for the teacher and the student. Some may apply generally to all students in a classroom; other ideas may be more appropriate for a small group or for an individual. Some are useful at all grade levels while others are specifically geared to elementary, middle school or high school students.

As in every chapter of *The Teacher's Toolbox for Differentiating Instruction*, some ideas are detailed in several paragraphs, and others are quick tips described in a few lines. Pick and choose from the strategies suggested in this chapter. See what you would like to take back and use with your students. To make this resource easy for you to use, the highly practical ideas in "The Alternate Route" are grouped in the following eight categories:

- Tools to Use
- Textbook Strategies

- Tips for Written Assessment
- Pencil Grip Tips
- Strategies for Schedules
- Paper Slant Strategies
- 5 Sensible Solutions for Pencil Tappers
- Quick Ideas Too Good to Miss

The first three major strategies, **voice recognition, portable keyboards,** and **videotaping** offer something for every student in the classroom. They are particularly helpful in meeting individual needs for students who struggle.

TOOLS TO USE

Voice Recognition Computer Programs

Grades 5–12

Many students have wonderful ideas for stories that are well thought out. They may know the answers to their social studies questions and have practiced their spelling words correctly. Somehow, in trying to move from *thinking* to *writing*, everything falls apart. The process collapses. Stories lose their magic, answers to questions become garbled and spelling errors multiply. For students who can *tell it* but lose the concept in the time that it takes to *write it*, there can be a practical solution.

Many of these students are good candidates for a voice recognition computer program. There are several on the market for general use. Since most of us are able to speak much faster than we can write, many people use them to save time by speaking rather than using the keyboard to write. I use a brand that offers more than one version, including one designed specifically to recognize the higher voices of women and teens.

How It Works:

To use a voice recognition program, the user wears a headset with a microphone attached. It looks much like a hands-free telephone headset. Simply put, as the person speaks, what is said appears on the computer screen. While it can take as little as ten minutes for the most basic training, a significant amount of time and practice can be required to fully use and understand the computer program. The computer "learns" to recognize a voice when that individual practices reading several preselected paragraphs into the microphone.

READING LEVEL

An immediate problem occurs for some students who are low-level readers because the practice materials vary from sixth grade to eighth grade reading levels. If the individual cannot practice the readings, it is impossible to use the program.

☞ **The Practical Pointer:**

> A simple solution solved the problem. I sat next to a student who was a low-level reader. The student wore the headset and I quietly read what was on the screen to the student. The student then "echoed" what I said into the microphone.

A parent can assist by providing the necessary training time at home. Let me emphasize that any user should plan to invest in practice time before the program will consistently display on the monitor what was said by the speaker. Even then, expect a few nonsense words. Once the computer recognizes the student's voice, this can be an extremely effective tool for students in middle school, high school and college.

Several cell phone companies offer voice recognition as an option when making a cell phone call. Undoubtedly, this will soon become a standard feature. Beyond cell phone use, it is a safe prediction that all computer users will see rapid progress in the quality of voice recognition programs and the ease in using them.

Voice recognition can speed up the ability to write for all of ages. I lent my own voice recognition program to my 82 year-old father whose typing skills on the computer made writing letters a long and laborious task. Now he *speaks his letters* through voice recognition. It works very well for him and I am delighted! I don't expect to see my program returned any time soon.

Visit your local computer store to compare different brands of voice recognition programs to see which one is right for your students.

O—̄ KEY IDEA

While voice recognition can enable any individual to write more quickly, it is especially helpful in a school setting for those students who are experiencing a written language problem.

Portable Keyboard

Grades 2–12

Portable keyboards can help anyone write more quickly and more easily. Many adults use these convenient writing tools at home or at work as an alternative to the laptop computer. The cost is considerably less and these keyboards are easy to carry from one room in the house to another or to take along in the car. In fact, you may enjoy using one when taking notes at a meeting or writing a report.

ILLEGIBLE WRITING

As a compensating tool, the portable keyboard is a gift for a student who writes very slowly or whose writing is, or nearly is, illegible. You may be able to think of students you have worked with who have good ideas but who have trouble *writing them down.*

Students who have this difficulty may or may not have identified special needs. Any student who cannot read his or her own class notes, answers to study guide questions, or paragraphs will find that typing the responses offers tremendous help.

One of the most common brands of keyboards used in schools is the AlphaSmart™. Typically, each individual keyboard holds eight separate files allowing several students to use it at different times and save their work.

I have seen students make excellent progress using this tool. These were students who had been so frustrated with their writing skills in the past that they avoided any tasks involving writing. The change was remarkable.

People often ask if the individual keyboard is, in fact, a laptop computer. It is not. It has to be used in conjunction with a computer for printing purposes. Some newer models do not require a direct hookup to a computer to print.

You may want to check the Internet for more information on AlphaSmart and other individual keyboards. You can arrange to try one with a student for a few weeks at no cost to see if it would be appropriate and helpful. Students who have special needs commonly use personal keyboards. They are equally useful for all students. In fact, some school districts have enough portable keyboards for a lab setting so that an entire class may use them at once.

☞ **The Practical Pointer:**
In your school district, the best person to talk with about portable keyboards is the occupational therapist. The OT may already be using an AlphaSmart or a similar device with some students. You may find one available to try, or at least you may have an opportunity to observe firsthand how it can be used.

Video "Cloning"

Grades 4–12

One of the challenges in today's classroom is how to reach and teach students at so many different levels with so many different learning needs. A common problem occurs when some students understand a concept and are ready to move on but other students need to go over it again.

Have you considered videotaping the instructional part of your lesson? Later, those students who need reinforcement can watch the lesson again on video. It provides consistency, particularly when there is a paraprofessional in the classroom who will be reviewing content. This strategy helps students who are struggling but also gives the teacher time occasionally to provide enrichment for those students who understand the basic concepts and need "stretch" activities.

Videotaping for the Substitute

Grades K–12

Seeing a substitute teacher in the classroom has a negative impact on some students. Many younger children do not do well with change and this new person may not say everything, do everything or handle everything the way *their* teacher does it. This can be very disconcerting for them. For older students, walking into the class and finding a substitute teacher may not be disconcerting. It may provoke feelings of joy and some students may even feel like it is a day off.

When you know ahead of time that you will be attending a conference or will be out of the classroom for another reason, consider preparing a short videotape. The purpose will vary depending on the grade level and subject area.

For primary students, the purpose may be to reassure students. Even though you will not be there that day, they will see your face and hear you telling them when you will return. Perhaps you might talk about what will happen during the Morning Meeting or tell them about a story that the substitute will read to them.

As a secondary teacher, you may elect to videotape the key part of the lesson for continued consistency. You may want to take ten minutes to review concepts from the day before or explain an assignment. Of course, a few carefully chosen words about expectations, accountability and behavior may not be a bad idea, either.

 The Practical Pointer:
One parent of three small children told me that he liked the videotaping idea for himself as a parent. Since he traveled frequently on business, he decided that he would videotape himself reading a bedtime story and saying goodnight to his young children before he left on his trip. We talked about counting the days he would be gone on the video and also telling the children which day he would return.

A Mouse in the Corner

Grades K–12

Just as you might consider videotaping for the substitute teacher, consider having the substitute videotape segments of your classes in your absence. It will give you a sense of what students learned, how they behaved and where you might begin when you return. Like the camera on the school bus, a video in the classroom can act as a deterrent when behavior is an issue.

Videotaping can also help you in evaluating the effectiveness of the substitute teacher. Would you like to have this person in your classroom on another occasion? Are there any suggestions you can make to better assist the substitute in your absence? How did your students interact with the substitute? It allows you to be the mouse in the corner and help to maintain a positive learning environment in your absence.

Video Feedback

Grades K–12

A strategy that helps both you as a teacher and your students is to videotape yourself regularly and evaluate your teaching. After watching the tape, you might want to show it to a colleague or mentor for feedback. Ask students for input. Students care that you care about your teaching and your students. What do they like about your class? What do they see that you are missing? What would they like to do differently?

⊶ KEY IDEA

Videotaping in a classroom requires parent permission. Many schools include a parent permission form as part of the registration process. For the safety of students, the videotape is used only in the classroom. Once the need for the tape has been completed, the tape is erased.

The Learning Basket

Grades K–12

A highly practical strategy for high-need students in the general classroom is the **Learning Basket.** The goal is to accommodate individual needs and modify content as part of differentiating instruction for all learners. There are times, though, when the classroom teacher cannot adapt every activity for students with significant needs.

The student may be functioning at a level well below grade level and some of the content may not be appropriate. A variety of short, appropriate activities can be available for that student based on objectives as stated in the student's Individual Educational Plan.

The **Learning Basket** is a solution that is designed for occasional use. It is not meant to supplant the general curriculum but to enhance it by offering additional choices for the high-need student.

A COLLECTION OF TASKS AND ACTIVITIES

The **Learning Basket** may be a plastic container for elementary students or a three-ring binder with pockets at the secondary level. Rotate a variety of brief activities and tasks in and out of the **Learning Basket** so that at any one time there may be five or six options.

At the elementary level, a popular activity to include is *scrambled eggs*. Use the plastic colored eggs that open to hold math problems, words to arrange in sentences or synonyms and antonyms. There can be a dozen eggs in a carton, each with a different task or problem inside. Depending on the time frame, the student will perform three or four tasks. These activities support classroom content and are also designed to assist with remediation.

At the secondary level, pockets in the three-ring binder may hold a highlighted chapter outline, an audio summary, a computer disk, a modified study guide or a variety of other content-related tasks.

All activities used should be age-appropriate, relate to specific goals for that student and should reflect sound educational purpose.

This strategy is detailed with numerous examples in *Inclusion: A Fresh Look — Practical Strategies to Help All Students Succeed*. For more information, please contact Covington Cove Publications (Toll Free: 1–888-LEARN-11.)

TEXTBOOK STRATEGIES

Acetate Alternative

Grades 1–12

A sensible solution for students with difficulty copying questions out of a text or math problems from a book is to circumvent the problem by using a sheet of acetate. Place the plastic on top of the page in the text so that the student can use a marker to answer questions or do the math problems without copying them onto paper. The transparency easily slides off the page and can be turned in for grading by the teacher.

The Practical Pointer:

Anchor the acetate to the page with paper clips so that it will not slide around. An alternative is to slide the page inside a report cover with the plastic binding away facing outside. The page will be secure.

Flyswatter Windows

Grades 1–5

A simple tool that helps many students is a **flyswatter window** or a **note card with a view** to use while reading or working on a math page. The purpose is to narrow the field of vision for a student who is easily distracted. The flyswatter or note card serves as "white space" preventing the students from seeing too many lines of print at one time or becoming overwhelmed by too many math problems.

HOW TO MAKE IT:

Use a razor blade or artist's knife to cut a rectangle cut from a plastic flyswatter or note card to create a window that helps a student see just one word, phrase or math problem at a time while blocking out the surrounding material.

 The Practical Pointer:

If you would like to make several windows of different sizes and shapes for a student, note cards work best. After cutting the rectangles and squares to fit the desired sizes, use a paper punch to make a hole in each corner, and then slip the cards onto a key ring. The student can match the size to fit the material that the student is working on. This practical solution is an effective tool that many students enjoy.

Personal Highlighter on a Stick

Grades 1–7

The personal highlighter takes the **window** concept one step further. The difference between the window described previously and the **Personal Highlighter** is the yellow cellophane that highlights the text as the student reads. The **Personal Highlighter** causes the print to stand out on the page helping the student focus on the task.

HOW TO MAKE IT:

Using yellow cellophane, tape, a craft stick and a note card, the student can make a **Personal Highlighter** in a matter of minutes. A rectangle that corresponds to three or four lines of print is cut from the note card. Cut yellow cellophane slightly larger than the opening and tape it in place. The craft stick makes a simple handle when stapled to the bottom of the card.

Like the **note card with a view** and the **flyswatter window, Personal Highlighters** can be made

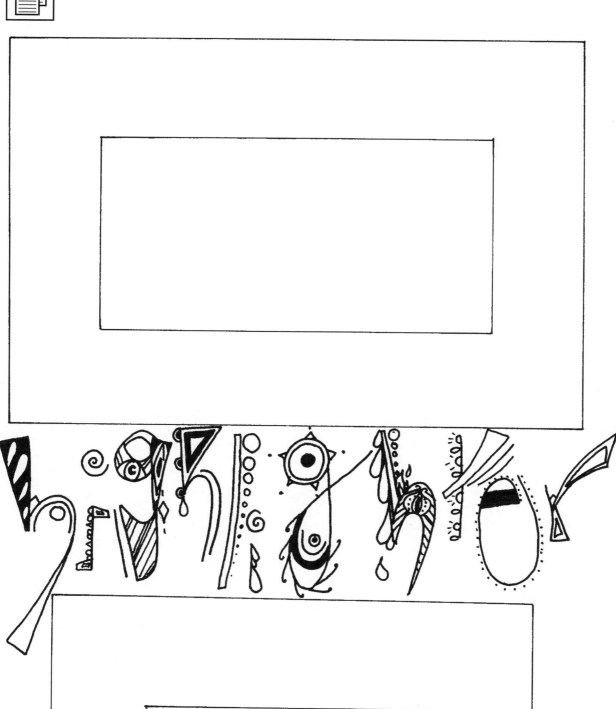

in a variety of sizes. Attaching them to a key ring works well for storage. The key ring strategy is especially helpful for use with math problems that call for different sizes and shapes. **Personal Highlighters** require very little production time but provide a lot of impact.

Reading Ruler

Grades 1–5

It looks like a ruler in size and shape but it is actually a plastic highlighting strip that students use as they read down the page. I purchase inexpensive "see through" yellow plastic folders to cut into strips about an inch and a half wide. One folder can be used to produce several **Reading Rulers**. Select a width for the strip that corresponds with three or four lines of type.

☞ **The Practical Pointer:**
The **Reading Rulers** are sturdy and can serve as bookmarks when not in use.

Magnifying Glass

Grades 2–12

Enlarging print size is a simple but effective strategy for making textbooks user-friendly. For computer-generated study guides, increasing the font size is a quick solution. Textbooks present a more challenging problem. An inexpensive plastic magnifying glass is a useful tool to enlarge print easily and quickly.

☞ **The Practical Pointer:**
Both craft stores and travel stores sell flat magnifiers that students can slide down the page while reading. Students can use them as book marks when not in use. Note that some attach directly to a book holder enabling the reader to move it easily to a specific part of the page.

Jeweler's Eyepiece

Grades 2–12

If there are detailed diagrams and maps, a round jeweler's eyepiece is a helpful tool for any student in the classroom. When students are examining original sources with small print, the jeweler's eyepiece enables them to enlarge key points.

A Page Turner!

Grades K–4

Young children and students at any grade level who experience fine-motor difficulty often struggle with turning pages in a book. Hefty Tabs™ can make a world of difference. The thumb-sized, stiff plastic tabs are easy to grasp and simplify the task.

Arrange the tabs in descending order, one per page, along the right hand pages of a book. A child will be able to grasp each tab and turn the page easily. Hefty Tabs come in five colors and can be ordered by calling Covington Cove Publications at 1–888-LEARN-11.

Find It!

Grades K–12

Hefty Tabs have many additional uses, as well. Students can use the tabs to mark frequently used sections of a text such as the glossary, index, charts and graphs.

Within a chapter, students can use them to flag key points and vocabulary. I like them because they can be repositioned as needed, are removable and can be written on with a permanent marker. For some students, the tabs work better than a bookmark, which can slide out. When students share a book, tabs in different colors indicate specific pages for specific students.

TECHNIQUES FOR WRITTEN ASSESSMENTS

Bubble Grid Tip

Grades 4–6

A challenging task for some students is a written assessment that requires a separate answer sheet. Many students with special needs, in particular, find that the most difficult type of answer sheet is the bubble grid. I have worked with students who knew the answers to many of the questions. That was not the problem. The problem came in matching the question to the correct line on the answer sheet and then entering the response.

As any teacher knows, when a student fills in the answer to *question 6* on *line 7*, all of their answers from that point on will be wrong. Students may skip a question that they are unsure of with the intention of coming back to it later. In doing so, they may "get off by one." The score does not reflect what they know; it simply reflects the difficulty that they experience in using the machine scored answer grid.

It can be extremely frustrating. One option is to allow students to write their answers on the test itself. If this will not be allowed, sticky notes provide a sensible solution.

Using two sticky notes in different colors, students place *one beneath the question* and the *second beneath the line on the answer sheet* to make sure that both the question and the answer line match.

As they continue with the assessment, students simply move the sticky notes down both the assessment and the answer grid. They check each question and answer line for a match. It will take a little more time and effort to do this, but the results will be worthwhile.

The Scribe

Grades 1–4

When I have worked with young children in primary grades who have had to fill in a bubble sheet on a reading test, I have found that some children were unable to use the sticky note technique described previously. Their difficulty with spatial relationships meant that it was hard to find the numbers in each column and line them up correctly. The additional problem of poor motor skills made the manipulation of sticky notes overwhelming.

The purpose of the assessment was not to measure the ability to fill in a bubble. The format became more important than the content and prevented some children from demonstrating understanding.

It was clear that some students needed help. Because adult volunteers were not available to assist, I invited students who were at least two years older than the students who needed help to visit the classroom and act as scribes.

The job of the scribe was not to *give* the answer but to simply *record* the answer that the younger student selected on the assessment. The benefit went both ways. The younger child received much needed assistance and the older student left the classroom walking just a bit taller that day.

Label It!

Grades 2–12

Some students experience extreme difficulty recalling the terms for fill-in-the-blank sections on a test. Several strategies may help these students including the use of mnemonics, acrostics, visualizing picture cues or acting out the word.

For some students, recalling from long-term memory or even short-term memory simply will not work. These students will not be able to recall the specific term even though they may have a good grasp of the content itself.

A time-efficient strategy for these individuals is to provide the terms on return address labels. This enables students to recognize the answer. It changes the objective from *recall* to *recognition* but the modification allows students to select the answer from choices given. It is then a matter of quickly peeling off the term and affixing it next to the number on the assessment.

Word Bank

Grades 3–12

For the student who can quickly write the responses on a fill-in-the-blank assessment but needs the choices for recognition due to a memory deficit, the traditional **Word Bank** is adequate. The **Word Bank** may be provided on a note card and lists the terms. This modification meets the need of that student without providing more help than is actually needed.

When this modification is specified on an Individualized Educational Plan for a student with special needs, there should be no question that the **Word Bank** is provided.

O⸺🗝 KEY IDEA

It bears repeating that the objective drives the activity. If writing the response will take a significant amount of time away from actually completing a larger number of questions, consider using the labels. This strategy accomplishes the same purpose.

☞ **The Practical Pointer:**
A **Word Bank** may be very much needed for a few other students without identified special needs. One teacher told me that under the latter circumstances, she offered any student a **Word Bank** for five points off the total assessment points.

These students made a decision to receive the **Word Bank** at a cost of five points and perhaps increase their overall score significantly, or forgo the **Word Bank** and keep the five points. In her view, this motivated any student who really did not need the **Word Bank** to go it alone.

The Flexible Folder

Grades 3–7

Some students feel overwhelmed when looking at the whole page of any assessment. Sometimes it is not essential to view the entire page as part of the assessment. When that is the case, use a plain manila folder and cut three or four horizontal strips from the outside to the fold.

The student can place the assessment inside the folder and lift a 3" or 4" strip to reveal only a portion of the material at one time. When that section is complete, the student can close that segment and open the next one. There is a sense of accomplishment as each segment is finished.

☞ **The Practical Pointer:**
Use a paper clip or "chip clip" to keep the folder and paper secure.

PENCIL GRIP TECHNIQUES

The Nontraditional Grip

Grades K–3

Some younger students and students who experience fine-motor difficulties sometimes struggle with the traditional pencil grip. Encourage these students to move the pencil over so that it rests *between* the index finger and the middle finger extending up between the first and second knuckles.

This may seem awkward to us because we have used the traditional grip for so long. It actually feels more stable to some individuals of any age because the thumb, index finger and middle finger are all in contact with the pencil point.

Some young children discover this independently and prefer it even when they are encouraged to use the more traditional grip. One of my children expressed a preference for this grip in first grade and has used it ever since.

⊶ KEY IDEA

By the fourth grade, a student has established a way to hold a pencil. Even when the grip is what may be called "the power grip," using the whole fist, it is very unlikely that the grip will change. Sometimes those students who grip the pencil in their fists are good candidates for the individual keyboards described earlier in this chapter because their writing is often difficult to read.

Mouse Pad Pressure

Grades K–3

When you have young writers who press so hard on the paper that the pencil lead breaks, try this simple strategy. Place their paper on a foam computer mouse pad. If the pencil pokes through the paper, there is too much pressure. It is a clear signal to the student to lighten up a bit!

Elastic Pencil Grips

Grades K–3

A quick solution for the student who has a difficult time grasping a pencil or pen is to wind a rubber band around the writing utensil. It makes it slightly thicker and will not slip.

Grasp a Ball

Grades K–3

Here is a tip for helping children who have fine-motor difficulty and find it tedious to hold a pencil. Offer a whiffle golf ball, small sponge or piece of clay to grasp in the palm of the hand while holding a pencil. It will make writing easier.

☞ **The Practical Pointer:**
Adults who have trouble writing due to arthritis may discover that this same technique works for them, too.

To the Rescue

Grades K–5

For the students who repeatedly drop a pencil, Velcro can come to the rescue. Attach a piece of Velcro to the corner of the desk and the corresponding part to the end of the pencil. Voila! There is always a place to rest the pencil and it will not roll off the desk. After several sharpenings, a new pencil will be needed. Simply add a new piece of Velcro. It is simple and it works.

The Magic Glove

Grades K–3

Turn a child's gardening glove into a useful tool for a child who has diffi-culty holding a paintbrush for an art project. Attach the paintbrush to the glove by Velcro or tape so that it will not fall out of the child's grasp. The child will enjoy painting without feeling frustrated. A pencil, pen or marker can be attached the same way.

Getting the Slant

Grades K–5

Most desks in classrooms today have a flat writing surface. While this works well for most students, some individuals find it easier to write on a slant. To compensate for the flat surface, use Velcro and a large, empty three-ring binder. Just turn the binder sideways with the rings toward the upper edge of the desk to create a comfortable writing slant. Attach it to the surface with small pieces of Velcro. It can be removed easily when other students are using the desk.

Toothbrush Holders

Grades K–2

Here is a quick tip for holding pencils. Tape an unbreakable toothbrush holder to the desk as a handy pencil and pen holder. It will usually accommodate as many as four writing utensils and will make it easier for a student to select one.

STRATEGIES FOR SCHEDULES

Picture Wallet

Grades 1–6

The **Picture Wallet** helps a high-need student compensate for difficulty in following a daily schedule at school. I am thinking of the plastic insert for photos that many people carry in their wallets.

Take photographs of the student engaged in each setting along with the specific teacher or staff member. For example, there may be a photograph of the child sitting at a computer in the computer lab with the media specialist near by. Another shows the student going through the lunch line with a tray and a cafeteria worker in the background. Another shows the student in the art room working on a project with the art teacher. Photos are then cropped to fit the plastic wallet and arranged in order for the day.

When the schedule changes and some classes do not meet, photographs can be removed, exchanged or rearranged. Extra photos can be stored in the dollar bill section. The student can put the wallet in a pocket or backpack and use it as needed.

While this strategy is suggested for elementary students, some older students with disabilities may find the **Picture Wallet** an inconspicuous way to follow the class schedule. As many teachers know, a limited number of our students at the secondary level struggle with telling time. They compensate by following the crowd. To help these students, a label can be added in the corner of the photo that indicates the time for the class.

☞ **The Practical Pointer:**
Indicate time in the same format as clocks in the school. If the school has face clocks, use a small picture depicting the time. If clocks in the building are digital, use that format so that the student will easily match the time with the clock.

Cue Cards

Grades K–5

This visual strategy shows the schedule for the day's activities in order. It uses a hands-on approach that involves the student throughout the day. Materials needed include indoor-outdoor carpeting, several kitchen countertop samples made of laminate and pictures to suggest each activity in your schedule.

How To Make It:

Cut a piece of indoor-outdoor carpeting about a foot long and five inches high. This will become the base for a schedule that is easily transported from desk to circle time to the media center.

Collect a variety of countertop samples that measure about two inches by three inches from the kitchen display area in your local home improvement store. There is no charge for these samples and the store manager will be happy to save discontinued colors and patterns for your use at school.

Collect clip-art pictures or actual photographs of all the activities in your daily schedule. Affix the pictures to the front of the countertop tiles. Add a small piece of the loopy part of the Velcro above the picture. Do the same on the back of the tile. The carpet piece will function as the fuzzy Velcro attachment.

Arrange the day's activities in order on the piece of carpeting. As the student completes each activity, the student can turn over the corresponding tile. By the end of the day, all the tiles will be turned over giving the student a well-earned sense of accomplishment.

☞ **The Practical Pointer:**
A student can also remove a tile after completing an activity and drop it through a slit in the plastic lid of a coffee can. For some younger students, this would be easier than turning over the tile and reattaching it to the carpet.

On the Board

Grades K–5

Some teachers like to provide the schedule for the day on the blackboard or white board. When second grade teacher Heidi Fritz told me that several of her students struggled with following her written schedule, I suggested that she try adding a *sequential picture schedule* along the chalk ledge.

She laminated 8" by 11" pictures depicting subjects throughout the day, including the related arts classes that changed daily. All of the pictures were stored in a basket. The job of "Picture Schedule" was added to her weekly job chart. One student each week was responsible for arranging the visual schedule along the chalk ledge corresponding to the word schedule on the board.

As the class finished each subject, the student in charge of the visual schedule would go to

the ledge and remove the corresponding picture. At any time during the day, students could look at the chalk ledge and see the next activity.

☞ **The Practical Pointer:**

Full-day kindergarten and first grade teachers may wish to display pictures for the morning activities *only* in the morning and wait to display the afternoon schedule until *after lunch* to avoid confusion.

Changeable Schedules

Grades K–8

Here is still another idea for students who have difficulty following a schedule. A personal version of the schedule located on the desk can be extremely helpful. Middle school teachers might consider laminating the daily school schedule to each desk for all students.

At the elementary level, the related arts classes change every day in many schools. To avoid confusion, use Velcro to create a changeable picture schedule using time slots. If computer class meets on Monday at 10:00, the student finds a laminated picture of a computer attached by Velcro to the time slot.

Then on Tuesday, that picture is changed to a picture of a paintbrush to indicate art. Perhaps Wednesday is library day and a picture of a book is attached. It is simple but clear for students.

Some of our youngest students are very literal when it comes to schedules. A first grade teacher told me that on the day before the winter break, she walked her students to music and rushed back to the classroom to take everything down from December and get the room ready for January. As you can imagine, she wanted to go home over the break and relax knowing that her classroom was ready for the New Year.

By the time her students returned, the January calendar was on the wall, a new winter bulletin board was up; "December" had been packed up and tucked away.

One little boy looked around the room and was devastated.

"I guess I missed Christmas!" he said sadly.

She quickly reassured him that all was not lost. It was a reminder to her, though, just how literal some of our students can be.

☞ **The Practical Pointer:**

Some primary teachers may choose to use the changeable Velcro schedules with the entire class. If so, partners can help each other change their schedules each day. When only a few students will use the changeable schedule, special student helpers can take turns providing assistance.

PAPER SLANT STRATEGIES

Right-Angle Slant

Grades K–4

This is a quick tip to assist some left-handed children and others who write with a hand "curled around." The first step is to examine how their paper is slanted on the desk. It may be placed incorrectly, often slanted for a right-handed person instead.

Simply laminate a small right angle onto the desk. The student places the corner of the paper in the angle as a guide. Locate it so that the left-handed student uses the angle to slant the paper in one direction while the right-handed student can use the same angle to slant the paper in the other direction.

The Triangle

Grades K–4

Here is another tip for helping students get the correct slant for writing. Ask students to clasp their hands in front of them toward the upper end of their desks. A partner or the teacher can slip a piece of paper inside the triangle created by their arms and hands.

Line up the long side of the paper on the *left* for *left-handed students*. Line up the long side on the *right* for *right-handed students*. Students can chant: "*Long side left—left; long side right—right.*" The paper will be at the correct slant.

Laminate the Paper

Grades K–2

One teacher told me that what worked for her was to laminate a piece of lined paper to each desk. It was slanted for the dominant hand of the student who sat in the desk. When students used an erasable marker, they wrote directly on the laminated paper. When students used a separate piece of paper, they simply placed it over the sample, lined it up, and were ready to go!

5 SENSIBLE SOLUTIONS FOR PENCIL TAPPERS

Tap on Your Lap

Grades 1–12

Let's talk about the "pencil tappers" for a moment. You cannot ignore them. They Tap! Tap! Tap! constantly. A quick solution is to encourage them to tap on their laps. It won't make noise.

Tapping Foam

Grades 1–12

Another option is to provide a small piece of foam rubber for tapping. It can be taped to the corner of the desk for silent tapping.

The Quiet End

Grades 1–4

A third tip is to tape a cotton ball to the eraser-end of a pencil. "Tap with the quiet end, Charlie . . ."

Use a Straw

Grades 1–4

Another option for those tapping students is to just hand the student a straw. Students can tap quietly to their heart's content.

Headphone Tapping

Grades 2–6

Provide a headset for a student who likes the sound of a pencil tapping. Encourage the student to tap on an earphone. They will be able to hear the tapping but it will be very quiet and will not disturb the rest of the class.

QUICK IDEAS TOO GOOD TO MISS

The following section of "The Alternate Route" contains quick tips with general grades levels listed. You may wish to consider strategies that are listed for all grade levels, even those you do not teach. Over the years, I have adapted many of these ideas for a broad range of students, especially for those students who have special needs.

Book Holders: 5 Tools

Grades 2–12

Some students find it easier to read a book or worksheet that is raised at a vertical angle. In many classrooms, you will see students who figure this out on their own by propping

their materials against other books to create a slant. Let me suggest five tools that work well for this purpose. There are actual **book holders** that are available at most office supply stores. Several other types of holders that I have used include things that you may already have at home. **Cookbook stands, decorative plate holders,** and **craft design holders** are all readily available.

While these items are fairly low in cost, you can make your own book holder at no cost at all. Use a **wire coat hanger.** Just bend the long hanger wire creating a lip in front to hold the edge of the book and bend the hook backward to create a stand to prop it up. Voila!

Weighted Paper Holder

Grades 1–5

Weighted paper holders are designed to hold papers upright. The commercially made paper holders look like a sphere cut in half with a slit across the top. Just as you can easily make your own book holder, you can make a paper holder by taping a clothespin to the edge of the desk. The student squeezes it open to insert the paper. It works well.

Skid Proof It!

Grades K–4

The waffle-style foam pad used underneath area rugs is an excellent nonskid material for a variety of practical uses in the classroom. If you have a student who constantly drops pencils and books, try the nonskid fabric in two different ways. It is an excellent solution for a quick pencil grip and slippery books. See the next descriptions for details.

Nonskid Grip

Grades 1–4

Create a secure pencil grip by cutting a 2'' square of the nonskid pad and rolling it around any writing utensil. The student will be able to hold on to it much more easily. The occupational therapist who works with students in your building may offer many additional commercially made pencil grips. This material works well as a back up and is quite inexpensive.

Hold It!

Grades K–4

To prevent books from sliding off the desk, cut an 8'' by 11'' piece of the nonskid pad to place beneath a textbook on a slippery table. The book will stay put!

KEY IDEA

Sometimes small accommodations can make a large difference.

Photo Album Packet

Grades 2–5

When some students receive a work packet or several pages at a time, it is not long before the materials are dog-eared, wrinkled and a few pages have disappeared. A few students' names may come to mind as you think about this . . . There is a simple solution.

Use a magnetic photo album. Papers are inserted into the pages and they will be stored neatly in order. A student can write directly on the plastic with a marker. Corrections can be made easily by wiping off the marker and trying again.

Paper Contrast

Grades 2–12

Using black ink on goldenrod-yellow paper creates the greatest contrast between type and paper. Black ink on green, pink or blue paper can be much more difficult to read because it does not create the same contrast.

It has been quite a while since any of us has used a ditto. Remember those? They were extremely difficult for many students to read. It had nothing to do with a disability and everything to do with poor contrast between ink and paper. That purple ink on white was the most difficult color contrast to read.

 The Practical Pointer:
Some teachers color-code assignments by paper color. Because of the difficulty created with some colors of paper, it may be more effective to ask students color-code the pages by marking the upper right-hand corner of each page with a marker.

Type Size on Paper

Grades 2–12

Think about how you, as an adult, react to print that is too small to read easily. The information sheets that are packed with medications can be a case in point. Restaurant menus are another issue altogether. (A savvy restaurant manager solves this by lending reading glasses to diners who forget their own!)

For our students, adequate print size makes a difference between a student completing an assignment and getting too discouraged to finish. A good rule of thumb is to use type size on handouts no smaller than 12 point for any grade level. For young children, consider size 14 or greater.

5-by-5 Rule

Grades 2–12

The rule of thumb on an overhead projector regarding the number of words read easily at one time is surprisingly small. The **5-by-5 Rule** suggests that no more than five words appear across on an overhead transparency and no more than five words appear vertically. The total number does not exceed 25 words.

☞ **The Practical Pointer:**

This is a general suggestion. Each teacher will want to evaluate how many words can be read easily from the back of the room on the screen. As an observer often sitting in the back, I find that the overhead projector is frequently placed very close to the screen due to lack of space. As a result, the image is sometimes very small and difficult to read beyond the first several feet. As a rule, a transparency that can be read without projection from a distance of ten feet is adequate in size.

Lighting is another factor, of course, that affects visibility of the image. An overhead transparency that is easy to read during First Period at 8 A.M. may be difficult to read during Fifth Period at 1 P.M. in a room without shades.

The 60-Second Rule

Grades 1–12

Another quick tip for using the overhead has to do with the length of time an overhead or a PowerPoint slide remains on the screen. Sixty seconds sounds like a long time for an image to remain visible but it is the typical length of time needed to assimilate the information. Speaking again from an observer's point of view, too often the slide or overhead is changed before students have had the opportunity to fully comprehend it and complete writing any notes.

Arms Length

Grades 2–12

PowerPoint is being used more and more today in classrooms. Print size for a slide from PowerPoint is large enough when it can be held and read at arm's length.

Carbonless Copy Paper

Grades 4–12

Some students are unable to take notes or are unable to read their notes later because they are illegible. A simple solution is the use of carbonless copy paper. On a rotating basis, peers use carbonless copy paper and act as designated note takers. When possible, use the *three-color* carbonless paper. The *white sheet* can be given to the student needing assistance, the note taker retains the *yellow copy*, and the *pink copy* is a tremendous help for the special education teacher in summarizing content or for the speech pathologist in working on vocabulary.

Rulers with Ridges

Grades K–2

For a student who has difficulty holding a ruler, purchase the type that have a raised ridge down the middle. The student will be able to hold it easily for measuring.

Paper with Raised Lines

Grades K–2

Like the ruler with a raised ridge, lined paper also comes with slightly raised lines to create a three-dimensional effect and prevent a student from writing "downhill." I found that it worked well to keep students "in line!"

Puff Paint Lines

Grades K–2

To create a sample of raised lines for a student, consider using a type of puff paint. It will work well on a small scale and keep writing in a straight line. I have also used puff paint to create a three-dimensional box forming raised borders to assist a child in learning to limit writing size.

Sticky Wicks

Grades K–5

Sticky Wicks are much like pipe cleaners with a tacky substance that will adhere temporarily to paper. These colorful sticks, which can be found in toy stores and craft stores, can be used effectively for two different compensating strategies.

Use them to make three dimensional, color-coded graphic organizers by shaping them into loops around parts of the web. These colorful tools can also be used to create boundaries and boxes to help students write answers within a defined area.

Transparency Tip

Grades K–12

The postage-stamp moistener is a wonderful tool to erase a portion of an overhead transparency. Too often a spray bottle wets too much of the sheet. The wheel dampens just the line or two that you want to erase. Then blot with a tissue.

Stamp Pads

Grades K–4

Some students experience extreme difficulty writing their name on a page. I am thinking particularly of students who have trouble in the area of fine-motor skills. This basic task can take them five minutes and, for them, it is laborious and frustrating.

An alternate route is needed. A practical solution is to provide a rubber stamp with their name on it and an inkpad. These inexpensive, personalized stamps can be ordered through any business supply store.

It becomes a matter of stamping the name of the top of each page. This basic requirement is completed quickly so that the student can spend the time needed on the learning task.

☞ **The Practical Pointer:**
Remind the student to turn the inkpad upside down at the end of the day. It will be ready to use the next morning.

⊶ KEY IDEA

Putting a name on the page is required on every paper but it is not the objective of the assignment. The objective should drive the activity. That is where the time should be spent and effort should be directed.

Field Trip Photos

Grades K–5

A camera is an essential tool to bring along on a field trip. Take the pictures yourself or designate a photographer to record the event. Back at school, the pictures can be used to help students recall the event. It is especially helpful to use when students need to write about the experience. Students can select a photo from the trip and write about that part of the experience.

Sequencing the Experience

Grades K–5

The concept of sequencing can also be taught using field trip photos. The trip can be recreated visually from start to finish. An option is to provide some of the photos in sequential order leaving gaps where the student's task is to fill in the missing photos.

Taping the Directions

Grades 1–4

A quick tool for to use when giving oral directions is the standard cassette tape recorder. While giving directions, simultaneously tape-record them so that an auditory learner may listen again later in a listening center, if necessary.

A Note Card on the Desk

Grades 1–4

Visual learners benefit when visual cues accompany oral directions. This may be on the board, but a few students may need a note card on the desk with the steps listed in words or portrayed in pictures.

SUMMARY

The strategies, tips, tools and techniques suggested in "The Alternate Route" are designed to help our students succeed by teaching students ways to help themselves. All of the strategies focus on helping a student work around a personal obstacle, weakness or disability. None of these strategies makes learning "too easy." These are tools that can be essential for a student. These are tools that, for some individuals, will become a way of life.

In fact, one adult who happens to have a learning disability told me about her own ongoing journey to find compensating strategies during her school years and now in her professional life. She said, "I have finally come to grips with the fact that it is not a matter of applying myself. It is not about trying harder or spending more time on something. It is all about recognizing that seemingly small skills make a big difference in my life. What may seem insignificant and even second nature to other people are, for me, essential skills to use for a lifetime."

Before you go on to another chapter, you may want to go back over "The Alternate Route." As in the previous chapters, star the "keepers" that you would like to try with your own students. If you are a parent, star the ones that you want to share with your child's teachers.

We must see that every child has equal opportunity, not to become equal, but to become different—to realize the unique potential he or she possesses.

–John Fischer

4

READ TO SUCCEED

Outside of a dog, a book is your best friend; inside of a dog, it's too dark to read.

–Groucho Marx

Children's author and university professor of teacher education, Mem Fox, encourages parents to read at least three stories a day to their children. By the time they start kindergarten, she says, children need to have heard more than 1,000 stories and memorized at least six nursery rhymes. Why so many? The average first grader has a reading vocabulary of 1,000 words at the end of the year. The listening vocabulary is so much greater! That same first grader understands over 10,000 words that are heard.

"When we read aloud, we're making the unfamiliar familiar—the print, the unfamiliar language and the information," explained Ms. Fox. This familiarity is critical to learning to read, as every teacher knows. Unfortunately, not every student comes to school with this critical experience of being read to on a daily basis. A superintendent of a large city school district told me recently that many of his students begin school not knowing which direction a book opens, that a page is read from top to bottom, and that words are read left to right. Reading is completely unfamiliar to them. They are beginning their school experience at a tremendous disadvantage.

Unless we can help them make rapid gains, the outlook is discouraging. Any experienced first grade teacher will tell you that students who are struggling with reading at the end of first grade will continue to struggle two and three years later. This presents an enormous challenge for teachers in upper elementary, middle school and high school. A reality in today's classroom is that there will be a wide range of readers in every classroom at every grade level.

O⟐ KEY IDEA

As teachers, we hope that students will enter our classrooms reading on grade level. The hope is often a far cry from the reality.

While some students will be on grade level and some students will be reading significantly above grade level, an increasing number of students will be significantly below.

In fact, I frequently meet many teachers who report that they often have very high-level readers and very low-level readers in their classes, with few in between. Adapting their reading content for such variation can be extremely difficult. It is not an overstatement to suggest that dealing with such a broad range of reading levels is one of the most critical challenges facing many classroom teachers today.

A fifth grade teacher came up to me during a break at a seminar that I was giving.

He said, "Linda, can I tell you something?" He sounded angry.

"Sure, of course," was my response.

He began by saying evenly, "I teach fifth grade. I teach fifth grade content and use fifth grade textbooks."

"Fifth grade is an important year," I responded.

"What I'd like to tell you is that I don't teach *second grade!* My textbooks aren't *second grade books,*" he added vehemently. He wasn't finished.

"And another thing," he added, "I don't teach *special education."*

This conversation was suddenly beginning to sound familiar. He was extremely frustrated. What would you say? How would you respond?

I said quietly, "We teach kids. That has to be our focus. Your students may all be in the fifth grade but some may be reading on a second grade level or even below. You have students who may be able to *learn fifth grade material* but they may *not be able to read it.* I am sure that you are an excellent teacher and you face an enormous challenge."

We cannot ignore teaching reading skills but we also must help students compensate so that the fifth grade curriculum is not beyond reach. In today's classroom, the challenge faced by this teacher is universal.

"Read to Succeed" offers numerous concrete strategies that can be used with a wide range of readers. Some strategies focus on listening as a teaching tool for the low-level reader. As in the other chapters, you are invited to pick and choose among the strategies, tips, tools and techniques. Grade level applications listed are only approximate. As you differentiate instruction for your own learners, adapt and adjust the ideas to fit your needs. See which strategies appeal to you.

To use this chapter more easily, you will find topics arranged in the following categories:

- Read . . . Read . . . Read . . .
- 16 Vocabulary Strategies
- Text Tools
- Raising the Score
- Reading and Writing
- A Word About Poetry
- Quick Tips and Tools

READ . . . READ. . . . READ . . .

Catch the Language!

Grades K–12

There is an old saying that goes, "Language is more caught than taught." The more words that a child hears, the larger the vocabulary. Vocabulary must be *heard* before it can be *read*. Listening vocabulary develops at a very early age, perhaps even before birth. The auditory vocabulary grows at a rapid rate.

When that same child begins to read, the child is able to read a few words, then a few more. During the reading process, the auditory vocabulary continues to grow as the child listens to more and more new words. The number of words that a child hears and understands continues to exceed those words that a child can read independently until that child is reading at the *eighth grade reading level.*

One of the best ways to help a child become a better reader is to read to that child again and again. Every time teachers and parents read to children, auditory vocabulary increases. When parents of preschoolers ask me what they can do to prepare their children for school, the answer is always the same: Read to them. Snuggle up and read to them every day for at least 20 minutes. One of my favorite professors at the University of Minnesota was Dr. John Manning. He would repeat over and over, "Children come to school in two ways. They have been read to regularly or they haven't. What a difference this makes in school success!"

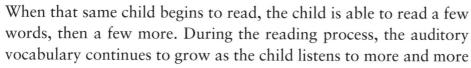

KEY IDEA

Listening vocabulary far exceeds visual vocabulary until the eighth grade reading level. Any student reading below the eighth grade reading level understands more of what is heard orally than what can be read independently.

This is a critical concept. Many of our eighth graders are not reading anywhere near the eighth grade reading level and may *never* read at that level. These students consistently understand more of what they *hear* than what they *read*. This may be true not only during their school experience but also throughout their lives.

When I taught high school students with learning disabilities, I worked with some juniors and seniors who were reading at the second grade level. It was very unlikely that, even with extensive remedial reading, these students would achieve high reading levels. Students do not typically gain a year of improvement for every year of remedial instruction when the gap is that large.

It did not mean that these students could not learn; it simply meant that these students would depend primarily on what they heard rather than what they read for information. For them, auditory and hands-on learning experiences were critical. Most of their learning did not occur through reading. To manage the high school curriculum, much of their course content was read to them.

"Is My Grandpa in that Box?"

Grades K–3

One way to reach the goal of reading 1,000 stories to every child by age five is to involve the extended family. Invite grandparents to read to their grandchildren from almost the moment of birth. It is a wonderful way for a child to recognize a grandparent's voice and to begin a close bonding relationship. In my own large family, my parents have always enjoyed reading to the grandchildren. Some of my siblings, though, live hundreds of miles away and have small children. They do not get to see each other as often as everyone would like.

THE CASSETTE RECORDER

As a holiday gift a few years ago, I gave my parents a cassette tape recorder, a detached microphone, blank tapes, and some of my favorite children's books. It was a simple solution. Since then, my parents have been reading to their grandchildren on tape and have sent the tapes along with the picture books to Sam, Lily and Allison. The grandchildren love listening to the stories and, despite the miles between them, the little ones have known their grandparents' voices from an early age. Now that Sam is old enough to hold a book by himself, he listens on the tape for Grandpa to "Ding!" a glass with a spoon telling him that it is time to turn the page.

I had an opportunity to listen to one of these special tapes recently. I smiled as I heard my 82-year-old father reading one of the same books that he read to Sam's father when *he* was a little boy. Then, I chuckled when I heard a telephone ringing on the tape.

"Whoops," I heard Grandpa say on the recording, "Just a minute, Sam, Grandpa has to answer the phone." There was a *clunk,* as the tape recorder was turned off, followed by another *clunk* as Grandpa turned the tape player back on again.

"Grandpa's back, Sam! That was your Aunt Linda on the phone. She sends you a kiss! Let's see now, where were we . . ."

Sam's parents say that he loves the part when the phone rings and Grandpa talks to him. One day, as a toddler, Sam took a good look at the tape recorder and demanded, "Is my grandpa in that box?"

☞ **The Practical Pointer:**

Even though a tape recorder often has a built-in microphone, using a separate microphone that plugs into the recorder and can be held closer to the mouth produces better sound quality. These microphones are inexpensive and are available at any discount store. While not "high tech," tape recorders are inexpensive, easy to operate and can be used anywhere.

⚷ KEY IDEA

It is critical that children see and hear their parents reading too. Encourage parents to use this same strategy. If there are children who attend day care, I always suggest that parents tape-record themselves while reading to their children. Then they can take the tape with the book to the day-care provider and ask the person to play it during the day. I have had parents call me later to tell me that naptime was so much better when their child could listen to a story read by dad or mom.

"Burning" the Book

Grades K–3

Instead of using a tape recorder, the computer can be used to create personalized *books on CD*. To do this, you will need to purchase a PC microphone to plug into the computer. You will also need a program such as Microsoft Word Media and a CD "burner" to create CDs. The advantage to this approach is that CD players are more common today in many households than tape recorders. The disadvantages are that this approach is more complicated and the equipment is more expensive.

☞ **The Practical Pointer:**

A great group baby shower gift is a collection of favorite children's books, microphone, blank CDs or tapes and tape recorder. It sends a wonderful message to the new parents about the value of reading and the books will be treasured long after the child has outgrown a pajama sleeper.

The Video Version

Grades K–3

Another strategy for out-of-town grandparents is to set up the video camera on a tripod and read to the grandchildren. Encourage grandparents to turn the book to the camera and hold it long enough for the child to see the picture easily before turning the page. I tell grandparents to imagine that they are reading to a whole group of children. It helps them take their time so that the reading pace and pictures are comfortable for children. Remind grandparents to poke their heads into the camera as they begin videotaping to say hello to the child and introduce the book.

☞ **The Practical Pointer:**
Some parents as well as grandparents have commented to me over the years that they are not good readers. This is the reason that they avoid reading to children. My response is always that children are not critical and they will hear only love in the words that are read to them. Curl up with a child and read. If reading "in person" is not possible, try one of the alternatives listed here.

Don't Stop Now!

Grades 2–6

Many parents already know the importance of reading to their children regularly. What they may not realize is the value of continuing to read aloud to their children *after the children have learned to read.* Some well-intentioned parents read to their children almost daily until this point but stop when their children are young readers. This frequently happens at about the second grade level. The parent may *listen* to the child read aloud but no longer *reads* to that child.

There is an enormous benefit to children when parents and teachers continue to read aloud at a level *just slightly higher* than children could read on their own. Every time we read aloud, we increase listening vocabulary, attention span, imagination and teach more content. As discussed in the previous section, we need to *hear* a word before we can *read* it on our own. Reading aloud significantly increases auditory vocabulary.

This is not just for young readers. Middle school and high school teachers can help their students increase both vocabulary and comprehension by reading aloud to their classes on a regular basis. I am not suggesting that secondary teachers consume a full class period by reading an entire textbook chapter to the class. Students would lose interest quickly.

Instead, I am suggesting that teachers select certain important passages or key points to read aloud. This might include relevant journal articles, an important section of a textbook, mathematical problems or a daily chapter from a novel. Many students who are reading on grade level will also find this enjoyable and helpful, especially those who are strong auditory learners.

☞ The Practical Pointer:

Being "read to" can be a joy at any age. Some adult couples find that reading aloud to each other increases a sense of closeness and creates an opportunity to talk afterward.

Literary Lunch

Grades K–5

Here is a quick idea to increase time to read during the day. Offer time to read during lunch in an elementary school. Just as we have different types of learners, we have students who have different preferences for how they relax during the school day. Some children need to step away from noise and activity for a short time just as some adults need a few minutes of quiet time to unwind.

The **Literary Lunch** gives students a choice between the cafeteria and a quiet room for reading during lunch. Supervision is always a concern. Since it is important for children to see adults reading, too, different staff members may elect to read quietly along with students. The **Literary Lunch** creates an opportunity for students to see the principal sitting down for 20 minutes with a good book.

Reading Recess

Grades K–3

In addition to lunchtime, recess offers another opportunity to increase reading during the day. While many students love recess and list it as their favorite elementary "subject," other students would rather curl up with a book. When we give students choices, we empower them and help them become independent learners.

⚲ KEY IDEA

As Jim Trelease says, "Reading is an accrued skill. The more you do it, the better you become."

Guest Readers

Grades K–3

Invite school board members, central office staff, community leaders, parents, grandparents and older students to be **Guest Readers** in your elementary building. They can select a book or you may provide a list of options for them to prepare and read to students. Some teachers tell me that it is a way of recruiting volunteers to assist in the classroom. A great time to use guest readers is during D.E.A.R.—Drop Everything And Read. Some students, especially low-level readers or nonreaders will benefit more from being read to during D.E.A.R. than just looking at pictures on their own.

☞ **The Practical Pointer:**
Tape-record your **Guest Reader** while the individual is reading. Without spending any extra time, you can add the book and story to your listening center. Students will increase vocabulary, imagination and attention span by listening to others read.

Guest Listeners

Grades 1–3

In today's diverse classroom, it is often difficult to find the time for primary students to read aloud to the teacher. Invite volunteer listeners from the community to come in during their lunch hour on a weekly basis to listen to students read. In Minneapolis, one program involves a large number of volunteers from City Hall including judges, attorneys, law enforcement officers and office staff. One judge commented, "I love Tuesdays. This is the best part of my day!" Not only does this benefit students, it also increases community support by providing an opportunity to see firsthand what is happening in schools.

Magazine Strategy

Grades K–12

Reading can be a function of opportunity. We can increase reading by just having materials available. Here's a simple and highly successful strategy that I used with high school, middle school and elementary students.

Magazines appeal to all levels of readers. Once a week I went to the media center and selected several back issues of the magazines that were most popular with students. My clue was looking for "dog-eared" copies. The back issues were usually located in a back room, not easily accessible to most students.

I brought them into the classroom and placed them on a table. As a class, we allocated 20 minutes for magazine reading. There was no quiz, no group activity, no hidden meaning. I had discovered at all grade levels that many of the students did not get any magazines at home. Neither parents nor their children subscribed to any publications. That was unfortunate because magazines can be a tremendous motivator for reading.

Often students who "don't like to read" will become immersed in magazines that interest them. Week after week, I noticed that the same students selected the same magazines.

Before parent conferences, I complied a list of students' favorite magazines, including the subscription information. When parents came for the conference, they received the list with the name of one magazine circled. I mentioned that it was a favorite of that student's and would be wonderful to receive it at home. I also mentioned magazines as a birthday or holiday gift idea.

Several parents of my students subscribed. The interesting part was the number of parents who told me that this had never occurred to them. Two years later, many students were still receiving a particular magazine. This simple strategy had long-term impact and the students truly enjoyed it.

KEY IDEA

Some adolescents who had been avid readers in elementary school suddenly read only what is assigned in middle and high school. This is partly due to their schedules, their social lives and the amount of required reading. For this age group, magazines serve an important function in encouraging reading for pleasure.

Best Sellers

Grades 9–12

What child has not traveled by spinning the globe?

–*Thurston Clarke*

A high school English teacher told me that he has increased the amount of reading his students *choose* to do through what he calls his **Bestsellers** program. He keeps books from the bestsellers list in his classroom and when students finish early, they can browse through them. Often students find books that appeal to them and read them. It is sort of a mini-library, he explained, and reading is completely voluntary. Most of the books are ones his students had not heard of—but they read them because they are there.

16 VOCABULARY STRATEGIES

A critical part of reading is the understanding and assimilation of vocabulary words. In this section of "Read to Succeed," 16 vocabulary strategies, tips and tools are suggested.

Applicable grades levels are suggested and several can be adapted for any content or grade level.

Lend Me an Ear

Grades K–4

This simple strategy helps elementary students focus on key vocabulary when the teacher is reading to the group. Laminate a 3″ x 5″ picture of an ear. It can be a drawing, clip-art, or cut from a magazine. Staple it to a craft stick.

Select a vocabulary word and write it beneath the ear using an erasable marker. Ask a student to listen for the word during the story and raise the stick when it is heard. That signals the teacher to stop and review the vocabulary meaning in context.

I have made four or five "ears" and dispersed them throughout the class so that several students could participate during one lesson. This strategy serves another purpose. It helps some students focus on listening for a specific word when the teacher is reading aloud. Parents might enjoy using **Lend Me an Ear** at home when reading to their children.

Eye Cue

Grades K–4

Use this in conjunctions with **Lend Me an Ear**. **Eye Cue** uses a similar approach with a picture of an eye. Again, a key vocabulary word is written in erasable marker. The difference is that student who holds the "eye" is watching for the word in print. The student then raises the **Eye Cue**. This strategy is used when the group is reading together and has the text in front of them. I have used both simultaneously. Some students listen for key words; others watch for them.

Address the Vocabulary!

Grades 4–12

An inexpensive address book makes an excellent management tool for placing vocabulary in alphabetical order. Instead of arranging vocabulary by unit or subject, the address book creates a mini-dictionary for each student. Frequently, you can find a variety of address books at the local Dollar Store. (Just don't ask the clerk there how much anything costs . . .)

Select an address book with adequate space for writing the word and definition. I prefer address books that are small, three-ring binders so that I can add pages, if needed, for common letters like "S" and "T."

When the address book strategy is used in a science class, students add vocabulary throughout the entire semester or school year. Reviewing terms for a final exam is a simple

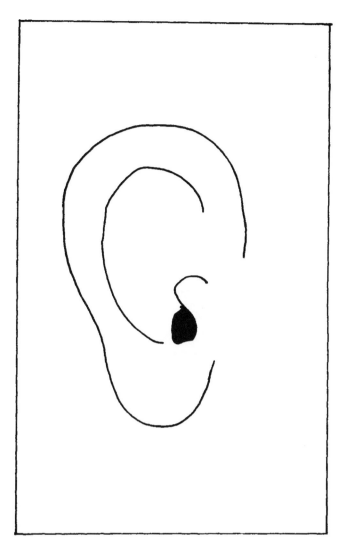

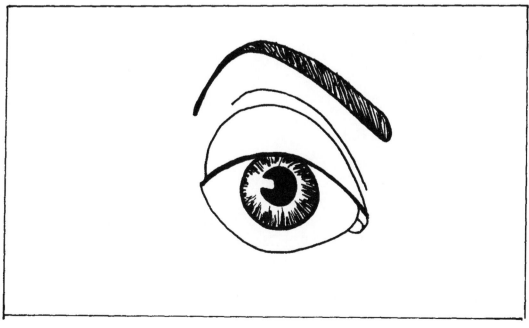

matter of paging through the book. All vocabulary for all units is located in one place in alphabetical order.

Personal Spell Check

Grades 3–5

Younger students can also use an address book as a personal "spell check." Troublesome words are continuously added to the book. When a student is writing and wants to check on a particular word for correct spelling, she or he can find it easily by beginning with the first letter. The strategy provides practice in alphabetizing, as well.

The Spiral Notebook

Grades 4–12

This next approach to vocabulary keeps all the words from every unit together in one place. I use a small spiral notebook made up of 3" x 5" note cards that are cut in half vertically up the center. The notebook now contains two stacks of cards attached to the spiral.

Next, ask students to number the corresponding left and right halves of each note card with the same number: 1–1, 2–2, 3–3 and so on. The notebook is now ready to use.

Each new vocabulary word is written on the left half of the card. The definition is written on the right half. Students can quickly flip through the left side when reviewing vocabulary words and recall the definitions. If a there is a word that the student cannot define, it is a simple matter of referring to the number on the card and flipping to the same number on the right to find the definition. This handy tool collects all the vocabulary from a semester or yearlong course for efficient and convenient review.

☞ **The Practical Pointer:**
Use a tab or sticky flag to mark the next open card in the spiral so that it is not necessary to flip through several weeks' worth of words to write a new word. The student may also wish to indicate the beginning of each new unit by a colored tab for easy reference.

Front and Back Flash Cards

Grades 6–12

This practical vocabulary strategy uses individual 3" x 5" note cards. It is different from the previous strategy that connected all of the cards by a spiral. It can be advantageous to keep all vocabulary together in one place, but there are also advantages in keeping the cards separate and focusing on vocabulary for the current unit only.

Front and Back Flashcards is a simple technique that lends itself to including more details on

Word:

Visual Cue:

Part of Speech

Pronuciation

Definition:

Sentence:

Unit _____

Pg. _____

each vocabulary card. The front of the card has two things: the *vocabulary word* and a *visual cue*. (See more details in the following section about the advantages of the visual cue.)

On the back of the card, there is room for several more details:

- upper left corner lists the *part of speech*
- upper right corner provides a *pronunciation guide*
- lower left corner indicates the *abbreviated name of the unit*
- lower right cites the *page number in the text*
- the *definition* is written in the center of the card
- beneath the definition is a *sentence using the word in context*

The card concept can be easily adapted depending on the amount of detail needed for the content, grade level and individual student.

Picture Cue

Grades K–12

As the old saying goes, a picture is worth a thousand words. A **Picture Cue** is particularly valuable in learning and assimilating new vocabulary at all grades levels. When the drawing is self-generated, it is much more memorable for a student than using a teacher-generated visual cue.

During staff development, I frequently ask teachers to draw a quick visual to depict the meaning of a given word. It is not an art contest. I often hear comments lamenting a serious lack of artistic ability, but level of talent has little impact on creating simple picture cues. The reason for the exercise is to give everyone an opportunity to see afterward what other individuals drew.

It is amazing to take a basic vocabulary word like "profit," provide just 30 seconds of drawing time, and see how many different interpretations there can be within the group. What would you draw? As you can imagine, there are always the predictable dollar signs, pots of gold, and graphs with the line edging ever upward.

There are also very unpredictable approaches as well. Let me share just one example. One person drew a duck and a fence. After I overheard several individuals sitting nearby discussing the "hidden meaning," I heard one person say, "See if *she* gets it!"

I took a long look and had to admit that I was stumped. A fellow named Robert had illustrated "profit" by a duck and a fence. . . H-m-m-m . . . Of course, it didn't matter if the rest of us were not making a connection; the visual cue only has to be relevant to the person using it. Finally, I had to give up. How did the duck and the fence suggest "profit"? The answer was simple, the artist explained, "When I think of 'profit,' I think of Bill

Gates!" Oh. I would never have figured that one out. Have you had a few students who would think along those same lines?

Act It Out

Grades 4–12

Just as the **Picture Cue** helps the visual learner, **Act It Out** is a tremendous vocabulary strategy for the kinesthetic learner. This can be used at all grade levels to reinforce new vocabulary. In the classroom, I placed students in cooperative groups and gave each group a word and 60 seconds to figure out how to **Act It Out** for the group. One of the words that I used with fifth graders was *export*.

It was especially interesting that two groups had the same word but chose very different ways to act it out. One group made paper airplanes. They stood up and flew them across the room. They were *exporting*. Another group with the same word took a completely different approach. Each member quickly ran around the room, grabbed something off a desk and ran out the door. They, too, were *exporting* but that looked more like *theft* to me! Eventually all of the students returned and the items were put back. **Act It Out** made quite an impression and students remembered those words.

Let me share one more example. A teacher told me that she made the mistake of teaching both *area* and *perimeter* during a short span of time. Her students were confused. Finally, she had everyone stand and come to the center of the room. She told students to extend their arms, twirl around and chant *"area, area, area."* Next, she had everyone walk around the outside edge of the room chanting *"perimeter, perimeter, perimeter."*

A few days later, the students were working quietly when one boy got up, walked to the side of the room chanting, *"perimeter, perimeter, perimeter."* He sat down and went back to work without another word. Now there is definitely a "hands-on" learner!

☞ **The Practical Pointer:**
Students can also write the word "perimeter" and circle the word "rim" within it as a reminder. Filling in an "a" in area can provide a visual cue for that word.

The Recipe Word Box

Grades 4–12

I have used all of the vocabulary strategies listed in this section successfully in different situations, but the **Recipe Word Box** remains one of my favorites. It is one of those tried and true tools for vocabulary that is simple and effective. The dividers are used to separate units. Students can use markers to color-code the upper corner of each card to indicate units. The recipe boxes can be stored easily in the classroom or at home. This is one of those strategies that is as effective for a college senior as it is for a fifth grader.

☞ **The Practical Pointer:**

When it is time to review, a student can pull the cards from one unit and separate vocabulary into piles of words that are already understood and words that need review.

Context Cues

Grades 4–12

Sheets of paper with vocabulary definitions stuffed in a folder are usually not very effective for assimilating new vocabulary. Learning meaning in context makes more sense. Sticky notes work very well for this purpose. Encourage students to write definitions of key words on sticky notes and place them directly underneath the word in the textbook. Later, when the student is reviewing, the definition will appear in context.

Peripheral Learning

Grades 6–12

A study strategy that can be useful to any student is **Peripheral Learning** because it can be applied to virtually any topic or subject area. The concept focuses on creating a visual memory by repeated exposure to content. Students who are strong visual learners will find the concept particularly appealing.

HOW IT WORKS:

To demonstrate the concept to students, you may wish to begin with three or four key vocabulary words that are part of a unit of study. Write the words in large print on oak tag board using a broad marker. Make sure that the print is large enough to be read easily from across the room.

Place the words on the wall in places where students will look frequently, such as *near the clock, above the door,* and *above the blackboard or white board.* Then, on separate oak tag board, write the meaning of each word in large print, again using with a broad marker. Tape the meaning beneath the word and call attention to it often during the unit in context.

Students will read the words on the wall during class. At some point, there may be a time when you want to assess students' understanding of the vocabulary and you may not want the meaning of the word to appear on the wall. Remove the meaning, but leave the word itself.

When students come to the word on an assessment, they will glance up at the location where the definition had been located. Often they will visualize the meaning that they had seen so often and will be able to define the term.

The Practical Pointer:
Math teachers can use **Peripheral Learning** with a formula and example. Students habitually look at both and create a visual model that they can "see" even when the example is not there.

Peripheral Learning in Color

Grades 6–12

One teacher told me that **peripheral learning in color** helped her students learn parts of speech during the grammar unit. She wrote each part of speech on a different color of bright oak tag board so that her students would associate both the location and color with the term. "Noun," defined with several examples, was on bright green oak tag board above the clock. "Verb," also defined and with examples, was on bright orange above the bulletin board. The room had a rainbow of bright grammar posters.

When it was time to take a standardized test, she originally planned to remove the posters but decided against it. Instead, she covered each poster with a blank piece of oak tag board in the same color.

During the test, she was amazed! She watched as students paused, looked up at the brightly colored blank posters and quickly wrote a response. Their assessment scores showed that **peripheral learning** made a huge difference.

Thinking back to your college years, you may have had experiences with **peripheral learning.** Can you recall being in a situation where you were taking an exam, perhaps in the infamous Blue Book? Did you remember being so close to recalling some important information that you could almost "see" the page of your notes? Unfortunately, the notes may not have been quite clear enough to help you, until you turned in your exam, that is.

Once out in the hallway, did you find that the information suddenly came back to you? That last part was due to stress. Visualizing your notebook page was part of **peripheral learning.**

We can teach peripheral learning to the whole class as an effective study tool. For those students who find this helpful, it is one more learning technique to add to their personal repertoire. They can use it while studying at home and continue to use it in postsecondary education.

Photo Flash Cards

Grades K–3

Some younger students benefit from using vocabulary photos to learn vocabulary. Digital cameras have made this strategy easy to implement. It is especially useful when students are very literal in their approach thus making photos, magazine pictures or even three-dimensional objects the best way for them to learn.

Word Wall

Grades K–5

In most elementary classroom where I have visited in recent years, there is **Word Wall** of some type. There can be many purposes including spelling, sight word recognition, synonyms, antonyms, story characters and vocabulary.

Using it for vocabulary is easy to do. Dedicate one section of wall space to creating a running record or new vocabulary as it is introduced. Words are added on large note cards. It is a convenient way for a teacher to call attention to key words frequently and review definitions.

☞ **The Practical Pointer:**
When wall space is at a premium, consider using a movable bulletin board or portable room divider. A folding screen works very well for an "addition" to wall space. Decorative screens can be found at garage sales and may be easily repainted or covered with fabric.

Key Ring Vocabulary

Grades 3–6

The use of key rings as a practical tool for holding flash cards has been highlighted in other chapters. Key rings are particularly effective in learning vocabulary. I encourage students to write the word on one side and the definition of the other. The words for one unit are hooked together on the key ring. As in the suggestion for learning spelling words, vocabulary cards can be eliminated from the ring once they are learned. This allows the student to concentrate on the more difficult words left on the ring. When all of the words have been mastered for the unit, the vocabulary is returned to the key ring and stored for review later.

Vocabulary Cut-Ups

Grades 2–5

The **Vocabulary Cut-Ups** strategy uses manila folders cut in strips. Write the vocabulary word with the definition following. Cut a jagged line between the word and the meaning to create a two-piece puzzle. Place several puzzles in an envelope. Students can work in pairs or individually to reconnect the jagged pieces to form the correct combination. Consider a wide variety of other uses besides vocabulary for the cut-ups.

TEXT TOOLS

Prereading

Grades 4–12

An effective strategy for struggling readers at all grade levels is **prereading.** A chapter in a textbook or story can be read aloud to the student the night before or the day before it is introduced in class. The key is to read it ahead of time. This way, vocabulary and content are familiar enough so that the material is already at a review point for the student.

Too often these students are in a continual mode of "catch-up." They read more slowly and may take longer to assimilate the information. The goal of **prereading** is to "front load" information ahead of time so that low-level readers are one step ahead instead of one behind.

Consistent Basis

When **prereading** is done on a regular basis, the student comes to class prepared to participate in class discussions. Several different individuals can assist with prereading to a students or group of students. Paraprofessionals, Title 1 teachers, Assurance of Mastery teachers, parents, peer tutors, community volunteers and special education staff can help with this.

In my own experience, regular **prereading** worked successfully because of the diligence of a parent. For high school students, this arrangement may be preferable for privacy reasons. No one at school is aware of it. The parent receives the syllabus ahead of time and stays one day ahead of the content.

It takes a great deal of time and commitment for a parent to read the material aloud nearly every night for classes such as social studies and English. While I have worked closely with parents who have done this, not every parent is able or willing to do so. It may be possible for parents to read part of the time but additional readers are needed for many students.

☞ **The Practical Pointer:**
When a parent decides to take on the **prereading** role, it helps tremendously if an additional copy of the text can be kept at home.

O⚷ KEY IDEA

Just because the student lacks the ability to read something does not necessarily mean that the student lacks the ability to comprehend it. The results can be impressive.

SQ3R (Survey, Question, Read, Recite, Review)

Grades 5–12

Learning how to read expository material such as textbooks, articles and original sources is critical. It is different from reading narrative material. A student can miss a few pages or an entire chapter of a novel and fill in the missing pieces very quickly. The story line carries the reader.

EXPOSITORY WRITING

This is not the case with a textbook. If a student misses a few pages of a social studies text or science chapter, a large amount of content is missed. In helping students become independent learners, we need to demonstrate this critical difference between reading narrative writing and expository writing. Understanding expository writing in textbooks creates the biggest challenge. The content requires the student to interact with the text in order to process the information. To do so requires essential comprehension skills.

READING PACE

Another issue centers on the reading pace of the student. The student should not read faster than that student's ability to assimilate complex concepts. It is not unusual to find it necessary to read expository content more than once to understand it. Each chapter may also contain important information in charts, pictures and headings that some students miss or ignore. Finally, the volume of content makes it essential that the student stop frequently to think through the concepts.

O⌐ KEY IDEA

Students need to learn the difference between reading narrative and expository content. Too often students think that both can be read at the same pace. In fact, they need to read expository material much more slowly, stopping frequently to assimilate what was read.

SQ3R REVISITED

The **Survey, Question, Read, Recite, Review** technique is worth revisiting as an effective approach to reading expository material. It is the workhorse of comprehension, a tried and true strategy that has been taught for years. You may have learned how to use it when you were in school. Many teachers train their students in how to use it today. The next section describes **SQ3R** but describes how the strategy can be taken one step further in increasing its effectiveness.

The SQ3R Spin-Off

Grades 4–12

The **SQ3R Spin-Off** refines the **SQ3R** technique by adding a questioning component at the end of each paragraph. Notice that the first few steps are identical to the basic **SQ3R** format. The strategy can be taught as an individual strategy but also works very well as a partner activity. For students at all reading levels, the **SQ3R Spin-Off** can be an effective tool for increasing reading comprehension.

O─┐ KEY IDEA

While the use of pairs is suggested for this activity, three students in a group can also work well. I am always particularly careful to make sure that students are comfortable reading aloud. When I ask adults about their best and worst school memories, reading aloud in class is often mentioned immediately in the "worst" memory category.

Some of our students feel the same way. Certainly a student who truly dreads reading aloud should never be forced to do so. That student could benefit just as much by pulling up a chair and joining two other students who would take turns reading. All three students could then participate in formulating questions.

The **SQ3R Spin-Off** requires very little class time to teach. If it is used frequently to introduce expository material, students will be able to use the technique on their own as a lifelong independent learning strategy.

☞ **The Practical Pointer:**
See the **Shoulder-to-Shoulder** technique in "All Together Now" for an excellent strategy to use when students are reading with a partner.

KWLS

Grades 4–12

Three words form the backbone for key questions of Donna Ogle's **KWLS** reading tool **Know, Want,** and **Learn.**

SQ3R SPIN-OFF

Step 1: *Survey* the section.
Look at the title and subtitles before beginning. Page through the section reading captions beneath photos and charts or graphs.

Step 2: *Skim questions* at the end of the section or chapter.

Step 3: *Learn critical vocabulary.*
Later in this chapter, you will find several applicable strategies for learning vocabulary.

At this juncture, the SQ3R Spin-Off differs from the original SQ3R.

Step 4: *Circle the last period of each paragraph* in the section to be read.

Step 5: *Read the first paragraph aloud.*
Complete steps 6 through 8 for each paragraph. Continue reading aloud, alternating paragraphs with a partner.
One reads while the other listens.

Step 6: *Stop at the circled period* at the end of each paragraph after it has been read.

Step 7: *The listener asks a question.*
"What was this about?" Questions may become more complex with practice. The essence of the question is always gleaning the main idea of the paragraph.

Step 8: *Answer the question.*

Step 9: *Switch roles.*
The reader becomes the listener and the listener becomes the reader.

What do you *know*?

What do you *want* to know?

What did you *learn*?

It has truly become a concrete strategy for helping students process information in content-area reading. I have used it with students from upper elementary grades through high school and in teaching adult education GED courses. My four children also were taught several variations of the KWL approach to interact with their reading in several different subjects. As I visit classrooms today, I find that teachers routinely adapt the concept to fit content, purpose, grade level and individual needs of students. An adaptation that helped my students was addition of a final question signaled by the letter "S" in the key word "Still." What do you *still* want to know?

How It Works:

What do you know?

I used the strategy most often in cooperative groups but I have observed students using it on an individual basis in many classrooms. The first question focuses on background knowledge. What information does a student or group of students bring to a topic? In a brief session not unlike brainstorming and using a series of columns, students quickly record facts, impressions and experiences that are already familiar.

Lists, phrases, visuals, photographs from trips, news articles and pictures from magazines are some of the pieces of information that may fill the first column. When necessary, students can expand the column provided to include a second page. I have also had students bring in three-dimensional objects to share as part of their personal background knowledge.

When one of my own children was in fifth grade, he asked me to bring a collection of historical artifacts that had been stored in a great-grandparent's attic. These formed an essential part of his prior knowledge on the subject.

What do you want to know?

Sharing background knowledge in any content area heightens interest in the topic. Students are naturally curious. The purpose of the second column is to formulate questions about the topic. Depending on the purpose, I have varied the format for this using whole group, small groups, one-on-one, and individual approaches.

Sometimes so many questions were formulated that additional paper was needed. Flip charts work well for cooperative groups in formulating questions. Assign one student the task of taking home the large sheets from the entire class and recording a composite of class questions.

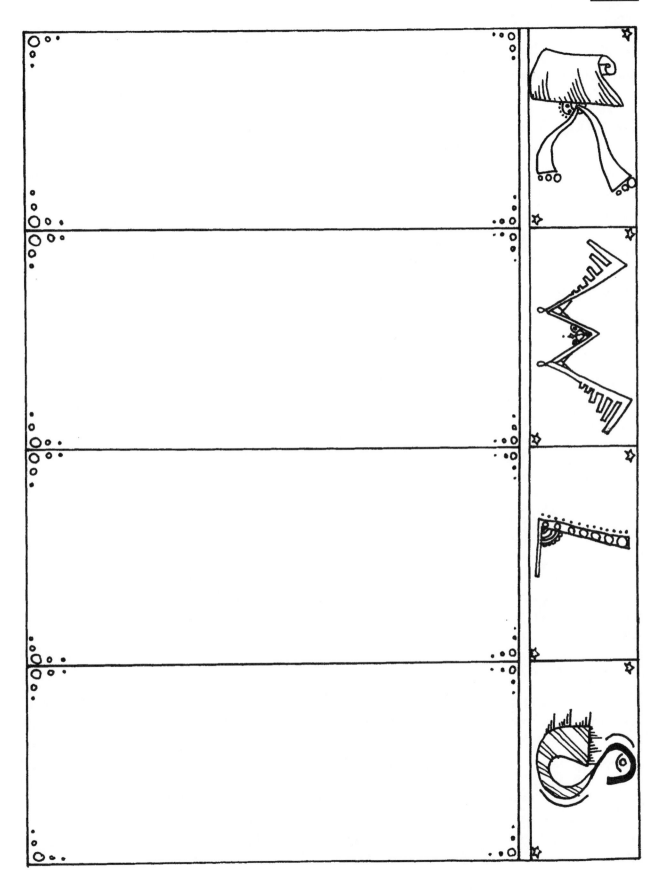

What did you learn?

Next, students read the text in combination with several other strategies that teach vocabulary, main idea and inference. Numerous other class activities enhance the content. Ultimately, students return to the **KWLS** format to record what they have learned. Using lists, phrases and comments, students describe what they have learned.

Students will analyze what they have learned to see if the new information also confirms their prior knowledge. Students sometimes discover significant gaps in their background knowledge or memory of what they thought they knew. They can make additions in the first column to correct any misinformation that they had at the outset.

The third column may not provide enough space to record all the new information learned but it is meant to serve as a model to teach the thought process. In addition, students will be demonstrating what they have learned in several ways beyond this written format. As part of differentiating instruction, students will use what they have learned to produce a final product that clearly shows some critical aspect of what they now know.

What do you still want to know?

The final question focuses on further study. Given the opportunity to learn more, students are asked to indicate what piques their interest. In many classrooms, this forms the basis for independent study as some students may elect to delve further into a subject of interest.

When I suggest this process to teachers, I find that many of them go through the logical process of **KWLS** without naming the strategy. One teacher told me, "I would say that I do that already. It makes sense to begin with finding out what my students know. It helps me plan how to approach the content. My current students may know more than the group that I had last year. I always adjust my plans. Finding out what students want to know is the next step. I make sure that my required content also fits their interest. Afterward we go back and evaluate. I've always taught this way. It just makes sense."

Place Cards from Above

Grades 2–12

Many students at all grade levels like to use a note card to keep their place as they read. Too often, they will place the card beneath the line of print and move it down the page line by line. It marks the place, but reading can be "choppy." It is more efficient to flip-flop this technique. Encourage students to hold the marker above the line of print. As they read, they will slide the marker down the page. The difference is that the eye moves more quickly than the time it takes for the hand to slide down to the next line. The result? Reading will be faster and smoother.

Watch It First

Grades 4–12

Often when a novel is be read by the entire class, the video version is shown afterward. Sometimes the purpose is to compare the book with the video, other times it is a reward. When there are students who are reading well below grade level, consider offering these students the option of watching the video *first*. While students will lose the opportunity to *imagine* characters and settings, they will gain an understanding of the story line, know the characters and be better able to participate in class discussions. For them, the benefits can outweigh the disadvantages.

☞ **The Practical Pointer:**

Some videos vary great greatly from the original book. When there is a discrepancy between the novel and the video, it is helpful if those differences are indicated ahead of time. Others follow the plot closely. An example is *Shiloh*, a popular novel by Phyllis Reynolds Naylor. The video version mirrors the book so there would be no confusion for students who view the video first.

RAISING THE SCORE

Reading Tests Aloud

Grades 2–12

Reading a paper-pencil assessment aloud can make a noticeable difference in raising grades for some students. I have had students who had failed a "book test" for a particular unit. The next unit test followed a very similar in format and level of difficulty. This time, I read the test orally. The same students who failed the previous test passed a second assessment with strong scores. Have you had the same experience with some of your own students? If so, you are not alone. Whenever I ask this question during a seminar, hands go up and heads are nodding.

WHO BENEFITS?

I found that this simple strategy of reading tests orally was successful over and over again for me during 22 years of teaching. One group of students who benefited included low-level readers who struggled when they *read* the questions but recognized the words when they *heard* them. Another group of students who benefited were often auditory learners who performed better when listening. While they were able to read independently, listening was their learning preference.

STANDARDIZED TESTS

A common issue centers on reading standardized tests aloud. Is it permitted? Should it be permitted? Students with special needs may have a clear statement written on an Independent Educational Plan (IEP) that specifies which sections must be read orally. For these students, permission is based on personal need.

If having material read orally is the way that they learn in the classroom on a daily basis, these students are often allowed to have specific sections read aloud. For students on Section 504 Plans, the same is true. They may qualify to have parts of standardized tests read orally. On a case-by-case basis and depending on the purpose of an assessment, permission may or may not be granted to read a section aloud. Ahead of time, check with a special education teacher and examine the language of the IEP in this area.

Most states now use standardized assessments at several grade levels. Often each state department of education will specify what accommodations are allowed and under what conditions.

For students without specific permission to have sections read to them, reading a standardized assessment aloud is usually not permitted. This can be very frustrating for parents and teachers alike who know that it would be very helpful for a particular student who may be a low-level reader or a strong auditory learner.

⊙┱ KEY IDEA

When a student has a history of struggling as a reader and performs substantially better on assessments that are read aloud, the student may be a candidate for a 504 Plan. It would have to be determined that the student currently has a disability that significantly affects that student's learning and ability to function. Further, the condition must be shown to have a major impact on the student's life to qualify for Section 504.

Subvocalizing for Auditory Learners

Grades 1–12

As a learning strategy, I have read classroom unit tests and other materials aloud to the entire group. One purpose was to help students discover if this helped them. When the response was favorable, I encouraged strong readers to experiment with subvocalizing, that is, reading aloud quietly to themselves. They could accomplish the same thing without teacher input. This was easy to try at home. In the classroom, students could elect to sit in study carrels and subvocalize without disturbing others.

Students liked having a choice in how a paper-pencil classroom assessment was administered. "If you would like to listen as I read the test aloud, sit on this side of the room and follow along. If you prefer to read it on your own, please sit on the that side of the room and work at your own pace."

☞ **The Practical Pointer:**

Much research has been done and much has been written about learning styles and learning preferences. Most likely you have discussed learning styles and the impact on learning in your own school. Stop for a moment, though, and think about the different styles including visual, auditory, kinesthetic and haptic or combination of styles. Which learning style characterizes most of us as teachers? Most people use a combination of learning styles, but which style is your own dominant style? The odds are that you answered "visual" to both questions.

O⊸ KEY IDEA

Research supports that the majority of teachers, at least 60 percent, are strong visual learners. I think the actual percentage is much higher. Whenever I ask a group of teachers in a seminar how many would consider themselves to be strong visual learners, a whopping 80 percent of the hands go up. It is overwhelming. I find the same response whether I ask a staff of 30 or a very large group of over 600 teachers.

The implications are enormous in our daily teaching. While we undoubtedly have some visual learners in our classrooms, we also have some strong auditory learners and some strong kinesthetic learners. When asked how we teach, most of us would say that we teach using a variety of styles. What we may not realize, however, is that most of us teach *more often in our own preferred style.*

Since most of us are visual learners ourselves, we tend to favor visual learning. That is why so much of schoolwork has been based on *reading,* the preference of visual learners. A key component of differentiating instruction in the classroom involves offering choices based on the learning preferences of all learners. As teachers we can strengthen our teaching by increasing kinesthetic and auditory activities to meet the learning preferences of *all* students.

Taping the Assessment and Other Materials

Grade Levels 4–12

Taping reading materials is not a new strategy, but it is a strategy worth revisiting. Recording textbooks, novels, directions and key points enables low-level readers to gain the same information through listening that other students gain through reading. Reading is an important skill. We need to continue to emphasize critical reading strategies while simultaneously recognizing the immediate need to present the content in a variety of ways.

Listening to content on tape is one such route. The fifth grade teacher, mentioned earlier, who felt frustrated by a student in his classroom who was reading at the second grade level, could have taped the social studies chapters for that student. In fact, taping was one of the first suggestions that I made.

O—🔑 KEY IDEA

Taping as a strategy is not intended to minimize the need to read. Instead, taping is a realistic tool for those students, especially secondary students, who are reading far below grade level. For them, the only way to master grade level content is to find an alternate route.

The Headset Solution

Grades 4–12

Taping solved a key problem in one school where I was consulting. Several secondary teachers felt that reading a test to the entire class would benefit *some* students but would be *distracting* for others. How could anyone meet the both needs simultaneously? One teacher said that he alternated how he delivered his written assessments. Sometimes he read the questions aloud to help the auditory learners; other times he deferred to the request of the visual learners for a quiet environment.

Taping the test and providing headsets in the classroom offered a viable solution. In fact, his approach became standard throughout the school with strong administrative support.

The principal required that each written assessment be complete and ready for taping 24 hours in advance. Then, paraprofessionals tape-recorded the questions. On the day of the written assessment, teachers offered tape players with headsets to their students. Those who needed to listen to the test while reading the questions could do both in the classroom without disturbing those students who preferred a quiet atmosphere. A taped test offered another advantage in that it allowed students to go back and replay questions over again for better understanding.

☞ **The Practical Pointer:**

Most teachers do not have time to tape all the materials used. Consider asking retired teachers, community volunteers or high school students who are skilled readers to do some taping. Some schools create a partnership with community businesses that provide volunteer readers as well as donations of audiotape and tape recorders.

 # KEY IDEA

All students can learn. Not all students learn in the same way or at the same rate. It bears repeating that not being able to read the social studies chapter, for example, does not mean that the student cannot understand the content.

READING AND WRITING

Creating a Wordless Book

Grades 2–8

Several years ago, our family packed the car and went on a road trip to the Black Hills of South Dakota. We had not gone more than a few miles when Annie, our youngest child, realized that she had forgotten her favorite stuffed animal, Jester the Monkey. There was considerable sadness for a while but soon Jester was forgotten.

At a rest area, my husband noticed the monkey's leg sticking out behind the cooler in the trunk. Keeping his discovery to himself, he had an idea. He kept Jester hidden from the rest of us but quietly took pictures of the little monkey everywhere we went throughout the trip. Jester had quite an adventure! When we arrived home, Annie found Jester just where she thought she left him, "sound asleep" on her bed.

A few days later, she woke up to find Jester clutching a gift. Annie unwrapped a photo album recording the entire trip to the Black Hills. Imagine her surprise when she discovered that Jester was in every picture! There was Jester wearing sunglasses outside the famous Corn Palace. There was Jester roasting a marshmallow at the campfire. There was Jester looking up at Mount Rushmore. There was Jester tucked in next to Annie in her sleeping bag. Jester was even reading a map at a rest area. Old Dad was pretty proud of himself for creating a wonderful wordless book that Annie treasures.

"You 'Flat Stanleyed' our trip," I laughed. He had no idea who Flat Stanley was but, if you are an elementary teacher, you know. For the uninitiated, stop in at your local library and you will be in for a treat. Your students can develop the same concept.

From Wordless to Words

Grades 6–8

Jester's excellent adventure became the basis for a creative writing unit with my middle school English students. I visited the local public library and filled two baskets with wordless picture books. Several of my eighth grade students were unfamiliar with wordless books. We spent a class period enjoying the library books. There was not a sound that day as students finished one and grabbed another.

The next day I brought in a basket of books using photographs as illustrations. Students poured over these books with equal interest.

The third day I explained the series of tasks that we would be engaged in during the next few weeks. Very briefly, the first task was to tell a story in photographs with the added requirement that each picture had to contain the same inanimate object. The eighth-graders were extremely creative.

The second task involved using the photo sequence to write the accompanying story. The overall goal was the same for all students: to write a children's story. The elements that were part of every narrative were discussed and these key concepts had to be included. Key vocabulary words that were essential to the unit were required for every student.

Beyond that, there was much room for differentiating instruction. Some students selected black and white photos; others used color; some elected to use hand-drawn cartoons. Topics included a myriad of subjects. Length of the stories varied greatly from student to student. Complexity varied based on ability and interest.

The third major task required proofreading by peers who followed a writing rubric. Community volunteers also came in to assist with proofreading.

The fourth task was to read the story to an audience of younger students. Each eighth-grader had to determine which grade level would most enjoy hearing the book. Every student read to a small group. Some of the eighth-graders with special needs were particularly delighted to share their books with younger children.

A final requirement was to create a "Writers' Expo" exhibit. Each student chose how to display the book and demonstrate the process that had been used to create the final product. Families and school staff members were invited. Students stood next to their displays, answered questions and talked about the writing process.

In this detailed example of differentiating instruction, each student completed a children's book that was different from every other book but contained all of the required elements.

As a generous gesture, some students donated their books to children in homeless shelters while others elected to keep them to remember the experience. Students felt empowered by the choices they had within the parameters of the writing project. Without exception, every student fully participated, learned a great deal about the writing process, and enjoyed the project.

⊙⌐ KEY IDEA

It should be noted that this was one of many, many writing projects for the eighth-graders. Writing a children's book taught specific creative writing skills; several other writing projects focused highlighted components of expository writing.

Comic Strip Writing

Grades 4–6

A quick writing technique that has many different adaptations is **comic strip writing.** One approach is to provide blank paper and have students retell a story or create their own story using the comic strip format. Another version that I have used is to give students a comic strip from the newspaper with the words removed. Students write their own story to correspond with the drawings. It is interesting how different their interpretation can be using the same drawings in the same sequence! Still another version involves providing the first two comic strip frames and students can finish the story using as many frames as they wish. The activity can be adapted to fit a very short time frame or developed as part of a larger writing task.

Human Proofreader

Grades 4–12

In writing, encourage students to have someone else read paragraphs and essays before turning them in to the teacher. Today many students make the mistake of relying completely on the computer for spelling and grammar checks. As you know, these systems are helpful but do not take the place of a **human proofreader.**

I chuckled when an admission counselor for a top university described some of the "bloopers" on admission essays that had not surfaced on spell check but were most definitely *not* what the writer had in mind. One prospective student expressed pride in her volunteer efforts at the local hospital as a *Candy Stripper!* Another student wrote lovingly about his mother and the influence that this *heroin* had on his life!

Students can be so close to their own writing that they will not notice common problems. See "All Together Now" for using the **Book It!** strategy as a practical and efficient tool to connect students for mutual proofreading.

Read It Aloud

Grades 4–12

Another helpful writing tip is to encourage students to read their papers aloud. They will catch awkward sentence structure and run-on sentences by listening to how their essay "sounds."

Ten-Line Journal

Grades 3–12

I took a lot of tests in Blue Books. When I really knew the answer, I just nailed it with a short answer. When I didn't know the answer and I was just going for a passing grade, I went for volume. I filled the book. It usually worked. Now that I think about it, that was kind of unfortunate, don't you think?

–Recent college graduate

When the U.S. Department of Education required students in fourth grade, eighth grade and twelfth grade to take a national writing exam four years ago, only about one-fourth of students were writing at grade level. There has been tremendous concern expressed that our students today will need an increased ability to communicate effectively in writing both in college and in the workplace.

The College Board is answering this concern by adding a 200-word handwritten essay to the SAT 1, beginning in 2005. In the SAT 1, students will have 20 minutes and no computer aids to check spelling or grammar.

What this means for students is the need for writing on a more frequent basis in the classroom. One way to increase writing without adding more than five minutes of class time each day is to incorporate the **Ten-Line Journal**. The goal is to have students quickly write ten lines on a given topic or subject area to continuously improve written language skills. Feedback is a critical part of it. Periodically students turn in their **Ten-Line Journals** for comments and writing suggestions. It is short but effective.

HOW TO MAKE IT:

To make a **Ten-Line Journal**, students fold four or five sheets of lined paper vertically. The size of the lines should be appropriate for the grade level and needs of the student. Add a cover of construction paper and staple along the fold. The journal can be used two or three times a week during a grading period as a convenient place for creative writing, a place to record results from a science lab, reactions to a novel, or retelling a story. I used the **Ten-Line Journal** as a writing tool for the *Question of the Day*.

Examples of questions would truly run the gamut:

> What advice would you give parents of teenagers today?
>
> If the product is 8, what is the question?
>
> Should every child have a pet? Why or why not?
>
> Who is your hero? Why?

The **Ten-Line Journal** creates brief, open-ended writing opportunities for every student in the classroom.

Hand in a Great Paper

Grades 4–8

In Brenda Goffen's classroom, students **Hand in a Great Paper** by giving themselves a hand, literally! A five-step system helps students check on basic requirements that are part of the writing rubric:

1. Holding up the *thumb* means check for *capitals*.

2. Adding the *index finger* signals proper *punctuation*.

3. Adding the *middle finger* verifies correct *spelling*.

4. The *ring finger* indicates *neatness*.

5. The *little finger* shows that it is *on time*.

One, two, three, four, five! The student is ready to **Hand in a Great Paper!**

Eye Contact Cue

Grades 4–12

Reading and writing are closely connected with oral communication skills. The ability to give reports and express thoughts in a speech are crucial skills today both in school and in the workplace.

This technique will assist students in maintaining eye contact with the audience and will increase their self-confidence while giving an oral report. First, to discourage students from reading a speech from note cards, have them write down only key points. Then encourage them to highlight phrases in color to serve as an cue to look up and make eye contact with the audience as that phase is spoken.

Highlighting makes it easy to locate the place to continue the speech. Use several different colors so that *green* cues the student to look up, make eye contact and return to the green part of the note card. The student continues. Then at the *yellow* phrase, the eye contact process is repeated.

 The Practical Pointer:
Select phrases to highlight that are easy to remember.

Write for the Eye, Speak for the Ear

Grades 6–12

Here is an additional tip for oral reports. When students are writing a report to hand in, keep in mind that the reader can reread a sentence that is unclear or is long and complex. When students are giving oral reports, the listener has only one opportunity to understand the message. Sentences need to be shorter and less complicated. A simple way to think about it is to **write for the eye** and **speak for the ear**. Remind students to practice oral reports aloud and tell the listener about the topic. An effective oral report will sound like a conversation and not be read word for word.

A WORD ABOUT POETRY

Poetry is news—News of the mind, news of the ear— and in the reading and hearing of it, poet and audience are fused.

–Bill Moyers, *author of* The Language of Life

Poetry Break

Grades K–12

One type of reading that we sometimes neglect is poetry. Do you take a one-minute poetry break any time during the day? The poem can be placed on the overhead for students to read together or follow along as the teacher reads. Poetry can also be used to teach. For example, a wonderful collection of poems that center on life in the animal kingdom is *Pig Tales and Humpback Whales* by biologist Jayne Buscho (ISBN 0–88739–308-X). The poet writes for all ages and fills each poem with accurate information about a wide range of creatures.

One of Jayne Buscho's poems, "Peculiar Primitive Platypus," is provided as a reproducible to enjoy with your students.

PECULIAR PRIMITIVE PLATYPUS

Created in haste from snippets of waste
And a hodgepodge of animal parts,
Its self esteem, an impossible dream
Before its life ever starts.

With an otter's frame, fur much the same,
A duck's bill and its webbed feet too,
A beaver's tail, eggs like a quail,
It's the size of a cockatoo.

Platypus at night, hidden from sight,
Leaves its burrow on Billabong Creek,
Then swims low, searching to and fro
For snails and worms with her beak.

From *Pig Tales and Humpback Whales,* ISBN 0-88739-308-X. Used by permission of Jayne Buscho.

In the spring of the year, Southern Hemisphere,
When October brings warm days,
Platypus makes a nest and soon is blest
With young from eggs that she lays.

Two "platys" grow for three months or so
In the nest among roots underground,
Fold webs on their feet and leave this retreat,
Then unfold them to paddle around.

It does seem strange Platypi don't change—
They've been here for millions of years!
It's a good guess it's due to success
Of parts they obtained from their peers.

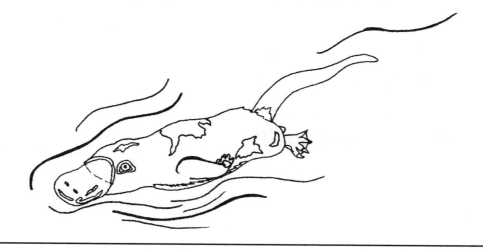

Four-Line Rhymes

Grades 4–8

Turn your students into poets by giving them a topic and asking them to create four lines that rhyme. This is a wonderful warmup activity before any topic to spur imaginative thinking. Students can enjoy reading their poems to each other. This activity can be ungraded and just for fun!

Free Verse

Grades 4–12

A choice as part of differentiating instruction may include writing free verse on any theme. This type of poetry is especially appealing to students because there are no confining rules of verse and no wrong answers. Every student can be highly creative in exploring thoughts, concepts and feelings.

Share a variety of examples with students of your own content to inspire them to begin. You may even wish to offer several optional "first lines" to choose from for students who find themselves staring at a blank page.

Shape Poems

Grades 2–12

Tell your students that the sky is *not* the limit here! Anything goes! The more creative, the better! Shape poems use a concept, thought or image to concrete visual poetry with words forming the shape. Inspiration may come from unit content, from inner feelings, from a photograph, from a memory or a past experience.

Shape poetry is fun! It can be a five-minute transition tool or a creative writing activity. It can be part of a group brainstorming session or an individual assignment. Encourage students to experiment with different media: pen and ink, watercolor, charcoal, computer, crayon, pipe cleaner or puff paint.

Weave poetry experiences into the fabric of your curriculum. Your students will enjoy the variety in both listening to poetry and creating their own poems.

QUICK TIPS AND TOOLS

Lifting the Letter

Grades K–2

This fun strategy reminds me of an old song about names. It went something like this: *"Linda, Linda, Bobinda, . . . Fe, Fi, Fo, Finda . . . Linda!"* The first word many children learn to read is their own name. As teachers, we can use that knowledge to build reading skills.

Make a large version of the child's name out of oak tag board. Staple several small flaps over the initial letter. If the name begins with a consonant, for example, create a flipbook of consonants with the top consonant spelling the child's name: Sammy. The child will say the name, then **Lift the Letter** repeatedly, practicing several consonant sounds, all in the context of rhyming with the child's name:

> Sammy, Tammy, Kammy, Bammy, Jammy

Then create a new name with flaps over the vowel. This time the child can **Lift the Letter** and rhyme with different vowel sounds.

> Sammy, Semmy, Simmy, Sommy, Summy

This same strategy can be applied to other words that the child learns.

O‑┓ KEY IDEA

We learn by connecting new information to what we already know.

 ### Penlight

Grades 1–4

Sometimes when a student reads, a parent or teacher will run an index finger under the words to help the child follow along. The problem is that the finger can cover the tails of letters that drop below the line, making the word hard to read. An inexpensive penlight, available at any hardware store, lights up the words without distortion. It is also useful in partner reading. One student can light up the words while another student reads.

 ### Sky Writing

Grades K–4

Penlights can be enthusiastically embraced by the whole class for "sky writing" in a darkened room. Hands-on learners love this idea! It also works well to "write in lights" on dark construction paper on a desk. It is an effective reinforcement technique and adds variety when reviewing spelling words, vocabulary or math facts.

Reading the Room

Grades K–3

A simple way to practice visual cues or word recognition is to **Read the Room.** Bring in an old pair of reading glasses with the lenses removed. Using a yardstick as a pointer and wearing the "reading glasses," a  student walks around the classroom on a visual mission. The student may be looking for words like "exit" or other posted words like "clock," "January," "desk" or "map."

After this student has located several words, other students may take turns finding and reading additional words. The same visual activity can focus on shapes or colors found in the room. For example, a student wears the special glasses and uses the pointer to find every item in *red* or every *circle* in the classroom.

☞ **The Practical Pointer:**
When the student is **Reading the Room** for shapes or colors, place a sample of the targeted shape or color made of construction paper on the end of the pointer for the student to match.

Tab the Location

Grades 3–12

Encourage students to locate frequently used sections of any text with removable tabs. Tabs can flag the current unit, section, chapter review, glossary, index, as well as key charts, maps and graphs. Color-coding makes finding specific sections easy and efficient.

Letting It Gel

Grades K–2

Letting It Gel is a highly tactile reading experience that works like finger paint without the mess! Use a quart-size zipper plastic bag for this idea. Squeeze about a cup of colored hair gel into the bag, zip and tape the opening closed. Primary students can practice drawing letters and writing words in the brightly colored gel.

Shaving Cream Letters

Grades K–2

Kindergarten teacher Sonja Erickson told me that she uses another strategy that is also very popular with her students. After students clear their tables of all items, she provides shaving cream to practice "writing." A pleasant side benefit of using the shaving cream is that the tables are sparkling clean afterward!

Cookie Sheet Letters

Grades K–2

Ms. Erickson also uses baking sheets with 1'' sides that she fills with sand for still another tactile alternative to practicing letter formation. On a given day in her classroom, students can choose among several tactile strategies for letters.

⊶ KEY IDEA

Too often, the learning style that we use least is the one that many of our students need most: kinesthetic learning. Hands-on! Hands-on! Hands-on!

Popcorn Reading

Grades K–2

Using reading material that a child can read at an independent or nearly independent level, the parent and child take turns reading one sentence at a time. The parent reads one sentence and the child follows. **Popcorn Reading** helps the child improve word recognition because typically many of the words are repeated over and over in the story. Hearing the parent read them reinforces the child's auditory vocabulary. The child is more likely to recognize the word in print within the context of the story. Through this strategy, the child is able to read aloud material that may become too long or too difficult to read independently. **Popcorn Reading** is fun for both parents and emerging readers. Using a penlight would be a helpful addition to the **Popcorn Reading** technique.

Parents often ask me for tips in reading with children at home. Just one idea is mentioned here but several more suggestions are described in the chapter entitled "Parents as Partners," in *Inclusion: A Fresh Look—Practical Strategies To Help All Students Succeed* (Covington Cove Publications, 1-888-LEARN-11).

Photo Bookmarks

Grades 1–5

Laminate a photograph of a student to use as a bookmark. It helps students see themselves as readers and serves the practical purpose of quickly identifying the owner of a book left on a table.

SUMMARY

Just the knowledge that a good book is awaiting one at the end of a long day makes that day happier.

–Kathleen Norris, author

Imagine a world where every child loves to read like Kathleen Norris. Imagine a world where every child is a successful reader! It is an attainable goal when we use a focused, results-based reading program that is highly structured for young children combined with multiple reading experiences and opportunities. We can accomplish the goals of improved reading within the framework of differentiating instruction for all learners. All students need a core curriculum that is rigorous and challenging. Then as part of the content, choices enable students to further develop individual strengths, interests and talents.

Reading for pleasure is also critical in improving reading skills. At all grade levels, students benefit from a print-rich environment filled with books, magazines and newspapers that students can read just because "they are there."

Because reading and writing are so closely connected, multiple and varied writing experiences across the content areas improve reading skills and enable students to express themselves clearly and concisely. Students need to be writing more every day. While some writing experiences are strictly creative in nature, are not corrected and promote writing for the sheer joy of writing, many other writing tasks create essential opportunities for feedback and improvement.

Combined with parent encouragement to read, read, read at home to and with their children, reading skills can improve and our students will "Read to Succeed."

5

MATH WORKS!

Do not worry about your difficulties in math. I can assure you that mine are greater.

—Albert Einstein

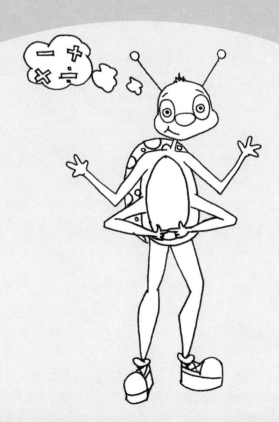

I can think of no other subject area in school than math that carries with it such strong feelings for students, parents and their teachers.

Among parents during my parent talks, math is the subject that generates memories and current beliefs—whether accurate or not—about lack of ability, lack of aptitude, and the assumption that this has been passed on genetically to their offspring.

"I was never any good in math, either."

"I can't help my child at home in math. It was always my worst subject."

"She's just like her father! Being good at math does not run in our family . . ."

"Math? Forget it!"

Of course not all parents feel this way but enough do to make it a concern. When parents voice their perceptions, their children can adopt the same view. Despite my suggestion that parents never tell their children that they were "never any good at math," they do. The subject of math evokes memories of failure in many parents second only to their memories of reading aloud in class.

Among elementary teachers who teach math and special education teachers at all grade levels who co-teach in math classes, there are often feelings of inadequacy and fear. Comments that surface most often center on lack of training.

"I just don't have a good background in math."

"Math was not my best subject."

"I'm finally learning algebra now co-teaching with an excellent math teacher."

"Math is not my strong point."

"I hate math."

Math teachers do not feel this way but many other teachers do and that is alarming.

Students themselves express fear and lack of self-confidence about this subject more than any other when I talk to them about school success.

"I never get it."

"It's too hard."

"The teacher goes too fast."

"Everything is going OK except math."

"It's my worst subject."

"I'm not any good in math."

There are many students who love math and cannot seem to get enough of it. Why do other students have such negative feelings? The more important question is how can we turn these feelings around? How can we help all students see math in a very positive light? I suspect that for middle and high school students some of the negative feelings are related to significant gaps in their learning along the way. They are missing key steps in the sequential process that are essential building blocks to understanding new concepts. For these students, math is difficult because pieces of the puzzle are missing.

By middle school and high school, it is often assumed that students "should have learned it last year" or the year before, or the year before that. In some cases, they did not. It was taught; they didn't learn it. Math skills march forward in sequence and students are left behind. No wonder it is so difficult for students who struggle, for students who "fall through the cracks," for students who have special needs.

"Math Works!" is not meant to fill in all the gaps. That would not be possible and that is not the purpose. Instead, the purpose of "Math Works!" is to focus on the need to teach math skills through hands-on experiences. You may be thinking, "I already do that." Chances are that much of your math instruction is hands-on. This chapter is a reminder that many students need to do it to understand it. What follows are concrete, highly practical examples of hands-on math in six categories.

- Multiplication Grid Tools and Techniques
- Paper Plate Manipulatives
- Manual Multiplication
- Strategies That Work
- Measurement Visuals
- Quick Tips and Tools

MULTIPLICATION GRID TOOLS AND TECHNIQUES

Using a Grid

Grades 3–8

Despite efforts to learn their multiplication facts, some students will never be able to recall that $7 \times 7 = 49$. Grids and calculators make it possible for these students to find the product in a different way other than memorization. They can then use that information for practical applications such as determining how much carpeting would be needed for a specific area. While the multiplication grid is not a new concept, there are a number of ways to assist students in using the grid more efficiently.

	1	2	3	4	5	6	7	8	9	10	11	12
1	1	2	3	4	5	6	7	8	9	10	11	12
2	2	4	6	8	10	12	14	16	18	20	22	24
3	3	6	9	12	15	18	21	24	27	30	33	36
4	4	8	12	16	20	24	28	32	36	40	44	48
5	5	10	15	20	25	30	35	40	45	50	55	60
6	6	12	18	24	30	36	42	48	54	60	66	72
7	7	14	21	28	35	42	49	56	63	70	77	84
8	8	16	24	32	40	48	56	64	72	80	88	96
9	9	18	27	36	45	54	63	72	81	90	99	108
10	10	20	30	40	50	60	70	80	90	100	110	120
11	11	22	33	44	55	66	77	88	99	110	121	132
12	12	24	36	48	60	72	84	96	108	120	132	144

The Right Angle

Grades 3–8

A common problem experienced by many students is difficulty locating the product on the grid. It can be visually overwhelming. A simple solution is to cut a 90-degree angle out of cardboard to use as a locator. Make the locator about 3″ wide and long enough to reach all numbers on the grid. A student solving the problem "3 × 4" places the right angle so that the "legs" line up with the numbers "3" and "4", respectively. The product, "12", will appear in the corner of the right angle.

☞ **The Practical Pointer:**

I use brightly colored tag board to make the right angle because it clearly separates the cardboard locator from the grid and blocks out much of the remaining grid. Laminating it makes it last longer. Improvising on the spot can be achieved by manipulating two sheets of paper to form a right angle. Slide them around the grid in the same manner.

Division Facts Inside Out

Grades 3–8

The multiplication grid also becomes an excellent tool for division facts by using the right angle locator as a guide. Work from the inside out by first locating the dividend in the corner of the right angle and the divisor with one "leg." The quotient will appear automatically at the other "leg."

Equivalent Fractions

Grades 4–8

Did you know that the traditional multiplication grid up to 12 is also an excellent tool for finding equivalent fractions? To see how this works, use two sheets of paper and a multiplication grid. First, cover all of the numbers across the top line of the grid. The number "1" is still exposed in the margin. Locate the number "2" beneath it down the side of the grid. With the second sheet of paper, cover the numbers horizontally across the grid beneath the number "2". Along the left side of the grid, numbers "1" and "2" are now the fraction ½. Look across the grid horizontally. Note that now you see ½, ²⁄₄, ³⁄₆, ⁴⁄₈, ⁵⁄₁₀, and so on all the way to ¹²⁄₂₄.

Next slide the first paper down to cover the horizontal row of numbers 1 through 12 leaving the number "2" exposed in the margin. Slide the second sheet beneath the number "3" in the left column. You have just created the fraction ⅔. Look horizontally and notice the equivalent fractions for ⅔ including ⁴⁄₆, ⁸⁄₁₂, ¹⁰⁄₁₅, and so on through ²⁴⁄₃₆.

Students can find equivalent fractions using the grid in this manner. While this approach will not teach the *concept* of dividing a whole into parts and its equivalents, it is a useful tool to check an answer or to assist students who cannot remember equivalent fractions.

Grid Strips

Grades 3–8

The previous strategy works effectively when dealing with fractions on the grid that are in consecutive order: $\frac{1}{2}$, $\frac{2}{3}$, $\frac{3}{4}$. When a student would like the equivalent fractions for $\frac{3}{5}$, there is a sensible solution. Cut the multiplication grid into horizontal strips. Then to create $\frac{3}{5}$ and its equivalents, lay the strip beginning with the number "3" on the desk and place the strip beginning with the number "5" directly underneath it. Voila! You suddenly have $\frac{3}{5}$, $\frac{6}{10}$, and $\frac{9}{15}$, and so on.

☞ **The Practical Pointer:**

Store the strips in an envelope in the math pocket of an accordion folder or in the plastic pouch in the three-ring binder. They will be ready to use when needed.

Finger Travel

Grades 3–8

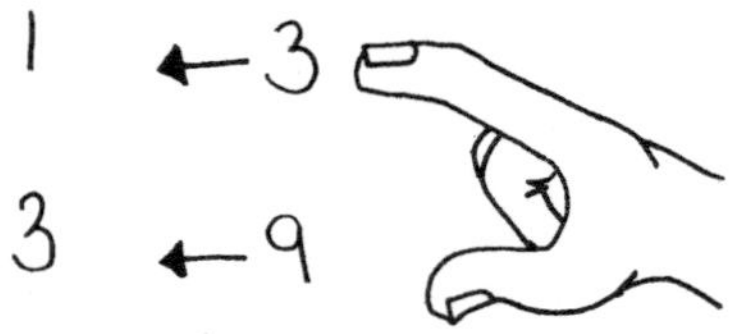

I have taught students to use a thumb and index finger to reduce a fraction with numbers in the same vertical column. Try it. Imagine that the fraction is $\frac{8}{24}$. It can be reduced. Within the grid, locate the fraction. Place your fight index finger on the number "8" and your thumb on the number "24". Next, slide the digits to the left as far as you can. Your finger and thumb are now at $\frac{1}{3}$. Every time you slide you hand to the left, you are reducing the fraction.

In this case, that new fraction is in lowest form. Imagine, instead, that the fraction is $\frac{10}{20}$. Place your index finger and thumb on the fraction. Slide all the way to the left as you did before. This time, you arrive at $\frac{2}{4}$, not reduced to lowest form.

Locate $\frac{2}{4}$ within the grid. The students become very adept at doing this. Slide your index finger up to the number "2" and place your thumb on the number "4". Now slide again to the left column. You have arrived at $\frac{1}{2}$, the lowest form. While students can also use a calculator for the same purpose, the grid is often readily available in the back of many upper elementary and middle school assignment notebooks.

Fill in the Grid

Grades 3–8

Still another effective use for the multiplication grid is to supply students with a blank grid for completion. Students practice their multiplication facts by filling the blanks: "$1 \times 1 = 1$", "$1 \times 2 = 2$". They create their own support tool. Some students need help checking for accuracy. The blank grid can also function as an answer sheet for multiplication problems using manipulatives.

PAPER PLATE MANIPULATIVES

Inexpensive paper plates work well as hands-on learning tools in your classroom. Strategies that use paper plate manipulatives are described next.

A Plate of Fractions

Grades 2–8

> *You better cut the pizza in four pieces*
> *because I'm not hungry enough to eat six.*
>
> –*Yogi Berra*

Most primary teachers rely on manipulatives for teaching mathematical concepts. We know that hands-on instruction is the best approach for many students, especially for students who struggle with math. But once students reach the upper elementary grades and middle school, we often reduce the use of manipulatives. Students at all grades levels benefit from the hands-on experience that manipulatives provide.

Teaching fractions is a concept that lends itself to frequent hands-on instruction. For example, when teaching or reviewing fractions, paper plates in a variety of colors make excellent manipulatives. Begin by giving each student two paper plates in different colors. I generally use the larger dinner plate size to demonstrate and give students the smaller dessert size to use as their manipulatives.

How To Make It:

Cut a slit in each plate from the outside to the center, the radius of each plate. Next, line up the two slits. Now slide the back plate over the front plate to display two different colors. Make a variety of fractions with the students. Students can follow your lead in creating ⅓, ⅔, and so on.

You may wish to draw lines on the paper plates to correspond to different fractions as guides. To show equivalent fractions, just add another plate in yet another color. Cut a slit as before from the outside to the center. This time, line up all three plates. Slide both of the bottom plates over the top plate. Slide one plate half way to create ½ and slide second a quarter turn to create ¼. Now students can clearly see the relationship and understand that ½ is the same as ¾.

☞ The Practical Pointer:
Traditional paper plates work well in colors but the vibrant, shiny plastic version has an advantage. You can see the fraction, such as ¼, on one side and then turn the plates over in your hand to display the remaining ¾ on the back. Students can see quickly that

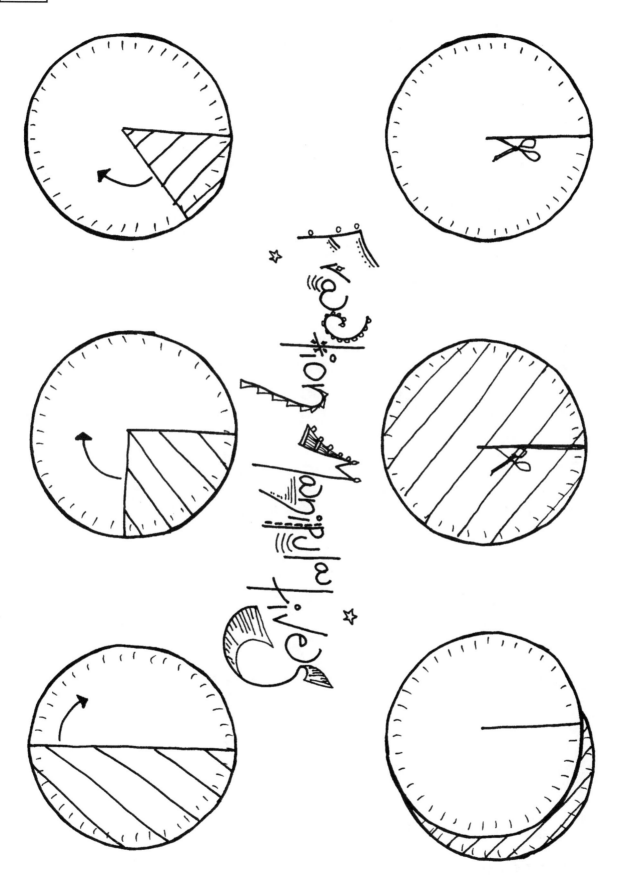

together the 4/4 make the whole. The disadvantage to the plastic plates is that they cannot be recycled. With care, though, they can last a long time.

Paper Plate Angles

Grades 4–9

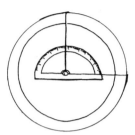

I was visiting an eighth grade math class recently. During the class, the teacher stood at the blackboard drawing angles and then asking students to calculate the size of the complimentary angle using calculators. It was apparent that students lost interest very quickly. Several students were off task. They were chatting, doodling, and one student began to doze. The problem was lack of involvement. The teacher was hard at work on the board but students had a passive role just watching her much of the time.

When the teacher and I were discussing ideas later, I wondered aloud if using paper plates would create more student engagement. What if each student had a set of paper plates and a protractor? Then, rather than the teacher drawing a 45-degree angle on the board, the students themselves could locate a 45-degree angle on the protractor and then slide the plates into the same angle. Next they could calculate the complimentary angle and create it by again sliding the plates.

A rather surprised group of ninth-graders were equipped with paper plates the next day. Everyone was awake and engaged! The teacher told me that everyone had fun, including her. The purpose is not to make class "fun," but to engage students because students who are involved and excited will learn more. They were not watching the teacher measure angles; they were discovering relationships on their own.

O— KEY IDEA

So many of our students need to be physically engaged in the task to learn. This thought is not new, but at times we need to remind ourselves as teachers to make our learning hands-on. Using the plates did not take any more class time than watching the teacher demonstrate and the impact was far greater.

Paper Plate Pie Graphs

Grades 4–6

Using three or four different colored plates, cooperative groups can make pie graphs that depict relationships on a wide range of topics. For example, a group may be asked to survey the class and family members regarding pizza preferences. After compiling their data on how many people selected cheese or pepperoni or sausage or vegetarian as their personal favorite, group members can depict the results using a paper plate pie graph in multiple colors. This simple, hands-on visual helps them understand the graphing concept quickly and easily.

Time on a Plate

Grades 1–3

This strategy helps students understand the concept of *60 minutes* in an hour. It can also be used to teach terminology such as *quarter-hour, half-hour, half past the hour* and *quarter to the hour*. In permanent marker, make a clock face on a paper plate showing the numbers by fives and supplying dots for the minutes in between.

Cut a slit as before from the outside to the center of the plate. Add a second plate in a contrasting color. Cut a slit in this plate as well. Place the second plate over the numbered one and slide the first plate through the slit to show five minutes, then slide the plate to show ten minutes and so on.

Students will need their own plates to manipulate. They will discover that 15 minutes make a quarter-hour as they see one-fourth of the plate covered. As more and more of the numbered plate is covered, students learn that 60 minutes are the total number of minutes in an hour. They can watch time go by! While this strategy will not show the hour hand, an immovable hand can be drawn on the plate as an example.

Paper Plate Review

Grades 5–12

Students can review addition facts, multiplication facts, story problems or algebra problems using the paper plate format. Students will be creating a review activity to share with a partner that can also be used later for self-study. It is a simple question-and-answer strategy. Ahead of time, students draw lines on a paper plate to divide it into an even number of pie-shaped sections. The number of sections depends on the space needed for the question or problem that will be written in the space.

Beginning with one problem or question in any pie section, the student will write the answer in the section immediately above it. Then a new question or problem is written in the next pie shape followed again by the answer. This continues until the plate is filled.

Use a second plate as a cover. It can be in a contrasting color, but basic white paper plates suffice. Cut a slit in the second plate from the outside to the center and place the blank plate over the first.

For the review activity, students trade plates so that are reviewing another student's questions and answers. Each student will begin by sliding the original plate to expose a question. The student answers the question or completes the problem. By sliding the plate, the student exposes the correct answer. This self-checking tool offers an alternative to review by worksheet or study guide.

Musical Notes

Grades 3–5

Paper plate manipulatives can be used in subjects other than math to illustrate concepts. In music, for example, use two contrasting paper plates to show the value of eighth notes, quarter notes, half notes and whole notes. An art teacher suggested making a color wheel using this same technique. Like so many other strategies, this strategy can be adapted and "tweaked" for a wide range of subject areas and grade levels. Sometimes the goal is simply variety. We are constantly looking for ways to teach the same concept using a different delivery or format that will hold students' interest and keep the concept fresh.

MANUAL MULTIPLICATION

Dressed to the Nines

Grades 3–12

Some of you are old hands at this manual strategy for the multiplying by nine. If not, **Dressed to the Nines** is one more surefire strategy for your students who struggle with the "nines" family of multiplication facts. It has particular appeal for the kinesthetic learner. I suggest using it as needed it all the way through high school and beyond because it can also help adults who have difficulty remembering their facts.

O⎯ KEY IDEA

I remind students that there is nothing wrong with using their fingers in math if it helps. Fingers are there when a calculator may not be. During my years of teaching adult education, I found that many adults were embarrassed to admit that they depended on their fingers for manual calculation. They were reassured to think of fingers as counting tools used by other capable, intelligent adults.

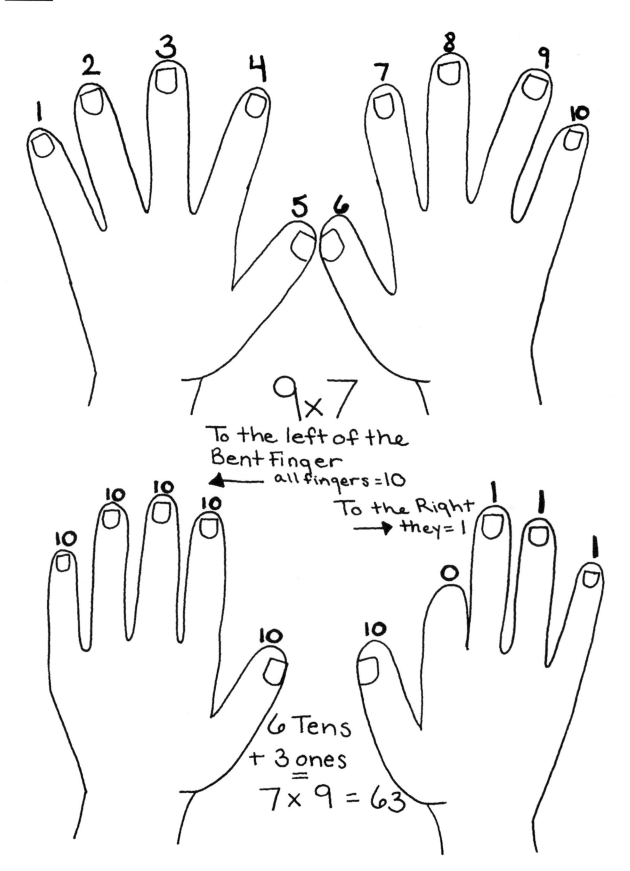

9×7

To the left of the
Bent Finger
all fingers = 10

To the Right
they = 1

6 Tens
+ 3 ones
=
$7 \times 9 = 63$

How To Use It:

Begin by holding your hands, palms down and fingers spread in front of you. For younger students, I put small stickers on their fingernails numbering from 1 to 10, left to right. The left hand is 1 through 5; the right is 6 through 10. To multiply any number 1 through 10 by 9, press down the number of choice: To multiply "2 × 9", depress finger number "2", the ring finger of the left hand.

Now look at your hands. Every digit *left* of the depressed finger is a *ten*. In this case, we have *1* ten. All the numbers to the *right* of the depressed finger are *ones*. Looking at both hands, we have a total of *8* ones. Add the tens to the ones and we have the product: *18*. Note that the finger you are multiplying is not counted in tens or ones.

Try another. Imagine that you are multiplying "6 × 9". Depress finger number "6", which is the right thumb. How many tens are to the left of the depressed digit? *5*. How many *ones* are to the right of the depressed digit? *4*. Add the tens and ones. The product is *54*.

☞ **The Practical Pointer:**
You may wish to teach this to all students but only those who find it helpful will use it regularly. Because it does not require paper or calculator, it is a quick and easy solution for those who forget the "nines." No one strategy will work for everyone. It will not work for students with serious fine-motor difficulties nor it will not teach the *concept* of multiplication. However, it is one more tool for success.

Make Your Own Nines Chart

Grades 3–8

This technique teaches students to create their own charts for the "nines." The first step is to make a list of the facts "9 × 0" through "9 × 10". Establish that "9 × 0 = 0". Then begin with "9 × 1 =". Subtract 1 from the multiplicand that will be multiplied by 9. Write it in parenthesis with a number that when added will equal the sum of 9.

For example, consider "9 × 3". Subtract 1 from 3, which equals 2. In parenthesis write 2 plus 7 for a sum of 9 (2 + 7) = 9. The two digits in the parentheses form the product 27.

$9 \times 0 = (0 + 0) = 0$ Product = 0

$9 \times 1 = (0 + 9) = 9$ Product = 9

$9 \times 2 = (1 + 8) = 9$ Product =18

$9 \times 3 = (2 + 7) = 9$ Product = 27

$9 \times 4 = (3 + 6) = 9$ Product = 36

$9 \times 5 = (4 + 5) = 9$ Product = 45

$9 \times 6 = (5 + 4) = 9$ Product = 54

$9 \times 7 = (6 + 3) = 9$ Product = 63

$9 \times 8 = (7 + 2) = 9$ Product = 72

$9 \times 9 = (8 + 1) = 9$ Product = 81

$9 \times 10 = (9 + 0) = 9$ Product = 90

Students can use the procedure as a self-checking tool making certain that the digits in the product can be added to equal the sum of 9.

Finger Facts 6 through 10

Grades 3–12

This strategy serves a different purpose from **Dressed to the Nines.** This applies to those students who know the lower multiplication facts but struggle with the sixes, sevens, eights, nines and tens. In order to use this strategy, students must be adept at recalling multiplication facts through 5 in all number families. In other words, they know "7 × 3" but "7 × 8" is a problem; they already know "9 × 4" but stumble over "9 × 7".

☞ **The Practical Pointer:**

Do not teach both **Finger Facts 6 through 10** and **Dressed to the Nines** simultaneously or even in near progression. Use this strategy *only* with students who need it to avoid confusion. For students who like the **Finger Facts** technique, there is a tremendous accompanying feeling of success. For an individual, either it works very well or it is just not applicable.

When I taught this to high school math teachers, a tenth grade teacher called me later to tell me what a difference it made for one of his students. "This girl was walking on air when she left my room that day!" he said, "Finally, something that made her feel good about math. It was the first time I've seen her smile."

How To Use It:

Assume the same hand position as in the previous strategy: hands palms down with digits extended. This is where the similarity ends, however. Starting with the thumb, number the digits on each hand in the same way: thumb is 6; index finger is 7; middle finger is 8; ring finger is 9; little finger is 10. The only numbers that you will be multiplying are these: 6, 7, 8, 9, 10.

Select a problem like "7 × 7" to begin. The sevens are the index fingers. Turn your hands and make a bridge by touching the left and right index fingertips together. Thumbs go up. Fold the fingers that are under the bridge. Both hands together will look somewhat like the letter "H."

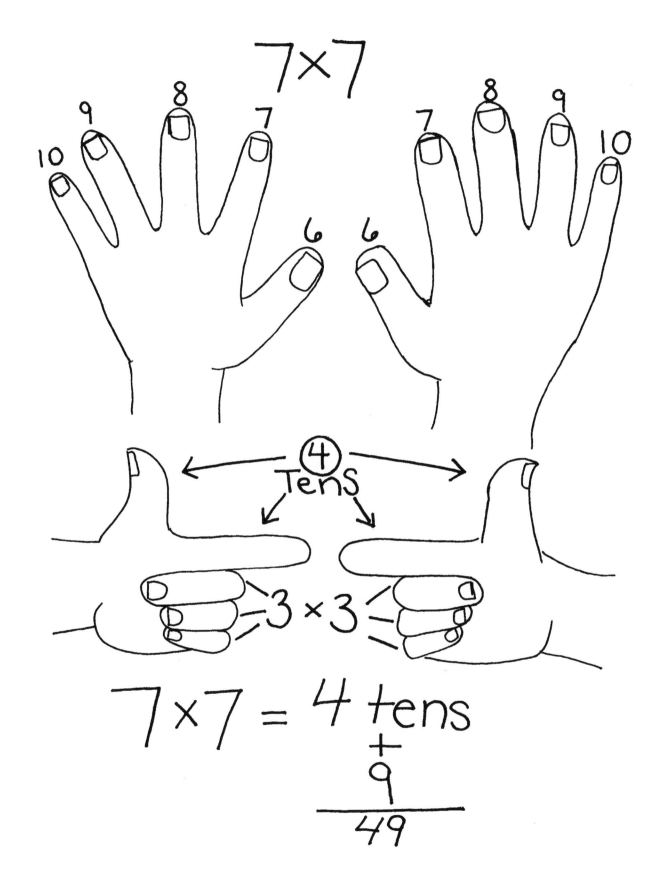

The digits that form the bridge and any digits above the bridge are counted as tens. Thus, in "7 × 7", the two index fingers that form the bridge and the two thumbs count as 4 tens. The remaining digits under the bridge will be multiplied. To do so, multiply the folded digits on one hand by the folded digits on the other: 3 digits × 3 digits equal 9. Now add the tens and ones together: "7 × 7" equals 4 tens plus 9 ones or 49. Try another for good measure.

Try "8 × 9". Touch a middle finger "8" to a ring finger "9" to form a bridge. Palms toward you; thumbs go up. Fold the digits under the bridge. As you look at your fingers, do you count 7 tens? You should have 3 on the "8" hand and 4 on the "9" hand. Remember that the digits making the bridge count as tens. Multiply the digit folded under the bridge on one hand times the digits folded under the bridge on the other hand. Did you multiply 2 folded digits on the "8" hand times 1 folded digit on the "9" hand? "2 × 1 = 2". Add the tens and ones. "8 × 7 = 72". (It does not matter which hand is 8 and which hand is 7.)

Sometimes "9 × 10" confuses students. Make the bridge: Ring finger to little finger. Thumbs go up. Do you count 9 tens? What is under the bridge? "1 × 0 = 0". So "9 × 10 = 90".

☞ **The Practical Pointer:**

Do not begin by teaching the sixes. Two of the sixes work but involve double-digit numbers: "6 × 6" and "6 × 7". These two can be taught more easily after several examples using sevens, eights, nines, and tens without involving sixes.

Try "6 × 6": Thumb to thumb, palms toward you, folding the remaining digits under the bridge. How many tens do you see? You see just 2; the two thumbs, but watch what happens when you multiply the folded digits on each hand. You will multiply "4 × 4" or 16. Add that product to the 2 tens and you have 36. "6 × 7" works the same way; you will have a double-digit product in the multiplication step. These are the only two that work this way and should be taught last.

☞ **The Practical Pointer:**

The bridge itself may be used every time or just during the learning process. After a student is adept at **Finger Facts**, students may not need to build a bridge. Instead, they can multiply with their hands held unobtrusively at their sides without making a physical connection. This will take practice. Many students love this strategy and find it useful forever. Many teachers, on the other hand, find it challenging to learn and are happy that they will not need to use it themselves!

STRATEGIES THAT WORK

Formulae Card

Grades 6–12

Encourage students to use a 4" × 6" note card to use as a quick reference tool. As each new formula is taught throughout the year, the students add the formula along with a step-by-step example to keep close at hand. The note card may be orange, green or another color that is easy to spot and can be clipped in the back of the math book or folder.

Red Dot Coins

Grades 1–5

When I was visiting an elementary math class, I watched students counting real coins on their tables. What was intriguing was that the teacher had used red nail polish to make dots on each silver coin: one dot on a nickel, two red dots on a dime, and five red dots on a quarter. Students dropped a handful of change on their tables and began counting the red dots by "fives" on all of the coins except pennies. Thus, one nickel, a dime, a quarter, and a penny sounded like this: "5, 10, 15, 20, 25, 30, 35, 40, 41—41 cents!"

In discussing this technique with the teacher, I learned that as soon as students understood coin values and were adept at addition, they ignored the red dots and added 25 + 10 + 5 and the penny. For those students who struggled with addition and coin value, it was a simple but effective tool.

Window Math

Grades 3–6

The focus of **Window Math** is to offer another alternative to help students succeed. Many students respond favorably to multiplication when it is presented in this format.

Make a window that corresponds to the number of digits when multiplied. For example, to multiply 2 digits by 2 digits, make a window of 4 squares, 2 above and 2 below. When multiplying 1 digit by 3 digits, make a window of 3 squares in a row. To multiply 3 digits by 3 digits, make a window of 9 squares, 3 on top, 3 in the middle and 3 below. The next step is to divide each square diagonally from lower left to upper right.

HOW TO MULTIPLY:

Step 1: One example of multiplying 2 digits by 2 digits, the window of 4 squares, will be used. Imagine that the multiplication problem is "24 × 36". Arrange the numbers "2" and "4" above the top squares and arrange the numbers "3" and "6" along the right hand side as shown in the reproducible.

Step 2: Next begin multiplying. Starting with the number along the upper right, multiply by the top right number. Write the answers in each square with the tens above the diagonal line and the ones below. Thus, "3 × 4 =12". The number "1" is above the

24 x 36 = 864

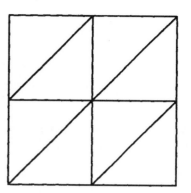

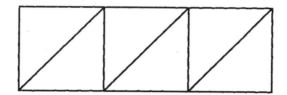

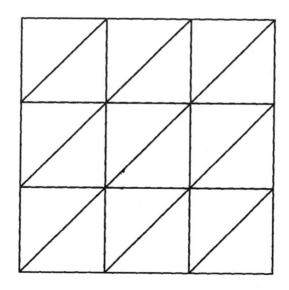

diagonal and the number "2" is below the diagonal. Then, "3 × 2 = 6". There are 0 tens above the diagonal and 6 ones below.

Step 3: Next start from the lower right, again multiplying by the top right number. Multiply "6 × 4 =24". Place the number "2" above the diagonal and the number "4" below. Continue by multiplying "6 × 2 = 12". Place "1" above the diagonal and "2" below.

Step 4: The window is filled and ready for the next step. Add the digits inside the squares in each diagonal row beginning on the lower right. Write the sums along the bottom and up along the left side of the window. Thus, the first diagonal is only the number "4". Write it below the line. Three digits form the next diagonal: "2 + 2 + 2 = 6". Write "6" below the line. Moving upward, the third diagonal is formed by three digits: "1 + 6 + 1 = 8". Write the number "8" along the left side of the window directly below the corresponding diagonal. The final diagonal contains only one digit: 0. Write "0" directly outside that diagonal.

Step 5: The answer to the multiplication problem will be the numbers from the top left down the side and across the bottom of the window. Omit the 0 and write 864 (24 × 36 = 864).

☞ **The Practical Pointer:**

It is one more option. It is not for everyone. Some students connect with the idea and love multiplying 10 or more digits by 10 or more digits. The same procedure is followed throughout.

O─┐ KEY IDEA

From a teaching standpoint, an advantage to using the window is that it shows all of the student's work. If there is an error, the window will display it.

What's Missing?

Grades 2–6

Get students up and moving to practice either addition facts or multiplication facts by playing **What's Missing?** in groups of three. Let's imagine that students are reinforcing multiplication facts. Each triad will use note cards with numbers written on them or a deck of playing cards. Each member of the triad has a different role and will rotate after each multiplication fact.

How To Play:

Two individuals draw one card each from the stack of note cards or playing cards and keep the card face down without looking at it. When they are ready, these students will raise their cards face out in front of their nose. They are unable to see which card they have drawn. The third person can see both cards and calls out the product of the numbers when multiplied.

Next, the students holding the cards face each other as they hold their cards in front of them. Each student knows the product and can see the other person's card. Without looking, what is the missing number needed to complete the multiplication fact? Each student calls out a number and then finally looks to see if the response was correct.

Cards are mixed back into the pile. Students rotate roles and continue with the math facts. It will move much more quickly in your classroom than it took to explain the procedure!

☞ The Practical Pointer:

This hands-on strategy is an alternative to using a math fact worksheet. It involves every learning style including visual, auditory and kinesthetic. Sometimes teachers tell me that they remember a similar version of this while they were in college but it was not in class and they were not reinforcing math facts. I always tell them to spare us the details . . .

MEASUREMENT VISUALS

The Measure Maniac

Grades 3–12

You might raise an eyebrow when you note that this is applicable through twelfth grade. It is just an illustration showing the value of using visuals. The whimsical **Measure Maniac** creates a strong picture showing the relationship among *cups, pints, quarts, half-gallons* and *gallon*. Visual representation of concepts like measurement can be a tremendous boost for all grade and age levels. Visuals work because new information is connected to the familiar. To use this, students must be familiar with the concept of measurement. By attaching this concept to the visual, a memorable association is created between measurement and the creature's anatomy! While most secondary students may not need this visual, some will. It is simply a tool to help those who need it. I like to tease other adults who, like myself, struggle with remembering how many cups are in a pint or quart. Put this on your refrigerator, I tell them, and the next time you're doubling that soup recipe, your troubles are over!

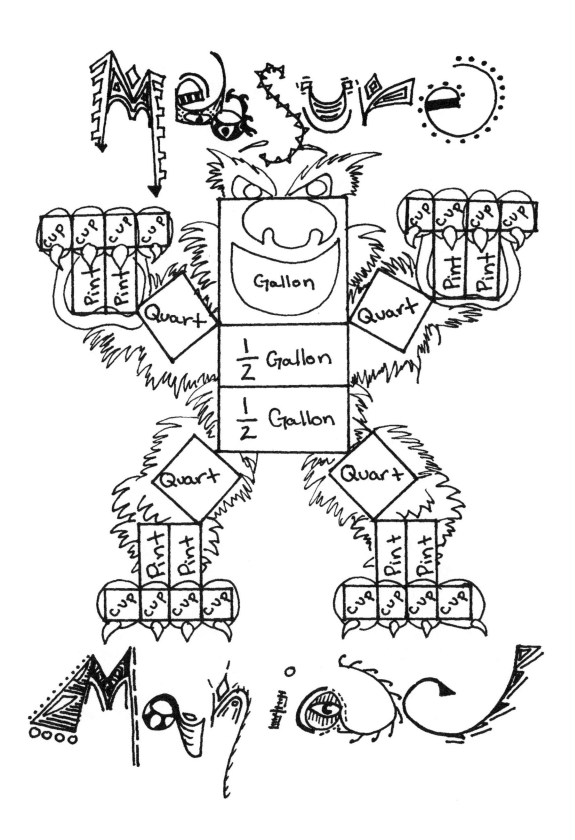

KEY IDEA

It is important that students see the relationships among the gallon, half-gallons, quarts, pints and cups. The easiest way to do this is by using manipulatives to stack in a variety of combinations on top of the gallon.

☞ **The Practical Pointer:**

Color-coding also helps students remember the measurements. Each student can select a different color scheme to decorate the reproducible **Measure Maniac.** Have students create their own creature using the same measurements. Some students like to make a bear or monkey or a person, for example, instead of the **Measure Maniac.** Once students have a firm visual image of just one appendage of the **Measure Maniac,** they will recall that 1 quart equals 2 pints and that 2 pints equals 4 cups. They can then multiply each measurement by 4 for the total number.

Two more examples follow for remembering the relationships among different measurements. I like to present all three to students. They will choose what will work best for them. It is even more effective if they invent their own. For our purposes here, I am using measurement as a visual example. As you think about your grade level and subject area, no doubt you will find multiple ways that you already use visuals in your teaching. Are there some other visuals that you might add to help your students succeed?

Gallon House

Grades 2–6

An alternative measurement visual that I have used is the **Gallon House.** Draw a simple house with a peaked roof. Draw 4 windows for *quarts.* Each window is divided into 4 sections representing *cups* with heavier lines down the middle to depict *pints.* A line from the peak to the bottom of the house divides the house in half creating *half-gallons.* Students like to add window boxes, flowers, a picket fence, or trees in the yard to personalize their house.

The Capital "G"

Grades 2–6

The third example is one that I taught my children many years ago but is one that I still demonstrate in classrooms today. Draw a large capital "G" on the board in the color of your choice. Students do the same on their individual whiteboards or on paper. Inside the lower "G, " draw 4 fairly large capital "Qs" in a contrasting color. Inside each "Q" draw 2 capital "Ps" in still another color. Finally, inside each "P" draw 2 capital "Cs" using a fourth color. You can see why it is important to begin with a very large "G." Students will have another visual for *cups, pints, quarts* and a *gallon*. Encourage them to select one that appeals to them and use that consistently until they are sure of their measurements.

QUICK TIPS AND TOOLS

Perimeter Fractions

Grades 2–5

Another fraction strategy uses a different type of manipulative. Students can create a multi-colored fraction pie using math manipulatives that hook together to form a circle. If the student is creating thirds, the student will hook manipulatives together to form a circle using the same number of each of three colors. The result is actually what we might call **Perimeter Fractions** because the colors divide the perimeter into equal pieces.

Jaws

Grades 2–4

The concepts of *greater than* and *less than* can be confusing for young students. A quick tip worth revisiting is to provide a strong visual cue using an alligator as a reminder. The jaws of the alligator open toward the greater number and form the symbol for "greater than."

The Movable Rectangle

Grades 2–4

How can one manipulative illustrate *three concepts* including the rectangle, the parallelo-gram and perimeter? Create a **Movable Rectangle** that transforms easily from one into the other using four metal brads and four strips of oak tag board.

It is best to use two different colors. The two shorter strips are of equal size and are one color. The two longer strips are of equal size in the other color. Poke a hole through the corner of each strip. Slip the metal brad through a short and long piece forming each of four corners of the *rectangle*. The metal brad allows the strips to move easily transforming the rectangle into a *parallelogram*. Then remove the metal brad from just one corner. Open the strips to form a one long line. Now the manipulative can be used to demonstrate the concept of *perimeter*.

Rectangle

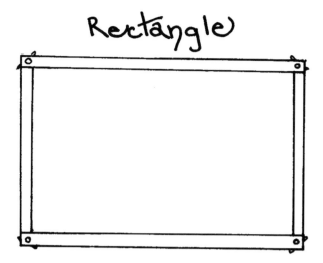

Parallelogram

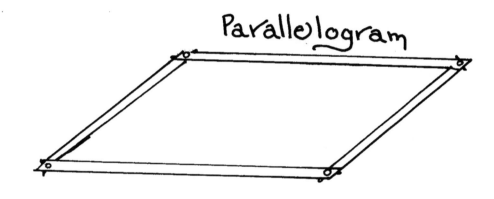

Perimeter

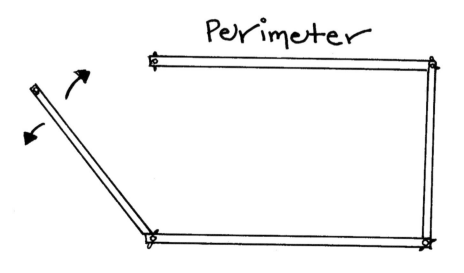

Clockworks

Grades 1–3

Did you know that a face clock is a simple tool for practicing addition to 12? As you look across a clock face, the numbers opposite each other add up to twelve: 11 + 1 = 12, 10 + 2 = 12, 9 + 3 = 12, and so on. I teach students that the number 12 stands alone. Circle 6 and add it again for the sum of 12. A quick tip is to have students use a ruler or note card to place beneath the numbers that they are adding so they are looking directly across the clock and do not add "downhill."

☞ **The Practical Pointer:**

The clock face is also a handy tool for practicing counting by fives. As students touch each 5-minute block, they will count by fives to 60: 5, 10, 15, 20, and so on.

Long Division by Hand

Grades 3–6

Long Division by Hand is a kinesthetic reminder of the steps in any long division problem. Students stand up for this activity. (They probably need a stretch.)

1. Clench each hand in a fist and crisscross the fists in front of your chest saying, "Divide!"

2. Unclench the fists and cross the arms on your chest forming an X-shape while saying, "Multiply!"

3. Use one hand to make a sweeping motion outward forming a subtraction sign while saying, "Subtract!"

4. Use both hands bringing palms down from your forehead to your chest while saying, "Bring down!"

The movements correspond to the steps: *divide, multiply, subtract, bring down.*

Students repeat the motions and words several times before beginning work on long division problems. The rehearsal helps many students follow the process correctly.

Long Division Acrostic

Grades 3–6

Encourage students to use acrostics to help them remember the steps in long division. A common example to begin with is *Dad, Mother, Sister,* and *Brother.*

Dad   ➜   Divide

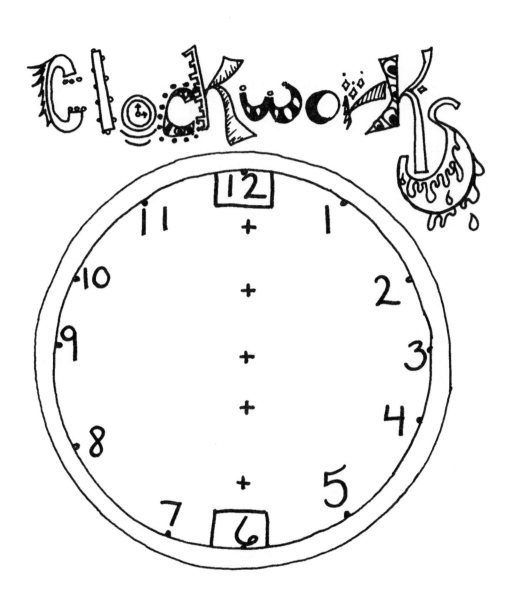

Mother   ➜   Multiply

Sister   ➜   Subtract

Brother   ➜   Bring down

Acrostics are most effective when students think about the concept and make up their own.

Gift-Wrapped Concepts

Grades K–6

One teacher used a very effective strategy for peripheral learning. During the summer, she created posters for math concepts that she would be studying with her students during the year. Her goal was to create a sense of anticipation and then provide review information that would be accessible throughout the year.

She created a series of posters and then wrapped each one with brightly colored gift wrap and a huge bow. Before her students arrived that first day of school, she hung the gifts all around the classroom. Her students were excited! She explained that as the year went by, together they would open all the gifts. As she began each unit, the class unwrapped the new gift amid much fanfare and a few edible treats. The new poster became a permanent review sheet available anytime a student needed it. By the end of the year, the class had indeed opened all the gifts demonstrating the key math concepts.

☞ **The Practical Pointer:**
While creating the posters took some time initially, once made they were ready to go for another year. The teacher left them on the wall and recovered them with new gift wrap. She unpacked the bows that had been carefully tucked away in a closet and reattached them to the gifts.

Number Line on Desk

Grades K–3

A vertical number line along the edge of each desk helps students remember that answers move *up* the number line when adding because adding makes numbers larger and answers move *down* when subtracting because subtracting makes numbers smaller.

Catalog Shopping

Grades 4–8

A high-interest approach to reviewing addition and calculating sales tax and shipping costs is to use catalogs that appeal to your students. In Minnesota, I have used catalogs for snowmobiles in the winter and other catalogs for personal watercraft in the spring. In addition to catalogs for "big ticket" items, I have also brought in some for less expensive items like sporting goods and clothing.

Students are given a budget and must purchase a minimum number of items. They have to calculate costs and determine how long it will take for an item to arrive. Money for expedited service has to come out of the existing budget. It can be a fun activity that students enjoy.

 The Practical Pointer:
Students can also shop on the Internet, but having the actual catalog to peruse appeals to them. They flip back and forth as they decide how to spend their "money."

Turn Your Paper Sideways

Grades 2–7

When working with multiple-digit numbers, a quick tip for keeping the digits correctly lined up in columns is to used lined paper turned sideways. The lines provide clear guidelines for columns. Graph paper with generously sized squares is an excellent tool for the same purpose but is more expensive than lined paper.

SUMMARY

"Math Works!" models hands-on math strategies that serve as reminders of the need to use a highly kinesthetic approach when teaching math skills. Many of our students learn best by doing. Most math programs in primary grades focus heavily on the use of manipulatives and learning by hands-on. As students move up through the grades into upper elementary and then to middle and high school, math skills rely less on manipulatives and more on calculators and paper-pencil skills.

Our goal is to focus on student success, which may involve changing negative attitudes in math to positive "can do" attitudes. Truly success breeds success. When our students—especially those who struggle—experience success in math, they will come back for more and believe that they can do it!

Believe . . . Achieve . . . Succeed!

6

STUDY POWER

*If you want to keep the lamp burning,
you have to keep putting oil in it.*

–Mother Teresa

*You have to know your stuff and then you have to know
that you know your stuff. You can't doubt yourself.*

*–Mansoor Alyeshmerni,
advice to his daughter, Bessie, as she started college*

*"I have to know my stuff and I have to know that I know my stuff! I can't
doubt myself!" I would say that before every test and pretty soon everybody
in my dorm was say saying it. It really helped. Now that I've graduated, I'm
going to say that all the way through law school!*

–Bessie Alyeshmerni

In "Study Power," strategies are suggested to help students understand what they are
learning, why, how to retain it—but most of all, how it fits within their frame of reference.
After all, current knowledge becomes the *prior* knowledge for the next step in learning.

- Knowing What You Know

- Remembering What You Know

- 17 Strategies for Class Notes

KNOWING WHAT YOU KNOW

One of the first steps in helping students become confident, independent learners at all
grade levels is to teach them the importance of connecting new information to what they
already know. As teachers, we can never assume what background our students bring to
the topic or that they are approaching new content from the same angle that we are.

BACKGROUND EXPERIENCE

Do you take the bus or does your mom pick you up after school?

–First-grader to his young teacher

Background experience shapes the view that anyone brings to any situation. Consider these two
different scenarios and what can be implied about background knowledge and experience.

A grandfather described taking his four-year-old granddaughter to a promotional event
featuring professional baseball players. The players were signing baseballs and the little girl
was lucky enough to receive one.

She asker her grandfather, "What did he write?"

After learning that the player wrote his name, the four-year-old was indignant, "Why did he do that? It's my ball!"

I chuckled at that story and also smiled recently when one of my children in college brought a group of friends home for the weekend. After encouraging them to make themselves comfortable, one young man opened the refrigerator and exclaimed, "Wow! Mrs. Tilton! A refrigerator that actually has food—and it's full!"

Both situations reveal information about the experiences of the speakers. The little girl had no idea what "autographing" was all about and college students forget all too quickly that a refrigerator can hold more than old Styrofoam containers and a can of beer. As I asked one of my own college sons before visiting his apartment, "Do I have to be up-to-date on my shots?"

"WHY DO WE HAVE TO LEARN THIS?"

Beginning with their first experiences in school, students need to be encouraged to ask this question and we need to have an answer. It is also critical that they know the "why" before beginning the assignment. To be accountable, students need to know how they will use the information, how it connects to what they already know, and how it connects to what they will learn next. This sets the stage for understanding the impact of prior knowledge to become the basis for new concepts.

Link It!

Grades 4–6

When beginning a new unit of study, here is a simple strategy to collect and assess what students already understand about a specific topic. Place students in groups and give each group several strips of construction paper.

Introduce the topic and ask students to record as many facts as they can about the topic on their strips of colored paper. Each group of students will create a chain by using glue to link their facts together. When each group has completed its chain, connect all the chains together to discover how much information the whole class has already collected.

☞ **The Practical Pointer:**
Color-coding the chains provided by each group gives the teacher fast feedback about how much each group knows and also provides accountability. Each group understands that the color will also indicate some measure of productivity and use of time.

KEY IDEA

We learn by connecting new information to what we already know. Helping our students understand this concept enables them to accomplish more on their own.

REMEMBERING WHAT YOU KNOW

Understanding Retention

Grades 6–12

As teachers, it is critical that we help our students in middle school and high school understand how most people retain information. This has an impact on how we teach but also in how students take responsibility for their own learning. Most likely you are already familiar with the numbers that follow but you may also want to share them with your students.

Without immediate review of material, we forget much of what we have just learned within 24 hours. How the material was presented has an enormous impact on how much we will retain.

- When we learn by *lecture*, we retain *5%*

- When we learn by *reading*, we retain *10%*

- When we learn by *A-V presentation*, we retain *20%*

- When we learn by *answering questions*, we retain *30%*

- When we learn by *discussion*, we retain *50%*

- When we learn by *immediate use*, we retain *90%*

For most of us, personal experience bears this out. Nowhere is this more apparent in my own experience than in computer use. When I asked one of my children how to do something on the computer recently, she explained it for the umpteenth time. I've looked at the manual. I've watched her do it. I've asked numerous questions. It was only when I said, "Move over. Watch me do it," that I really got a grasp.

I used the skill several times in succession. The next day, my 79-year-old mother happened to visit. Truly a life-long learner, she loves learning new skills on the computer. I had her pull up a chair so that I could teach her what I had learned. She learned in a fraction of the time that it took me. The fact that she is a quick learner helped, but learning by doing enabled her to learn even faster. It is no surprise that teaching her the skill reinforced my own learning.

As she left she said, "Now I've got to go home and teach your father or I'll never remember how to do this!" He is 82.

When learning becomes a hands-on experience for students with practical opportunities for immediate use, retention is much greater over time. As students discover how presentation in different ways affects retention, they can make choices that support their own learning preferences.

Chunking

Grades 2–12

As you think about a variety of ways to help your students assimilate the content in your curriculum, one strategy to consider is **chunking**. While the concept is not new, it is well worth revisiting. **Chunking** can be used effectively at all grade levels and in all subject areas to improve retention. It is simple and it works.

To illustrate the concept, use this demonstration with your students and perhaps with parents at Open House. Glance at the following four sets of letters for a few seconds. Then quickly cover them with your hand. Do not write them down. Then, keeping the letters covered, see if you can recall them and say them aloud in order.

CHU NKI GHE LPS

Could you do it? Did you get them all? From your own knowledge of brain research, you know that we can recall several disconnected items for a short period of time. For many adults, the limit is seven items, plus two or minus two. In my example, I asked you to recall twelve items, well beyond the limit for many of us. In fact, this is why I think that the nine-digit zip code has not caught on for many of us. It is just too long.

Now try a different example that will make the point about prior knowledge. Again, glance at what is written next and cover.

CHUNKING HELPS

With the letters covered, could you recall what was written? No problem this time. These were the *identical letters* in the *identical order* that I had used previously. The only change was that I *chunked* them in a different way. I grouped the letters to connect the letters with familiar information. It was much easier to recall because the letters now had meaning.

As part of good teaching, we "chunk" similar information together every day. When our students understand this, they can consciously do the same thing as they study on their own. Just an awareness of the value of **chunking** can assist parents in helping their children at home with homework.

Mnemonics: The Memory Tool

Grades 4–12

For content that is basic rote learning, such as essential vocabulary or sequential steps in a math operation, the **mnemonic** is an effective, dependable tool. A mnemonic uses a familiar word and attaches new meaning to each letter as a memory cue. Can you remember using **mnemonics** when you were in school?

For example, how did you learn the names of the Great Lakes? Did you learn the mnemonic *HOMES?*

> HOMES: Huron, Ontario, Michigan, Erie, and Superior

Did you learn the colors of the rainbow in order using this mnemonic: *ROY-G-BIV?*

> ROY-G-BIV: red, orange, yellow, green, blue, indigo, and violet

Can you think of others? Some people tell me that they can still recite all the cranial nerves that they learned in college because of a mnemonic. They haven't needed this information for years, they tell me, but it is stored in their brains for life!

O┱ KEY IDEA

Mnemonics serve a practical function in learning factual information efficiently so that a student can devote more time to higher-level thinking.

☞ **The Practical Pointer:**

This technique is most powerful when our students create their own mnemonics individually or in groups. They will remember more easily what they have created themselves.

Acrostics

Grades 4–12

Acrostics function the same way as a mnemonic but use a sentence or phrase.

> *Every Good Boy Does Fine* is an acrostic that most of us learned for the staff in music just as we learned the mnemonic, FACE, for the spaces between the lines.

> *Never Eat Shredded Wheat* helps young children remember directions: north, east, south, and west.

Please Excuse My Dear Aunt Sally provides the order of performing mathematical operations: parenthesis, exponents, multiplication, division, addition, and subtraction.

Dad, Mother, Sister, Brother indicates the sequential steps in long division: divide, multiply, subtract, and bring down.

George Elliot's Old Grandmother Ran A Pig Home Yesterday is a memory device from my childhood for spelling geography.

These are just a few examples. Students can create numerous acrostics to assist with basic learning.

☞ **The Practical Pointer:**
An acrostic is effective only when a student can remember both the sentence and what it signifies. One little boy asked me after reciting this acrostic several days in a row, "Dad, Mother, Sister, Brother. But why do we keep saying that?"

Singing for Retention

Grades K–3

At first, many students may not recognize the value of using music as a memory tool. Attaching new information to a familiar melody can enhance retention. Encourage students to *sing* math facts, vocabulary definitions and spelling words.

Most children learn the alphabet by singing it. Did you? Did you or your students have a problem with that pesky *Ellameno* or that extra "n" as in "*y n z*"? There is a simple solution for kindergarten and first grade teachers. Change the tune. Try singing the alphabet to the old nursery rhyme *Mary Had a Little Lamb*. It works like a charm.

> *Mary had a little lamb,*
>
> A - B - C - D - E - F - G
>
> *Little lamb, little lamb.*
>
> H - I - J - K - L - M
>
> *Mary had a little lamb.*
>
> N - O - P - Q - R - S - T
>
> *Its fleece was white as snow.*
>
> U - V - W - X - Y - Z

Voila! The *Ellameno* will never bother you again! Using melodies to other familiar childhood songs, such as *The Muffin Man*, work well for establishing routines for transition:

Did you know it's time for math?

Time for math, time for math?

Did you know it's time for math?

Today we'll learn new things!

Still another familiar melody, *Twinkle, Twinkle Little Star,* can be adapted to teach a phone number, complete with adding the area code at the end. Just sing the numbers instead of the words. Here's mine:

4 - 7 - 0 - 0 - 2 - 9 - 7

Twinkle, twinkle little star,

4 - 7 - 0 - 0 - 2 - 9 - 7

How I wonder where you are.

4 - 7 - 0 - 0 - 2 - 9 - 7

Up above the world so high,

4 - 7- 0 - 0 - 2 - 9 - 7

Like a diamond in the sky.

9 - 5 - 2 - 4 - 7 - 0

Twinkle, twinkle little star,

0 - 2 - 9 - 7 There you are!

How I wonder where you are!

The same melody can work for a troublesome spelling word such as "necessary." Note that the singer has to sing the "ss" together quickly!

n-e-c-e-ss-a-r-y

n-e-c-e-ss-a-r-y

Because not every spelling word will have exactly seven letters, improvising is a must and makes it fun. If you teach primary grades, you may already use singing to help students follow directions and retain information. Students can make up songs or make up words to familiar songs on their own to increase independent learning.

AT THE SECONDARY LEVEL

Your secondary students may not believe you at first, but this strategy applies to older students, as well. I've encouraged high school students who have struggled to remember math facts and vocabulary meanings to try *singing* them—in private. Several admitted later that this was effective for them.

While your students would never burst into song in class on their own, they might enjoy a short demonstration from you. Suggest it as simply another study tool. When the presentation is fun, everyone may be willing to give it a try and no one feels singled out.

☞ **The Practical Pointer:**
The students who benefit most from the singing strategy are often the same students who subvocalize while reading. Without realizing it, they will read aloud in a soft, audible voice. This helps them assimilate information while studying.

 KEY IDEA

Secondary students may immediately reject a strategy like this one before trying it because they perceive it as juvenile. So much lies is in how we present it. Our approach in presenting any strategy can be simply that here is another option, another tool, something that works for others and may work for you. Give it a try. Decide for yourself.

Hokey Pokey Learning

Grades K–5

I saw a bumper sticker recently that read *Is the Hokey Pokey really what it's all about?*

That poses an interesting question, doesn't it? I can't answer that but I do know that adding movement to singing can be an effective kinesthetic learning tool.

For example, you might begin with the traditional **Hokey Pokey** movements, lyrics, and music just for fun. Then adapt it to fit your content. Make up your own words. Change the movements but keep the familiar music. For young children, the **Hokey Pokey** can be a fun transition tool as you change from one activity to another. Enlist the help of your students in creating your own class version. Just two or three minutes of movement and music provide a much needed break and ease the shift from one subject to another.

If there is a current dance craze that appeals to older students, take a risk and get secondary students up and moving. They will be awake and engaged. While we cannot have students "Hokey Pokeying" their way through the day in tenth grade, we need to build in some kinesthetic involvement. See "High-Impact Review" for more than 25 classroom games and activities to reinforce content in a wide range of grade and subject areas.

Stick to It!

Grades 4–12

Among the countless uses for sticky notes is a technique to help students improve retention. The small notes can flag key words, main ideas or answers to study guide questions in both textbooks and class notes.

I encourage students to create a system that will work for how they learn best. One option that many students like is differentiating between the *top* of a notebook or text and the *side* to indicate what type of material the sticky note is citing.

Sticky notes protruding from the top are numbered with answers to questions on the study guide or chapter review. Sticky notes along the side of the notes or text are flagging main ideas or vocabulary. Since I am a strong advocate of color-coding, I suggest using three colors: pink for answers to questions, yellow for vocabulary and green for main ideas.

☞ **The Practical Pointer:**
The text and notes become interactive learning tools instead of materials to be used once. When the sticky notes contain key facts and vocabulary, they can also be peeled off and used later for review activities such as **Vocabulary Bingo**, **Tic-Tac-Know**, **Concentration** or **Jeopardy**.

17 STRATEGIES FOR CLASS NOTES

Pencils Down

Grades 4–12

Most teachers expect students to be able to take notes or copy key points listed on the overhead screen. Certainly this is a common expectation by the middle school level. As Mr. Park, an eighth-grade social studies teacher, said to me, "All I am asking them to do is copy. I put everything they need on the overhead. If they would just copy it, they would have it in their notes. It is very frustrating to see some of my students just sitting there!"

Many teachers share Mr. Park's frustration. It may be exasperating to watch as students "just sit there." There are two problems. The first problem is that some of our students cannot copy from the board or screen. When they attempt it, they will copy *letter by letter* in a slow and laborious effort that ends up as incomplete garble.

Students who cannot *listen and write* at the same time face the second problem. Some teachers continue teaching while expecting students to copy critical information simultaneously. This will not work for everyone. For some students, just listening to the teacher requires total concentration. A solution is to encourage these students to keep *pencils down and listen.* Wait until after the teacher finishes speaking, take a few moments to reflect, *then write.*

Copies of Notes

Grades 4–12

A teacher in one of my seminars had an experience that many of her students face daily. She was taking a graduate course during the summer. The instructor used numerous overheads in small print. She would try frantically to copy the information as he lectured.

One day she approached him after class. "Do you think that I could have a copy of your overheads? I can't write fast enough to copy all the information and also listen to your presentation."

The next day the professor arrived with a stack of handouts. He had made a class set of all the overhead transparencies that he would be using that day. He told the group that as long as he was making a set for one person, he decided to make them available to anyone who wanted a copy.

Without exception, the teacher told me, everyone eagerly took a set. She was elated because this enabled her to participate in the class without scrambling to take notes. The most interesting part was what the professor learned from the experience. The last day of class he told his graduate students, "I have never gotten through this much material in this course!" His students in the past had been spending too much time *copying* and not enough time *learning.*

⌐ KEY IDEA

Ask yourself if your students are copying information off the board or overhead screen that could be provided as a handout. During the discussion, students can highlight and color-code important points.

"Read Over" Instead of "Copy Over"

Grades 4–12

During my own teaching experience, I found that some teachers, especially at the secondary level, recognized that some students could not take notes during class. These teachers were willing to give a copy of the notes to certain students, provided that the students would "copy them over" on their own at home. The rationale for this approach has always been that when students themselves write the notes, they learn the content.

While this is true for some individuals, writing notes and copying notes are two different learning strategies and they do not work for all learners.

Spending homework time recopying what has already been written may take an unreasonable amount of time. It is worth questioning. Many parents have asked me about this issue over the years. The focus needs to remain on the objective as the driving force. That is a recurring theme throughout this book and bears repeating. Instead of "copying over" the notes, encourage the student *read the notes aloud* and *highlight key points*. This will take significantly less time but will enable the student to focus on learning concepts instead of physically copying content.

O—⟁ KEY IDEA

What is the objective? The objective should drive the activity. Is the objective copying or is it learning the course content?

Students need to discover what learning strategies work best for them. If "copying over" the notes is not an effective technique for their learning, students need to explore other options to reach the same end point of assimilating the content.

A second underlying theme worth repeating is that no one can afford to waste time during the learning process. How much are students expected to copy and is it the best use of students' time during that class? This is the important question.

For some individuals, copying notes takes time away from more challenging learning. This is *not* to say that copying notes should be eliminated for everyone. Copying a moderate amount of notes from a blackboard, white board or text is one option that some students find helpful as a learning tool. As part of differentiating instruction, we need to offer a variety of options within the framework of the content. The goal is to offer many different strategies in helping our students become independent learners.

O—⟁ KEY IDEA

Whether in the second grade or tenth grade, no student can afford to waste time in school. If a strategy is not working, it is time to investigate other options.

Skeletal Notes

Grades 4–12

Some teachers insist that providing a full set of notes actually discourages a student from participating in class. An alternative to the complete set of notes is to provide a **skeleton**. Partial notes are provided with blanks for the student to fill in. If there are four causes of the Civil War, for example, the skeleton contains the *first* and *third* causes of the war leaving blanks for the *second* and *fourth*. It is each student's responsibility to fill in those. Providing "every other one" on the skeleton rather than the first two consecutive responses builds in "catch up time" as the student is writing.

Despite this format, there may still be a few students whose notes are either incomplete or illegible. Under these circumstances, a copy of the notes could be provided later.

O—ı KEY IDEA

These students whose notes are illegible are excellent candidates for the personal keyboards described in "The Alternate Route."

Tape-Recorded Notes

Grades 6–12

I have a cousin who has been an emergency room physician for many years in a large urban hospital. On a given day, Bob may meet as many as 75 ambulances during his shift. He loves his work and his colleagues would tell you that Bob is a top-notch physician.

He was not a top-notch note taker in college and medical school, however. He learned best by listening and recording all of his classes on tape. The system worked well for him. Now, his daughter Madeline is experiencing the same difficulty in taking notes. The problem is not that she cannot learn the content; the problem is that some of his daughter's teachers are lowering her grades because her class notes are incomplete.

Not every student learns by simultaneously listening and writing. A sensible solution for students who struggle with taking written notes is to encourage them to use a basic cassette recorder to tape-record sections of the class period. Students can learn the content equally well by *listening instead of writing* and will be able to listen to the content again later on tape. Listening to the tape does not have to take an inordinate amount of time because students can fast forward through any parts of the material that are already understood.

Cornell Notes

Grades 4–12

An idea worth revisiting is the Cornell format for note taking. You may have used this yourself in high school or college because it is one of those essential strategies that work. My preference is to use the Cornell approach in conjunction with the skeletal strategy. Ahead of time, the notes are partially completed with the two-column Cornell format.

How To Use It:

If you decide to use the skeletal version, write the topic across the top of the page in preparation for class. Then divide the page into two vertical columns with the left column using about one-third of the page and the right column using the remaining two-thirds. Leave the left column blank except for the words *Passing Lane* written across the top.

I always tell students that this side of the page will help them *pass* an upcoming assessment. The skeletal outline appears on the right hand side and includes some of the main ideas and details. Adequate space is left for students to write their additions to the outline or graphic organizer. Depending on the grade level and individual student needs, lines to write on can prevent writing "downhill."

During the last few minutes of class, students use the space in the *Passing Lane* to generate one or two questions that would be answered by the notes they have just written. Initially, expect the most basic questions.

> What was this about?

> What happened in this chapter?

With practice, questions become more detailed and specific. Students learn that there is a connection between the questions on the left and the information on the right. This technique promotes the skill of processing the ideas and concepts learned. The process can be expanded in several ways described next.

Partner Review

Grades 4–12

The next day, students begin the class by folding their notes so that only the *Passing Lane* is exposed. Next they meet with a peer partner and ask each other their questions. It is interesting for students to discover that their notes may be different from a partner's even though the topic was the same. Students review from their own notes but also have an opportunity to learn what other students emphasized.

KEY IDEA

Partner Review is effective not only when using Cornell notes but also as a regular format for reinforcing content.

Assessment Input

Grades 4–12

As the teacher, you may decide to take the Cornell strategy another step further by collecting the student-generated questions and building them into an assessment. Doing this places even greater value on the procedure. It shifts ownership of learning to the students and empowers them as they see their own work becoming part of the assessment.

Visual Version

Grades 4–12

Cornell notes can be adapted for visual notes. The skeletal outline is provided on the right hand side as in the previous example but the left hand column is reserved for students to *draw* the concepts. The result will be a combination of words and simple illustrations. This approach can be especially effective for science diagrams, social studies maps, and characters in stories. Strong visual learners who love to draw will excel using the visual format.

Stick-Figure Notes

Grades 3–12

The students who like the visual version for Cornell notes will enjoy **Stick-Figure Notes**. Whenever students are focusing on characters, such as explorers in social studies, protagonists in a novel, or the subjects of biographies, this technique is effective. As the name suggests, the **Stick-Figure Notes** strategy uses a simple drawing of a character to create a vivid picture of the person.

The human shape becomes the vehicle for describing the character's qualities, thoughts and ideas through corresponding body parts. The concept is easily adapted for a variety of grade levels and students.

SECONDARY VERSION

At the secondary level, the information can be detailed and complex. Key thoughts are shown next to the head, beliefs are written near to the heart and travels are depicted near the feet. Personal strengths are listed next to the stick figure's flexed muscles. The hands

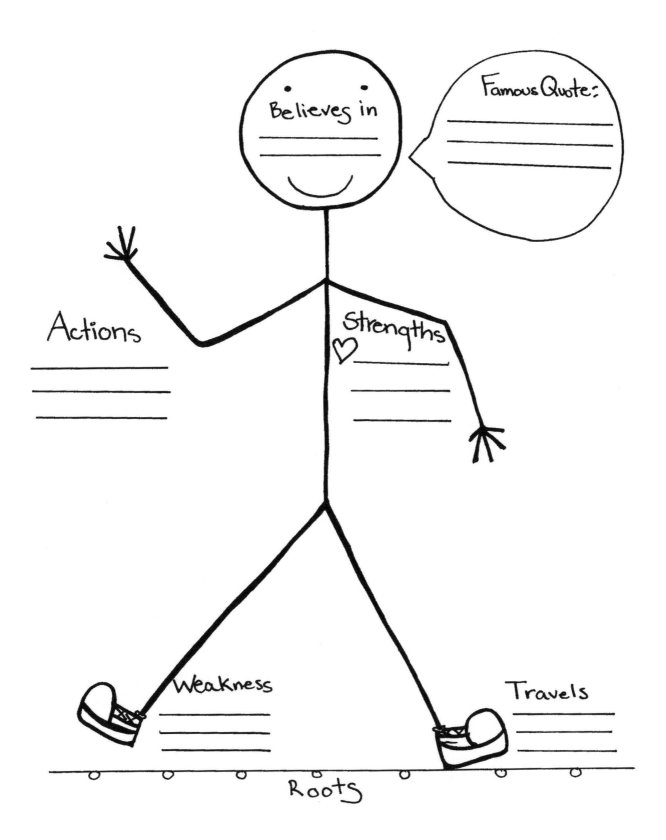

point to important actions. The character's roots are described beneath the feet. A cartoon bubble holds a notable quote.

As an English teacher, I was surprised to find hastily drawn stick figures in the margins of assessments. Several students reconstructed the characters from literary works to assist with recall before writing an essay.

ELEMENTARY VERSION

The stick figure has a different application at the elementary level. Students can select a favorite person to interview and then draw a large stick figure on butcher paper. Though simpler, the concept is the same. If a child interviews a grandfather, the child may recall something that the grandfather "always says" and write it in the bubble. The child often draws a self-portrait in the grandfather's heart. Strengths, travels and actions can be depicted in a very concrete way. This popular activity offers a basic introduction to character study.

Paper Airplane Learning

Grades 6–12

Class notes literally take flight as students share information with peers. You may be thinking that your students do not need encouragement in this department but **Paper Airplane Learning** definitely holds students' attention!

HOW IT WORKS:

Provide a skeletal outline for the lesson that day, similar to example using the Cornell note taking approach. There is a transparency copy on the overhead. One student stands at the overhead filling in the sample skeleton with a marker during class.

Save the last ten minutes of class for **Paper Airplane Learning**. On the back of the skeletal outline are dotted lines to form a paper airplane. It is essential to set clear ground rules. A key rule is obvious at the outset: Making the paper airplane comes at the end of the lesson *after* the skeletal outline is complete.

Students write their names on their completed outlines and then, *at the signal*, turn them over and quickly fold them into paper airplanes.

You can visualize the next part. All students send their airplanes into the air like mortarboards on Graduation Day. Airplanes must be flown *up into the air*, not aimed directly at a peer. Tell students to catch one and send it on. Each student is allowed three "take-offs."

Finally, students keep the last one that they catch. The homework assignment is to read that person's notes, make any additions or changes in a different color, and return it to the sender at the beginning of class the next day. (No flying this time!) It is interesting for students to see what other students have written on their notes. As the new class begins, students have already had an opportunity for a quick review.

 The Practical Pointer:

Making snowballs out of the skeletal notes is another approach that I have used. With certain groups of students, I have been concerned about the point of the airplane hitting someone. Snowballs eliminate this concern. The purpose of the activity is the same: to read another student's notes, add to them and review the content.

Write, Listen and Tell

Grades 4–12

Write, Listen and Tell is a technique useful in assisting students with processing new information. During the lesson, the teacher stops two or three different times and announces that it is time to **Write, Listen and Tell**. Students know the routine.

It is time to *stop* and *write* an idea or *draw* a visual on a sticky note depicting something that they have just learned. Next, students will stand up and get out of their seats. They will find their study partner, *listen* to what that person has learned, and *tell* that person what he or she has learned. This **Write, Listen and Tell** strategy is a simple tool with a huge payoff. It is especially helpful for those students who are unable to take notes and listen to the teacher simultaneously.

O⟶ KEY IDEA

We learn 80 percent of what we know through listening, a skill promoted by the *Write, Listen and Tell* approach.

 The Practical Pointer:

It is crucial that teacher remain *quiet* while students are writing or drawing. Give students a minute of silence to assimilate the information. Afterward they are ready to share with other students and go on to the next point. Students can easily apply this strategy to their own independent learning. Every few paragraphs in a text, students can stop, write or draw what they've learned and then summarize verbally to assist with retention.

Stop Draw

Grades 2–12

To check student understanding and retention of any subject from a science chapter to a novel to an art lesson, try this technique. At the beginning of the lesson, ask students to fold a blank piece of paper into fourths or eighths creating corresponding boxes. The number of squares needed depends on the grade level and complexity of the content. Next, ask students to number each box from left to right.

Throughout the lesson, stop frequently and say, "Stop Draw!" This is the cue for students to quickly think about what they have just learned and create a quick visual depiction. It can be a stick figure drawing, a diagram, a word or a visual reminder. There is no right or wrong response. Each student's response will be different.

When this is repeated several times, the students will have a sequential set of visual notes that may retell the story or highlight key points. Note that this may be carried over the next day if the lesson is continued.

☞ **The Practical Pointer:**
Many students who are adept at drawing prefer to take notes using a visual format on a routine basis. I watch for students who are constantly drawing cartoons in margins, on scratch paper or in their notebooks and encourage them to focus on visual notes.

Venn Diagrams

Grades 4–12

Note taking using the traditional Venn diagrams work well for topics that focus on comparison and contrast. Two interlocking circles will be the basic format. Students can use visual notes or words to label and fill in each circle.

☞ **The Practical Pointer:**
Encourage students to color-code their Venn diagrams by designating a color for each circle. They can write or draw in marker or simply highlight to color-code. After writing their notes in the interlocking section, they may wish to highlight commonalities with a third color creating a strong visual image.

Graphic Organizers

Grades K–12

The sky is the limit in the webbing process. Kindergartners learn the concept of webbing early in the year. A practical approach is to begin with "My Family." Before long, they are creating extensive webs through drawings, magazine pictures and photographs.

Visual learners often find that the web is an effective way to record class notes. The web is also an excellent tool to show relationships. From upper elementary through high school, encourage students to use markers to color-code the circles or squares to depict levels and groups of relationships as they make their webs.

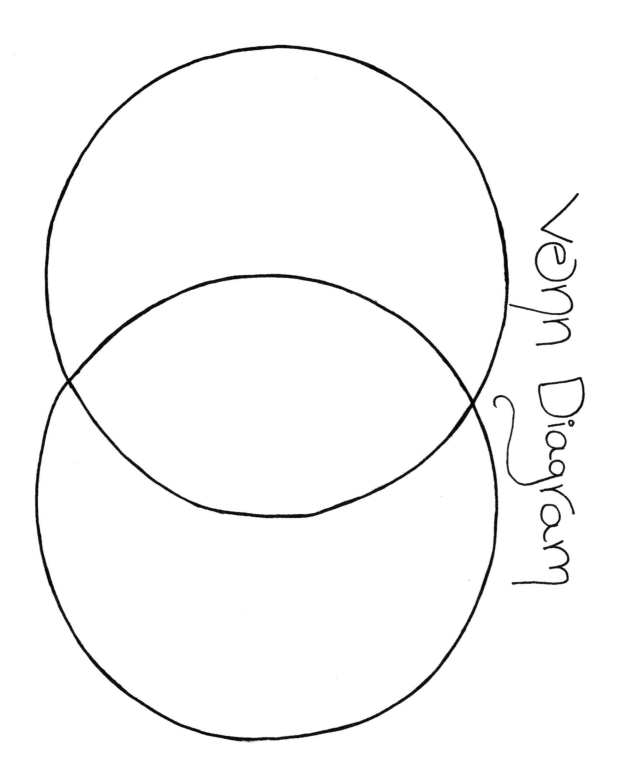

Venn Diagram

 The Teacher's Toolbox for Differentiating Instruction © Linda Tilton 1-888-LEARN-11

Outlines Still Work!

Grades 4–12

It is interesting, though, that some of my students over the years have preferred the traditional outline to webbing. For them, the linear format that the outline offers is easier to follow and makes more sense. Sometimes the web can be visually overwhelming.

For these students, the eye cannot focus on important concepts because there seems to be no order. When I have taught the traditional outline format using topic, mains ideas, details and supporting details, these students have found this technique more usable. Again creating a system of color-coding makes it easy to see the relationships among main ideas and levels of details.

T-Line Notes

Grades K–12

It might seem unlikely that any strategy for class notes could apply to all grades levels K–12. A strategy that spans the grade levels and content areas is the practical **T-Line** format. The **T-Line** strategy separates topics by arranging items into one of two columns. It is really a sorting strategy that can be very simple or quite complex.

PRIMARY GRADES

Very young children benefit from a simplified version of this by first arranging three-dimensional objects into two groups that are alike in some way. For example, toy trucks belong in one group; farm animals belong together in another. Children physically place the items into two different groupings.

Next, primary students can use photographs of objects and large paper divided into two columns by a thick black line. On the left side is a drawing of a house and on the right hand side is a depiction of the outdoors with a sun and blue sky. Children place the photographs either inside the house or outdoors as they begin to grasp the concepts of *like* and *different*.

Another step for students is to use pictures of children doing things. The students make decisions based on where the children would do what is described: Would the activity be *inside* and *outside*? As a group, students separate photographs of children watching TV on a couch and making cookies in a kitchen from pictures of children riding bikes in the sunshine and playing basketball in a park.

The process helps children determine what goes together. The product can form a basis for students telling about their selections.

MIDDLE AND HIGH SCHOOL USE

T-Lines become very sophisticated throughout middle school and high school. In math, use

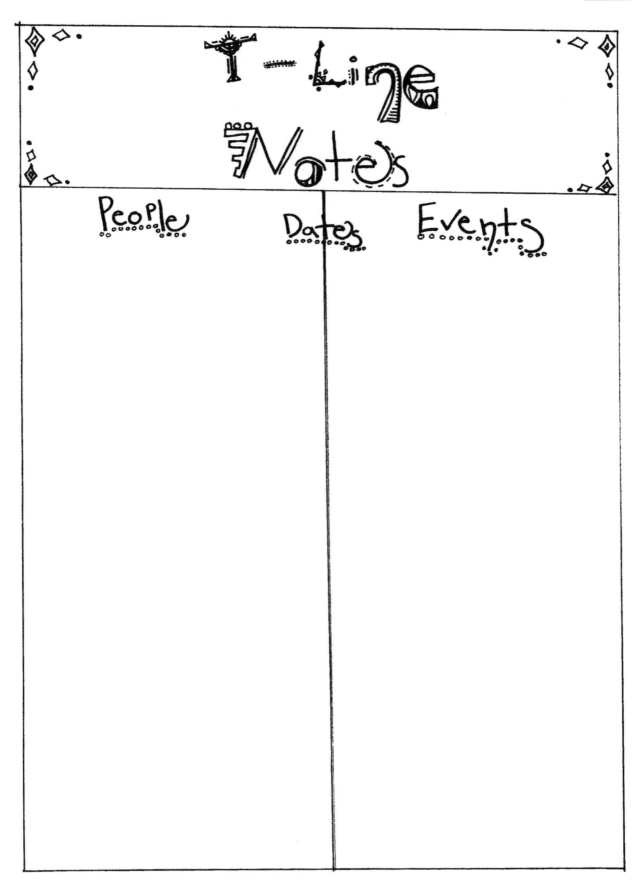

T-Line Notes

People   Dates   Events

T-Lines to help students with story problems by sorting essential information on one side of the line from extraneous information on the other.

This technique works especially well for vertical timelines. Students write the topic across the top of the page and then draw the "T" shape. *Who* will be in the left-hand column, *When* will be dates intersecting the vertical line going down the page and *What* in the right-hand column corresponds the event.

The middle school students in my English classes really enjoyed using the **T-Line** with a timeline during the initial stages of writing an autobiography. They listed each year of their lives vertically in the *When* column and indicated a key person or people in the *Who* column along with an important memory from that year in the *What* column. It made the project manageable in scope by helping them focus on a limited number of events.

☞ **The Practical Pointer:**

T-Line Notes also lend themselves to a partially completed skeletal outline. If the *What* is lengthy, I provide it and students fill in the *Who*. In using a timeline for class notes, I have always listed key dates ahead of time so that I can space them along the line to demonstrate the approximate relationship over time. It forms a visual continuum.

SUMMARY

"Study Power" focused on helping students understand how they assimilate new information. When students realize the impact of prior knowledge on learning new content, the stage is set for learning. Prior knowledge forms the basis for applying new information and creating a new frame of reference.

The young child was indignant when the baseball player signed *her* ball with *his* name, because she had already learned to "put your name on it" whether it was a paper, bag lunch or ball. Her response was dictated by what she knew. Suddenly and unexpectedly, prior knowledge was expanded to fit different information. She learned a whole new concept that day.

Because students do not all learn in the same way, they also need to learn what works for them. How one student takes notes or learns new content does not work for all students. They need options and choices. We provide these choices as we differentiate instruction. We go beyond our overall concepts, vocabulary and required "must know" information to a level that exposes our students to a whole new way of thinking.

What we want to see is the child in pursuit of knowledge,
and not the knowledge in pursuit of the child.

–George Bernard Shaw

7

HIGH IMPACT REVIEW

Learning is not a sit and get proposition . . .

–Classroom Teacher

We don't have time to play games. Students come. We review. I teach. They work. It's over. It's the same every day. It's very traditional. You don't know my school. No one would play games. This is the math department, Linda.

–Name withheld on request

A common misperception is that reviewing through the use of games takes more time and is less efficient than the traditional study guide or basic question-answer session. The high school math teacher was adamant that such frivolous use of time would never work. Actually, the level of student engagement and interest in activities suggested in "High-Impact Review" makes them very effective as review tools.

The same amount of time typically devoted to review of the lesson from the previous day can be used in a wide variety of ways to reach the same end. They are not meant to *add on* to what you are already doing. They are simply *different* ways of reinforcing content. No idea is suggested to the exclusion of other ideas including traditional review.

After much cajoling, the math teacher agreed to try a few games. It wasn't long before I got a phone call from her.

"All right. I tried some of the games and they loved them," she said. "Everyone was actually paying attention at one time. Now they ask every day if this is the day we're playing **Bluff**. They're telling me I'm their favorite teacher. Now what?"

It doesn't mean that you have to use these activities or ones that are similar every day. Use them on an occasional basis if that appeals to you and your students. We know that different students learn in different ways. I am guessing that some of the hands-on learners in that math class responded favorably to the games for that reason. It may also be safe to assume that other students liked the variety if, in fact, every day is the same. The fast-paced interaction in an activity such as **Bluff** is far different from a review sheet.

GAMES THAT TEACH

Students need both practice and review. There are many different ways to accomplish this. In most classrooms today, we have substantially reduced the number of worksheets, packets and study guides that we use with our students. The activities and games suggested in this chapter are a far cry from the monotonous drill-and-kill approach that was common in the past. A worksheet or study guide offers *one way* to reinforce concepts but does not differentiate instruction to meet the needs of all students.

Research supports that one of the best ways to raise quiz and test scores is *verbalizing the response, especially through self-questioning.* Many review games incorporate verbalizing and can be used as excellent learning tools and reinforcement strategies.

It is also worth noting that we are raising a generation of children of all ages who do not play games to the extent that previous generations have played them. There are strong reasons to promote a return to games inside and outside of the school setting.

Board games and other games teach thinking skills, negotiating skills, strategizing and camaraderie. Too often our students are adept at computer and video games that focus solely on individual strategies but do not involve the critical social piece of learning how to interact with others.

"High-Impact Review" is devoted to reinforcement activities and review strategies that focus on interacting with other people and studying aloud. All activities and strategies are easy to adapt for a variety of group sizes. Some activities can be used with the whole class; others work well in small groups or with partners, while others can be adapted for an individual student to use independently. Several lend themselves to a variety of group sizes depending on the purpose.

TEACHER-FRIENDLY AND TIME-EFFICIENT

All of the games cater to a variety of learning styles. The activities are hands-on, verbal, auditory and visual techniques that allow a teacher at times to reinforce the *same* concepts with all students but also allow for *differentiation by level and content.* Especially important is that all of these strategies, tips, tools and techniques can be effective in short segments of class time and all are teacher-friendly in terms of minimal preparation time.

Students have enthusiastically endorsed the review games selected for this chapter. Variety helps concentration. These activities produce the same end result of increased learning and retention in different ways. When students are actively engaged in their learning, higher scores can emerge.

K–12 APPLICATION

Many of the strategies can be adapted easily across all levels and content areas. Others apply more specifically certain grades. While general levels are suggested for each activity, consider expanding and adapting the game to suit your students.

☞ **The Practical Pointer:**
When using any of these review strategies, it can be useful to set a time limit and define the parameters at the outset. "We have six minutes to play **Toss It!**" or "The content reviewed today will come from Chapter Six."

These activities already generate high interest but I have found that occasionally providing a small edible reward further increases enthusiasm. I've been amazed at how hard students will work for a lemon drop during seventh hour!

POSITIVE RESULTS

The 26 high impact review and reinforcement activities are listed next to view at a glance. Some are games that I have used with my own students. Some are activities that other teachers have suggested. Some may be familiar and others will be new to you. Try them with your students and see the results!

26 HIGH IMPACT GAMES

- Bluff
- Innie-Outie Review
- Toss It!
- Blizzard, Snowstorm, Sleet and Flurries
- "I have . . . Who has . . .?"
- Silent "I have . . . Who has . . .?"
- Wordless "I have . . . Who has . . .?"
- ZAP!
- Simon Says
- Go Fish
- The Fish Pond
- Origami Partners
- Shout It Out!
- Shower Curtain Hopscotch
- Human Bingo
- Mancala
- Jigsaw Puzzles
- Checkers Review
- Pictionary Vocabulary
- Guesstures Review
- Tic-Tac-Know
- State Fair

- Soccer Ball Review

- Beach Ball Questions

- Concentration Lids

- Pots and Pans

Bluff

Grades 4–12

A teacher asked me to demonstrate **Bluff** in her ninth grade social studies health class using the chapter study guide and answer key. He said later that this activity generated more enthusiasm for that weekly study guide than he had seen in a long, long time. Very simply, **Bluff** is a question-answer review game that involves the entire class. It is fast-paced. Students described it as "fun!" The length of time needed for **Bluff** can vary but it certainly doesn't need to consume the entire class period. It can be a five- or ten-minute period used as transition from one activity to another during an 80-minute block class period or as a review activity at the end of class.

HOW IT WORKS:

Divide the class into two heterogeneous groups. It is simplest to divide the group right down the middle of the room. Designate one person per team to come to the board and keep score. There is friendly competition between teams, but it is *team-centered cooperation* rather individual competition.

Use study guide questions, vocabulary words, math problems, spelling words or other sources to formulate questions. Direct the first question to one side of the room. For example,

What is the capital of Minnesota?

Any member of that team may choose to stand and take a chance on being called on to give the response. Students who actually *know* the answer may stand as well as any member of that team who does *not* know the answer but would like would like to *bluff*. The moderator, usually the teacher, chooses any one of the students who is standing to give the answer.

If the person who is called on gives the right answer, a point is earned for *every person standing*. Even though some individuals who are standing may think that the capital of Minnesota is Des Moines, that doesn't matter in the point count. They were standing when the right answer was given.

Why would anyone bluff? The more individuals who stand, the more points that team will earn if the correct response is given.

If, on the other hand, the moderator calls on a person who is *bluffing* and answers *incorrectly*, no second chance is given and no points are earned or deducted for that round. All team members who were standing sit down and the same question is then posed to the other team.

This time, any member of second team who knows the answer or chooses to *bluff* will stand. The moderator again selects one person to answer. If that person answers correctly, points are awarded to that team based on the number of people standing.

This review strategy encourages all students in class to take a risk. As every teacher knows, there are students who are never willing to raise their hands in class because they are afraid of making a public mistake. The purpose of **Bluff** is not to encourage everyone to stand for every question, but to take a risk when the student has a good indication of the answer.

Because several students will stand at once, camaraderie is created in a low-stress situation. The worst that can happen is that when a student is called on, that student answers incorrectly and the question quickly shifts to the other team. Some students get it right; others will not. Many questions will be asked and students will always learn the correct answer.

☞ **The Practical Pointer:**
The goal is to include everyone. When **Bluff** is on the agenda, a teacher can quietly brief a hesitant student ahead of time by pulling the student aside as everyone is filing into class, "Remember yesterday when we were studying the capitals of states in the Midwest? Remember the capital of Minnesota?"

After some prompting, the student is prepared for that question and may take a risk later during **Bluff**. This student has the opportunity to shine in front of peers and earn some points for the team. That is a tremendous confidence-builder.

After students are used to playing **Bluff**, they can submit their own questions and take turns as moderators. This activity works especially well for chapter review. Expect your students to request **Bluff** often.

⌼ KEY IDEA

Like the math teacher, some high school teachers wonder if the activities suggested here apply to their juniors and seniors. They do. Games appeal to all ages from younger children through adulthood. As in anything, so much of the success depends on how we present the activity. If you teach secondary students, you may find that you will need to try these activities more than once before every student feels comfortable participating. Focus on results. I tell students "Here is a way to help you raise assessment scores and retain more information. Give it a try."

Innie–Outie Review

Grades 6–12

Innie-Outie Review is an excellent review technique for factual knowledge because it focuses on student-generated questions for review. As homework the night before or as an in-class activity ahead of time, each student writes five questions and answers on a note card.

The questions will vary based on the complexity of content, grade level and the ability of each student. Simple examples might include:

> Define the word "export."
>
> List two causes of the Civil War.
>
> What is the product of 5 × 5?

How It Works:

This activity requires some physical space. Students need to push desks or tables to one side of the room. Weather permitting, you may elect to take the class outside. Other options include using an empty room or hallway.

Divide the class in half. With note cards in hand, the two groups from two large circles, one inside the other. One circle faces *in* while the other circle faces *out* so that each person is looking at a partner, not unlike a square dance.

If the teacher says, "Inside!" each student standing in the inner circle selects a question from his or her personal question card to ask the partner. Note that all the "inside" students are asking their questions *simultaneously*. Each outside partner responds to the specific question asked by his or her partner. If the person responding does not know the answer, the questioner gives the answer.

Next, the teacher directs everyone to *move one step to the right*. The circles move in two different directions and everyone now faces a new partner. This time the teacher may direct, "Outside!" The process is repeated only now the questioners are standing in the "outer" circle. It is their turn to select and ask a question. The "inside" students respond. As before, the questioner provides the correct response if needed. Students then take another step to the right and face a new partner. The teacher again states either "Inside!" or "Outside!" and the process continues.

By changing partners constantly, all students are exposed to a wide variety of levels and types of questions. While a struggling student may ask basic factual questions, another student may ask more challenging questions. By repeating the process five or six times, very little class time is used but every student is exposed to several questions.

☞ **The Practical Pointer:**

Teachers frequently ask me how often students hold blank cards with no questions ready to ask because they haven't done their homework. The answer is, "Usually not more than once!" Having to stand in front of five different peers and make up questions on the spot is challenging. Most students discover that it is easier to prepare ahead of time.

Teachers also ask if this works well in large classes. I have used it in groups of 25 and larger. Occasionally, I have divided the group into two sets of circles when the space was available.

⚷ KEY IDEA

Any student can learn to use this same technique during independent study. The focus is on results. Creating note cards of self-generated questions makes review fast and convenient, particularly when a student needs to review a large volume of material covering a semester or full year.

 Toss It!

Grades 4–12

This is a variation of that tried and true classroom basketball game involving questions and answers, a wad of paper and the wastebasket. Why improve upon a good thing, you ask? Variety. I observed this version in an eighth grade classroom and found raucous acceptance by the whole group. Students like the added excitement of scoring one, three or five points for a correct response. Like **Bluff**, this review activity works well with the entire class; another option involves creating two games of smaller groups—one in front and one in back of the classroom.

HOW IT WORKS:

For this reinforcement activity, you will need to construct a backboard that can be tilted against a wall. To make it durable, you might consider plywood that measures about five feet across and four feet high. Five holes are cut in the plywood: a larger round center hole and smaller round ones in each of the four corners. The center hole is a *three-point* hole, the corners are worth *five points* and the backboard itself is worth *one point*. You will also need a beanbag, tennis ball, small rubber ball or a wad of paper to toss.

As in the previous games, this activity also calls for dividing the class into two groups. Each team sends one person at a time to respond to a random question, solve a math problem, define a word or list examples. The teacher, as moderator, is in an excellent position to adapt the level of question to the particular student. The first team sends a student to the **Toss It!** line. The moderator asks a question.

Who attended the Treaty of Versailles?

If the student responds correctly, that student has *earned the opportunity* to **Toss It!** Note that no point is earned for the correct response alone, this simply gives the student a chance to toss.

Standing at the **Toss It!** line, the student will toss an item at the backboard. If it goes through the center three-point hole, the team earns three points; if the student tosses it through the five-point corner hole, five points are earned; if the student just hits the board, one point is earned. If the student misses altogether, no points are earned. To clarify, points are earned through the toss. An incorrect response disqualifies the students from tossing the object.

Have you worked with students who struggle with content but very likely would throw a five-point toss? This is their chance to gain stature before their peers. As the teacher moves quickly through the questions, a variety of levels are included. Naturally some questions will be more difficult than others. The teacher has the indisputable authority in selecting content. In my experience, I found that the fast pace reduced comments from students that one person received a question that was more difficult or less difficult than another.

☞ **The Practical Pointer:**
A strip of masking tape on the floor can designate the **Toss It!** line. On a tile floor, a streak of shoe polish may be more popular with the custodian. This is easier to clean than the residue left by tape.

⌐ KEY IDEA

Frequent short spurts of review are often more effective than long sessions. Ask any college student who has spent the night before an exam "cramming" to learn the material. It would have been far easier in the long run to invest in a few minutes each night staying caught up.

Blizzard, Snowstorm, Sleet and Flurries

Grades 6–12

Try this review strategy with the whole group or in cooperative groups. As in the previous activities, the purpose to is to reinforce current content or material from previous units. It

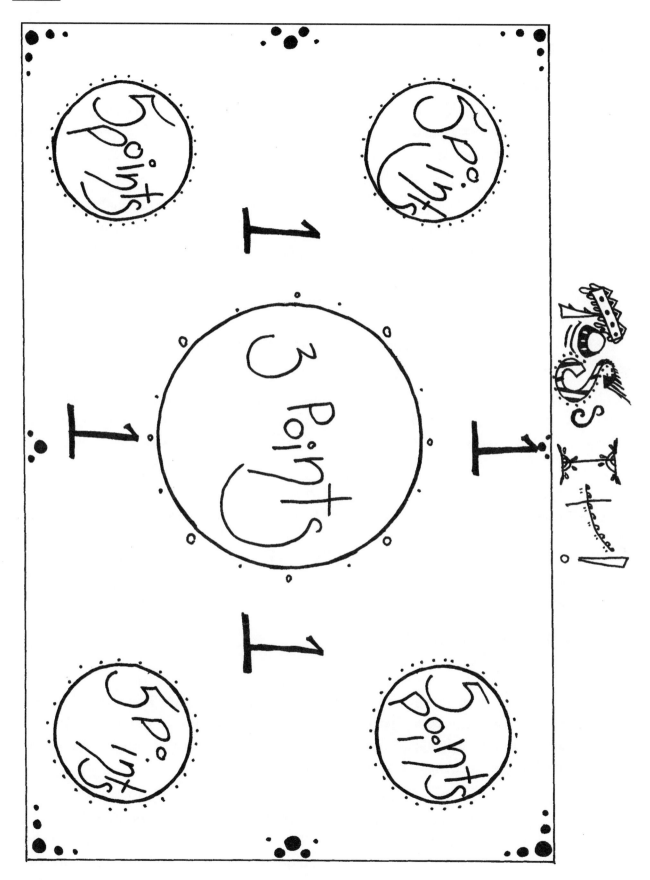

uses verbal questioning but this time students themselves select the level of difficulty in answering a question.

HOW IT WORKS:

Typically, the class is divided into two teams. The teams take turns and are allotted one question per turn. A designated participant chooses one of the following words: *blizzard, snowstorm, sleet,* or *flurries.* Here in Minnesota, a blizzard is the most severe weather condition in wintertime, and thus, it is the most challenging level of question.

A correct answer earns four points. A *snowstorm* indicates severe weather but is a notch below a *blizzard,* so questions at this level rate three points. Moving down in point value, *sleet* is worth two points followed by *flurries* or questions earning a single point.

After the student selects a level of difficulty, the moderator asks a question. Points for correct answers are earned as described. Only *one question* is posed to each student to keep the pace moving quickly from player to player. If the student's response is incorrect, the turn moves to another player on the opposite team who then selects any level of difficulty and receives a new question.

Students in your region of the country may not have practical experience with terms such as *blizzard* or *snowstorm* (and they should rejoice!). Adapt the activity by substituting different weather terms or vocabulary words to rate questions that fit your region of the country. You may also want to change terms with the seasons or times of the year.

☞ **The Practical Pointer:**

This activity can be student-led as well as teacher-led. Note cards in a recipe box are a good way to collect and store questions for each unit. When students need a five-minute break, **Blizzard, Snowstorm, Sleet, and Flurries** provides repetition, fast feedback and reinforcement. Any of these activities can be used to summarize content during the last few minutes of a class period.

"I Have . . . Who Has . . . ?"

Grades K–12

The previous review strategies in this chapter targeted students in upper elementary through high school. "I have . . . Who has . . . ?" works well for *all* grades K–12. It is an effective alternative to using study guides and worksheets. Like the other reinforcement and review strategies, it focuses on auditory reinforcement.

"I have . . . Who has . . . ?" works well as a whole group activity and I used it most often in that format. It is quick, energizing and gave me the feedback that I needed. It is also an excellent tool for differentiating instruction. "I have . . . Who has . . . ?" engages the entire class simultaneously but it can be easily adapted for small groups so that questions and pace can be adjusted for different levels and individual needs.

How It Works:

Each student receives a card with an *answer* to a question followed by a *new question*. The answer and question on that card do not match. The activity will ultimately create a circle as questions are asked and answered. While any student could begin the activity by asking the question on a card, it simplifies the process when one student receives a card with the words "Start Here" in the middle of the card above the new question.

That student begins by asking, "Who has . . . ?" This activity trains each student to listen carefully to the question. Someone in the group holds the card with the answer to that question on the top of the card. The student holding the card with the correct response calls out, "I have . . ." filling in the response and then asks the next "Who has . . . ?"

The activity continues until it has come full circle. The person who started with a question holds the final card with the answer. Content may include math facts, test review questions, vocabulary words, place value, telling time, shapes, colors, conversation in foreign language, art terms or concepts from music appreciation. The sky truly is the limit. One math teacher had his students work algebra problems and then the student with the answer would shout, "I have . . ."

○━ KEY IDEA

The goal is active reinforcement of concepts but "I have . . . Who has . . ." also creates an opportunity for every student to excel in front of peers. A teacher may elect to carefully hand out the cards so that a particular student receives a card that the student can answer correctly. The teacher may also cue Lisa, for example, ahead of time, to listen for Corey's question to enable her to respond correctly.

Silent "I Have . . . Who Has . . . ?"

Grades 3–6

A silent variation of the same game focuses on cooperation. Students receive cards and the object is to arrange themselves *in consecutive order* without speaking. Through looking at each other's cards and assisting each other, they will form a circle.

☞ **The Practical Pointer:**

When using this activity with younger students, a few suggestions may make it go more smoothly. Initially, a teacher may choose to hand out the cards *in order* to get students

I have:

Who has:

I have:

Who has:

I have:

Who has:

I have:

Who has:

I have:

Who has:

accustomed to the format. Also, younger children may be instructed to look at their cards and then *hold the cards behind them* until their turn to avoid confusion.

I found it helpful, too, to use both the *front* and *back* of the card for primary students. The *question was on the front* and the student turned it over to find the *answer on the back*.

Wordless "I Have . . . Who Has . . . ?"

Grades K–1

Finally, kindergarteners can play a wordless version. Several children can hold triangles, squares or circles. The teacher asks, "Who has . . . ?" and all the children with triangles, for example, hold up triangles.

ZAP!

Grades K–12

The **ZAP!** strategy spans all grade levels and content areas as an effective review activity with positive results. A French teacher used **ZAP!** with her fourth-year French students the day before a written assessment. She was delighted when every single quiz score went up. She credits **ZAP!** with the positive outcome.

The concept is simple. Students sit in small groups of three or four students. **ZAP!** can be adapted for a classroom filled with students functioning on many different levels. While it depends on your specific purpose, you may want to select students for each group based on skill level. This way, you can differentiate content to challenge the students in each group. Everyone is playing **ZAP!** but the content varies as students reinforce completely different concepts.

How It Works:

On each table, there is a container such as a lunch bag, coffee can or basket to hold what that group needs to reinforce. Topics may include color or letter recognition for younger students; multiplication facts or states and capitals for third or fourth graders; algebra problems, science chapter questions, or vocabulary for secondary students.

Craft sticks, tongue depressors, note cards or strips of paper are used for the questions or terms to be defined. Included is a *wild card* such as the word **ZAP!** The wild card may be any word or term that the teacher or class selects. Changing the wild card to fit the theme of each unit adds interest.

To play, each student takes a turn by drawing one item from the container. The student reads the question aloud and responds verbally as needed. If the response is correct, that student keeps the item and earns a point. If the response is incorrect, the student returns the question to the bag. Play continues as the next person takes a turn. Typically, only one turn per person is allowed to keep **ZAP!** moving quickly.

Students participate verbally in the response, auditorially by listening to the other responses and, of course, kinesthetically by grabbing the item from the bag. Eventually, someone will draw the wild card, **ZAP!** That person loses all points gained so far and must drop the cards back into the container.

☞ **The Practical Pointer:**

When some young children lose all their points with the **ZAP!** card, they begin to cry. We do not want that to happen. The goal is to reinforce, not devastate. **ZAP!** rules can be adapted easily so that a player who loses has to return only *one* item to the container and is allowed to keep the rest.

SURPRISES ARE MEANT FOR BIRTHDAYS . . .

Secondary students will be much more attentive while playing **ZAP!** when actual test questions for the following day are included in the container. I tell them, "Here's your chance to practice! You may want to pay special attention today to what is in your **ZAP!** bag. Expect to see very similar questions tomorrow on the assessment . . . "

With the adequate review that **ZAP!** provides, students know what to expect ahead of time. There is a verbal rehearsal but there is also an opportunity to review and strengthen areas that are weak. It should be noted that in preparing for an assessment, one student per group has an answer key and acts as a referee so that students are sure of the correct response.

In more typical **ZAP!** situations, no answer key is provided and students in the group act as general referees. They are generally quick to correct a peer.

O⚷ KEY IDEA

The bottom line is that we want our students to succeed. Activities like ZAP! provide opportunities to practice and review in a format that is much more fun and effective than using a traditional study guide or worksheet.

☞ **The Practical Pointer:**

Encourage students to create their own versions of **ZAP!** to help them study independently. They may wish to use create sets of **ZAP!** cards, color-coded by chapter, to review concepts throughout the semester. The simplest way to do this is to use a marker to code the upper corner of the note card. Vocabulary and concept cards from a chapter on the 13 colonies, for example, may be marked with a red line; cards from the next chapter can be color-coded in blue. Periodically, a student can spend as little as five minutes to keep knowledge of vocabulary and concepts current.

Simon Says

Grades K–6

The old childhood game of **Simon Says** becomes fresh and effective in whole group or small group review. At the end of a lesson, two minutes of quick review provides fast feedback for the teacher. While I have used **Simon Says** most often with elementary students, I have also used it with middle and high school students. The results were positive! It was especially useful as a relaxation tool just before an assessment to jog short-term memory and promote positive self-talk.

HOW IT WORKS:

Everyone stands. As the teacher, you may elect to be the moderator or may ask one or two students to prepare ahead of time for the role. Use maps, diagrams, vocabulary, questions written on the overhead, chapter review, individual white boards and scratch paper as sources of questions.

Let's imagine that it is science class and students have been studying anatomy. The moderator directs students to follow along:

"Simon Says . . . Touch your patellas!"

Students bend over and touch their kneecaps.

"Simon Says . . . Touch your mandella!"

Students touch their jawbones.

"Simon Says. .. Shout out the scientific name for your collarbone!"

Students shout, "Clavicle!!"

"What is this bone back here?" (Pointing to scapula)

Some students shout, "Scapula!"

Others shout, "You didn't say, '*Simon Says!*'"

"Simon Says . . . Take a deep breath!"

They follow along.

"Simon Says . . . Wiggle! Wiggle all over!"

They can definitely do this part with enthusiasm!

"Simon Says . . . Clap your hands and get a good score on your assessment!"

Students applaud.

"Simon Says . . . Shout, 'I can do it!'"

Students shout, "I can do it!"

"Simon Says . . . Sit down quietly . . ."

Students sit down.

Game over!

☞ **The Practical Pointer:**
You, as the teacher, decide whether you want everyone to remain standing even after being caught by Simon. In my own experience, I have approached every question as a new opportunity. No one is "out." No one loses. No one sits down. Everyone stays engaged and continues to participate. Students compete against their own knowledge. It is a learning experience.

Go Fish

Grades 1–3

This review activity is reminiscent of the card game, *Go to the Dump*. Did you play that when you were a child? If you have young children of your own, it may be a favorite at your house today.

HOW IT WORKS:

Instead of traditional playing cards, **Go Fish** uses word recognition or vocabulary cards. A double set of words can be made for grades one and two; a triple set for grade three. As in *Go to the Dump*, one student shuffles and deals seven cards to each player from the pile. You remember the rest. The partner begins,

"Give me all of your_____."

"Go fish. Give me all of your____."

When a player has a two of a kind in grades one and two or three of a kind in grade three, the player removes those cards from the hand. The first player out of cards wins.

The Fish Pond

Grades K–3

The fish pond strategy can be used with small groups of primary students to review a number of skills such as math facts, vocabulary meanings or spelling words.

HOW IT WORKS:

Use a stick and attach a lightweight cord on the end to make a fishing pole. A ruler and string will work. Tape a magnet to the end of the cord. For "bait," make a school of fish, laminate them and place a metal paper clip on each one. On each, write targeted words with a wipe-off marker so that the fish can be used over and over. If you prefer, make sets of fish with spelling words, for example, and then laminate each set. Drop the fish into a dry "pond" made out of a shallow pan.

Students take turns fishing. If the students are catching spelling words, they will look at their catch, say it, turn it over and spell it. If an error is made, the fish is thrown back into the pond.

☞ **The Practical Pointer:**
Goldfish crackers make a nice group reward at the end of the activity.

Origami Partners

Grades 4–12

You may remember this as a paper folding game from recess in elementary school. Bring it indoors and resurrect it as a review tool. The goals of reinforcement and review will be a little different from the playground version.

HOW IT WORKS:

First follow these steps for making the origami. Each student needs a square piece of paper. Fold all corners into the center. Turn it over. Now fold the new corners into the center. Turn it over again and there will be four flaps. Insert thumbs and index fingers under the flaps so that the square can be manipulated in and out. Do you remember this? Does this look familiar?

From this point a number of variations can be used for review. A simple approach is to label the four squares in four different colors. Turn the origami over and number the triangles from one through eight in the upper corners. Beneath each number, students will write a question. The eight questions may involve reviewing vocabulary meanings, math facts, chapter questions, spelling words, or any current topic in your curriculum.

Define: Import

Spell: Outcome

Multiply: 8 × 7

Students record the correct response directly underneath each flap.

Now everyone is ready to meet with a partner. One person holds the origami while the partner selects a color. If it is blue, the holder opens and closes spelling, B-L-U-E. Four

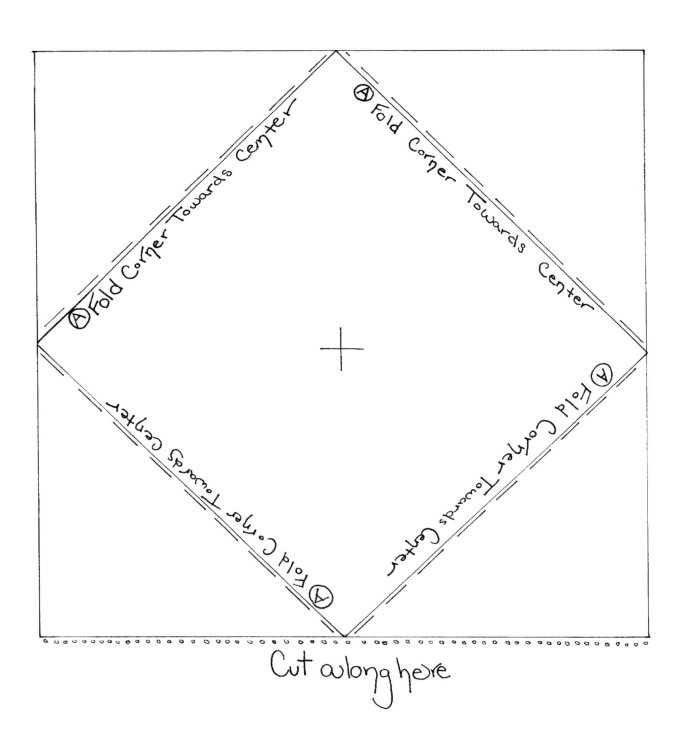

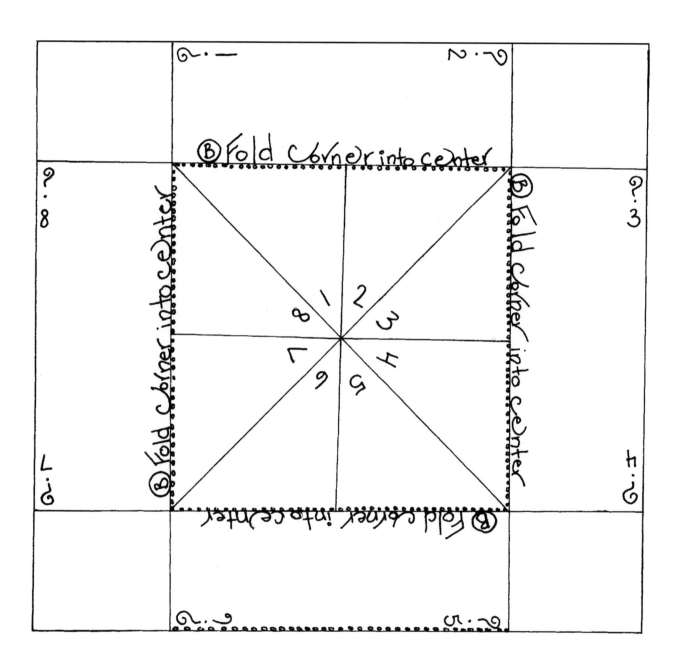

numbers are exposed. The partner chooses a number. The student holding the paper reads the question. The partner responds and lifts the flap to check the answer. Review continues until the partner has answered all eight questions. Roles are reversed and play begins again.

Do not be surprised if some students continue to play on the playground during recess. Older students like the opportunity to be kids. This is a good transition tool during a block class at the secondary level. Students can stand up, move around and review at the same time.

 The Practical Pointer:

> The first time that you use this for reinforcement, you may want to provide the template with two versions of the questions already included. Each partner receives a different version. This provides an example of questions to use but gives students experience in how to play. Afterward, students can make up the questions for other students to use.

Shout It Out

Grades 3–6

A card game that many of us played as children can be adapted for partners reviewing addition or multiplication facts. We called it "War" but I chose a different title in my classroom, **Shout It Out!** Each student sits on the floor with a partner and a deck of cards. The first player deals the cards into two piles, face down.

Simultaneous, both partners turn over a card. If the objective is to review multiplication facts, the person to call out the product first, takes the pair. Play continues. If the players turn over the cards with the same number, they shout, "Same!" and place three more cards face down, turning a fourth card over. Once again, the objective is to shout the product. The player with the most cards at the end of the time limit is the winner.

Shower Curtain Hopscotch

Grades K–3

Inexpensive white plastic shower curtains make wonderful kinesthetic tools to practice a variety of skills with primary students.

How It Works:

For **Shower Curtain Hopscotch** with addition facts, use a permanent marker to draw a hopscotch board on the plastic sheet. Make the squares large enough for a child to stand on in a traditional hopscotch format of ten squares laid out in a single, double, single, double, single pattern. Number the squares one through ten. This becomes a permanent hopscotch board that can be used over and over with different content.

Write addition facts on large note cards. Lay one card on each square.

To play, students take turns rolling a small pebble or plastic toy to see where it lands. The student will hop in the one foot, two feet pattern, stopping at the stone. The student states the sum of the fact on the card. If correct, the child gets another turn. If an error is made, the turn moves to the next child.

Children can practice color recognition, sight words, and addition or subtraction facts to name a few applications. You may wish to make several hopscotch "curtains" so that students can play in small groups. One practical way to differentiate instruction is to provide the same activity but at different levels. One group may be reviewing the doubles: 1 + 1, 2 + 2, 3 + 3. Another group may be reviewing a mixture of single-digit problems while a third group may be review double-digit addition. The materials are based on the needs of the students. The shower curtains can be folded and stored when not in use.

 The Practical Pointer:

Purchase shower curtains sale-priced at discount stores for under a dollar.

Suggest to parents that they play **Hopscotch Spelling** with their children at home. Review the weekly spelling list with the whole family. Even toddlers can "play." Use the same shower curtain format with lines drawn in permanent marker. Simply make new spelling cards each week to place in each space. When a child lands on a space, the child will see the word, say it and spell it.

Human Bingo

Grades 1–5

Human Bingo can be a quick transition activity to get everyone up and moving. This activity also uses the inexpensive plastic shower curtains.

HOW IT WORKS:

Ahead of time, use permanent markers to draw 20 squares on each of two plastic shower curtains. Like the hopscotch game, the bingo boards are reusable. The **Human Bingo** boards look just like the typical game cards only much larger.

Two games will be played simultaneously so that all students will be actively engaged and involved. Divide students into four groups, assigning two groups to each of two teams. Borrow the pullover "jerseys" from the physical education department so that one team in each group can be designated by color. Students hold cards for vocabulary cards, sight words, colors or math facts.

When you call a number, such as "G 15," add a word or math fact that the group might be studying. If you are working on compound words, it may sound like this: "*G 15 house-boat.*" The student with the *houseboat* card moves to stand on the "G 15" square. Call the next number and compound word. Play continues.

Just as in regular Bingo, the game ends when "Bingo!" is called. Four corners of the same color jerseys counts as a "win" as does any diagonal, horizontal or vertical line in the same color.

Mancala

Grades K–12

Mancala is an excellent strategy game that spans ages 5 to 105. This game does not involve reading, questions or content review. It is strictly a strategy game that promotes thinking skills and social skills.

While there is a computer version of **Mancala** that can be played individually, that version lacks the tactile aspect of physically moving the "counters" and interacting with a partner. There are a variety of ways to play **Mancala**.

I have included one version in "High-Impact Review" along with the description of materials needed for students to make their own games.

MATERIALS:

To make **Mancala**, students will need an egg carton, two margarine tubs and 36 items to use as counters. Counters may be multicolored "jewels" from craft stores, a variety of buttons, acorns, pebbles or even small candies. Counters typically are not all one color and do not form a set.

HOW TO PLAY:

Two students play at a time. There may be several games going on simultaneously in a classroom. Students sit opposite each other with an egg carton between them. One margarine tub, the "cala" is taped to each end of the egg carton. The six egg carton cups in front of a player and the margarine tub to the player's right belong to that player.

In this version, each player begins with 18 counters and drops three in each of the six egg carton cups on that player's side. The first player starts by scooping counters from any one of his or her egg carton cups and dropping them one-by-one in consecutive cups moving in a counterclockwise direction, including the player's own cala.

Note that a counter will be dropped in one's own cala but never in the opponent's cala. It remains the first player's turn as long as the last counter dropped lands in one of the player's own cups or cala. The object is to acquire more counters in one's own cala than the opponent acquires in the other cala.

The second player repeats the process. The first player has another turn and play continues in the same manner.

The game stops when either player has emptied all the cups on that player's side. The winner is the player with more counters in his or her cala.

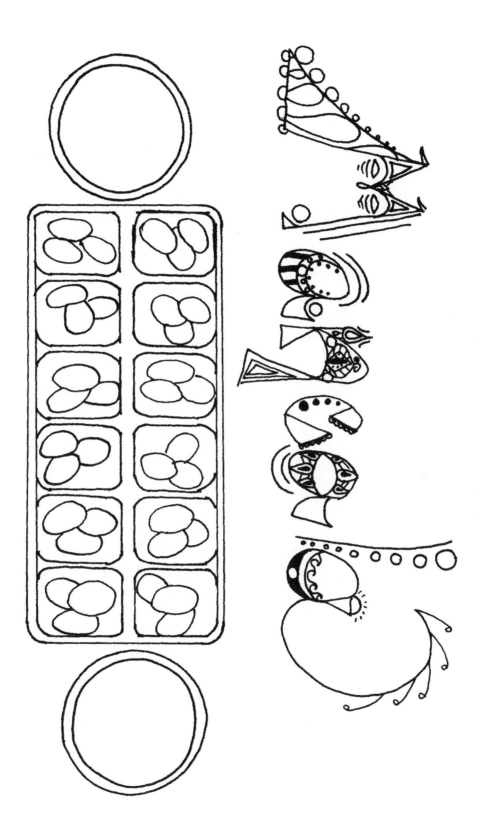

When students finish early or need a break, **Mancala** is an excellent game to have available. It can also be an excellent addition for use with a partner in a station. Consider setting up a **Mancala** tournament using a round robin format. Students are enthusiastic! This game can be adapted easily to fit individual needs. Change it. Try different versions. All students will benefit from the skill development in thinking through the strategies. Enjoy it with your students and with your own family at home.

☞ **The Practical Pointer:**
Your local public library is an excellent resource for rules and a wide variety of versions for playing **Mancala**.

Jigsaw Puzzles

Grades 3–12

Another tool for teaching skills of a different nature is the **jigsaw puzzle**. This activity requires patience, perseverance, visual perception and thinking skills. It is also fun and builds camaraderie among students. One secondary teacher whom I admire always has a puzzle set up on a card table in his room. He said that he almost always finds a cluster of students at the puzzle table before or after class. Some students arrive extra early or stop by after school with friends.

What amazes this teacher most is just how many of his students tell him that they have never done this before. They have never put a jigsaw puzzle together.

☞ **The Practical Pointer:**
After using them for several years now, this teacher has amassed quite a collection of puzzles. He suggests asking parents to donate jigsaw puzzles that may be gathering dust next to the Monopoly game on a closet shelf.

Checkers Review

Grades 2–5

When my daughter was in seventh grade, her friend, Julie, noticed an antique checkerboard on a table in our home and commented that she had never played checkers.

Like the jigsaw puzzle example, it was indicative of the fact that many of our children are growing up without experiences we may take for granted. I invited Julie to play on the spot. (My own child was mortified and gave me *the look* but Julie didn't mind.) By the time Julie left our house that day, she had played checkers—and liked it.

We were playing the traditional checkers but even this simple game can be adapted for review and reinforcement. I enjoy using checkers with elementary students to review multiplication facts. Instead of the plastic disks, I use two colors of one-inch square ceramic tiles from the local home improvement store. With a permanent marker, I write one fact on each tile.

The tiles are set up in the usual checkers format and the usual rules apply. The only difference is that to make a move, a player must first give the product for the fact on the tile, for example, "4 × 4 = 16." If a player is going to "jump" another tile, the player must give the correct product for the fact for that tile as well. In the event of an error, a player forfeits a move.

Vocabulary works well as another choice for checkers. To move, the player must define the word. In still another way to play, focus on word recognition. Make a set of common sight words on tiles. The player must read the word aloud before making a move.

 The Practical Pointer:
Look for large boxes of tiles in discontinued colors in the tile department of any home improvement store. The price is right and several different permanent sets of checkers can be made for reinforcement. When students have ten minutes, they can go to the bin and pick a bag of checkers. Each bag reinforces a different skill.

Pictionary Vocabulary

Grades 4–12

Commercial games like **Pictionary**® are easily adapted for review, especially for secondary students. This is an especially effective tool to review high school science and social studies. This game that features drawing objects and concepts was very popular at one time. Chances are that it will be at least somewhat familiar to many students.

How to Play:

Pictionary is another team game. As in most of the other team games suggested, the competition leans toward cooperation and includes all students. Select concepts or vocabulary words to reinforce. Divide the class into two heterogeneous teams. Each team will take turns sending a contestant to the blackboard or white board to draw the secret vocabulary words or concepts while team members provide clues. It is the contestant's job to figure out what the drawing represents.

Guesstures Review

Grades 4–12

For those of you who have not played the commercial game, **Guesstures**®, it is similar to charades in that players *act out* a word or concept. Instead of using the set of words packaged with **Guesstures**, incorporate your own vocabulary. The object of the game is for the team members to determine what word or concept an individual is depicting and do so within a time limit.

How to Play:

Make a set of cards using concepts or vocabulary. On each card, indicate two choices of words for different point values. Words or concepts that are more difficult to act out are worth more points than the simpler concepts. As in **Pictionary**, divide the group into two teams.

Each team selects one person who will draw a card, choose which word to use and act it out. A toaster-like timer runs while teammates attempt to guess the word. If they are successful before the buzzer goes off, the team earns the points listed on the card.

Play shifts to the other team where the same procedure is followed. Students can be extremely creative in their interpretation. The kinesthetic learners will find this activity especially helpful in recalling the terms or concepts later.

Tic-Tac-Know

Grades 4–12

I observed an eleventh grade science class in which the teacher turned Tic-Tac-Toe into **Tic-Tac-Know**. Students sat with a partner and were given a blank Tic-Tac-Toe board with squares. The partners filled in the grid with questions or terms from the current unit.

Then, the informational **Tic-Tac-Know** boards were circulated giving students an opportunity to play another team's game. In order to place an "X" or an "O" on a square, a player had to answer the question or define the term correctly. An incorrect answer resulted in a lost turn.

☞ **The Practical Pointer:**

Students created their own games for their peers. Their ownership made a significant difference in the enthusiasm and high interest demonstrated in the activity. This teacher allotted class time for students to make the **Tic-Tac-Know** boards. When time is an issue, an alternative would be offering extra credit to anyone who would like to make the boards at home and bring them to class.

State Fair

Grades 4–12

State Fair offers a versatile format for reviewing information learned earlier. Divide a sheet of paper into sections and label topics from the previous day or several days. Students meet in cooperative groups with notes, texts and study guides focusing on the content.

Each group receives a copy of the **State Fair** format and a coin to toss. Students place the paper on the floor several feet from group members. Taking turns, a person will toss the coin. Where it lands determines the category that a student must describe. That student has the option of telling something learned from that category. If the category names a character from a novel, one quality must be mentioned; if the category is broad like causes of the civil war, the student must name one.

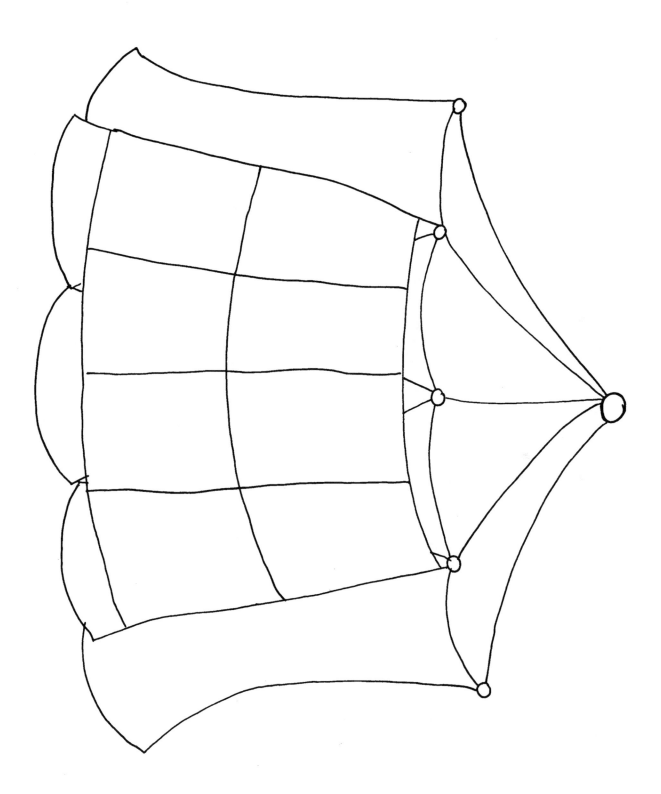

The pace is rapid as students take turns tossing the coin, aiming for a category of choice. Since several students will land on the same category during the time frame, several different responses will be mentioned for all group members to hear.

Soccer Ball Review

Grades 4–12

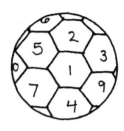

An extremely popular five-minute review strategy that I have I used is **Soccer Ball Review**. It is simple and always ready to go. Take a soccer ball and number the sections with a permanent marker. Ask all the students to stand. Toss the ball into the crowd. Whoever catches the ball calls out the number closest to their left thumb. *"Six!"* The moderator, usually the teacher, asks *question 6* from the study guide or chapter review. It not only gives everyone a stretch break but also facilitates a quick review. **Soccer Ball Review** also works to trigger enthusiastic brainstorming. Students toss the ball to one another and shout out an idea as the ball is caught.

O⚷ KEY IDEA

It bears repeating that one of the best ways to increase retention is by studying aloud.

Beach Ball Questions

Grades 1–5

An inflatable plastic beach ball becomes the vehicle for asking questions on a topic. There is enough space in each colored section to write a question in permanent marker. I used this in connection with reading stories. Adapt the **Beach Ball Questions** to fit the grade level and purpose. Questions might include:

> What is the theme?
>
> Who are the characters?
>
> What is the setting?
>
> What did you predict would happen?
>
> What happened?
>
> Who is the protagonist?
>
> What does "plot" mean?
>
> How did it end?

Other questions might ask about artwork, why a student liked or disliked a story or whether we read other stories by the same author. The procedure is similar to **Soccer Ball Review**. Students stand and toss the ball to each other. In this case, call out "left hand" or "right hand" to determine which question will be answered.

☞ **The Practical Pointer:**

Several beach balls can be used if students are working in literature circles so that every group has a ball. Use this technique before reading a story to anticipate and predict what might happen or afterward as a discussion starter.

Concentration Lids

Grades K–5

This next review strategy is one that I often suggest to parents as an activity to use at home. Use it to review vocabulary words, sight word recognition, states and capitals, telling time, place value, fractions or decimals.

In the traditional concentration game, players match pairs of identical pictures or playing cards. Cards begin face down and each player turns over one card and tries to recall the location of the "match." **Concentration Lids** follows the same format but is tailored for specific content and the needs of students. It can be played individually like solitaire, with a partner or in a small group.

AHEAD OF TIME . . .

Send a note home asking parents to save the round plastic lids from gallon water jugs and milk containers. Since the lids come in a variety of colors, sets can be color-coded. On the under side of the cover, glue a small piece of paper with whatever will be reviewed such as an addition fact, sight word, a clock with the time indicated, vocabulary, a state capital, fractions or decimals. As in regular concentration, make a double set. I make several different games and label sets in plastic bags.

HOW TO PLAY:

Individuals, partners, or groups receive a set. Students spread out the lids, plain side up, on the floor or table, moving them around to mix them.

If **Concentration Lids** is being played in a partner arrangement, the first player takes a turn by turning any two lids over. If they match, the player keeps those two and continues playing until no match is found. At that time, it is the second player's turn and play continues. The game ends when all the lids have been matched. The player with the greater number of pairs wins.

VARIATIONS

One option is to use questions and answers. Instead of a match, one lid is the answer to another: one lid has "4 + 2 = ?"and the corresponding lid has the sum "6." One lid has the vocabulary word; another gives the meaning. One lid has the state; another gives the capital. One lid has the color word; another shows the color.

Another approach requires the player to give the correct product, "35," for example, when the two matching lids state the math fact: "5 × 7 = ?" If the response given is incorrect, the lids must be turned over again.

☞ **The Practical Pointer:**

Store bags within easy reach of students. They can grab a bag for a quick review when there are five minutes left before lunch or when an active change of pace is needed.

Pots and Pans

Grades 2–7

Pots and Pans can be adapted for recalling facts, reviewing foreign language vocabulary, reinforcing synonyms, antonyms, teaching analogies or reviewing math facts. The format can be applied to a wide range of topics and grade levels.

HOW IT WORKS:

Sets of the content to be reinforced are created ahead of time on note cards or quarter-sheets of paper. Students line up with their backs to the moderator, usually the teacher or a paraprofessional. One card is taped to the back of each student. Somewhere in the room is another student wearing the card that goes together like **Pots and Pans**.

Students move around the room asking questions that can be answered by "yes" or "no." Each student may ask another student just one question before moving on to another person. As the teacher, you may set a limit on the number of questions asked. The goal may be to find the partner within five questions or within ten questions. The partners typically find each other and may earn free time, a small treat, a bonus point or simply have time to talk.

☞ **The Practical Pointer:**

Pots and Pans is an excellent transition tool. It gets students up and moving while creating an opportunity to review at the same time.

SUMMARY

Many traditional games have been adapted for use as review tools by teachers for years and years. How many of you have used *Jeopardy, Baseball,* or *Wheel of Fortune* on a regular basis? Can you remember playing *Stump the Expert* or *Seven Up* as an elementary student? If you are not already using games, you may consider resurrecting games from the past and adding some of the games suggested in "High Impact Review."

Games teach many life skills. Through a variety of games, students learn cooperation, following the rules, self-control, winning or losing gracefully, getting along with others and, of course, taking turns. The activities and games suggested in "High Impact Review" focus on all of these skills whether in teams, small groups, or with partners. Some are useful as individual activities. With few exceptions, the games and activities presented in this chapter provide an added benefit of using the format as a vehicle to review and reinforce content. The exceptions, such as **Mancala,** focus on developing general thinking skills as players plan and strategize the next move.

COMPETITION

Some teachers avoid any type of competitive game making all activities cooperative in nature. Student do need to learn to work together cooperatively in our classrooms, but creating some situations in which students compete against each other are not necessarily negative. So much is in how competition is presented. Competition is part of life. We cannot escape it. Some children thrive on it while others do not. Card games like **Shout It Out!** allow competition without aggressive behavior. That is the part that can create problems in the classroom.

COMPUTER GAMES

While the focus of the "High Impact Review" has been on low-tech but effective interactive games, the category of **Computer Games** encompasses a broad category of games that appeal to our students and can reinforce a wide range of goals and objectives. The media specialist in your building will be able to offer the most recent games to enhance your content and interest your students. Students themselves can be excellent resources for new computer games.

FRIDAY GAME DAY

Friday Game Day can be a great way to end the week. It may actually be **Friday Game *Hour*** or **Friday Game *20 Minutes*,** but it can be a joyful time of reviewing or simply connecting as members of the learning community using a combination of both traditional games and computer games.

FAMILY GAME NIGHT

Encourage parents to play games with their children at home. Many of us have a variety of games tucked away in our closets. Get them out. Make them available. Younger children will opt for spending an evening playing board games with parents over watching TV. Games offer a fun way for children to have the full attention of a parent that a passive activity like watching a movie does not provide. Promoting **Family Game Night** is something that teachers of elementary students can include in a newsletter or on a Web site.

Teenagers may not relish the idea of sitting down with parents for an evening of games.

However, question-and-answer games like the various trivia games attract the high school crowd when left on the kitchen table. More than once, I have found my own teenagers playing **Trivial Pursuit**® with their friends simply because the game was there. Would they have gone to the closet to get it? I doubt it. I do know that I hear a lot of laughing and a lot of talking during the process. That is perhaps the final point in promoting games. Games are fun! Whether used as an occasional learning reinforcement and review tool, or simply "for the fun of it," games are enjoyable and bring people together sharing the common bond of laughter.

8

ALL TOGETHER NOW

Get your students talking to each other, not just to you or the air.

—Wayne C. Booth

I am in the service industry. When I look at job applicants, I know what I want. I can teach someone with a degree in geology to become a better geologist because I have years of experience in the field and I know what our clients want and need.

I want to hire someone who knows how to get along with people. I want someone who can work in a group and be part of a team. I can't teach that. I want someone who will provide a good value for the money my clients are paying. Hiring someone who cannot function as part of a group and will not pull their weight would be my greatest nightmare. A person like that could ruin my business.

—Small Business Owner

In an interview on National Public Radio, this business owner was describing the traits he values most in young people new to the job market. The ability to get along with others was at the top of his list. It is hard to think of a business or industry today that would not require these same skills.

Interpersonal skills help students succeed now in the academic setting but teach critical skills needed to succeed later in the workplace. Group interaction skills are essential as part of our goal of differentiating instruction for all learners. Students need to learn content but few people function in isolation. The nature of some tasks and choices may call for independent work but a variety of tasks may be best addressed in pairs, triads or quads.

GROUP INTERACTION SKILLS

In our classrooms, practical use of interpersonal skills can be incorporated in a number of ways encompassing many different aspects. Critical skills include acceptance of other group members, respect for each individual, an understanding of various group roles, a willingness to learn together, the ability to ask for help in large group, and flexibility in using a variety of group response techniques. The group strategies suggested in "All Together Now" focus on several components of creating groups and group interaction.

- Partnerships
- Group Roles
- Calling on Students
- Group Evaluation

- Group Study Strategies
- Raising the Group Grade
- 6 Strategies for Asking for Help
- 16 Every Student Response Strategies

"WHO IS IN MY GROUP?"

This chapter offers strategies for selecting students to act as partners or members of a larger group. A key question always concerns whether students choose their own groups or whether the teacher selects groups or whether a random system is used to determine the make up of each group. In practice, students benefit from having all three types of group experiences.

CHOOSING THEIR OWN

When I was observing in a middle school English class, I watched with sadness as students scurried to create groups while one student waited. No one approached him to join them.

Only when everyone else had moved their desks and had begun the specified task did the teacher notice that this student was left sitting alone. "Jared, join this group," the teacher told him. Jared moved reluctantly over to the assigned group. While no one was rude, no one welcomed him. I had the impression from watching Jared that this was probably not the first time that he was not chosen.

Some students enjoy choosing their own partners or groups. Unfortunately, the students who do not are often the last ones picked. Children need to learn from an early age that including others in an important part of life. The **Book It!** strategy in this chapter is a way of grouping students that encourages everyone to work with a variety of partners and groups. Students have some control over who will be in a group but parameters are clear and ultimately, everyone will have an opportunity to work with everyone else.

TEACHER SELECTED

Some teachers post lists of group members. Periodically the lists change and groups are reshuffled. Many teachers carefully choose group members based on skills, personalities, interests, gender and the topic. A fourth grade teacher commented, "I never leave this to chance. I do change groups but most of the time, I am careful not to place a top student with a very low student. What works best, in my view, is placing students together who are fairly close in ability. Behavior is also an important factor that I take into consideration. There are students who would never get anything done if they are within ten feet of each other."

RANDOM GROUPING

A college professor who always groups students randomly by drawing names had this to say:

> *In the workplace when you are working on a project, you won't get to*

choose group members. Sometimes you will work with people you will probably like; other times you will be with individuals whom you may not. Some will do their share; others will do very little or just enough to get by. Sometimes a group member will be the type of individual who will try to take over and do the whole thing without group input. Learn to deal with these situations. Now and later, make it work.

In the K–12 learning community, we as teachers can create numerous opportunities to teach essential group skills. Some of our younger students are years away from the workplace but they will be interacting with other people every day of their lives. What the college professor had to say about random grouping has merit. Our students need to learn how to function in a variety of group situations. Certainly some of the time they need to be told basically the same thing: These are the people in your group. Make it work. **Draw a Card** is just one quick technique described in the chapter for arranging random grouping.

GROUP ROLES

Who is Doing What?

Grades 3–12

Once students have been placed in groups, critical time is often wasted while students decide who will record, who will be the timekeeper and who will facilitate. To focus time on task, you may opt to determine roles by an attribute of the day.

The person with the next birthday is the recorder today.

The group member who has the shortest hair is timekeeper.

The person with the most buttons will be facilitator.

The person whose name is closest to the beginning of the alphabet . . .

The person who has the most pets, oldest pets . . .

The person who is wearing the most colors . . .

I have discovered, as you would expect, that it is best to avoid any attribute that will generate a great deal of discussion. Some of you may be thinking that you have students who will start a discussion about any topic in the universe. I have tried and eliminated topics such as:

The person who got up the earliest . . .

The person who stayed up the latest . . .

Any remaining roles are assumed in order by moving to the right. If the recorder has been determined, then the person to the recorder's right will be the timekeeper and then the person to that person's right will facilitate, and so on. It is a strategy that is quick, easy and gets the job done.

One Pencil, One Paper

Grades 3–12

A quick tip for any group activity in which one person is to record all responses is to allow only *one pencil and one paper* per group. The recorder controls both. The paper may be the large poster paper or regular notebook paper depending on how the information will be used later. Ask all other group members to put away their writing utensils and paper so that they truly depend on the recorder to write for the group.

Stopwatch

Grades 3–12

A stopwatch can be an effective motivational tool for the timekeeper. If you have allotted seven minutes for the brainstorming segment, the timekeeper sets the stopwatch and calls time for that and each subsequent segment of the activity. There is an old saying that the work expands to fill the time. A clearly delineated format for the timing of the group task helps students accomplish the work efficiently.

Tape-Record It!

Grades 3–12

Tape-recording group work serves several purposes. One of the biggest issues with group work is keeping group members on task. Use a dettached microphone that plugs into a basic cassette recorder. The only person who can speak is the individual holding and speaking into the microphone. Not only does this encourage members to speak one at a time, it also creates an auditory record of how time was used. Students know that the teacher can listen later in evaluating the group process.

PARTNERSHIPS

Book It!

Grades 3–12

Frequently in today's classroom, we want our students to work together in pairs, triads, quads or even larger groups. Some teachers set up "partnerships" that will last several weeks or even an entire semester. I see this most often in science classes for lab partners.

When it works, it works very well. Some students, however, do not work well together for an extended period of time. Personalities, ability level, social or behavioral issues and commitment to the task are some of the factors that can influence the success or failure of a group. Just about every student can and should learn to work with a wide range of individuals on a limited basis.

An alternative to being "joined at the hip" for an extended period of time is creating a series of very brief partnerships within the class so that over time virtually every student has an opportunity to work with every other student.

This can be easily accomplished by arranging appointments to be become partners through the use of **Book It!** Each student is provided with a blank page from an appointment book. It is an enlarged version of the typical appointment book that students see in their doctor's or orthodontist's offices. Lines are provided making it easy to schedule appointments.

How It Works:

Students are told that they have just three minutes to fill all their appointments. As students dash about the room, you will hear Michaela asking Gina, "Will you be my 5:00 appointment?" Students are strongly advised by the teacher that the only acceptable answer in that classroom is the affirmative. Michaela writes Gina's name in the 5:00 slot and Gina fills in her appointment page at 5:00 with Michaela's name. They now have an "appointment."

And so it goes during the three minutes. Many teachers find that they will need slots for triads for certain class activities. Simply provide two slots at 3:00, for example, so that Jackson will write both Kristen and Bailey on his calendar. Simultaneously, Kristen will fill in Jackson and Bailey while Bailey writes Jackson and Kristen.

A similar plan can be made for a group of four students. When the time limit is up, students with blank appointments raise their hands and are paired with anyone else who has an opening.

Later in the day, the teacher may want students to find a partner for **Write, Listen and Tell.** The teacher instructs students that it is time for their 7:00 appointment. A partnership is born for that activity! Students move quickly to their appointments and the task is completed.

The next day, 1:00 appointments sit together to proofread their essays. The 3:00 triad meets during science for lab work.

Students fill out new appointment pages at the discretion of the teacher. I found that every two or three weeks works well. The advantage of using this technique for putting students into groups is the constant mixing. Students learn that each partnership is brief in duration. Because of this, students are far more willing to work with a variety of classmates.

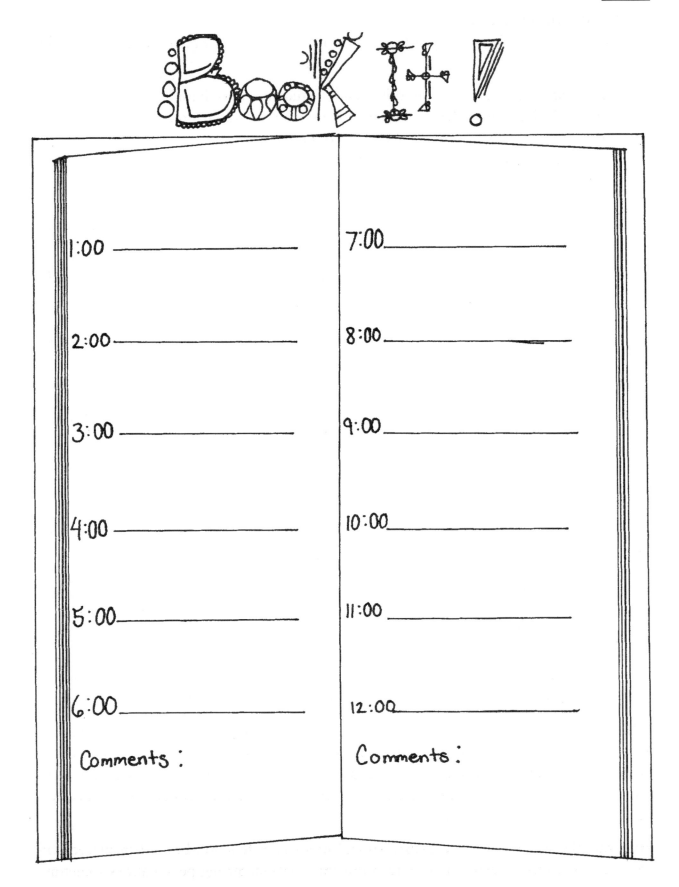

Book It!

1:00 _____

2:00 _____

3:00 _____

4:00 _____

5:00 _____

6:00 _____

Comments :

7:00 _____

8:00 _____

9:00 _____

10:00 _____

11:00 _____

12:00 _____

Comments :

☞ **The Practical Pointer:**

Here are five tips for setting clear ground rules to make this strategy work successfully.

1. *It is essential to dictate how many times the same name can appear on the appointment page.* Two middle school students who happened to be "best friends" filled **Book It!** with each other's names. I discovered this when these students were always together for any **Book It!** activity. My rule: One name can be repeated twice provided that person's name was not on the previous page.

2. *Indicate how many male and female names are required for gender equity.*

3. *Spread the fun.* Insist that students include at least five new names that were not on the previous page.

4. *Ahead of time, encourage particularly sensitive students to* first approach *several of the students who potentially could be left out.* Make sure that no one has an empty page or has very few filled appointments. It helps to discuss this with the entire class ahead of time. Everyone needs to feel included and valued as a member of the learning community.

5. *Primary teachers may wish to simplify* **Book It!** *by inserting a limited number of appointment slots.* In fact, any teacher can have students fill in fewer appointments limiting the total to five or six. On some occasions, you might tell them, "Fill in six appointments and then take the rest of the day off!" That suggestion is not to be taken literally!

Book It! sounds more complicated than it is in practice. Students soon learn the process and it actually saves time in the classroom. The best part is that it provides students with the experience of getting to know every class member.

Craft Stick Partners

Grades K–4

Another strategy for putting students into groups or with a partner is to write each name on a craft stick and place it in an empty orange juice can. As the teacher, you can quickly grab four sticks creating Group One; grab four more to create Group Two, and so on.

While it appears that names are drawn completely at random, this is not always the case. Sometimes it is necessary to separate certain students and sometimes it is advantageous to place certain students together. Here is a quick but effective tip that for worked for me. Use tiny color-coded marks on the ends of a few of the sticks to designate whatever you need to know in grouping students.

For example, students with identified special needs may function best when placed with specific classmates. Green dots provided this information. Strong personalities sometimes needed to work in different groups at times. Blue dots designated these strong personalities. Behavior issues often created the biggest barrier to successful group interaction and the tiny red dots indicated which students should not be placed together. As I grabbed my sticks for each group, I made sure that the "red dots" were spread out a bit. No one was singled out but it helped set the stage for positive group dynamics.

O—ᴈ KEY IDEA

The dots were not always used. At times, groups were formed entirely by chance. The purpose of the group activity determined how students were placed. Over time, every student had the opportunity to be in a group with every other student.

Draw a Card

Grades 4–12

A quick strategy for random placement of students in groups is using a deck of playing cards. Ahead of time, the teacher has created sets of cards creating as many groups as needed with up to four students per group. As students arrive for class, they draw a card. The student who drew the three of clubs will join the other students who drew the remaining three's to form a group. It is fast and there are no disputes. Trading is not allowed. The group exists for that day only. Another day, a different group will be formed.

CALLING ON STUDENTS

Who Hasn't Been Called On?

Grades K–12

Students need to be accountable for their learning. Participating in class discussions is part of that accountability and also gives students the opportunity to contribute their personal insight.

As every teacher knows, sometimes the same students respond again and again. Other students may want a chance to respond but never seem to get their hands up fast enough. Still others are content to assume a very passive role in class and avoid participating in the discussion.

At all grade levels, I have occasionally used craft sticks not to group students but as a way of calling on students. Only some questions were "craft stick" questions. Other questions and discussion focused on the more traditional approach using volunteers. Elementary students like the craft stick technique because it added a bit of mystery and excitement.

My goal was to increase participation and attentiveness. Everyone had an equal chance of being called on and an equal chance to participate. However, each person had the opportunity to say "Pass" one time. In that case, I quickly drew another name. Once used, though, the pass could not be used again during the same class period. My purpose was to encourage students to contribute to the discussion. Often a hesitant student would respond, thinking that the pass option might be needed later.

⚬⟲ KEY IDEA

Since the two bottom-line rules in my classroom were No put-downs and No sarcasm, students knew that it was safe to respond in any way without fear of embarrassment. Everyone was expected to demonstrate respect for others. I wanted to create an atmosphere in which students were willing to take a risk.

Photo Seating Chart

Grades 1–12

The first day of school, take a picture of each student to make a photographic seating chart. This will help secondary teachers get to know their students much more quickly. These charts can also be useful in encouraging participation by giving the teacher fast feedback about which students are responding in class.

After a student has contributed to a discussion, place a small sticky note over the picture. Use it for a single class or over a period of two or three days. Are there students on the seating chart without a sticky note at the end of class? Is this a consistent pattern? How can these students be encouraged to participate? It is a gentle reminder for the teacher to make sure that everyone is included.

☞ **The Practical Pointer:**
Leave a seating chart made up of photographs in the substitute folder with names under the photos. It will help the substitute teacher connect names and faces much more easily.

GROUP EVALUATION

Watching the Process

Grades 4–12

Using the video camera has been mentioned in several different contexts in the *The Teacher's Toolbox for Differentiating Instruction*. As a tool for evaluating group interaction, video-taping is effective from the perspective of both teacher and students. After obtaining parent permission to videotape in the classroom, video segments of group interaction.

Later, the entire class can evaluate what went well and target goals for improvement. The video also enables the teacher to see how members of each group relate to each other, use the time and focus on the task. A student can act as the roving cameraperson. Just seeing the camera can become an incentive for students to stay on task.

Raising the Group Grade

Grades 6–12

We truly learn a concept when we teach someone else. **Raising the Group Grade** gives students the opportunity to teach concepts to others in a group setting. A common problem that I have encountered repeatedly has been the reluctance of very capable students to be in a group with a student who struggles academically.

This strategy creates a positive climate and a positive outcome for students at all levels.

WIN-WIN SITUATION

When students are assigned to groups for review, all students are told that when the grade of any group member goes up on the next assessment when compared to the previous assessment, every member of that group receives a certain number of bonus points.

Suddenly, those students who need peer tutoring most become more desirable to have in a group because their grades have room to improve. With help, those grades will go up and every member of the group will receive bonus points. In a group filled with top students who are already achieving nearly perfect scores, raising those scores can be extremely difficult.

I have watched students take on a whole new attitude as mentors in this situation. They not only go over notes and explain concepts to students who are struggling, but they encourage those students on the day of the assessment and ask about the results. It is a win-win situation.

WIIFM

Grades K–12

Raising the Group Grade is meant for occasional use. The acronym **WIIFM** stands for

What's in it for me? Middle and high school students may be naturally altruistic in some cases but it not realistic to expect them to want to tutor students who are struggling on a daily basis. In fact, as educators, we need to guard against turning more able students into extra teachers. There is a place for both roles in the differentiated classroom. Top students need to be challenged by stretch activities as well.

I have had frequent conversations with parents who were concerned when their children spent too much time helping peers and their need for challenging tasks was being ignored. It is a fine line. As teachers, we know that teaching someone else is often the best way to solidify personal understanding of concepts. When we offer a wide range of opportunities for a wide range of students, we truly differentiate our instruction to meet everyone's needs.

Peer Evaluation

Grades 4–12

A discussion of group interaction would not be complete without some comments on grading work completed in groups. This is an issue that comes up frequently. In some situations, one or two students put forth substantially more effort than others. When the group gets one grade, there can be a lot of resentment on the part of the "worker bees" toward other students who coast along without contributing equally. The next time there is a group activity, there is resistance and teamwork falls apart.

One option satisfies most students and works in the best interest of everyone. Two different forms of group grades are assigned: one by the teacher and the other by the students themselves.

A PRACTICAL SOLUTION

The first grade is the teacher's grade, which is a composite group grade for the product. Everyone receives that same grade. The students determine the second grade. Each student in the group assigns a grade for effort. This grade assesses the participation of every group member and is based on 100 total points. If there are four members in the group and everyone has participated equally, each person receives 25 points. Students are honest in this assessment. If one person has done all the work, that student takes all of the effort points. Those students who contribute very little also end up being quite honest. They recognize who has put in the effort and are usually very open to giving credit where credit is due.

The teacher takes these evaluation points from each student and figures them into the final grade for the task. This procedure strongly encourages group participation because everyone who contributes earns points. It also recognizes that equal participation does not always happen. In those situations, the academic reward belongs to those who earned it.

Self-Evaluation

Grades 4–12

In individual assignments, a very telling strategy to use with students is to ask them to write a **Self-Evaluation** describing their personal progress in class. As teachers, we learn much from what students write about themselves. Some students can be overly critical of their work and need help in portraying a more realistic picture.

One high school teacher commented that he has carried one student's self-evaluation in his wallet for years as a reminder of what school can be like on a daily basis. This senior student wrote, "I think I deserve a D. I have to graduate. I'm a good kid, really I am. I just need more time."

The teacher's comment was:

> *This young man worked more slowly than many of the students in my class. He earned a solid C but he saw himself as a D student only because of his pace. Here was a kid, a good kid, who perceived that speed was the ultimate goal in finishing assignments. He was not fast but he was dependable and he stuck with it. I've kept this piece of paper in my wallet since then because it reminds me that not everyone learns at the same pace. He taught me to encourage all students to do their best* at their own speed.

O—ꜩ KEY IDEA

Everyone learns at a different pace. It is an important message to convey to our students.

GROUP STUDY STRATEGIES

Were you ever in a study group in college? Did it help you learn? One of my sons in college delayed a trip home until after his weekly study group met for economics. He commented, "I always know more at midnight than I knew at 10:00. I usually find out that I knew a little more than some people but a lot less than a few others. Study Group is one thing I can't miss!"

Bring the Card!

Grades 6–12

This strategy is presented here as a group review technique, but it can also be used on an individual basis, as well. **Bring the Card** can be used with students in the upper elementary grades and is effective throughout middle school, high school, and in postsecondary training.

How It Works:

Students know ahead of time that the day of a written assessment, they will be able to bring a note card with them and use it during the exam. In my experience, I have found **Bring the Card** to be a highly motivating technique. It teaches skills that can be applied in reviewing for any class, whether or not students will be allowed to bring the card to the assessment.

Full Sheet

About three days before an assessment, students gather in groups with the task of reviewing all content from a unit of study. One person is the recorder and is given a *full sheet* of blank paper.

The members of the group use notes, textbook and concepts from class discussions. Then they begin to call out key points. The recorder quickly lists the points on the paper. There is a time limit for the process that is determined by the teacher based on grade level and volume of content.

Half-Sheet

The next day, the same group meets with the list from the previous day but now has a new task of reducing the review facts to just a *half-sheet* of paper. Students need to determine what information they already know. Again time is limited to just minutes of class time.

Note Card

Finally, the day before the assessment, students in the group receive only a *quarter-sheet* to record their review facts. As they leave class that day, each student receives a 3" x 5" or 4" x 6" note card. At home, they have the option of writing *whatever they can fit* on the card *in whatever size* they can write or type knowing that they can bring the card into the assessment the following day.

O─┰ KEY IDEA

Some students write or type in minute print to fit the maximum amount of material on the card. One of my students used seven-point type on the computer to fit just about the entire science unit on a note card. The interesting part for many students is that, like my student, they discovered that they never actually needed the card during the assessment.

By that time, they had reviewed the content repeatedly during several short sessions and they knew the material thoroughly. Some students do rely on the card, however, and it teaches them a very effective technique that brings positive results. The group process makes the approach visual, kinesthetic and auditory.

☞ **The Practical Pointer:**

Ask students to compare test results using this strategy to test results when they reviewed all at once the night before. "Cramming" is rarely effective.

Fact in My Pocket

Grades K–4

This is a group strategy with an individual twist. It can be used to reinforce a troublesome math fact, spelling word or other concept that needs practice. It lends itself to application as a classwide activity using the same fact or concept for each student. However, it can also be used as part of differentiating instruction by tailoring the fact or concept to individual needs.

HOW IT WORKS:

The teacher provides a small slip of paper with a *Word of the Day* or *Fact of the Day* for students to pick up as they arrive in the classroom each morning. For purposes of explanation, let's assume that everyone has the same fact on this particular day. Examples may include *Spell "export"* or *7 + 4= 11* or *The capital of New York is Albany.* The group goes over the word or fact and then each child tucks the slip into a pocket.

Whenever the student is in the hall, or in the lunch line, or perhaps walking into the media center, someone may stop the student and ask, "What is the fact in your pocket?"

The goal is for the student to recall the fact without looking and respond, "The Fact in My Pocket is 7 + 4 = 11!"

If the student forgets the answer, the student can pull the slip of paper out of the pocket and review it on the spot. This can occur several times a day. Parents can also be part of the activity. "What is the fact in your pocket today?" a parent may ask at dinner.

☞ **The Practical Pointer:**

Initially, giving every student the same **Fact in My Pocket** helps students understand the strategy. Most often, though, different students will need different concepts to review. Facts can easily be tailored to fit individual needs. For one child, it may be a spelling word; for another, a challenging math fact. This study strategy takes only moments during a day but provides fast feedback and reinforcement.

Shoulder-to-Shoulder

Grades 4–12

When students are studying together as partners, reading aloud is often involved. I have discovered that when partners sit **shoulder-to-shoulder** but facing opposite directions, a couple of good things happen.

First, the noise level is substantially reduced. When one student is facing forward and the other is facing backward, their heads are quite close together. This allows them to read to each other and still be heard in softer voices. One teacher explained it as reading in a "6-inch voice," that is, a voice that can be heard no farther away than six inches. When students sit knee-to-knee, they are at least 12 inches apart. That "12-inch voice" easily raises the classroom noise level to a far greater level.

A second result of sitting shoulder-to-shoulder is the reduced likelihood of students being off task. They are not facing each other. They are not looking at each other. They are less tempted to tease, "bug" or otherwise distract each other from the task at hand.

Up and Moving

Grades 6–12

Getting students out of their chairs and into motion is a way to coax group participation and involvement at all grade levels. Groups of children in the primary grades love to "be the ones" who gets to come up and write on the board.

Middle and high school students can do the same thing. Invite ten students to come to the board in pairs to solve the same five algebra problems as students in their seats. Ask two students to work together filling in the skeletal outline on the overhead during social studies. One of the goals of differentiating instruction is to keep the content but change the delivery to personalize instruction. Any change from the ordinary, any change from the usual that gets students up and moving will spark interest and increase group participation.

The Movable Test

Grades 6–12

This strategy can turn an individual assessment into a group task when the focus is on teamwork. Instead of the usual on-the-desk format for a paper-pencil assessment, consider providing a different type of assessment. When students arrive, they will find an assessment that has questions posted throughout the room. Questions are written in large print on the wall, on the door, on the bulletin board, with an arrow on the map and projected onto the overhead screen. Kinesthetic learners thrive with this testing strategy since motion is what they love. Working in groups, students move from question to question, reaching consensus on a response. Questions may be answered in any order so that the entire class is not clustered around the same question.

7 STRATEGIES FOR ASKING FOR HELP

In a classroom setting, the ability to ask for and get the help that is needed requires students to learn both patience and persistence. Here are seven different approaches to teach students how to give and get help in a large group setting.

H.E.L.P. Partners

Grades 4–6

When students work in groups or with a partner, too often they try to help each other by simply giving the answer without allowing the peer to arrive at the answer independently. The **H.E.L.P.** tool teaches peers how to offer assistance effectively. I observed this technique in a fifth grade classroom and it worked well. The teacher taught all students how to **H.E.L.P.** each other. The entire process takes only minutes.

When a student gets "stuck" trying to recall the capital of New York, for example, the student can approach a partner for **H.E.L.P.**

1. The first step is for the helper to give a **H**int.
   "Do you remember when we looked at the map of New York?"

2. The next step is to **E**ncourage the partner to guess.
   "What city did you think it might be?"

3. The third step is to **L**ist some options.
   "I can't give you the answer but I'll give you three choices: Albany, Buffalo, or New York City."

4. Finally, the helper provides the **P**age number or other location of the answer.
   "Look on page 84, right-hand column."

   H: Hint

   E: Encourage guessing

   L: List options

   P: Page number

As I watched students working together, I saw them following the steps in the acronym, resisting the impulse to immediately provide the answer.

Colored Cups

Grades 1–5

A system using three colors of paper cups helped a computer teacher I know encourage her students to ask for help but kept hands free to continue working. Each student had a set of three brightly colored cups: blue, yellow and red. They were kept on the computer monitor upside down and stacked.

When everything was going well and no help was needed, the blue cup was on top and the others were stacked inside. If there were problems and the student was getting confused, the student changed the cup order so that the yellow cup was on top, hiding the other colors. If the student was completely stumped and needed help as soon as possible, the red cup went on top and meant, "Help!!"

☞ **The Practical Pointer:**

> If you teach primary grades, you may wish to stick to one cup—red. Keep it simple! If a student needs help, up goes the red cup. I can think of several students who would raise their hands to ask if the problem required a red cup or a yellow one . . .

Name Card Sideways

Grades 1–5

Here is a quick tip to teach your students an alternative to raising their hands when they need help. Have each student make a fold-over name card for the corner of the desk. When they need help, tell them tip it sideways. As you circulate during independent work time, seeing a **name card sideways** will let you know immediately who needs help.

Help Card

Grades 1–5

As part of doing more on their own, we want to encourage students to skip the problem or question that is too difficult and go on to the next one. Too often, students will assume that if they need help, they should stop and wait. Undoubtedly you have admonished students, "If you come to one that you cannot do, skip that and try the next one."

As a reminder, provide a **Help Card** that is a basic fold-over tent card. *Help* is written on the side that faces the teacher. On the side facing the student is a different message: *Keep Working.*

Take a Number

Grades 2–12

Write numbers on small sticky notes and place them on the board. When a student needs help, the student walks to the board, takes a number, sits down and continues working until the number is called. Glancing at the board, the teacher can quickly see what number to call next.

Collect the numbers so that they can be used over and over. This works effectively in any subject area and at any grade level, from elementary students who need math help to proofreading papers with high school students.

Name on Board

Grades 2–12

Similar to taking a number, this approach also gives students a quick breather when they are having trouble. They will get up, go to the board and write their names in order. Just as we all know, "Your call will be answered in the order received," our students learn patience in waiting their turn. They also learn to be accountable by taking responsibility for seeking and receiving help.

First Call for Help

Grades 4–12

If there are students in the classroom who have a good understanding of the content and would like to act as designated teaching assistants, they can help their peers when the teacher is busy helping someone else. Students are told, "The following individuals have volunteered to be teaching assistants today. If I am busy, go to one of these four people. They can help you. If your question is still not answered, I will help you as soon as I can."

As in **Raising the Group Grade**, it is important that capable students are not overused as assistants at the expense of their own learning. Rotate teaching assistant duties so that top students who consistently "finish early," have time for the challenge of stretch activities that go beyond general expectations of the curriculum.

16 EVERY STUDENT RESPONSE TECHNIQUES

Every Student Response techniques or **ESR** can be used in a variety of ways in a large group setting to meet several different purposes. The main objective is to involve every student in the class in participation. I've selected 16 **ESR** techniques to describe here. You may have many others to add to the list.

Every Student Response techniques address two common problems. The first one involves the student who sits back passively and lets the other students do the work. In **ESR** strategies, there is no opportunity to sit back. Everyone participates as a group. It is easy for the teacher to monitor. **ESR** is also nonthreatening because everyone is engaged and no one is singled out.

A second common problem, solved by **ESR**, is encouraging some of the more eager students to wait and give classmates a turn. There are students who *know* the answer and want the teacher to *know* that they *know* it. The simplest way to do that is to shout it out, but doing so doesn't give other students the chance they need think it through. Several of the **ESR** approaches listed allow students a quick way to signal that they know the answer without giving it away.

Some of these **ESR** techniques are appropriate for all grade levels K–12 across the content areas as indicated. Others apply more specifically to primary, middle or upper grades. The grade levels listed are suggestions only. Choose and use! Change and adapt to fit your needs and those of your students.

Thumbs Up, Sideways, Fist

Grades K–12

Perhaps the most basic **ESR** format involves **thumbs up** for "yes" or "agree," **thumbs sideways** for "no" or "disagree" and a **closed fist** for "I don't know." The whole group participates providing fast feedback for the teacher in checking for understanding.

 The Practical Pointer:

For many years, I used **thumbs up** and **thumbs down**. A wise math teacher suggested that the whole concept of **thumbs down** often has a negative connotation. Just because someone disagrees, it may simply reflect another point of view, not necessarily negative. He made a good point. **Thumbs sideways** is neutral. I adopted his approach.

White Board Response

Grades K–12

Individual **white boards** make some of the best **ESR** tools. While purchased white boards or white board clipboards can be expensive, there are affordable alternatives. Take yourself on a personal field trip to your local home improvement store. Stop in the wallboard (paneling) section or bathroom shower section and purchase a large sheet of either one. Ask the clerk to cut it into approximately 8'' x 11'' sections. Voila!

Bring dry-erase markers and several old socks to class. Students can generate their own responses to questions or work on an algebra problem. When you signal, every student holds up a response. A study partner can check to make sure that a partner is on track. The boards are excellent when students are moving around the classroom during a science experiment, meeting outdoors in groups, or sitting on the floor.

9" Plates

Grades K–12

The glossy disposable plates make an inexpensive alternative to whiteboards for **ESR**. While not as durable, they function in the same way. It is handy to keep a stack in the closet. I frequently suggest this idea to parents to use with a child at home or in the car. The plates act as a transportable writing surface for practicing spelling, math facts or vocabulary. Consider laminating manila folders to use with dry-erase markers as still another tool for **ESR**.

Chalkboards

Grades K–12

Individual **chalkboards** also function like white boards for **ESR**. Some teachers have told me that they make them for their students. Did you know that there is spray paint available that turns cardboard into a chalkboard? Chalk dust can be messy but students enjoy using the small chalkboards. The goal is to create a variety of writing surfaces.

Shapes or Colors on a Stick

Grades K–3

Primary teachers and parents of young children will find that children love practicing shapes and colors when they are mounted on a craft sticks and laminated. These **ESR** tools allow all students to participate simultaneously when asked, "Hold up the square shape!" or "Raise the yellow piece." Paint samples from the hardware store work well for teaching colors when laminated and attached to a stick.

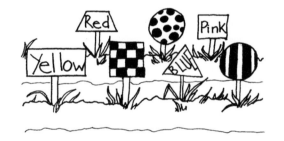

☞ **The Practical Pointer:**

I encourage parents to make this part of what I call "glove compartment learning." This means collecting a bag of learning materials to keep in the car. It can include books, a spiral notebook and a pencil, magazines or catalogs, small toys and simple learning tools like shapes and colors. Use them during all of those "wait times" in the car on the way to soccer or while waiting for a sibling at piano lessons.

A Movable Fan

Grades K–4

An easy **ESR** strategy to practice math facts or identify numbers is to cut tag board into narrow strips and write a single number on each one. Attach them at one end with a metal brad to create a movable fan of numbers. When asked the sum of "6 + 6," each student arranges the fan so that "1" and "2" are displayed to make "12." As a group, the fans are held in the air and the teacher can see quickly that everyone understands.

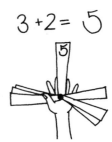

True-False Quick Check

Grades 4–12

I write the words *True* and *False* on two different colors of construction paper and glue the 5" x 7" rectangles back to back. Every student has one rectangle laminated and mounted on a craft stick to use as an **ESR** quick check on content. Holding up the card to display either *True* or *False* is an alternative to the paper-pencil quiz. It saves class time while still providing reinforcement for the student and feedback for the teacher.

Yes-No Cards

Grades 4–12

Similar to *True* and *False* cards, the *Yes* and *No* cards are constructed the same way but serve a different purpose. I have used them as discussion **ESR** tools to show consensus in the group. "Raise your *Yes* card if you think . . . It looks like the majority of you agree on this. Who can tell us why you feel this way?" It encourages nonthreatening participation. Everyone raises a card but a volunteer offers an explanation.

Multiple Choice Strips

Grades 4–12

Use **ESR** as an alternative to the traditional multiple choice assessment. Students lay four different colors of construction paper strips on their desks. As multiple choice questions are read aloud, students hold up red for "A," blue for "B," yellow for "C" and green for "All of the above." It is an effective way to teach students how to take a multiple choice assessment successfully by analyzing each question together. Some students see *All of the Above* on an assessment and immediately select it without thinking it through. This also helps the teacher discover which if any of the questions are confusing and need to be restructured.

Vote With Your Feet

Grades K–12

Have your students been sitting too long? Do they need to move around? This is a whole-body **ESR** technique! Students get up and *vote with their feet* to respond to oral true-false questions, yes-no statements or concepts. To begin, everyone stands. Then those who believe that a statement is true, for example, remain on their feet. Those who believe that it is false sit down. To begin the next question, all students are back on their feet and the process is repeated by standing for true and sitting for false.

In a slightly different format, I have asked all students to stand in a row. Step *forward* for to vote true, step *back* to vote false. When this is fast-paced, it creates a refreshing breather during a lesson.

Tell Your Hand

Grades K–4

To discourage students from shouting out the answer, try this approach. When asking a question in class, tell students to raise one hand when they are ready to respond. Next, have them cover their mouth gently with the other hand and *whisper* the answer into their palm. Students can show that they know and even *say* the answer quietly so that other students have the time they need to process the information.

Close Your Eyes, Raise Your Hand

Grades K–4

Younger children love it when the teacher asks the class to sit quietly and close their eyes! The elementary teacher may say, "Close your eyes. The question is What is 5+5? Raise your hand as soon as you know the sum!" Students respond by raising their hands. To make the activity totally nonthreatening, have students lower their hands before opening their eyes. It gives the teacher fast feedback on facts without putting anyone on the spot.

Although high school students would also love to hear the teacher instruct them to close their eyes, this idea is best limited to elementary students.

Hit the Buzzer

Grades K–4

One of the favorite and most requested **ESR** strategies of the elementary children I've taught is called **Hit the Buzzer**. When there are just five minutes left before recess, lunch or the end of the day, this rambunctious technique can be a great way to review factual content quickly and enthusiastically.

Students imagine that there is a game show buzzer perched on their desk or table. Clasping their hands together with interlocking fingers poised above the imaginary buzzer, students listen for the first question. They signal their response by slamming the buzzer. After waiting for responses, the teacher calls on one student to give the answer. This gives students who need more time to process the question the time they need. It goes without saying that some students get carried away in the frenzy and **Hit the Buzzer** before they know the answer. Most often, though, they formulate a response first. Students love **Hit the Buzzer**, and the class is completely engaged!

☞ **The Practical Pointer:**
If you have a student in the class who startles easily, you will not be able to use this idea. However, two quieter options are listed next that may be more appropriate.

Hand on Shoulder or Hands on Head

Grades K–4

A less raucous **ESR** technique is simply telling students to indicate that they know the answer by placing a hand on the opposite shoulder or placing both hands on top of their head. When the teacher sees that everyone has had an opportunity to respond nonverbally, one student is called on to respond aloud. You will not get as many requests for this version of **ESR**, but students will still be enthusiastic. The goal is variety! variety! variety!

Five Fingers

Grades 1–4

Use the hand as an **ESR** tool for any topic that lends itself to a list of five categories or five items. For example, when introducing a new chapter of a text or a story, you may ask students to hold up their hands in a fist. Then ask who can find the *title*. Students hold up their thumbs as they read it together.

Students lower their hands, as they get ready to add the index finger. Next tell them raise their hand with both the thumb and index finger extended when they are ready to *predict* what the chapter is about.

Next they will add the middle finger to show that they have looked at the *pictures*.

Students will add the ring finger to show that they are ready to *preview* the headings and subheadings together.

Finally, they extend their hands with all fingers and thumb extended to show that they have read the first *paragraph*.

Palm Up, Palm Down

Grades 6–12

I wanted to increase participation but also be sensitive to the anxiety level of a hesitant student. A simple solution was to arrange a private signal with that student as a way of indicating to me whether or not the student knew the answer. After asking the question, the student would turn a *palm up* to show, "Yes, call on me, I know the answer," or *palm down,* "No, don't call on me this time." This quiet signal allowed the highly anxious student to relax knowing that he would not be called on when he was not ready.

O—⚷ KEY IDEA

Every Student Response strategies promote cooperation and offer opportunities to reinforce the whole class. They provide fast feedback for the teacher and students alike. *ESR* strategies are easy to use and do not require more than a few minutes of class time. This list can help you create several more *Every Student Response* strategies.

SUMMARY

"Two heads are better than one" is a saying often used in promoting the benefits of collaboration among adults. The same is true when students put their heads together to learn and study as members of a group. Ideas and strategies emerge from the group process that no one person would have thought of individually. In our classrooms, learning to work as a team and function effectively as members of a larger group is a process that begins with respect, openness and a sense of belonging together as members of a community of learners.

What lies behind us and what lies before us are tiny matters compared to lies within us.

–*Ralph Waldo Emerson*

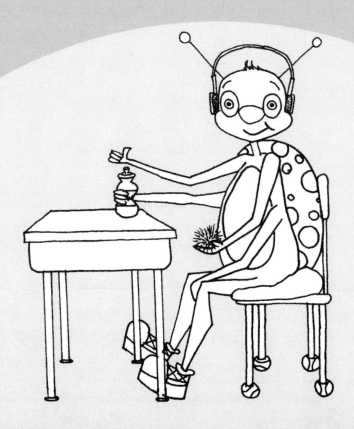

CREATURE COMFORTS

If you learn from hard knocks, you can also learn from soft touches.

–Carolyn Kenmore

9

Students typically spend an average of seven hours each day in school. Multiply that by 180 days each school year and it is no surprise that creating a comfortable environment, conducive to teaching and learning makes a critical difference. "Creature Comforts" matter.

This chapter focuses on a broad range of strategies, tips, tools and techniques that generate a hospitable climate for learning. Topics include amplification so that students can hear easily, noise management, physical comfort, lighting considerations, focusing tools, manipulatives for fidgeting students as well as ways to cope with and corral the nomadic learner.

- The Amplified Classroom
- Types of Microphones
- Low-Tech Amplification
- Positioned for Comfort
- Reducing the Noise Level
- Focusing Tools
- Lighting Tips and Tools
- Tips and Tools for Fidgeters
- Nomadic Learners
- Quick Tips for Creature Comforts

THE AMPLIFIED CLASSROOM

Let's Hear It!

Grades K–12

A microphone is an extremely effective tool for classroom use. I have included it in "Creature Comforts" because a microphone benefits every student in the classroom. Many of our students are missing a lot of what is said in our classes because they cannot hear it. This includes not only those students who have a mild hearing impairment, but also many other students who are distracted by typical classroom noise.

All of us struggle with competing sounds every day. In the classroom, the competition is great. As a frequent classroom visitor, I find that often I have to work very hard to hear both teacher and student comments. It is understandable that many of our students give up and turn their attention elsewhere.

A SENSIBLE SOLUTION

The microphone is a tremendous tool to use *daily*. If that is not possible, consider using it on an occasional basis. Whenever I mention this strategy during a seminar, teachers who have not used one ask several good questions:

> What are the benefits?
>
> How many school districts are wiring every teacher?
>
> Is this workable on a practical basis?
>
> Who pays for a microphone?
>
> Are there inexpensive ways to accomplish the same thing?
>
> How can we convince our administration that we need them?
>
> How can this be done in an old building?
>
> What if a class is co-taught?
>
> Will this work in a building that was built during the "open classroom" era?

Let me first explain how this benefits all students and then offer some very inexpensive, realistic alternatives to the more sophisticated microphones on the market. I can also add suggestions that may sway the administration to invest in at least some portable microphone systems.

WHY A MICROPHONE?

Think about the background noise that is common in most classrooms. Students drop books and pencils. There are side conversations. People cough. A custodian vacuums the hallway. Chairs scrape on tile floors. Paper is shuffled. The fan of the overhead projector adds noise. The drone of the air conditioner or heating unit clicks on and off. Noise continually competes for our students' attention. Our students learn as much as 80 percent of content by listening. If they cannot hear it, they miss a lot.

OBSERVATION

As teachers, we learn so much by observing our students. Sitting in the back during a classroom observation offers a great vantage point for me to see how many students are actively engaged in an activity, whether they are on the right page, and how many are not paying attention to the lesson. Their attention may be focused on a variety of other sounds and distractions that they hear. "Tuning out" happens for a variety of reasons; not being able to hear easily adds to the problem.

In teaching, we often compensate for background noise by increasing the volume of our own voice. We sometimes think that speaking in a louder voice works. To some degree it can be successful but, as the day goes by, we distort our voices by continuing to increase the volume. The distortion becomes even harder to listen to and we lose more students.

WIRING EVERY TEACHER

Some schools are, in fact, "wiring every teacher" with a lavaliere microphone. When purchasing a microphone for every teacher all at one time is not financially feasible, some schools start with a few, often beginning in the primary classrooms, and add more microphones every year. The reason for beginning at the primary level is that the nature of the activities creates the greatest demand for a microphone.

THE GOAL

The goal of using a microphone is to amplify our voices just a notch above our usual speaking level. In doing so, we block out much of that extraneous noise. The fan of the overhead projector no longer distracts. The teacher can be heard above a side conversation. The voice is not distorted.

Ideally the best type of microphone for classroom use is a lavaliere microphone that clips onto clothing near the face leaving the hands free. When a student is responding to a question, the teacher can easily remove the microphone and hold it so that the student can speak directly into it.

VOICE SAVER

For many teachers, the microphone is a necessity after years of straining their voices while teaching. Some veteran teachers experience hoarseness to the extent that students cannot hear them easily without amplification. An inexpensive microphone is often adequate under these circumstances. See the section entitled **The "Hip" Speaker**.

Amplified Reports

Grades 2–12

There are two key times when it is especially helpful for students to use a microphone on a regular basis. The first is when students are giving reports. Often their voices simply do not project to the back of the room. During an observation, I watch as peers sitting near me in the back pay attention to student reports initially but then quickly lose interest.

Amplified Reading

Grades 2–12

The second key time when students should use a microphone is when we ask for volunteers to read a paragraph to the group. Students often bury their faces in the book making it hard for anyone sitting more than a few feet way to hear them.

Solving these two problems does not require full-time microphone use. Some schools own one or two portable systems allowing teachers to check them out ahead of time on an as-needed basis.

Using a Microphone

Grades K–12

Many times before a staff development session that will last all day, the organizer will assure me, "You won't need a microphone in that room. We use that room all the time and we never use one."

Actually, I *do* need a microphone even when the room is relatively small and the group is not large. It enables adults to listen and participate more easily. We know that no one is listening *all of the time* to anyone whether it is the facilitator or colleagues. In any given meeting, adults tune in and out just like our students. Some people may be thinking through what else needs to be done that day, their grocery list, or their evening plans.

THE EXPERIMENT

Even in a relatively small space, it can be difficult for motivated listeners to hear the person who is speaking and stay connected. To illustrate the point, consider this experiment that I conduct with the graduate students in my Hamline University course. The class meets in a typical college classroom; there are approximately 25–30 individuals who are working on their masters' degrees or are simply taking the course out of personal interest.

For the first hour of a two-hour class, I wear the lavaliere microphone. Then I take it off and continue with the class. Invariably someone asks, "Will you put the microphone back on?"

That is my opportunity to find out whether participants were more "tuned in" when I wore the microphone, when I did not, or whether the microphone made a difference at all.

The response is always the same. Everyone agrees that they were *more* attentive *more* of the time when the microphone was used. It was simply easier to listen.

☞ **The Practical Pointer:**
Try this same experiment with your school board. Be sure to turn your back to the group and continue talking as many of us do as we walk toward the white board or blackboard in a classroom. Ask school board members when it was easier to hear.

While *all* students benefit from classroom microphone use, the students who will benefit the most are those students with attention deficit disorder who cannot block out all of the sounds competing for their attention.

TYPES OF MICROPHONES

Lavaliere Microphones

Grades K–12

In the classroom, the best microphone is wired through a system to speakers in the walls so that sound is evenly dispersed throughout the room. Four speakers, with two in the back of the room and two more in the front, are ideal. In fact, in primary classrooms, speakers would be mounted at a lower height so that they would be at ear level when children are seated. Speakers for older students would be mounted just a bit higher.

The easiest and least expensive time to wire the room for speakers is when the building is under construction. Even if the microphone and speakers are not in the budget, it is advantageous to install the speaker wire since the wire itself is very inexpensive. Microphones and speakers can be added later. Some schools that are already built cannot add speaker wire through the walls but can install one or two speakers in a suspended ceiling at a fairly reasonable cost.

The "Hip" Speaker

Grades K–12

Think of the microphones worn by salespeople at the State Fair or a shopping mall when they are demonstrating how a gizmo can slice, dice and chop. At a fraction of the cost of the typical lavaliere microphone, these clip-on microphones are connected to a small speaker worn on a belt or waistband. The sound quality will not be the same as the expensive lavaliere sound system. This self-contained system is adequate, however, for most classrooms. In fact, these microphones are popular with physical education teachers who need to speak to large groups of students in gymnasiums or outdoors on the playing field.

There are several advantages to these microphones in addition to the reasonable cost. Because they are worn on the teacher's hip, the speaker is close to ear level for most students when seated. It will be louder for students located close by. In a classroom, preferential seating near the teacher should be given to students with a mild hearing loss or attention deficit disorder. Another advantage is that these units operate on rechargeable batteries that can be plugged in each night so that they are ready for use each day.

Hand-Held Microphones

Grades K–12

Less desirable than the lavaliere microphone or the hands-free hip unit is the cordless hand-held variety. The amplification works very well but it is less convenient and more cumbersome because the speaker must hold it. In my own experience using a hand-held unit, I find that it can be distracting to put the microphone down when I need to use both hands and remember to pick it up afterward.

Microphone on a Stick

Grades K–12

An alternative is to use a microphone stand. Unfortunately, few cordless hand-held microphones are equipped this way. Usually microphones with stands are attached to a cord, which significantly limits movement. The biggest problem for me is getting the cords tangled on chair legs as I move about the room.

☞ **The Practical Pointer:**

A simple solution is to eliminate the wrap-around problem is to tape the cord to the floor with duct tape. The obvious disadvantage is that it allows the speaker even less movement, confining the speaker to one spot. A student would have to come to the front of the room to read a paragraph or give a report.

Inexpensive Alternatives

Grades K–12

You may think that a microphone is not a realistic strategy for your classroom because of the cost. While there are school districts where all teachers are now wired with lavaliere microphones, your school district may not be able to do this. Don't give up on this valuable strategy. There are workable, inexpensive alternatives. Two inexpensive versions are listed next.

KARAOKE ANYONE?

Since the premise of this resource book is to offer effective and *inexpensive* strategies, let's consider reasonable alternatives to using the lavaliere microphone system. One inexpensive option to "state of the art" amplification is a basic karaoke machine. Karaoke has been described as the fad that just won't die! You may have a karaoke machine yourself. If not, ask your students if anyone has one at home.

The amplification is adequate, and though it is unlikely that you would use it all the time, it is a sensible solution for key times when you need it most. The microphone itself may need occasional replacement, but a new one can be purchased at low-cost from a discount store. Who knows? You may just burst into song on a Monday morning!

CHILDREN'S MICROPHONES

Toy microphones can achieve adequate voice amplification. These tend to be battery operated and cannot be used all day. They can, however, be used for occasions when the activity is particularly noisy, for oral reports or when a student is reading aloud. Toy microphones will serve the purpose, too, of helping students gain practical experience and confidence in using a microphone.

Wired for Co-Teaching

Grades K–12

A microphone can be part of a co-taught class. When both teachers are taking active roles and are tag-team teaching, both teachers need to be heard. In one option, the designated "lead teacher" on a particular day wears the microphone and passes it the second teacher when necessary.

In another option, both teachers wear microphones that are connected to each other. It should be noted that when the co-teachers are working in small groups, the microphone system would be turned off since there would not be a need for amplification during that time.

Open Classrooms

Grades K–12

Schools without walls may prevent the use of microphones. The biggest concern that I hear from teachers in this structural arrangement is the distraction already created by another teacher's voice from across the way. This occurs without amplification. Amplifying this would only add more problems.

O—ᴈ KEY IDEA

The open classroom environment is extremely difficult for certain students who are easily distracted. Despite comments such as, "They will get used to it," some students never do.

☞ **The Practical Pointer:**
When there is no other option, seat students who have the most difficulty blocking out competing noises near the teacher. They should sit as far as physically possible from the next classroom space. Ideally, the best suggestion is to explore ways to create separate spaces and control noise levels from adjoining classrooms.

Involving the Community

Grades K–12

Having access to a microphone is so valuable that it is worth asking for help in the community. Local businesses will sometimes underwrite the cost of portable microphone systems that can travel from classroom to classroom.

Parent groups and individual parents have sometimes purchased microphone systems for their local school. Explain the purpose and ask for help.

Occasionally, resourceful teachers have been successful in locating older but working "stand alone" microphone systems that businesses are no longer using. Companies may be willing to donate them to schools and receive a tax benefit for the value.

☞ **The Practical Pointer:**

In a search for used equipment, be sure to inquire at country clubs, rotary organizations, hotels, places of worship and convention facilities. They have been good sources for schools in the past.

LOW-TECH AMPLIFICATION

Two very simple tools are described next and make excellent tools for amplification when working one-on-one with primary students and teaching sounds.

Elbow Pipe Amplifier

Grades K–3

Take yourself on a "teacher's" field trip to your local home improvement store. You may want to start a list of several inexpensive items mentioned in *The Teacher's Toolbox for Differentiating Instruction* that you may wish to purchase.

If you are a primary teacher, the elbow pipe in the plumbing department is something that you will want to add to your list! Look under your kitchen sink for a sample. The newer ones are about two inches in diameter and are made of plastic.

HOW TO USE IT:

Using an elbow pipe is simple but effective. When you are teaching sounds, have the student speak into one end of the pipe. The other end curves around to the students' ear. It is an amplification tool. Purchase another section to form an "S" shape. Now turn the top piece outward and you can speak into the child's ear and your voice will be amplified.

Soda Bottle Speaker

Grades K–2

Here is another low-tech version of a way to amplify sounds. The top of a soda bottle works like an old earphone. Simply cut several inches off the top of a plastic two-liter soda bottle. Speak into the wide end of the piece. Sound going into the ear will be amplified. This simple technique helps students who are having trouble differentiating between two similar sounds.

POSITIONED FOR COMFORT

*Seat on the seat; feet on the floor. That is just the way
I have to have it in my classroom.*

–Fourth Grade Teacher

Assistance from the Occupational Therapist

Grades K–5

Although we expect our students to sit on typical chairs at school every day, we could hardly have designed a less comfortable seat. One size truly does not fit all and many chairs are too big or too small for the students who spend time on them throughout the day.

Invite the occupational therapist into your classroom to evaluate students for proper fit in desks or chairs. Some desks are adjustable for elementary students providing the good fit necessary to enable the student to sit just the way that fourth grade teacher would like.

Proper fit creates two right angles as the student sits: one right angle is formed by sitting upright and bending the legs from the hip; the second right angle is formed by the bend in the knee.

At the secondary level, it would be impossible fit every desk to every student each class period because so many different students share the same desks during the day. A feasible option may be to include a few larger desks and a few smaller desks in addition to the standard size in each classroom. This would provide some choices.

Therapy Ball

Grades K–4

Explore the possibility of a therapy ball for the classroom. A "class set" is unlikely but ask the occupational therapist whether a single therapy ball would be available for your students. The therapy ball is large enough for a small child to sit on comfortably and it rests on a disk to prevent rolling. What makes it so pleasant is that the therapy ball is soft and conforms to the individual.

Carpet Squares

Grades K–5

An alternative that adds comfort is a carpet square on the seat of a desk. Many students like to use carpet squares both for desks and for sitting on the floor. The local floor store would be happy to provide carpet samples for this purpose in discontinued colors.

O⌐ᴚ KEY IDEA

Check with your local fire marshal to see if carpet samples are allowed in your classroom before asking your local carpet dealer for 30 samples.

Learn at the Lectern

Grades 2–12

Some students who act out are just responding to the discomfort of sitting in a desk for any length of time. A practical solution is to offer the opportunity to stand while still participating in class.

If you look in storage closets at school, you are likely to find an extra metal lectern that no one is using. It can be placed on a desk or table off to the side of the room. Invite any student to take a turn standing at the lectern as an alternative to sitting during class. That student can read, lean on it, write and still participate actively in class while in a standing position.

Music Stand Learning

Grades 2–12

A music stand also gives a student the chance to stand and learn. It can be placed at the side of the room so that a student will not block anyone's view. Since the height of a music stand is adjustable, the music stand offers the option of placing a book at a comfortable level for reading. Students will not be able to *write* on a music stand, however, because it will not offer enough stability.

Bookshelf Learning

Grades 4–12

When students want to stand but need to take notes or do math problems, consider allowing students to use a *bookcase, ledge,* or *file cabinet* for a makeshift stand-up desk.

Several students can line up along the bookcase at one time making it easier to use than the music stand or lectern.

Rocking Chair

Grades 4–8

It is hard to surpass the comfort of a rocking chair for independent reading at any age. While rocking chairs are almost required at the primary level, they are rarely found in upper elementary classrooms or beyond. Since beanbag chairs and overstuffed furniture have been eliminated from most classrooms by the fire code, the wooden rocking chair remains as a staple for reading comfort. I would like to see one available in every class-room for a student to enjoy a novel or pick up a newspaper when there are a few minutes of free time.

Lapboard

Grades K–12

Lapboards create a movable writing surface that students can carry to different areas of the room, use in an auditorium setting, take outdoors, or use while sitting on the floor. They can be made of inexpensive wallboard that has been cut into clipboard-sized pieces. Far less expensive than individual clipboards, lapboards enable students to write comfort-ably in locations other than at a desk or table.

Turn the Chair Around

Grades 1–8

If you have a student who likes to rock back on a chair tilting danger-ously on two chair legs, invite the student to turn the chair around and straddle it. This offers a change of position and, without a back to lean on, the student is less likely to lean backward.

Office Chair Option

Grades 3–8

I had a child with special needs who rocked in the chair frequently. For this child, turning the chair around was not a practical solution. We brought in an office chair with arms that was designed to rock back and forth safely. It worked well for that student. While the rocking was slightly distracting to others at first, before long no one noticed.

Camping Pillow

Grades K–3

A quick solution to the problem of the uncomfortable desk chair is the camping pillow inflated just enough to create a cushion. The student who fidgets will appreciate the "wiggle room."

Beach Ball Comfort

Grades K–3

Semi-inflated beach balls also function as chair cushions. These creature comforts may seem unnecessary for many students. There are some students, though, for whom the difference they make will be significant.

☞ **The Practical Pointer:**
   Purchase both camping pillows and beach balls on clearance at the end of the season. I
   have found both for 75 percent off regular price.

O─┓ KEY IDEA

Creature comforts do matter and reduce discipline problems.

Hoola Hoop Boundaries

Grades K–2

I have found that inexpensive Hoola Hoops create personal space for students who need it. Particularly during Circle Time when students gather on the rug, a few students may elect to sit in the space created by the Hoola Hoop. It provides a bit more room and sets boundaries for all concerned. There will not be enough room for every student to use one but not every student will ask for one. The Hoola Hoop can be a special treat.

Stabilize It!

Grades 1–12

The rubber tips used on crutches work well attached to a desk with uneven legs. The desk will not rock or slide around. Can you imagine sitting in a "rocky" chair or desk for 180 school days? That can be both distracting and irritating.

REDUCING THE NOISE LEVEL

Tennis Anyone?

Grades 1–12

Cut a slit in used tennis balls and place them under chair legs on a tile floor. Presto! Quiet movement. Students can slide chairs easily without screeching. This simple strategy can save the nerves of both teachers and students over the course of a school year.

☞ **The Practical Pointer:**

Well-used tennis balls are the best choice because the fuzz will have been worn off. New tennis balls have a distinctive odor and also tend to "shed," both of which may create problems for students with allergies.

Also, for children or adults who use a walker, tennis balls are helpful in allowing the walker to slide easily across the floor. These are preferable to using rubber tips that will not slide and force the individual to repeatedly lift the walker during movement.

Put a Box Over It!

Grades K–12

Often when I am in a classroom, I will notice the same phenomenon—whether it is a third grade room, middle school English, or high school social studies. At the very moment that the teacher is making a key point or facilitating discussion, a student will get up, walk right in front of the teacher, and grind away at the pencil sharpener. R-R-R-R! Does the pencil really need sharpening that urgently or does the student simply want to get up and walk around? Most often, I suggest that it is the latter. Then the student will return to the desk unfazed.

There is a practical solution for this behavior that annoys both teacher and other students. **Put a box over it**—the pencil sharpener, that is, not the student. When it is not an appropriate time to sharpen pencils, the box provides a clear and very simple signal. During work time, the box can be removed and the sharpener is open for business.

Music for the Class

Grades K–12

A creature comfort that many teachers use during independent work is soft, instrumental music. The volume is set at a level that is barely audible but loud enough to hear. In fact, when the noise level in the classroom exceeds the music volume, it is a signal to students that they are too loud during that activity. Generally, music is a popular addition. If only a few students seem to respond positively to the music, however, the teacher may wish to consider allowing these students to listen on headphones at designated times.

Headphones with Music

Grades 2–12

The auditory learner may find that headphones with instrumental music will increase

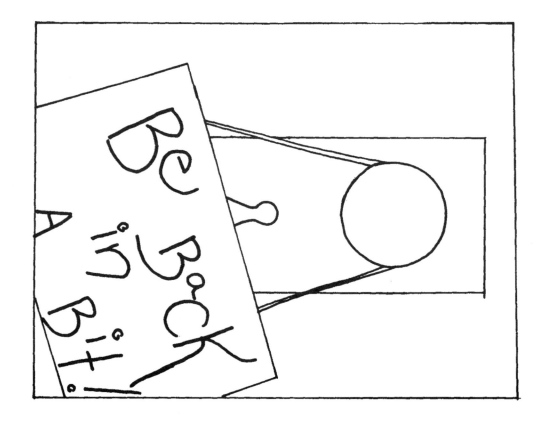

concentration during individual work time. Some people believe that 60 beats per minute is the ideal tempo for background music, although much depends on individual preference. Some students prefer the sounds of nature. There are numerous, inexpensive collections to choose from in this category.

Quiet Headphones

Grades 3–12

Not every auditory learner finds music a benefit to concentration. Some people need a quiet atmosphere for individual work. Have you tried wearing headphones *without* any music?

In a typical classroom, there is a lot of background noise. An elementary classroom has an ongoing hum of activity. There are children's voices, pencils dropping, the sound of papers rattling, and general movement. There are often too many sounds to tune out for a highly auditory learner.

For some children and adults the use of quiet headphones helps to block out extraneous sounds and noise. Among the options are expensive headphones that emit an auditory signal that acts like "white noise" and overshadows unwanted sounds. Another option is the high quality *quiet headphones* designed for this purpose that will significantly reduce background noise. The cost of the high-tech model is prohibitive for classroom use but ordinary headphones serve the purpose.

More affordable and more easily available are common headphones that reduce some unwanted noise. Wearing headphones can also cue the student wearing them, as well as classmates, that this is quiet independent work time. Strategies like this appeal to some students but may become another distraction for others. It is worth a try.

☞ **The Practical Pointer:**
I am noticing more and more adults wearing headphones on airplanes. Are they listening to music or a book on tape or do they simply want quiet time? Other travelers are less likely to strike up a conversation with a person wearing headphones.

Basic Sign Language

Grades K–12

A quiet and inclusive strategy for classroom communication involves basic sign language. Teach the class to spell out common requests such as going to the restroom, a locker or drinking fountain. Then include students in creating common hand signals for borrowing a pencil, turning out the lights or asking teacher to repeat directions. Noise will be reduced without any loss in effective communication. Exposure to sign language is important at all grade levels since it is a means of communication that everyone may find useful in the community or workplace.

Study Carrel Option

Grades 2–12

For the student who is bothered by distractions, consider offering a study carrel as an option at times. If an actual study carrel is not available, teach students to make their own by standing two manila folders on their sides to accomplish the same purpose. While it will not block any significant amount of noise, it will give the student a sense of privacy and the perception of control over the environment. A cardboard box with the bottom and end cut off works well also.

FOCUSING TOOLS

Practicing the Directions

Grades K–12

I teach very young children to highlight key words in directions. Together we *circle* the word "circle." We *underline* the word "underline." We *draw a box* around the phrase "draw a box." Using a highlighter, we *do* what the directions tell the student to do. In doing this, the students have already completed the task once and have practiced the directions.

The Human Highlighter

Grades K–12

Highlighting notes, study guides and review sheets is effective at all grade levels. Color-coding adds a dimension that provides more information for the student. For strong kinesthetic learners, the act of highlighting itself acts as a reinforcement of the learning process.

Unless we teach our students *how* and *what* to highlight on the paper, they tend to highlight anything and everything ending up with yellow page! How many of you have seen that? I know that I have done this myself. To reread key points means rereading the whole paper but in *yellow* the next time.

To teach highlighting skills, we need to focus students' attention on what is important. We may want to call attention to major concepts, key words, locations on a map, a math problem, phrases in music or a detail in artwork. The overhead projector is a wonderful tool to use in teaching these skills. As the teacher, you can transform yourself into an effective and memorable **Human Highlighter**. This may not be your fantasy but it works. *You become the strategy* by holding bright tag board on a stick in front of your overhead screen!

HOW IT WORKS:

Staple a brightly colored piece of oak tag board onto a paint stick or fly swatter. Stand in front of your overhead screen where the overhead image is projected. Hold the **Human Highlighter** against the screen focusing on the important image. Then lift the image forward a few inches to enlarge it slightly, making it float before your students' eyes. It is truly magical!

They will wonder if David Copperfield is paying them a visit. Color is the key. Suddenly you have made a ho-hum transparency jump off the screen and come to life in color. The best part is that you are directing students' attention to focus on a specific part of the image.

If students have a copy on their desks of the same overhead, they can highlight that same vocabulary word or idea with their markers.

☞ **The Practical Pointer:**

I make **Human Highlighters** in a variety of colors and shapes depending on my purpose. When teaching parts of speech, I like to make several color-coded **Human Highlighters** on flyswatters out of oak tag so that each part of speech has its own color. When I focus on a single word in a sentence on the overhead, a noun will always be highlighted in green; verb will always be highlighted in orange and so on. The same is true for operational signs in math. An addition sign may be yellow, for example, and subtraction may be pink.

DOL Magic Wand

Grades K–4

Many elementary teachers use "daily oral language" as an exercise to begin the day. The sentence of the day is written on the overhead. Students need to examine it for errors, copy it, and make corrections. In practice, a better description might be *daily written language.*

Students love coming to the board. Select a student to act as the **Human Highlighter** by using the **Magic Wand** to lift the errors off the screen, tell what changes should be made and why. You will have more volunteers than you can use for this one!

☞ **The Practical Pointer:**

Some students find it extremely difficult to copy the DOL sentence off the board or overhead. A simple solution is to *provide a copy* for the student at their desk. They will skip the copying and get right to the objective. Their task is cross out errors and quickly make the necessary corrections on paper directly above the mistake.

Flip It and Frame It!

Grades 1–12

The back of the **Human Highlighter** can be used help students focus on a key point on the overhead. A simple approach is to use a flyswatter, but any size oak tag board can work well and can be adapted to fit your needs.

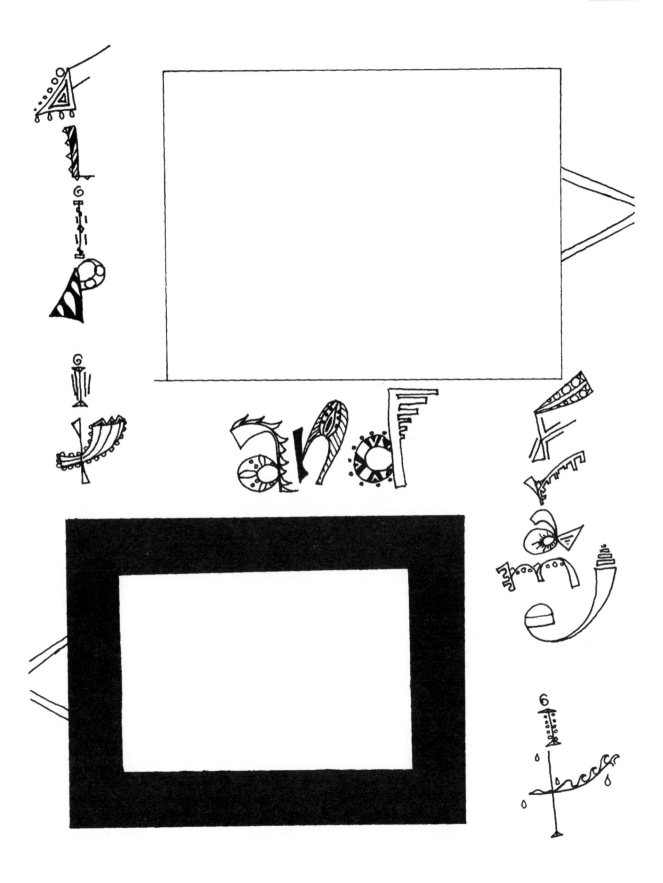

How To Make It:

Cut a square of white oak tag board and staple it to the flyswatter. Draw a strong, thick square with a broad marker about an inch inside the perimeter of the oak tag. When you use this with your overhead, attention will be drawn inside the square, your area of focus.

I flip back and forth. I use my **Human Highlighter** to lift images off the screen in color, and then flip over to **Frame** a key word or part of a map. The **Frame** is not necessarily in color, but is used to block out some of the surrounding material. It is similar to the **Window Concept** for students mentioned later in "Creature Comforts."

Color Your White Board!

Grades K–12

One of the challenges we face as teachers is to continually grab our students' interest and help them stay focused on the discussion, concept or lesson. When you are writing on a white board, you are most likely already color-coding by using different colored markers. Another way to draw students' attention to a particular word, letter or other point of emphasis is to create color shading that is the white board equivalent of the **Human Highlighter**.

How To Make It:

Cut a frame from oak tag board with a border about two inches wide. Then cut colored cellophane about an inch larger than the opening. Tape it securely to the back on all sides.

You are finished—for a minimal expenditure, you have a see-through tinted block of color. Hold it over a key word or math problem on your white board and you can highlight it in color. Grocery stores offer plastic wrap in different colors seasonally, so you can quickly make several of these in a variety of colors and sizes. Students like the novelty and quickly focus on what you have highlighted in color.

☞ **The Practical Pointer:**
Use a hair dryer to blow hot air on the cellophane, shrinking it to fit tightly.

Highlighting Tape

Grades K–12

Many times it is helpful for a student to highlight textbooks, maps, "Big Books," music and other nonconsumable materials. College students spend upwards of $600 a year to purchase their books and, for them, highlighting is a way of life. Most of us got through college by both highlighting and writing notes in the margins. The best college text in the bookstore was often a "used" book that had already been highlighted.

At the K–12 level, I don't see school districts or parents underwriting that cost in our public schools. The reality is that school districts use textbooks seven years or longer. Our students cannot write in most books even though several students would benefit from high-lighting key points and making notes in the margins.

In fact, we have our students so well trained *not* to write in their books that a child gasped as she watched an author at a bookstore autographing his own book. "That man is *writing* in the book!"

Highlighting tape offers a practical solution. It enables students to color-code materials and write notes in margins on the tape. After the student is finished using the materials, highlighting tape can be removed from most materials without damage. The tape, which is available in six colors and a variety of widths, can be written on with pencil or pen.

Contact Covington Cove Publications at 1-888-LEARN-11 to order. Packages are available but you can ask for any combination of sizes and colors that would work best for you. Please note that it is wise to test all materials before use.

☞ **The Practical Pointer:**
> I laminate a 4" x 6" note card and attach strips of all six colors of highlighting tape. Each student has a card to use in class. Students examine a section in the text by high-lighting the main idea in yellow, a key vocabulary word in green, the city in purple and the name of a person in orange. The colors cause the highlighted items to jump off the page during discussion.

At the end of the class period, students peel off the highlighting tape and replace it on the laminated card to use again another day.

⟳ KEY IDEA

Highlighting by tape or marker often helps kinesthetic learners assimilate the information. It enables these students to make reading a truly hands-on task.

Highlighting by Book Covers

Grades 4–12

Many schools require students to cover their textbooks to protect covers and make the books last longer. Office supply stores carry rolls of plastic designed for this purpose. The tacky substance on the plastic sticks to the books but is also removable. It is see-through and available in a variety of prints but also in bright solid colors.

This same material can be used much like a larger version of highlighting tape. It works well for creating a variety of shapes to use in highlighting key points on bulletin boards, posters and other materials that you may want to display during class.

☞ **The Practical Pointer:**
You may wish to cut large exclamation points, question marks, stars, smiles, rectangles, triangles, circles and other shapes in a variety of colors out of the plastic. Just as the laminated note card stores strips of highlighting tape, you can laminate larger paper to hold these colorful accents. After using them, replace them on the laminated sheets and they are ready to use over and over.

Maxi Pointer

Grades K–12

The traditional pointer has always been a useful focusing tool in directing students' attention on the white board or blackboard. Jazz up that yardstick or wooden pointer by adding a tag board hand with the index finger in the pointing position. Use a bright color for greater impact. You can purchase these through teaching catalogs but you can make your own in just minutes for a fraction of the cost.

Mini Pointer

Grades 1–12

When you use your overhead projector, you also want to direct students' attention to a particular point. A pen or pencil can do the job in a basic sort of way but you can also make a mini pointer that has much greater impact. Younger students call it the *magic hand*.

HOW TO MAKE IT:

Use a craft stick or tongue depressor for the arm. Select a "hand pointing" from clip-art on your computer. Print a copy on a clear overhead transparency. Cut out the hand and staple it to the "arm."

The advantage of the transparent hand is that your content will be visible as you slide the hand over your material on the overhead projector. In less time than it took to describe it, you can create a mini pointer!

Laser Sharp

Grades 1–12

A laser is a great focusing tool for your overhead screen, white board or blackboard. Here is a quick tip for using a laser. Unless you have a very steady hand, you may consider pointing with a small circular motion. The point of light will move smoothly. Trying to hold a laser perfectly still often creates a shaky point of light, which can be distracting to watch.

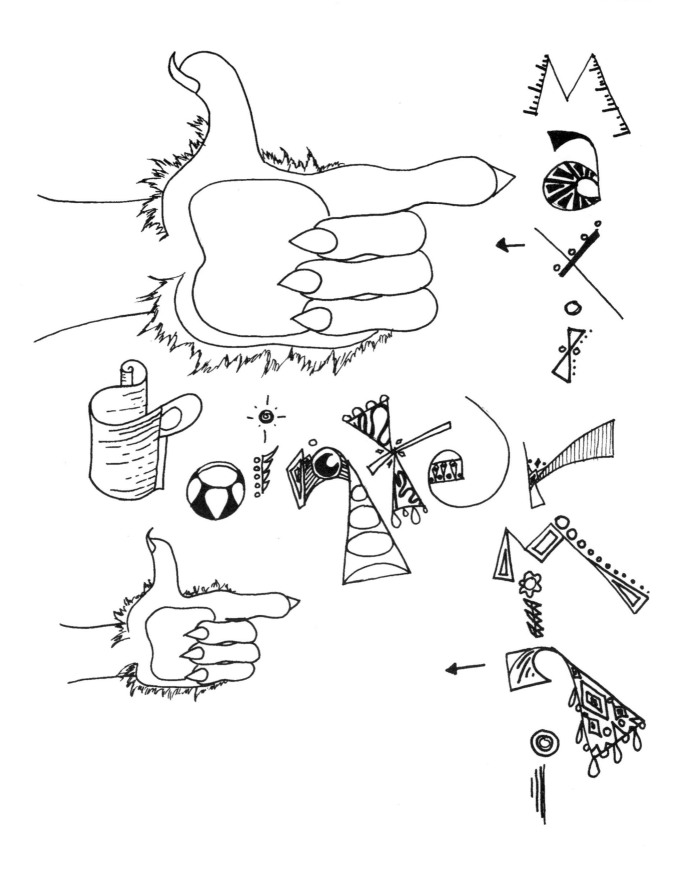

Clip It!

Grades K–3

A practical solution for the student who needs a gentle reminder to stay focused is to clip a clothespin or "chip clip" to the paper, book or activity that is the current task. Quiet encouragement to "Work on your clip!" may be all that is needed. When the task is completed, the clip comes off and the student places the paper where it belongs.

☞ **The Practical Pointer:**

If you decide to use a wooden clothespin, you can write a note on it to the student like one of these:

Do this now!

You can do it!

Keep working!

Focus and finish!

Work in Progress

Grades K–5

When students leave the classroom to go to music or art, a quick tip is to have them place all unfinished work on a personal clipboard. Later, students know that their first priority is to finish what was left on the clipboard before beginning another task.

At home, they can follow the same procedure. When it is time to take a break, stop for dinner, leave for basketball or band practice, students can clip the paper on the clipboard and know just where to begin again.

"SALLAME!"

Grades K–5

A verbal focusing tool used by fourth grade teacher Annemarie Regan was quick and to the point. When she said, "SALLAME!" students knew that she was telling her class, "Students, **all** eyes are on **me**!" That meant, "Pencils down. Look at me because this is important."

SLANT

Grades 2–6

Cecil Mercer, at the University of Florida, is famous for **SLANT**, another verbal focusing tool. This acronym describes behavior that effective students use for classroom success.

SLANT is one of those strategies that has withstood the test of time because it works. Perhaps you remember a variation of this when you were a student.

Sit up straight

Lean forward

Ask questions

Nod occasionally

Take notes

While not many high school students would not be too eager to sit up straight, they would discover that assuming an attentive position can actually help them focus on learning and consciously put them in a receptive frame of mind. You may want to adapt the acronym to suit your grade level and subject area.

It's in the Bag!

Grades K-8

A quick tip for creating interest is to use a drawstring bag or a zippered pillowcase that contains an item that relates to content that day. Place the bag on the desk or hang it from a hook before students arrive. Refer to it and perhaps provide clues. Students will wonder what is in the bag and when the time comes, they will be focused on its contents!

LIGHTING TIPS AND TOOLS

Reducing Glare in Print

Grades 2–12

Some students experience significant difficulty with glare from overhead lights. This is particularly noticeable when reading glossy paper used in some textbooks. To cut the glare, try laying a colored transparency over their reading materials to see if they find it easier to read.

While not everyone will notice a difference, some students will tell you that it is a major improvement. Over the years, a number of parents have been very enthusiastic about the success of using these transparencies with their children. So much depends on the lighting in the room, the glossiness of the page, and contrast between print and paper. In some cases, the novelty of using the transparency may be part of the appeal. Regardless, if it seems to work, I encourage students to stick with it.

Overhead Projector Glare

Grades K–12

When projecting an image from the overhead projector onto a white board, there can be significant glare for students. Looking at the reflection of the bright light bulb can be extremely fatiguing. Reduce the glare by laying a light gray or green transparency on the overhead projector first and then placing your own transparencies over that.

☞ **The Practical Pointer:**
The teacher is facing away from the white board and may be unaware of how intense the glare can be for students. Stand in the back of your classroom for the students' view.

Natural Light

Grades K–12

In some classrooms where I have visited, I have noticed that all ceiling lights were turned off. Natural lighting was used as much as possible. Floor lamps and table lamps were used when needed. The effect was both pleasant and relaxing. If this idea appeals to you, check with your local fire marshal to see what adaptations or wiring considerations would be needed to meet the fire code.

Miniature Book Lights

Grades 4–12

For some students, overhead fluorescent lights make reading in the classroom difficult. The small portable reading lights project light directly on the task. I use a miniature book light at home for reading in bed. There are several brands available that work well in the classroom because the lights operate on batteries as well as using an outlet.

Some teachers have brought in table lamps and floor lights using soft light bulbs because increased light directly on a task can help some students concentrate and read more easily. The key to lighting is to make sure that student is not reading in a shadow.

☞ **The Practical Pointer:**
Lighting that shines over the shoulder of the nondominant hand will not create a shadow when the child is writing.

TIPS AND TOOLS FOR FIDGETERS

Teachers and parents sometimes ask, "When is that child ever going to sit still?" In a word, the answer may be, "Never."

It seems to be just the way that child is "wired." To a great degree, the child probably will not grow out of it. Tolerance for sitting still will always be at different levels for different people. I can think of some adult friends who have a short tolerance for sitting in a restaurant having dinner. When the limit is reached for one person, the party is over because that individual stands up and gets ready to leave. Before long, everyone else follows.

ADULTS FIDGET TOO

Take a good look around during your next staff meeting at school. You will see several people who are content to sit quietly. See, though, if you notice other adults who are "fidgeters," doing a variety of things throughout the meeting. There are the ever-present doodlers. Then are the foot jigglers and finger tappers. One person may be watching a window shade moving slightly in the breeze. Another person may be listening intently to the loud ticking of a watch. You may see at least one "multitasker" who is cutting triangles out of construction paper for a class activity. Someone else may be thumbing through a catalog, flagging items. A few may be grading papers. Sound familiar?

Might some of these behaviors be considered inappropriate during a meeting? Possibly. Does it mean that these individuals are not participating or listening? Not necessarily. Looks truly can be deceiving. All of the staff members mentioned may be able to give you an accurate account of the meeting despite the appearance of distraction.

FIDGETS WITH A PURPOSE

I had a fascinating experience in this regard when I attended a three-day business seminar. On the table near each person attending were three items: a small container of clay, a miniature slinky and putty in a plastic egg.

The instructor made no mention of the items at any time. After the first hour or so, I noticed that some individuals opened the clay and began to roll it into long snakes, sniffing that characteristic smell. You can be sure that it had been quite a while since these business leaders had smelled clay and played with it. A few other individuals absently stretched the putty or wadded it into a ball. I saw a few others working the slinky back and forth as they listened to the instructor.

Maybe it was the teacher in me, but I waited, as did a few other rather obedient souls, for the instructor to tell us to do something constructive with the materials. That directive never came. On the last day, I finally asked the seminar leader if I had missed "the good part." I wondered aloud if I had made a trip to the restroom and missed some amazing concept that involved these three tools.

He laughed, "I put them out because there are always people who need something to do. Over the years, I've learned that if I provide some options for everyone to touch and look at, people are more attentive, more comfortable, and they stay in the room. Without them, they get up more often and leave the room to get coffee or make a phone call."

What the seminar leader discovered from experience was the value of the fidget. Adults and children are often very similar in this regard. Are you a fidgeter? What works for you? Our students can be very creative in this department. If we do not provide or suggest something that is acceptable in our classroom, they will manage to meet this need in ways that we may find annoying or at least distracting.

I've always provided a basket of acceptable fidgets that students may use during class. The first reaction of many teachers is that we cannot teach when 25 or 30 students are playing with a wide array of "toys." The fact is 25 or 30 students will not need fidgets. It will be only a few. Calling a fidget a toy is really not accurate. It is meant to be a tool that can actually help the some students increase concentration.

KEY IDEA

If a fidget does become a toy and distracts the student, it defeats the purpose. It should be removed and the student must move on to another choice. A fidget is not the focus but is an item that a student handles unconsciously.

In this section of "Creature Comforts," several fidgets are mentioned. See which ones appeal to you, would be acceptable in your classroom, and would also appeal to your students. There are a variety of choices for the visual, auditory and kinesthetic learner. Pick and choose.

Because options for fidgeting span the ages, grade levels suggested are very broad. In fact, adults use many of the fidgets mentioned. Perhaps you can add several ideas of your own to the list!

Pipe Cleaners

Grades K–12

A pipe cleaner makes an excellent fidget because it is quiet and does not draw attention to the user. A student can twist it, bend it and wind it around a finger while participating in the class discussion.

Cellophane Tape

Grades 2–12

Tape rolled backward around an index finger makes a good tactile fidget. The individual can inconspicuously tap the tape with a thumb satisfying the need for movement. This suggestion came from a woman who discovered that it worked for her. She carried a small tape dispenser in her purse and used her fidget at meetings, religious services and events such as concerts where she would be sitting for any length of time. It helped her relax and no one else noticed.

Velcro®

Grades K–12

This material, mentioned for other uses earlier in "The Alternate Route," can also be used as a fidget. This three-dimensional material works well for tactile stimulation that some individuals find calming. Attach the fuzzy portion of Velcro® underneath a desk or table for a student to touch. Note that you may want to attach only the fuzzy part without the interlocking part that connects with it in actual use. This way you can avoid listening to "R-I-I-I-P! R-I-I-I-P!" throughout the class.

Water Bottles

Grades 2–12

A **water bottle** makes an effective fidget. When I mention this in a seminar, more than one teacher has asked if this has led to squirting, water fights and total mayhem.

The first step is to set the ground rules. Only *clear* water bottles with pull-up tops will be allowed to avoid spills. Of course, any squirting results in the water bottle being removed from that student with no second chances. When can students fill it? Determine specific times for this. Only water is allowed in the bottles for obvious reasons. We don't want them filling up on caffeine during class.

From the perspective of promoting good health, the water bottle is a way to encourage students to drink more water. Aren't all of us supposed to drink several glasses each day? Also, it is preferable that students chew on the top of a water bottle than on the other common choices including sleeves, pencils or necklines of shirts. In fact, encouraging the use of a water bottle helped one fourth-grader who would unconsciously suck her thumb when under stress. When she had the water bottle, she chewed on the top instead. It was socially acceptable and it worked.

☞ **The Practical Pointer:**
As you would expect, many of the students bring a water bottle to class when it is first suggested. What typically happens is that interest drops quickly. It is not too long before only a few students keep a water bottle on their desks. This is the pattern with most fidgets. Only those students who really need these tools remain interested.

The Stress Ball

Grades 2–12

At the checkout counter of many stores, you can purchase a commercially made "stress ball." For both adults and students, clutching and squeezing the stress ball reduces stress during a variety of situations. Taking tests, reading aloud and being called on to answer are just some of the situations that can provoke feelings of stress in school. For some students, squeezing a stress ball helps them relax.

HOW TO MAKE IT:

In the classroom, I have found that students enjoy making their own stress balls by using balloons filled with flour, salt, rice or sand. Create a funnel by cutting off several inches from the top of a plastic soda bottle. Stretch a 12-inch helium-quality balloon over the lip of the funnel. Pour the material of choice through the funnel to fill the balloon lightly.

☞ **The Practical Pointer:**

Have students stand over a sink to do this. Students should not blow up the balloon because it will weaken the fabric. The stress ball will be small. I like to add a tablespoon of vegetable oil to the balloon before tying it closed. When the student is kneading the balloon, the oil moves around coating the material inside. In the event of a puncture, the dampened material is less likely to create much of a mess.

O⚿ KEY IDEA

Please note that some students are allergic to latex. These students should not come into contact with latex balloons. To avoid skin rashes, check with parents and the school nurse before using.

Doodle Pad

Grades 2–12

When I observed a high science class not long ago, I watched as the teacher gave each student a copy of the study guide entitled *Ecological Systems of the World*. Before you could say Jack Robinson, one student near me had immediately filled in every "O" in the title and had decorated the corner of his study guide with snow-topped mountains and a skier swooshing down the hill.

I ask you, is this student a doodler? We have all had them in class. They draw, doodle, decorate and create cartoons. This may not have been a problem on a study guide but the student could not or should not decorate his textbooks the same way.

Offering students the option of keeping a doodle pad handy on the corner of the desk meets this need. Local businesses often give away small pads of paper for advertising purposes. I collect them and pass them to students for doodling.

Doodle Along

Grades 3–12

Here is a quick tip to use whenever you are reading aloud to your students. Invite anyone to "doodle along" on scratch paper as you read. It helps many students focus and increases concentration. In fact, if we do not provide an acceptable place to draw, doodlers will find an alternative outlet on their hands, the desk or the edge of the text.

Paper Clip

Grades 3–12

A fidget can be as simple as a paper clip. You know the twisted paper clips that we find near the phone at home or on the floor? They are usually the work of a fidgeter. A paper clip can be offered as a fidget, especially for older students who would never choose an item that would single them out from others.

Elastic Fidgets

Grades 1–7

Another simple fidget is a rubber band. For a student who needed something quiet to do during discussions, I have offered the wrapped elastics designed to use on hair. The student would stretch it in different directions but pay close attentive and make pertinent comments on the topic. A teacher asked me, "Just exactly how long did the student play with the elastic before shooting it across the room?" For this student, that never happened. I can think of other students for whom a rubber band would only lead to disaster.

The fidget has to fit the student. Ground rules need to be clear ahead of time. If a student shoots the elastic, that is the end of it.

☞ **The Practical Pointer:**
As with so many things, it is all in how an idea is presented. I continually stress with students that we all learn in different ways with different tools. Fidgets are learning tools for some individuals who concentrate better while using them. When we as teachers make the option available to anyone who is interested, the use of fidgets becomes acceptable to the group. In the process we are also increasing students' understanding of different learning needs.

Fabric Fidgets

Grades K–5

A basket of small fabric swatches creates a variety of tactile fidgets. Pieces of corduroy, velvet, silk, terry cloth and other fabrics can be available for students to select and touch. The fabric fidget is unobtrusive, offers limitless choices, and will not disturb others.

"Chomper"

Grades 3–5

Most people would not think of the staple remover as an impromptu tool for a fidgeting student. Quite by accident, it became a favorite fidget for Chad, a third-grader, who picked up it when he was standing next to his teacher's desk. As the teacher explained a word problem in his math assignment, Chad listened as he continuously squeezed the staple remover. Chad took **"Chomper"** back to his desk and made it his personal pet. Whenever he felt the urge to wiggle, Chad "worked" the staple remover.

Postage Stamp Moistener

Grades K–3

When we need postage stamps, most of us purchase the peel-and-stick variety for daily use. There are, however, inexpensive postage stamp moisteners still available in office supply stores. I mention them for several handy uses, one of which falls within the fidget category.

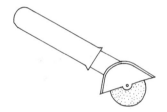

The postage stamp moistener is basically a tube that can be removed and filled with water. It is then attached to a small wheel that is a sponge. As the wheel is rolled over postage stamps, it moistens them and is a great alternative to licking.

I had a student who needed a fidget on the spur of the moment. Other attempts to redirect his fidgeting behavior had failed in the past. I emptied the water from the postage stamp moistener and handed it to him. It worked. He liked to roll the wheel back and forth in his hand. The tactile approach helped him relax when he felt agitated.

This tool would not be an option for some other students who would shred the foam wheel into smithereens in a matter of seconds. No one idea works for everyone!

☞ **The Practical Pointer:**
The primary reason that I had the postage stamp moistener in the classroom was not to moisten stamps but to erase small segments on an overhead transparency. It works well, far better than a spray bottle for erasing a single word or math problem.

Water Writing

Grades K–3

Still another use for the postage stamp moistener is for water writing. Fill the moistener with water. Give a student construction paper to "write on" or allow the student to write in water on the desk. Not only was this an effective fidget but also it cleaned the desk at the same time!

Beanbag Fidgets

Grades K–3

A small beanbag makes an excellent fidget because it is easy to make and is often already available in the elementary classroom. To avoid distracting others, the beanbag can be limited to use in a lap or pocket.

Woven Balls

Grades K–5

The small woven balls filled with seeds or pebbles are other options for fidgets. They appeal to students because the balls can be manipulated and offer tactile interest. Many students already own these and are delighted to bring them out at specified times.

Clay

Grades K–4

Consider including a small chunk of clay in a container of fidgets. It can be squeezed, shaped, rolled and stretched. Clay normally does not create much of a distraction because it is not new or unusual. Other students typically will ignore it.

Small Sponge

Grades K–3

Like clay, a small sponge can be squeezed repeatedly and can be helpful when a student may be experiencing stress during an assessment. Clutched in the hand, it is not visible to others, making it another effective choice for older students.

The Pocket Fidget

Grades K–5

Small toys from children's meals at fast food restaurants can be effective **Pocket Fidgets**. Student may choose one at the beginning of class but there is one rule: *Keep it in your* *pocket or under the desk*. It is out of sight but can occupy a student during a story or discussion without interfering with listening.

Visual Fidget

Grades K–12

The lava lamp has made a comeback not only as décor but also as a visual fidget. Have you considered adding a lava lamp to your classroom? Although it may not have crossed your mind, it is an option. The random movement of the shapes in the lava lamp can be relaxing and helps some students concentrate. These students will watch the bubbles move and reconfigure into various shapes while they are listening to a novel being read aloud or discussing the causes of the Civil War.

The lava lamp is to the visual learner what the stress ball is to the kinesthetic learner. It provides a visual focus that can actually *assist* in concentration rather than *distract*.

The visual fidget need not be electric. You can purchase small plastic desktop containers that may feature a boat rocking gently in blue water. You have seen these in gift stores. Perhaps you already have one at home. Consider placing it on the edge of your desk. Watch your students. Some will be mesmerized.

How To Make It:

Your students may enjoy making their own visual fidgets with clear plastic water bottles, food coloring, oil, water and small objects such as Monopoly game pieces. Experiment a bit with the amount of oil.

With the top screwed on tightly, the student can turn the bottle upside down and watch the object inside slide slowly down to the bottom. Once a student is pleased with the effect, use permanent glue to seal the top onto the bottle.

As with the other fidgets, only some of the students will use their visual fidget on a regular basis. For others, it will be a creative project to make but interest in the fidget will subside quickly.

Secret Signal

Grades K–5

If a student distracts others by tapping, humming or making other noises, it makes sense to establish a secret signal. For one student, I would make eye contact and then touch my earlobe. That served as our secret signal to stop tapping, snapping his fingers or discontinue some other behavior. Often that gentle reminder was all that was needed.

Gum

Grades 4–6

Gum is prohibited in most schools for obvious reasons. There are exceptions to every rule and the rule banning gum may be circumvented for certain students in certain situations. I am thinking about individuals who hum as they work, for example. They are unaware that they are humming and are a source of annoyance to people around them. You may know an adult who hums. Suggest chewing gum. It is difficult to hum and chew gum simultaneously!

Students may make other noises as well. One little boy continuously made the sound of a sprinkler that oscillates while shooting spurts of water. Ch-ch-ch-ch-chu! Ch-ch-ch-ch-chu! He was completely unaware that he was doing this.

Chewing gum became the remedy in this situation too. Try using the secret signal technique first to make the student aware of the behavior. When this achieves only limited results, a stick of gum may be the solution.

Sunflower Seeds

Grades 3–6

Eating shelled sunflower seeds is an alternative to gum for the student who makes verbal noises. Some teachers find this idea more palatable, shall we say. In addition to managing verbal sounds, I have used sunflower seeds successfully to discourage a student from chewing on pencils, wads of paper and her hair.

As the teacher, you will determine, of course, what is acceptable and appropriate in your classroom at your particular grade level. Sunflower seeds, for example, would not be an option for some teachers under any circumstances. Other teachers are comfortable with food in the classroom and, depending on the situation, may find sunflower seeds a good choice.

⚷ KEY IDEA

There is not a right way or a better way. These suggestions for fidgets are meant to provide many different options. Choose and use.

Kick It

Grades 2–5

Do you have students who continually kick the leg of the desk in front of them? Again, students are often unaware that the *Kick! Kick! Kick!* can be distracting and annoying.

One elementary teacher found a reasonable solution. She purchased very wide **rubber bands** at an office supply store and placed one between the metal legs on the front of each desk. Students could kick the rubber band as much as they wished and not make a sound.

Bungee Cord Sanity

Grades 2–5

A **bungee cord** wrapped around the legs of the desk also offers a quick solution if kicking chair legs is a problem that is limited to just a few students in the classroom. Bungee cords are more expensive than rubber bands but are much more durable. Wrap the cord around the legs of the desk, creating a "U" shape. The strategy will meet the needs of the "kickers" without distracting other students.

Rotate the Desk

Grades 1–5

Some students find a variety of personal fidgets to choose from by digging around in their desks. Desks that open toward the student can offer so many distractions that the student is not participating in the class activity. There is a sensible solution. Just turn the desk around so that the opening faces out. To reach anything inside, a student would have to get up walk around to the other side. Very few students will take this route.

Close the Drawer

Grades 1–5

Another solution to the distraction of the open desk is to add a cardboard drawer. Cut a box to fit the opening so that it acts like a drawer that slides in and out. It is actually much easier to find things when they are needed in a drawer that pulls out. When the drawer is closed, the contents are not available.

O—⚷ KEY IDEA

It is highly unlikely that all 25 or 30 students in any one classroom will have a need for a fidget. By making it an option for anyone at specified times, the fidget becomes an acceptable choice. No one is singled out. The use of a fidget is neither strongly encouraged nor is it strongly discouraged. Just as that business instructor provided the choices for adults attending a seminar, we need to provide choices for our students in our classrooms.

NOMADIC LEARNERS

What about those students who just get up and take a little field trip around the room during class? This happens at all grade levels. Some students seem to have a need to wander. They get up and take for a short break. They may sharpen a pencil or ask for a Hall Pass. Some teachers have said, "I cannot possibly have 30 students wandering around my classroom!"

Just as it unlikely that all 30 students will be using fidgets, it is equally unlikely that everyone will be cruising the room. If we build in enough movement during the class period, students will be less likely to move on their own.

There are several strategies to try with the young nomads depending on the grade level and needs of the individual student.

Masking Tape

Grades 1–3

A quick idea to use with a student who continually gets up and wanders is to create a masking tape boundary. A generous square on the floor surrounding the student's desk sets the clear limit for "travel." Clarify times when the student can get up and move about within bounds but not go beyond the tape.

Mini Field Trip

Grades 1–5

There are students who need to leave the classroom at times. To take care of this, more than a few teachers have developed a sudden urge to send a messenger to the office. An eager student is out the door with a quickly written note.

The school secretary probably receives one or two of these nonurgent messages every day. A first grade teacher mentioned that she has used this simple strategy for so many years now that she uses a special blue envelope for the purpose. The secretary sees the blue envelope and knows the drill: Greet the student, initial a piece of paper and send the messenger back.

After a quick field trip, the student is able to settle down and join the rest of the class.

A Home Away from Home

Grades 1–5

The nomadic learner cannot sit in any one location for a significant amount of time. If you have the luxury of an extra desk in your classroom or can locate one in a storage room, the spare desk can become an optional seating choice. You can explain to the student, "If you would like to change seats for awhile, you are invited to leave your home base and sit in your second home. If you choose to do this, you need to participate in the activities and do your work." It is amazing how revitalizing a change of scene can be!

Weighted Vest

Grades K–5

Here's a tip that comes from a hair salon. Whenever I have my hair cut, the stylist covers me with a plastic cape and places a lightly weighted collar over my shoulders. The purpose is to hold the cape down away from my neck during the haircut. It feels like someone is pressing gently on my shoulders. It is a very calming and relaxing experience.

Some of our students feel that same way while wearing a **weighted vest**. It is not particularly heavy but it is an effective tool. It has the same calming effect and is a comforting reminder for some younger children who need help staying in their seat.

☞ **The Practical Pointer:**

To make an inexpensive weighted collar or vest, use an existing vest and sew some metal washers into the lining. Test it. It should feel comfortable, not heavy.

Lap Buddy

Grades K–3

Similar to the weighted vest but less conspicuous is the **Lap Buddy**. This is simply a five-pound bag sewn closed after being filled with sand, small pebbles or another material. It is spread comfortably across the lap as a quiet signal for younger students to stay with the group, or in the desk or on the carpet. When it is time to get up, the Lap Buddy is put away.

The Office

Grades 1–5

Dave Kollitz, a fourth grade teacher, shared this strategy with me. He has used it for years, he told me, with great success. He acquired an extra student desk, moved it to the side of the room and named it **The Office**. He made a sign with the words "Occupied" on one side and "Unoccupied" on the other.

He never *sends* anyone to **The Office** as a punishment. Instead, students *choose* to go there when it is unoccupied for some quiet time.

This simple strategy significantly reduced behavior problems in Mr. Kollitz's classroom. Often when a conflict was developing, one student would walk over to **The Office**, flip the sign to

"Occupied," and take a "time out" without missing any of the lesson. Students knew when they needed a breather from peers, noise and activities. Before **The Office** was an option, students had more frequent outbursts and experienced more difficulty in the classroom.

Mr. Kollitz grinned as he told me that on more than one occasion, he would have liked to go to **The Office** and flip that sign to "Occupied."

Exercise Bike

Grades 2–5

A middle school teacher had a rather novel approach to dealing with nomadic learners. She brought her exercise bike to school. After all, she wasn't using it, she said. During times when the class was reading, she invited anyone to take a turn and peddle away. There was a bookrack on the front next to the water bottle holder. It was a very nice set up.

At first, *everyone* wanted a turn. It was quite a novelty. It wasn't long, though, before only a few students were interested in riding the bike. This is typical. If we offer the opportunity to all students with little fanfare and mention that this might help some students concentrate, we usually find that after a while, only those students who need it continue using it.

QUICK TIPS FOR CREATURE COMFORTS

Comfortable Cardholders

Grades K–2

Here is a simple way to create cardholders for playing cards or flash cards so that young children can hold them easily. This strategy is equally effective for students who have difficulty with fine-motor skills. Use two round margarine tub lids joined outside to outside by a metal brad through the center. Children can grasp the tool "clam style" and slide the cards between the lids. Cards will be held securely even when turned upside down.

Game Box Tip

Grades K–2

Make another version of a cardholder by inverting a game box with a lid. Cards will fit easily along the sides in the space created between the bottom and lid of the box. Once cards are in place, hands are free and each card is clearly visible.

After a While, Crocodile

Grades K–2

This technique helps students wait until a later time to share a story or show something from home that is unrelated to the current activity. Create a poster in the shape of a crocodile. When a child interrupts an activity to "tell" about something, put the student's name on a sticky note and ask the child to place it on the crocodile.

When there are a few free minutes before recess or while waiting in line to go to lunch, the teacher removes a name from the crocodile and asks the student to share the story. Some students will have forgotten what seemed so important earlier. Just knowing that they will have an opportunity to share **After a While, Crocodile**, allows young children to refocus on the current task.

SUMMARY

One size truly does not fit all when it comes to "Creature Comforts." Just as comfort is always a factor for adults, comfort matters for students. Part of differentiating instruction is recognizing that just as we need to provide choices for students within parameters of learning content, we must also provide choices in other aspects of learning.

Different students have different tolerance levels for noise, different preferences for sitting or standing, different needs for fidgeting and different ways of focusing. Celebrating these differences does not "water down," diminish, lower standards, or compromise expectations. On the contrary, celebrating differences in individual preferences enriches the learning environment and spurs creativity.

In order to be irreplaceable, one must always be different.

–Coco Chanel

10

EXPECT THE BEST

It's a funny thing about life; if you refuse to accept anything but the best, you very often get it.

—W. Somerset Maugham

> *I am convinced that life is 10% what happens to me*
> *and 90% how I react to it.*
> —*Charles Swindoll*

As part of being accountable, our students must see the direct relationship between action and consequences. Our goal is to teach that relationship but also to provide numerous opportunities to make good choices in a variety of situations. We must expect the best. When we do, more often than not, we will get it.

Nowhere is there a more direct relationship between action and consequence than in receiving a speeding ticket. I was reminded of this the time my college son was pulled over by flashing lights while driving to a ski area during spring break.

When the phone rang and our son was on the other end of the line, we were surprised. It was not his habit to call and check on the folks back home the day after leaving. Was everything all right? He assured us that everything was going fine.

Then he paused. There was one thing . . . that would be the matter of a speeding ticket. The reason he called was not so much to tell us about the $90 fine but to see what we could do about it.

We wondered aloud exactly what that might be. We also wondered why he thought this should become our problem. Not only was our son incensed that his spring break savings had just been severely depleted, but the circumstances were almost too much for him to bear. To hear him tell it, the situation was so unfair! He was pulled over while driving *down a hill* and in a friend's car that *just crept up* when he wasn't used to it. What really irked our son was that he thought that *they didn't give tickets in Montana!* (They do.)

"Can't you do something? Can't you call somebody?" Sean pleaded.

We paused and assured him that no, we could *not do* anything nor could we *call* someone. (What exactly did he think we would say if we had any idea whom to call?) We told him there was nothing *we* could do but what *he* should do immediately was to pay the ticket. There was one more thing, we told him. If the insurance rates went up later, he could pay that bill, too.

It was a tough lesson. The consequences were swift and severe. The good news is that he has watched his speed ever since.

When we can closely connect behavior to a logical consequence, the more effective the consequence will be. This chapter is not about consequences alone; it is about giving our students chances to feel proud of themselves by making good choices. It is about using strategies, tips, tools and techniques that focus on the positive yet hold the student accountable for actions.

"Expect the Best" is divided into six categories:

- Circumventing the Problem
- Interventions
- Managing Behavior
- Student Involvement
- Peer Power
- Focus on the Positive

CIRCUMVENTING THE PROBLEM

Courtesy for All

Grades K–12

While most people do not consult Emily Post for etiquette today, one thing that has not gone out of style is courtesy. When all members of the learning community of any age use words that reflect common courtesy and respect, the atmosphere is more conducive to positive behavior.

Please

Thank you

Excuse me

I'm sorry

May I . . .

I appreciate . . .

Would you be willing . . .

Students and teachers alike should expect to hear these words and others like them on a regular basis. Courtesy ensures that everyone is treated kindly with mutual respect. The same is true of language. Everyone has a right to expect appropriate language. As one teacher tells her students, "This is your place of work, your place of employment. Certain language is acceptable in the workplace. You cannot say certain things here."

Avoiding Escalation

Grades K–12

This strategy actually works backward by understanding what has triggered negative behavior in the past. Common triggers include academic frustration, waiting for help, boredom, lack of control over the situation, lack of choice in activities and personality conflicts. There are also environmental triggers such as an overcrowded classroom, a room that may be too hot, noise, uncomfortable chairs or undesirable seating arrangements.

Once there is an understanding of the triggers, it may be possible to adjust some factors to prevent some of the negative behavior in the future. For factors that cannot be changed, help may be provided for the student in anticipating and dealing with those triggers in an acceptable way.

Location! Location! Location!

Grades 1–12

Many times we provide preferential seating for a student who has issues with behavior and who is also easily distracted. Often our choice is front and center, right in the thick of things. Sometimes that works. More often than not, that location exacerbates the problem. There are often more auditory and visual distractions here than in any other location in the room.

There can be just too much to look at for a student who is sitting near the teacher's desk. This same student may be more likely to engage in attention-seeking behaviors in the midst of activity. Seated back a few rows, surrounded by students who are typically highly motivated and on-task can be a better choice. The other students act as role models and will not encourage the negative behavior.

Students with behavior issues often need help staying on task. Consider seating them away from distractions. A study carrel can be a good option at times. It reduces the opportunity to touch, listen and watch things that will take the child away from the task at hand.

I am reminded of Tyler, a highly distractible second-grader, who tended to act out. He focused best away from distractions. Unfortunately, his second grade classroom was highly stimulating in every way with colorful bulletin boards and a myriad of things dangling from the ceiling. "Mrs. Tilton," Tyler confided, "there's no place to give my eyes a rest."

☞ **The Practical Pointer:**
Placing a desk near a section of the wall that is blank, a bulletin board with just a few items or a corner of the room with nothing hanging from the ceiling can have a calming effect on students like Tyler.

Visit a Teacher

Grades 3–6

At times when a student is agitated, it can be helpful for the student to leave the room for a few minutes and "cool off" in a different classroom. A simple solution is to set up a reciprocal arrangement with another teacher for these situations. Teachers have agreed ahead of time that students can "visit" each other's classrooms until they are calm and ready to return. I found that this strategy worked best when the teachers involved taught different grade levels.

The student leaving third grade would be more likely to regain composure quietly in a fifth grade classroom than at the same grade level. Likewise, the fifth grade student would sit quietly in the third grade room.

☞ **The Practical Pointer:**

The purpose is not to call attention to the visitor but to give both teacher and student a breather from dealing with the behavior. For the student, having a safe place to go outside of the classroom was often a relief. Sometimes students I worked with knew that they needed a breather and asked if they could take a short break.

Choices, Choices, Choices

Grades K–12

Differentiating instruction celebrates individual differences and recognizes that there are all different types of learners. Choice is an integral part of the process within the larger framework of the overall theme. When a student has options, there can be a substantial reduction in negative behavior.

The choices may be as small as which of two activities to do *first* or whether to use a word processor instead of writing a paragraph. There is much power entrusted to the student when we present options in the form of choices to be made. In themselves, the choices will not affect the learning outcomes or the content of a unit. For the student, though, the ability to make choices within the classroom setting is extremely important.

☞ **The Practical Pointer:**

Adults make dozens of choices every day. We often take this autonomy for granted. Students feel empowered and in control of the situation when they learn that, even though certain things must be done, there is room for choice within specified parameters.

Tranquil Lighting

Grades K–12

A quick tip to help students relax and reduce stress is to turn off the lights for a few minutes. It can help everyone unwind, even the teacher. Turning off the lights changes the atmosphere while creating a sense of tranquility.

☞ **The Practical Pointer:**

When the fluorescent lights in a classroom are too bright and garish, they make the room unpleasant. Students feel edgy. I am sure that I am not the only teacher who has asked the custodian to come in with a ladder and remove a few of the light bulbs throughout the room. It changes the effect.

INTERVENTIONS

Sit Down

Grades K–12

A quick tip for dealing with a student's behavior is to sit down to talk with a student. This position enables the teacher to meet the student at or near eye level. It prevents the teacher from towering over the student who may then feel so defensive that the behavior worsens.

○—ⁿ KEY IDEA

Avoid making a small problem bigger.

"I" Statements

Grades K–12

In any relationship, but especially when conflict may be involved, beginning any statement with "I" will generally be received in a much more positive vein than beginning with "you." Compare these two sets of comments.

> "*I* need you to listen to me."

>> instead of:

> "*You* must listen to me."

> "*I* need you to sit down now."

>> instead of:

> "*You* sit down now!"

The use of "you" puts the listener on the defensive immediately. The use of "I" focuses attention on what the speaker needs and wants. It can be more effective with our most challenging students to use the "I" centered approach and switch the focus to our own needs.

The implied "you" has the same negative effect as stating it. When we deal with students, our first reaction, as teachers, may be to use the abrupt version:

> "Sit down."

"Be quiet."

"Stop that."

"Eyes on me."

Changing to "I" statements makes the same command less confrontational. We are clearly not providing a choice, but how it is stated makes a difference.

Masking Tape Strips

Grades K–5

When a certain negative behavior is being targeted, it can be monitored by this strategy. Tear several short strips of masking tape and place them along the edge of the student's desk. The number of strips depends on the grade level of the student, the length of time involved, and the demands of the particular situation. There may be five; there may be three. The student's goal is to keep all of the strips for the designated time frame.

They serve as a wordless reminder of the targeted behavior. If a problem occurs, the teacher can quietly remove one of the strips from the desk. A second incident results in the removal of another strip of tape. Students need to know clearly what behavior will result in the loss of tape. In any situation involving behavior, there should be no surprises.

At the end of the designated time, the student or teacher records the number of *success strips*. If the student maintains the desirable behavior without losing all of the strips on a given day, there may a reward or simply a verbal compliment. The goal is to reduce the number of reminder strips so that, ultimately, the student no longer needs the visual cue.

☞ **The Practical Pointer:**
> If some students do not cooperate with the strategy by pulling all the strips off their desks, try Plan B—place the masking tape strips within view of the student but out of reach on the teacher's desk.

Stop Sign

Grades K–5

A simple technique to stop negative behavior is to use a small red **stop sign** mounted on a craft stick. Without saying a word or interrupting the flow of the lesson, the teacher can quietly make eye contact with a student and hold the **stop sign** just high enough for the student to see it.

The **stop sign** can also be useful when the teacher is circulating about the room as students are working in groups or individually. Just clip it to a clipboard that the teacher may carry to make notes and, again, hold it up near a student or group of students who are acting out. It serves as a first warning to change the behavior.

Point of Light

Grades 6–12

One high school teacher told me that his version of the **stop sign** for secondary students was to use a laser beam. He aimed it at the desktop of a student who was talking or was otherwise distracted. The **point of light** dancing on the desk usually got the student's attention.

O—⚷ KEY IDEA

The teacher mentioned that he was very cautious, as anyone would be, to make sure that the laser was directed downward and not into anyone's eyes.

Proximity

Grades K–12

One of the first techniques that every new teacher learns from experience is managing behavior by proximity. The more frequently we stand *near* students who act out, the better they behave. When we move throughout the room on a constant basis, we can easily approach any student who is acting out. Without a word, that proximity can be enough of a deterrent to continuing the behavior.

When I first started teaching I was given an old bit of advice that rings true today: *Out of your seat and on your feet.* Keep moving. One of the pluses in a co-taught classroom is the presence of *two* adults who stay in close proximity to students who need them.

Agitation Box

Grades K–5

A technique to help students manage stress and calm down when they are upset is using the **Agitation Box**. It can be a mid-sized plastic storage bin or shoebox that contains several items that are age-appropriate:

- clay

- sponge to squeeze

- a small soft ball

- elastic to stretch

- watercolor paints and paintbrush
- paper and markers or crayons
- small CD player and instrumental music and headphones
- quiet headphones without music
- gum, hard candy or sunflower seeds, if acceptable and appropriate
- computer disks of calming activities
- books and stories on tape
- glue stick, construction paper and blunt-nosed scissors

Location matters. Invite the student to go to a quiet place in a study carrel or relax in a carpeted area where there is comfortable furniture. Another option is to allow the student to go to a designated location outside the classroom. An adult should always accompany the child if the child is extremely agitated.

☞ **The Practical Pointer:**
Before giving the **Agitation Box** to a student, examine contents for any items that are not appropriate or could be dangerous, such as hard candy, for certain students.

Anger Writing

Grade 6–12

A quick tip for older students who are upset is to encourage **Anger Writing**. It is simple, safe and effective. After giving students paper and a pencil, I tell them, "Write whatever you would like to say to that person, whomever it is—friend, teacher, parent, coach, team-mate . . . It is all right to be so angry that you want to *say* those words aloud, but don't. Writing it all down will help. Then tear it up! You will not ever give that piece of paper to that person and I will never read it."

☞ **The Practical Pointer:**
Be sure to watch as that paper is torn to smithereens.

Send Later

Grades 6–12

Most people use e-mail today on a daily basis. In many ways, it saves time. Unfortunately, it also allows an individual to type an angry message and hit the *Send* button before thinking through the ramifications of doing so. Just as students can use **Anger Writing** as a tool to express anger without actually delivering the message, they can also be reminded to always consider the **Send Later** option with highly charged e-mail. **Send Later** is like a safety valve. It gives the writer the opportunity to consider the impact and repercussions of sending the e-mail. Once sent, there is no second chance to take back the angry words.

Anger Drawing

Grades 2–5

An effective technique for younger students is **Anger Drawing**. Provide paper and crayons, markers or pencils and encourage students to draw continuously until the agitation disappears. Some students scribble in circles, not drawing anything discernable, other students draw a picture of the situation including people and objects.

The goal is similar to that of **Anger Writing**. In a safe atmosphere, students can vent the anger in a way that does not create more problems or accelerate the conflict.

One-on-One Time

Grades K–12

A middle school teacher had a student who was routinely disrupting her physical education class. She noticed one day after school that this same young man was extremely upset. When she asked what was wrong, the student told her that someone had opened the door to the darkroom in the photography lab and all of his photos had been ruined. Photography was his hobby and he had spent a lot of time in the lab. He wanted to know how someone could be so careless. How could someone do that?

The teacher listened intently. The student was angry. After agreeing that it was very frustrating and also agreeing that someone had been extremely inconsiderate, the teacher made this comment, "I think I know a little about how you feel right now. I spend a lot of time planning activities for my class. This is very important to me, just like your photography is important to you. When you come to my class and disrupt it, my plans fall apart. I also feel angry."

The student listened. They talked some more and the teacher realized that for the first time the student understood. From then on, he became the class helper.

This is a true story. The value of one-on-one time cannot be overestimated. That time together, combined with the honest exchange, made a significant difference in behavior. It is unlikely that every situation will work out so well. Wouldn't it be nice if it did?

MANAGING BEHAVIOR

Chart It!

Grades 4–12

As teachers, many of us insist that we ignore the negative and reward the positive when it comes to behavior. I wonder if we really do. Here is a technique to measure positive and negative interactions each week with a few targeted students.

Think about two or three students who currently "push your buttons." Highlight their names on the seating chart and keep it within reach during class. Every time there is an interaction with one of the students listed, indicate whether is it positive or negative. For each positive interaction, draw a plus sign near the student's name in the margin; if it is negative, add a minus.

At the end of the week, tally the pluses and minuses. Which number is higher? If there are more minuses, we may *think* that we are ignoring the negative, but we are reinforcing it. That self-fulfilling prophecy has just gotten stronger. This can be an eye-opener!

The Instant Replay

Grades 3–12

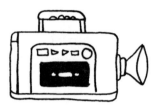

I have used a video camera in the classroom for several different strategies mentioned in other chapters. Cooperative group work was often videotaped so that we could analyze the group process afterward. In that situation, we talked about what worked well, what presented some difficulties, and set some goals for the next group task.

The video camera can also be an effective tool for managing behavior. It gives you an opportunity to "catch them being good," as the saying goes, and captures it on video to prove it. Using the camera unobtrusively, you can videotape your students doing the right thing. Show them the proof later. Students are pleased to see their positive behavior on video and it can be extremely reinforcing.

"Good for you, Dustin! Watch what a great job you were doing as the recorder in your cooperative group. Look! See that? You waited and gave other people a chance to share their opinions. You were terrific! I thought you'd like to see how you looked. Congratulations! I'm proud of you!"

Improving the View

Grades 3–12

Another way that I used the video camera was to record behavior that needed to be addressed as part of a behavior plan. For example, when a middle school student was creating significant problems in my class, I wanted to involve the parent. I knew, though, that if the parent came to observe, the student certainly was not going to behave that way on that particular day.

While videotaping a segment of the lesson for students who were absent, I "caught" the negative behavior on tape. I requested that the parent and the eighth-grader come in together and watch the video.

There were two significant benefits to this strategy. The first was that the student seemed surprised by his own behavior on tape. He had no idea how his behavior *looked* to his peers. Watching himself helped him realize that his attention-getting behavior came across as immature and silly. Afterward, he made an effort to tone it down. Increased parental support was the second benefit. A phone call and just talking about it would not have had the same impact as viewing it.

Middle School Punch Power

Grades 5–8

In a middle school that I visited, I noticed that classroom behavior on the Blue Team was monitored by a punch card system. Students moved as a group from one core class to another. As they entered the classroom, one student handed the teacher the class set of note cards on a large key ring.

When I asked about it, I learned that the cards had the names of all of the students in the group. During class, the cards were kept on the teacher's desk. If a student acted out, the teacher thumbed though the ring of cards and used an ordinary paper punch to "record" the infraction.

Students worked toward group goals and individual goals. The team earned popcorn and other rewards when the total number of round holes punched in all classes went down from the previous week. Some individuals were also working on personal goals to reduce round punches. The teacher did not say a single word to the group; punching a card sent a strong nonverbal message. This simple strategy also generated peer pressure for positive behavior so that the entire group could enjoy a reward at the end of the week.

☞ **The Practical Pointer:**
The Blue Team received a new set of cards every Monday so that each week represented a fresh start and a new opportunity to make positive choices.

The Star Punch

Grades 5–8

The round paper-punched holes in the previous description indicated *negative* behavior. The Blue Team also had star-shaped punches that were earned for exceptional behavior on the *positive* side. For example, students earned a **Star Punch** for making an extra effort to help a student who was struggling or for exhibiting exemplary behavior during a cooperative group activity or for making significant progress toward a personal behavior goal.

☞ **The Practical Pointer:**
A **Star Punch** offset a negative punch. Any student could atone for negative behavior by making a conscious choice to do something positive.

Write It Down

Grades K–12

Even the palest ink is better than the most retentive memory.

–Old proverb

Ask hallway monitors, playground supervisors and teachers on lunchroom duty to carry a notebook. An effective and efficient strategy to reduce undesirable behavior is to record the incident immediately when it occurs. Just seeing the notebook acts as a deterrent. Write down what happened on the spot. Have the students involved read it. Tell them, "This is what I saw. This is how I am reporting it."

This is not an invitation to discuss or dispute the written record. That is not the purpose. Students can present their side later in the office or during peer mediation. The purpose is simply to record what happened from the perspective of the adult in charge. Writing it down has tremendous impact and carries significant weight in dealing with the situation.

Photo Collateral

Grades 4–8

Students begin class with a laminated photo on the edge of the desk. If a students needs to borrow a pencil, the photo is used for collateral. If the student acts out, the student turns in the photo as collateral until it is earned back by positive behavior. At the end of the class period, a bonus point is awarded to any student who has not used the photo as collateral.

Random Points

Grade 4–12

Maria Ramirez, a middle school social studies teacher, uses a behavior strategy that takes only moments but is very effective. Before she begins each of her five classes, she draws one card from a stack. Each card has 0–10 points written on it. The cards are face down and she does not look at the card selected.

Students know that she has randomly selected the number of extra credit behavior points that can be earned by every student that day. The opportunity is there to earn those points but the responsibility lies with each student.

During class, Mrs. Ramirez jots down the names of students who disrupt, sleep or prevent other students from learning. At the end of the hour, Mrs. Ramirez turns over the card. Every student who cooperated, participated, and showed effort will earn the extra points. It is not about an "A" paper or getting a good score. It is all about attitude and effort.

A student assistant records the points in the grade book. Admittedly, the system is subjective and, if there is any doubt, Mrs. Ramirez awards the points. Her students like the system, she told me. "My students usually agree with me on points. They want our classroom to be a place where they can learn. They are frustrated in classes where students make learning impossible."

☞ **The Practical Pointer:**

A student who is absent cannot make up the behavior points. These points reflect behavior and attitude in class on a given day. The system encourages stellar attendance. Mrs. Ramirez commented, "My students tend to make their orthodontia appointments during their other classes . . ." As the saying goes, *must be present to win!*

Daily Points

Grades 6–12

I used a chart in my classroom for daily points that had nothing to do with academic points and everything to do with behavior, organization and effort. It is worth noting that when students began consistently earning their daily points, academic improvement was not far behind.

HOW IT WORKS:

If this technique appeals to you, it is easy to implement and monitor. Twelve points can be earned daily: 1 point for a bringing a pencil and 3 effort points for each "third" of the 48-minute class period.

Every student kept a point sheet on the corner of the desk during class. I focused on student responsibility and student ownership. It was their job to immediately record 1 point for a pencil or pen when they arrived. If they quickly borrowed one before class, they still earned the point. I wanted students ready to work.

KITCHEN TIMER

Monitoring was not complicated. One student set a basic kitchen timer for 18 minutes. When we heard the "ding!" students recorded their points. As a group, we operated on the honor system. I had the final say but generally a look or a shake of the head was all that was needed to admonish a student not to award any unearned points. It was a level playing field.

I also included a section for comments from the students as part of the self-evaluation. Absenteeism was recorded here as well as reasons for being out of the classroom part of the class period. Students could also make any comments about their points for the day or

Daily Points	Pencil	Part 1	Part 2	Part 3	Total	NAME _____
						Week of _____
Monday						
						comments
Tuesday						
						comments
Wednesday						
						comments
Thursday						
						comments
Friday						
						comments
					Weekly Total	

comments on the activities. They often complimented themselves on good days, "Great job!" or vented frustrations, "I just can't work in a group!"

SELF-MONITORING

Walking around the classroom, I was able to spot-check point sheets. When I started the system, I tried to keep the point sheets and award the point total myself each day. This worked when I taught small groups of students in a special education resource room setting but it was too cumbersome to work in a regular classroom. I switched to self-monitoring and found that it worked well.

Sporadically, there were group rewards such a "No Homework Night" or a popcorn break. The real reward came from each individual's point total for the quarter. I factored these points into the grade for daily work. These effort points could *raise* a student's grade one step. That could make a significant difference for some students in either making the honor roll or passing the class. It should be noted that I did not use the effort points in a punitive manner. Earning few points would never be used to *lower* an academic average. I wanted students to see effort points as a "boost" available to any student willing to put forth the effort.

Banking It!

Grades 6–9

Max Rosenberg, a ninth grade math teacher, told me that he had been feeling a certain amount of burnout after spending every day with ninth-graders. They frequently challenged his patience as only ninth-graders can. That all changed when he implemented the **Banking System** in his classes. In fact, he was astounded that such a simple strategy could have such tremendous impact on behavior!

HOW IT WORKS:

Everyone began class with $5 each day. There was no real money involved but Mr. Rosenberg discovered that cash, even when it is just pretend, motivated ninth-graders more than points. Everyone started with Five Bucks, as he referred to it. One student was the designated Banker for the month and kept a class list on the desk. That role earned the student extra pay.

During class, any infraction cost a student in the pocketbook. "That will be a buck, Jack," Mr. Rosenberg would say without stopping class. The Banker deducted $1 from Jack's cash for the day. Students knew the rules. Arriving late cost a dollar. Unfinished homework could get expensive.

IMMEDIATE GRATIFICATION

At the end of the month, there was an auction where students could spend their earnings.

Mr. Rosenberg went to the Dollar Store to find prizes and asked community members for small donations. Students could also bring in items for the auction. Candy, free time, soft drinks and coupons for local fast food were just some of the items in the auction. The teacher and students had fun during the event.

LONG-TERM REWARDS

Not every student spent all or even some of their earnings at the auction. The system allowed for this short-term reward but students could choose to save their money. At the end of the quarter, students with high earnings and a hefty savings account could spend it on a major purchase, such as extra credit points on the quarter test. If they had earned Five Bucks every single day during the quarter, they had the option of purchasing their daily work grade as their quarter grade. They did not have to take the quarter test.

Mr. Rosenberg noted that the students who earned and saved enough points to opt for the daily work grade were almost always those students who would do well on the quarter test anyway. His students were learning that choices needed to be made. Students were accountable for their earnings and took control of their own spending. There were many lessons learned.

Designated Rules

Grades K–12

Students need boundaries. They need rules—not fifty of them—but they need to know what is acceptable behavior in each classroom. When rules are limited in number and are posted clearly, students are more likely to follow them.

Some schools have universal rules that are the same in every classroom. In other schools, teachers determine their own. Some teachers create rules on an as-needed basis. Still others work with students to jointly determine what rules are needed to make that classroom run smoothly.

There is no single way to handle classroom rules, of course. What is important is that rules, once made, are clearly posted and consistently enforced.

The Unwritten Rules

Grades K–12

A tricky part of the "hidden curriculum" for many students at the middle and high school levels are the *assumed* or *unwritten rules*. These are in addition to the posted rules that are stated clearly.

A typical middle or high school student may see six to eight teachers in a given day. Classroom management and expectations for acceptable behavior in those six to eight classrooms may vary significantly.

Consider these examples, all of which I have observed in visiting classrooms in recent months. A student attends First Hour. The bell rings and it clearly signals: Be quiet and class begins. Second Hour is different. The bell rings and everyone is still chatting, including the teacher. A different noise level is tolerated and class begins eventually but not at the moment that the bell rings.

In Third Hour, the same student forgets a pencil and wants to go to the locker. In that class, the teacher says, "Go ahead." In another class, the teacher would have simply handed the student a pencil. In still another class, I heard a teacher say, "I guess you won't have anything to write with today."

Later in the day, a student talks to a friend during class. There does not appear to be a problem. The same student does the same thing in the following class and gets a detention, leaving the student to wonder, "What did I do?"

O—ʒ KEY IDEA

Most students quickly figure out the demands of this "hidden curriculum" when it comes to behavior. Some students, especially students with special needs, find this confusing. Teachers can help by clearly explaining both written and unwritten rules of each classroom.

☞ **The Practical Pointer:**

As teachers, we learn so much by observing not only our students, but also other teachers in our own buildings. Arrange to observe in several other classes during part of a day. Watch for the unwritten rules. It helps us understand the variation in classroom management styles and why going from class to class can present difficulties for some of our students.

Picture Rules

Grades K–3

Many teachers post classroom rules on the wall. A technique that works well for nonreaders is to create photo rules next to each rule. The picture is simply an example of the rule in the positive format. *Hands to Yourself* shows students standing near each other without touching. While this applies only to primary students, it is also a reminder to discuss with older students exactly what the rules mean.

Relaxation Tapes

Grades K–12

Have you ever tried using relaxation tapes for a few minutes each day in your classroom? Soothing music can help students unwind and can also reduce anxiety just before any type of assessment.

Other relaxation tapes use progressive muscle relaxation. This strategy helps the listener tighten and relax different groups of muscles beginning at the feet and moving upward. Just like the soothing music, progressive muscle relaxation is useful before any stressful situation and creates a calm atmosphere. I encourage students to try this strategy whenever they need extra help in feeling relaxed.

☞ **The Practical Pointer:**
These tapes can be so relaxing that the hardest part is for the teacher to remain alert!

Visualization

Grades 6–12

Another tool for managing behavior is visualization. This is an idea that some people find very effective as a calming device when they feel tense and upset. It does not take a lot of class time and, with practice, can take only moments. The teacher leads the class initially but gradually students learn to do this on their own.

In my own experience, I have begun by asking students to think of a place where they feel completely relaxed. Next I create a visual image for them of a place that I can picture such as a beautiful beach on a warm sunny day. Using all of the senses and a variety of descriptive words, I try to make the image come alive drawing the students into the scene.

After trying this together, I have encouraged older students to recall a place where they have been that suggests relaxation, peacefulness and tranquility. No one else has to be aware that they are doing this. Creating a very clear picture and seeing themselves in that place enables them to relax and then refocus on the task at hand.

STUDENT INVOLVEMENT

Greeting Committees

Grades K–12

I sat down with a group of teachers to discuss strategies that have worked for us in improving the climate and behavior of students in a building. One point we all agreed on was that schools with some form of greeting committees had students who consistently behaved better.

Perhaps the greeting committees contributed to a feeling of overall well-being in the building. Perhaps the greeting committees sent a message that everyone cared about each other in the learning community.

Of one thing we were sure, the greeting committee was an uncomplicated strategy that made a significant impact. As you think about the students you come into contact with daily, are there students who need consistency in their lives? For some of our students, we, their teachers, provide that consistency. The way we greet them can shape their day. Being acknowledged as they walk down the hall or enter a classroom or sit down with other students can make a world of difference.

At the secondary level, the greeting committee could be as simple as asking every teacher to stand in the doorway between classes and personally greet students. Even though many teachers typically use that time to prepare for the next class, time spent greeting students is invaluable. Many teachers do this every day. One high school teacher told me that he has done this for years.

He told me, "No one enters my classroom until we shake hands and make eye contact. The eyes truly are the windows to the soul. Some days I can tell that world history is far from being the most important thing going on in that young person's life that day . . ."

At the elementary level, some teachers offer their students a choice of the three "H's" as they arrive at school. Students know that they can choose to receive a:

- High Five   • Handshake   • Hug

O⟶🗝 KEY IDEA

Greeting students sends a clear message that we are glad that they are here at school. Imagine guests arriving in our own homes. We would all get up if we were seated, go to the door, greet them, make them feel welcome, and tell them how happy we are to see them.

School Ambassadors

Grades K–5

Another approach to the greeting committee at the elementary level is using **School Ambassadors**. Students sign up on a rotating basis to greet other students at the buses and in school entryways every day. From the moment a student arrives at school, that student is greeted with an enthusiastic, "Hello, _____. I'm glad you're here today!"

The Practical Pointer:

In some schools, the Parent Teacher Organization provides T-shirts with a logo on the front such as *Silver Oaks School Ambassador*. Ambassadors for the day stop in the office and pick up a shirt to wear while greeting students. The **Ambassadors** are easily identified and the shirts add prestige to the program.

Student Ushers

Grades 1–12

A dilemma faced by school staff everywhere is encouraging parents to attend school events. Too often the same parents come to Open House, conferences, or to hear speakers, and are present at student activities. Can you identify these parents in your school? While these parents are most welcome, the greater concern is reaching out to a wider audience and involving more parents, especially parents of students who struggle in school.

It makes sense that parents are more likely to attend school events when their own children are directly involved. Enlist students to act as ushers at events such as Open House and parent-teacher conferences. Elementary students can wear sandwich board signs and act as guides who direct parents to classrooms, take parents on school tours, and invite them to the cafeteria for coffee. They can assist with serving cookies and bars.

It can be a good idea to involve students who have behavior problems as ushers. Surrounded by adults, they probably will not act out. The positive role gives them a chance to shine and encourages their parents to attend.

Middle and high school students can assist at Open House by overseeing tables where parents pick up student schedules and nametags. They, too, can give school tours and serve refreshments.

At this level, students facilitate their own parent-student-teacher conference. Students can plan it, bring samples of work and manage the conference. Extra credit can be an incentive. Some teachers provide three points if a student attends and three more points if a parent also attends.

 The Practical Pointer:

The more student work and projects that are displayed during these events, the more likely it is that parents will attend. Photography and sculpture exhibits from art class, science projects, pictures from athletic events—any and all evidence that the school belongs to the students will entice parents to attend. That ownership transfers to parents in the form of home-school support.

Delegate a Job

Grades K–12

We never know how high we are till we are called to rise.

–Emily Dickinson

One of the best management strategies that I have used for students with behavior issues is delegating a job. Every student needs responsibility and a sense of purpose, something to create a connection to the school, a reason to show up and become a contributing member of the learning community.

Let me share an example. I was a mentor for a middle school teacher who was working on her master's degree in special education. We spent a lot of time discussing one of her students, Amelia, who was constantly disrupting every one of her classes. Amelia's classroom teachers were frustrated. Every teacher wanted her out of class. In fact, Amelia spent much more time in the office and in the special education resource room than in any classroom.

She was falling further and further behind academically. It was not that Amelia lacked ability. She was bright. But she had spent too much time out of the classroom during her elementary years and too much time in the resource room environment. Amelia needed the stimulation of the regular classroom. However, when Amelia attended class, her negative behavior diverted attention away from the content.

The school was providing as much help as possible. Amelia was receiving counseling and she had a behavior plan in place. The question was: Could Amelia learn to manage her behavior so that she could remain in the regular classroom setting? There was no question that her behavior was difficult.

There were glimpses, though, of a very kind, sensitive, hurting child who covered these qualities with much negative bravado. Amelia's special education teacher believed that there had to be a way to turn Amelia's behavior around.

After much discussion, we offered Amelia a "job." Would she like to spend a class period each day assisting at the elementary school with some of the students who had severe and profound disabilities? The building was located next door making access feasible. She jumped at the idea.

In that setting, Amelia was nothing short of amazing. Her best qualities surfaced immediately. For one class period each day, Amelia did not have to show off, act out or talk back. She was aching to feel important, needed and valued. In her new role, she was all of these. At times, Amelia was allowed to leave her classes early to help the elementary students. At the end of the school year, she wrote thank you notes to her teachers and asked if she could be part of the summer program.

The question many teachers would ask at this point is this: How was Amelia's behavior in her regular classes? In a word, better. She was not perfect. After all, she had had many years of practice on the negative side. No one changes overnight.

In fact, whenever Amelia would slip backward and be sent back to the office, the principal advocated taking away her job with the elementary students. "Make her earn it," the principal said. I strongly disagreed. "Don't take away the *one* thing that has worked for this child."

O⎯ KEY IDEA

If there is one thing that is working, build on it. It may be participating in a sport, drama, band, a club, or an after school job that provides a sense of purpose and a feeling of success. If that is taken away, what does the student have left?

PEER POWER

Peers Can Help

Grades 4–12

Think about what can happen when a disruptive student is assigned to a cooperative group. Sometimes other students groan, make comments, and turn away from that student. Behavior becomes worse under those circumstances. We need to teach peers effective ways to encourage good behavior by modeling positive comments and actions.

Peers set the standard and tone for what is acceptable behavior; teachers can use this powerful force in the classroom. I was reminded of the powers of peers when I was observing in a co-taught classroom. I had been told there were students with behavior disorders in that setting, but I could not identify the students. Everyone fit in and everyone participated.

It was only later when I was talking with the special education teacher in the resource room that a student came in, jumped up on top of a desk and sat with his feet on the chair. The teacher stopped and said, "What are you doing, Max? You didn't behave like this in history class. Why are you behaving like this in my classroom?"

"This is special ed," Max replied. Very telling . . . This student recognized the level of acceptable behavior in a regular classroom. He consciously chose to fit in with peers there but clearly chose a different standard of behavior in the resource room.

Peer Mediation

Grades K–12

You may want to investigate implementing a **Peer Mediation** program in your school. It can be an effective tool for primary grades through high school. The premise is that peer mediators can be trained in the skills needed to address conflict in a nonviolent way.

At the primary level, **Peer Mediation** curbs the relentless "tattling" that occurs both on the playground and in the classroom. For older students, **Peer Mediation** helps students become accountable in taking ownership for potentially dangerous disputes.

 The Practical Pointer:

All students—mediators and those involved in a dispute—should be seated at a table. The individuals directly involved in a conflict sit on the same side of the table so that they are not looking directly at each other as they talk. Instead, they are looking at the mediator as they discuss the issues. Avoiding face-to-face contact reduces the opportunity for greater escalation.

Student Guest

Grades K–5

When a student is working on improving social skills, allowing that student to invite a guest from another classroom is an effective strategy. The guest is usually a neighborhood friend who visits for one class period as a reward.

While a variety of days and times could be selected to include a *student guest*, **Friday Game Time** worked well for my students. It was the end of the week. The strategy involved several components, all of which focused on developing social skills with peers.

The student introduced the guest of honor to the class and showed the guest some of the activities that the class had been engaged in during the week. If it happened to be Game Day, the guest selected the game. Not only was the guest in a position of honor during that time, the student host felt very much in control and shared the elevated status as well.

FOCUS ON THE POSITIVE

As the saying goes, it is easier to stay out of trouble than to get out of trouble.

Ask Me!

Grades K–3

A little boy named Jacob was walking down the hall in the primary building where I was visiting. I noticed that he was wearing a tag on string looped around his neck. On the card were just two words: **Ask Me!**

The teacher next to me paused and said, "Jacob, ask you what?"

Jacob replied with a smile, "Ask me what I did just exactly right today."

"OK, Jacob, what did you do that was just right today?"

"I talked in a quiet voice at Morning Meeting today!" Jacob told us proudly.

"Jacob! That is wonderful news! You are terrific! Good for you!" We both put in our positive two cents even though we could only guess why Jacob was working on turning down the volume. It didn't matter that we knew any details. The whole point was giving Jacob the opportunity to tell in his own words what he had accomplished.

 The Practical Pointer:
When used sparingly, an **Ask Me** sign can be promoted as a special honor for primary children to wear home from school. It can encourage parents and children to talk in more detail about the day other than the typical conversation:

> Parent: *"How was school today?"*
> Child: *"Good."*

End of discussion.

Under My Wing

Grades 6–12

Several schools have an **Under My Wing** program for students with behavioral concerns. The purpose is to provide a small number of students with extra support from caring adults.

There are students at all grade levels who would benefit from the **Under My Wing** program. At the middle school and high school levels, students typically come into contact with six, seven or eight adults every day. Some students who need extra attention are sometimes overlooked.

How It Works:

It is very informal. During a staff meeting, the names of particular students are mentioned for the **Under My Wing** program. Within the entire school staff including teaching staff, administration, office staff, custodial staff, coaching staff and all other support staff, there may be a particular adult who offers to make a special effort to connect with that student. Usually this adult already has some relationship with the young person.

Sometimes it is the attendance secretary who has gotten to know a student and has provided encouragement or a welcome smile. The adult may be a teacher who has had the student in the past. Sometimes it may be the custodian who sees the student in the hallways before or after school. Perhaps it is a coach.

This adult makes a point of seeking out the student, greeting the student by name, asking about interests, taking a special interest in grades or assignments and being available to talk. The goal is simply to increase support.

KEY IDEA

There are teachers and other staff members who do this as a matter of course. They do not need a program. They do not need to call it anything. It is just what they do. The students helped by these individuals are so fortunate. There are other students, though, who seem to get lost in the shuffle. This informal program calls attention to these kids and looks for a "match."

Accepting a Compliment

Grades K–12

Unfortunately, some of our students have learned to function only in a negative way. Over time, their entire persona becomes based "being one of the worst." That is what they expect and, too often, is what others expect of them.

Turning that view around is not easy. Many students will resist because hearing a positive comment is not in their comfort zone. Accepting a compliment or any positive feedback is so difficult that they will act out or make an inappropriate remark that results in a reprimand.

Creating low-stress situations in which all of our students can practice saying "Thank you" and learn to accept a compliment gracefully makes these students feel more comfortable hearing positive comments. Very gradually, a different self-image begins to emerge as the student builds a more positive self-concept.

It Looks Like This

Grades K–3

For a highly practical reminder of what a desirable behavior looks like, tape a photograph of the student "doing the right thing" to the desk. For example, if an ongoing problem involves the student blurting out answers without raising a hand, take a picture of the child with a hand raised. Tape it to the desk as a visual reminder. The visual cue along with verbal praise when the desired behavior occurs will help the student get the picture!

SUMMARY

The state of Minnesota recorded 56,000 out-of-school suspensions in 2001; more than half of those were for fighting or disorderly conduct. Of that number 1,800 involved children in grades K–2. For these younger students, the suspensions added up to 150,000 hours of missed time in school.

"We know that if kids are not in school, they're not learning," one school board member said. Suspending such young children may seem extreme and school districts look at out-of-school suspensions very seriously. The behavior that preceded this action, however, was extreme for the age group.

Two-thirds of the out-of-school kindergarten suspensions were for fighting. Behavior included kicking other people and spitting in their faces. Sixteen percent of kindergarten suspensions involved weapons. Parents of other students were adamant that such behavior should not be tolerated in their child's classroom.

There were 110 out-of-school suspensions for kindergartners last year but this figure jumped to well over 1,000 involving second-graders during the same school year and nearly 2,500 at the fifth grade level. The greatest number of suspensions occurred among eighth-graders with 9,354 suspensions recorded, followed closely by ninth-graders and seventh-graders, respectively.

While the numbers are incomplete and some students may account for more than one suspension, the situation is alarming. The trend could represent any state, even though these specific numbers come from Minnesota.

In another example, it may not surprise you that out of 235 referrals for behavior in one building, eight students were involved in 110 of the incidents. This statistic was taken from a middle school in the northeast. Would these numbers be typical of your own building? Would you be able to identify these eight students? It could fit most schools. Does it have to be this way? I hope not.

My hope is that we can tap into the potential of students who disrupt and that we can make changes. My hope is that these students will experience academic success so that acting out is not a reaction to learning itself. My hope is that we can teach students adequate coping skills.

One teacher who works primarily with students who have behavioral disorders described it this way, "I always tell my students, 'You do not have to throw a chair to get my attention. Ask for help. If I can't help you, I will find someone who can.' I am there for them. I want them to know that there are many caring adults who are willing to help in any way possible."

As educators and parents, our expectations must be high. We need to expect positive behavior from our students in every school, in every location. We need to provide clear guidance supported by practical tools and strategies to help students develop positive behavior. We need to "Expect the Best."

Behind every "behavior problem" is a story to be heard
and a heart to be healed.
–Anonymous

INNER STRENGTH, OUTER CONFIDENCE

Within your heart, keep one still, secret spot where dreams may go.

—Louise Driscoll

Every child has value; every child has talent. Not every child, though, shines in the traditional academic talent applauded so often in the typical K–12 setting. Do you know people who "came into their own" after high school or later in life? Sometimes these were individuals for whom success in school was evasive but, as adults, experienced success in many different forms. Isn't this a common scenario at many high school reunions? How many of us, who have a few reunions under our belts, can recall several "success stories" that were not apparent during the school years?

RETHINKING SUCCESS

One of our roles as teachers is to help all of our students see their personal value and discover personal strengths. In some cases, this occurs despite significant struggles in school. Most of us would agree that there are many different types of success.

I think about Nick, a young man for whom success did not fit typical school standards. Nick struggled with both reading and writing skills. His spelling was too far off to be corrected by a computerized spelling checker. "Nick, Nick, Nick," I would tell him, "Always ask a human to proofread your spelling!"

Yet Nick was extremely lucky. He had a music teacher in high school who looked beyond reading levels, test scores and spelling. She noticed that Nick had an exceptional ability to compose music "by ear." Nick could not read music, but he was a highly gifted composer. She nurtured that talent and truly made a tremendous difference in his life.

Because of one teacher who believed in him and with the strong support of his parents, Nick developed his gift into a vocation. Despite struggling at the college level and dropping out of two different schools, Nick is very much a success today. He is employed full time doing what he loves in music. He is confident and happy. I just received an invitation to his wedding. Probably the best news of all is that Nick is marrying a teacher! Spelling should not be much of a problem in the future . . .

Just as success can be defined in many ways for different individuals, positive self-esteem emerges for each person through a variety of experiences. The two are closely connected. One way of developing self-esteem is by doing what is difficult and then overcoming the obstacles. Through tremendous challenges, a strong sense of self emerges and self-confidence grows.

As adults, it can be helpful to recall some of these challenges that we have experienced in our own lives. How did we develop self-esteem? What were some of the experiences that we dealt with perhaps many years ago that shaped our lives?

PERSONAL CHALLENGE AND SUCCESS

Try to recall an example from your own life that had an effect on developing strong self-esteem. Think about a challenge that was difficult for you but one that you ultimately overcame. Think of something that was very important to you at the time. At the outset, it may have seemed impossible. Think about how that situation made you feel. Most of all think about the long-term impact of both the struggle and the success.

As a college student, I remember wanting to teach swimming lessons and work as a lifeguard during the summer. To become certified as a water-safety instructor required extensive training over several months beginning with a rigorous, long-endurance swimming test.

On the first day of the course, we were told to swim 100 laps. I couldn't finish. Most of the other individuals swam on the men's university swim team. They were strong swimmers, and, compared to me, were in far superior condition. The instructor told me after that first class that I would never pass the course and strongly suggested that I quit.

Being told that I would not succeed became a motivator for me. I decided not to quit and practiced daily, building my endurance and strength. I spent hours and hours at the pool. I passed the course. The instructor thanked me later for not giving up.

"You taught me something," she said, "I gave up on you but you never gave up on yourself. I won't do that to someone else."

I was fortunate enough to be hired as a lifeguard and swimming instructor that summer and all through college. I was the first to recognize my personal limits. Working at a pool rather than a large swimming beach was the right choice for me. Teaching swimming became my favorite summer job. It was both extremely rewarding and, in retrospect, probably what led me into the field of education.

Even more rewarding was the inner strength that I gained from that training course. In the many years since, there have been times when I have recalled being in that pool, swimming those laps. I have called upon that same inner strength in so many other situations since then.

I believe that it is important for each of us to think about the many experiences that together shaped our own inner strength. Self-esteem does not come from experiences that are easy. It develops from facing tough challenges and overcoming obstacles. It comes from positive results.

Many of our students deal with enormous challenges on a daily basis. These may be students with special needs who are struggling to succeed in the classroom with peers. Other students face the typical challenges of growing up, which can be daunting. Building self-esteem involves helping our students focus on results and personal accomplishments despite challenges and obstacles. Ultimately, we want to help our students become individuals who feel empowered, capable and self-confident.

O—¬ KEY IDEA

A pattern of overcoming obstacles and experiencing success builds strong self-esteem. Eleanor Roosevelt said it so well, "You must do the thing you think you cannot do."

Being valued by others is another important part of building strong self-esteem. In our learning communities, every individual must be treated with respect and be viewed in a positive light. As teachers, we can exert powerful influence by creating a classroom atmosphere where acceptance, belonging and mutual respect become the norm.

O—¬ KEY IDEA

Toward these goals of acceptance, belonging and respect, two overall rules have always formed critical cornerstones of my classroom: No put-downs and No sarcasm.

The strategies, tips, tools and techniques and ideas suggested in "Inner Strength, Outer Confidence" offer opportunities to celebrate the value of each person and the strength of the group.

These practical ideas are divided into 11 categories and focus broadly on the importance of each individual and the respect due each person in the classroom. More than any other chapter, the strategies listed here can be adapted for a wide range of grade levels because they are based on the broad beliefs that everyone belongs and everyone is accepted. Choose and use. Change and adapt. Have fun with these ideas as you make them part of your curriculum.

- Photo Finish
- Getting to Know You
- Phone Home
- Snail Mail and E-Mail
- Good Tickets
- Put It in Writing
- Class Affirmations

- Backscratchers
- Bookends
- What Goes Around Comes Around
- Options for Rewards

PHOTO FINISH

Photo Bulletin Board

Grades K–12

When I arrived at a high school math class recently, I noticed that students rushed in and were gathered around a bulletin board. Students were laughing, talking and seemed very excited. Dan Ryan, the teacher, explained that he had just changed his photo display. Every month he took a roll of candid pictures of his students in a variety of class situations: working in cooperative groups, talking before the bell, entering or leaving class and just being "kids."

He posted new photos at the beginning of the month and gave away the pictures that he took down. The manager of a local convenience store donated a roll of free film and developing every month making the bulletin board truly priceless!

Mr. Ryan told me that many of his students moved frequently. Some were in foster care and few had recent pictures of themselves. He showed me the photos of his own family on his desk. Through his bulletin board, he wanted to send a message to his students that they, too, were "family." In fact, Mr. Ryan told his students that he liked looking up from his desk after school and seeing their faces. The high school kids loved hearing that and seeing their pictures. The best part of taking pictures every month, Mr. Ryan explained, was the opportunity it gave him to get to know his students.

Class Quilt

Grades K–6

This simple, space-saving strategy holds papers and art on the wall or in the hallway. Displaying students' work instills confidence and demonstrates pride in their efforts. You will need as many plastic page protectors as there are students in the class. Tape them together *on the back* leaving an *opening in the front* of each page protector.

Place a small headshot photo of each student in the lower right hand corner of each page protector, giving each student a "home page" where they will insert a drawing, paragraph or "Proud Paper" to display. The movable quilt can be used to display work on a rotating basis and can be especially inviting as a focal point during Fall Open House or to create visual interest while parents are waiting at conference time.

KEY IDEA

The quilt is powerful because every student is represented individually but is symbolically connected to everyone else as members of the same learning community.

Photo Affirmation

Grades K–12

Students enjoy seeing their photographs on the quilt display. Whether or not you decide to create a class quilt, chances are that you display students' work from time to time. Using a photograph personalizes any student work that is displayed. It also reminds students that their work is an extension of themselves. At all grade levels, student work, art exhibits, and science projects displayed throughout the school are ways of recognizing a job well done. Adding a photograph promotes pride and self-confidence.

☞ **The Practical Pointer:**
> Show your students examples from the local newspaper of photographs accompanying descriptions of accomplishments by adults in the business arena. This gives more credence to having students' photos displayed as part of the way we recognize success.

Rotating Artwork

Grades K–12

Several years ago, my local school district began framing student artwork to decorate the district administration building. It was a simple strategy to implement and has been very popular in our community.

Each month teachers from all grade levels submit new artwork to be considered for framing. A committee of volunteers selects pieces to be matted by the high school art department and hung throughout the district offices.

The young artists and their parents visit the building each month to see their work displayed. Not only is the rotating art a delight to the eye, it also reminds the administrative staff to focus on children.

☞ **The Practical Pointer:**
> Select large, simple frames that will be appropriate to use over and over for artwork. Replacement is fast and easy because the frames are numbered and placed on the same hooks each month. Consider displaying sculpture and other three-dimensional projects in a lighted case in the entryway.

Artwork at Home

Grades K–5

Many parents display children's artwork and papers at home on the refrigerator and cupboard doors. Encourage parents to also purchase some simple, inexpensive picture frames. Artwork takes on special significance when children see it framed at home on a wall.

Like the committee in the administration building, the children themselves can assist in rotating their work throughout the school year. It is another way of affirming personal pride in their work.

☞ **The Practical Pointer:**
Some of my favorite pieces of artwork on the walls of our family home were done by my own children and placed in permanent frames. To me, each one tells a story and holds memories more valuable than any piece of professional art.

Family Photos

Grades K–5

Encourage students to bring in family photos that can be taped inside a folder or attached to a key ring. One primary teacher installed small hooks on the wall for students to hang key rings of photos. During free time, a popular choice was to look through the key rings of classmates' pictures. Family pets were always included in this strategy.

Class Photo Album

Grades K–5

During projects and activities, any teacher may want to keep a disposable camera available (unless there is access to a digital camera). Take pictures and create a running record of progress made during the year. When parents arrive for conferences or **Treats on Tuesdays** (described in the next section), they can see at a glance what the class has been doing. Younger children will enjoy taking the photo album home overnight to show their families. It is a great conversation starter!

GETTING TO KNOW YOU

Tell Me More

Grades K–12

When I was attending Fall Open House for one of my own high school age children, Kari Mich, a social studies teacher, used a simple technique to gather information about her students so that she could get to know them better. This strategy was a wonderful way to connect with parents and promote positive communication. At the same time, it was an effective way to show that she cared about each person as an individual, not just as a student in fourth period social studies.

She placed a 3" x 5" note card at each student's place the night of Open House. When parents arrived, she asked all of us to take two minutes to write down some information about our children: hobbies, sports, outside interests, as well as any academic or personal concerns that the teacher should know.

All of us did as she asked and turned in the cards. As one parent was leaving the room, she stopped by the teacher's desk. I heard her confide in the teacher, "Thank you! I'm so glad you gave me the opportunity to let you know . . ." The teacher had provided a short but effective way to open communication. Later this same teacher used far less personal information from the cards to ask her students about their activities and get to know them better.

Any teacher could use the same note card technique at Open House as Ms. Mich used. Another time to use the cards may be while parents are waiting their turn at school conferences.

Mystery Student Cards

Grades 4–12

The **Mystery Student Card** strategy is similar to **Tell Me More** except that the students themselves fill out a **Getting to Know You** card on the first day of class. It can include any information that the student chooses to share such as hobbies, interests, sports, and trivia.

For example, one student wrote, "I had the unique experience of having four different casts in six months."

Another wrote, "I play soccer and hockey like a lot of people in this class, but how many other people built a foosball table this summer?"

"I am easy to identify because I am always drawing cartoons," wrote another.

Periodically, or as a transition between activities, the teacher draws one of the **Mystery Student Cards** and reads the identifying information aloud. Classmates will guess the name. Expect high school students to request, " Is there time for a **Mystery Student Card?**" The activity takes less than a minute but helps class members gel as a team.

Class Dictionary

Grades K–5

A great way to start the year and help classmates get to know each other is by creating a class dictionary. First names only are used and each child's name will be followed by a pronunciation guide, picture or drawing, and whatever family information the parent and child choose to include.

The definition describes what makes that child unique. What hobbies, interests, pets, sports, favorite books help to define the child? Adapt and adjust this strategy depending on the grade level of the students. Every student has a full-page entry. Creating the entry can become a parent-child activity.

The teacher begins by sharing his or her entry. If there is a paraprofessional in the room or a co-teacher, those individuals create their own entries, as well.

☞ **The Practical Pointer:**
Assemble the class dictionary alphabetically in a magnetic photo album. Keep it available for children to enjoy when they have free time or as a choice of reading material during *D.E.A.R.—Drop Everything And Read*. The plastic cover sheets will keep the entries clean so that each can be returned to the owner at the end of the year.

All About Me Video

Grades K–5

An ongoing strategy that creates a visual record of student progress throughout the school year is the **All About Me Video**. Each child has a blank videotape as the year begins. In my own elementary building, several parent volunteers assisted with videotaping students periodically. Options include showing the individual student reading, telling stories, giving reports, displaying artwork and participating in activities. The composite became a story on tape of the child's experience that year. It is given to the parent as a gift at the end of the year.

☞ **The Practical Pointer:**
Some schools begin each child's video during kindergarten and continue the process throughout the elementary years. At the end of fifth grade, the child has an **All About Me Video** that spans the full elementary experience. Should a family move during the elementary years, the parent receives the video as a farewell gift from the school.

PowerPoint Autobiography

Grades 6–12

For middle and high school students, creating a **PowerPoint Autobiography** is both a learning experience and, when completed, a tool to show future employers. It demonstrates skills and provides background. Work-Study Coordinator Ellen Shaughnessy commented that this experience was the most popular activity she has used with her students in the last few years. Each student enjoyed creating the **PowerPoint Autobiography** and several students with special needs incorporated it as part of a transition plan from school to work.

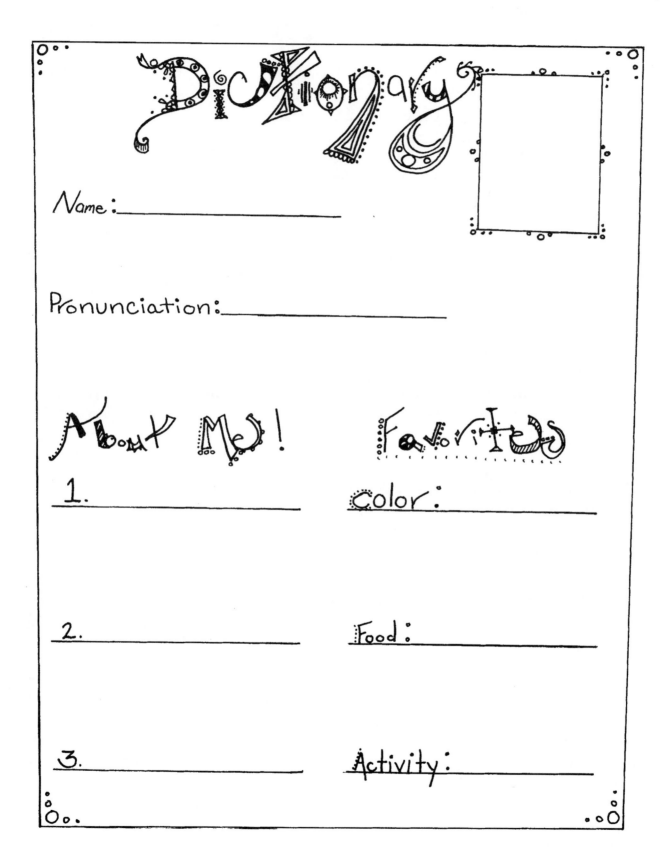

Dictionary

Name: _____

Pronunciation: _____

About Me!

1. _____

2. _____

3. _____

Favorites

Color: _____

Food: _____

Activity: _____

Lunch with a Teacher

Grades K–8

A positive reward for elementary and middle school students is eating a brown bag **Lunch with a Teacher.** Consider the benefits of spending one-on-one time with a student in a relaxed atmosphere. Younger students are often amazed that teachers even eat! You know how it is when you run into a young student outside of school in a grocery store or at the mall. Did the student look at you as if you were from outer space?

Lunch with a Teacher creates a special closeness and provides a time for the teacher to get to know the student in a way that is difficult in the larger classroom environment. In the course of the school year, an elementary teacher would schedule 25 or 30 lunch dates with students out of a possible 180 lunches. Middle school teachers have many more students but not every student would select Lunch With a Teacher. If the concept appeals to you, give it a try. Ask someone to take a picture of your lunchtime together. This lunch will become a special memory for the each student.

There are teachers who do this every day with the entire class in some school districts and so, for their students, **Lunch with the Principal** might be a novel idea instead. Some teachers rely on that short lunchtime as a much-needed break from children and an opportunity to recharge for the afternoon. For these teachers, this idea is not an option that they would choose to use.

Treats on Tuesdays

Grades K–5

Several years ago, the second Tuesday of every month was a special morning in the elementary classrooms of my children's school. Parents were invited to stop at school on their way to work to visit classrooms, see students' work on display, and get to know other parents and students. Children would act as hosts serving simple refreshments. It was brief and informal with no program or planned activity. Siblings were welcome. The time before school seemed to work better for many families than an event in the evening.

Originally, the school targeted specific guests each time. One Tuesday was dedicated to *Donuts for Dads;* another was called *Muffins for Moms.* I adopted the same concept for my own classroom but made the invitation more inclusive to reflect families today. I called it **Treats on Tuesdays.** Everyone was welcome. Each student could invite someone special. As you know, an increasing number of grandparents are raising grandchildren today. They came too. Parents, day-care providers, sometimes a special friend or neighbor stopped by. It was a simple way for students to demonstrate pride in their school and foster open communication between home and school.

Star of the Week

Grades K–3

When students arrive for the new school year, they will meet the first **Star of the Week—** their teacher! They will get to know their teacher through photographs, words and stories assembled on a large poster. During that first week, the teacher may choose to bring in a pet, invite special guests, demonstrate crafts, display hobbies, and share favorite foods, books, music and items that have special memories.

If there is a co-teacher or student teacher, that individual may be the next **Star of the Week**. A letter to parents explains the concept and asks parents to select first and second choices for a week to "star" their child. Many students like to be **Star of the Week** when they are celebrating a birthday.

Classmates may learn about family customs, may meet grandparents, baby brothers and the family ferret. The **Star of the Week** takes on special duties, sits in a place of honor during Morning Meeting, and chooses a favorite story to have read. Everyone gets a turn for this special honor sometime during the school year.

☞ **The Practical Pointer:**

Many teachers begin the **Star of the Week** for students about a month after school has begun to give families adequate time to gather photos and create a poster. Some parents schedule a few hours off work to visit the classroom during that special week and have lunch with their child.

Student Teacher for a Week

Grades 1–4

Teacher Brad Sampson shared this wonderful idea with me that his second graders loved. He noticed that there was an extra teacher's desk in the storage room at school. It gave him an idea. He moved it into his classroom and placed it next to his own desk for the designated **Student Teacher of the Week.**

The purpose was to give students a glimpse of life as a teacher but also to build self-confidence and enhance self-esteem. For one week during the school year, each student moved everything out of his or her own desk and spread out for a week in the large desk next to Mr. Sampson. The view from this direction was new and interesting. Whenever there were papers to pass, Mr. Sampson asked the Student Teacher to assist.

When a message needed to be taken to the office, Mr. Sampson knew just whom to ask. Everyone loved the swivel chair that could be adjusted to just the right height. The behavior of the Student Teacher was exemplary. It was noteworthy, added Mr. Sampson that the positive behavior carried over when the student returned to a regular desk.

When asked at the end of the year what students liked about being in Mr. Sampson's room, being Student Teacher ranked at the top of the list.

"I just wonder if the Student Teacher strategy planted a seed in some future educators . . ." mused Mr. Sampson. As someone who grew up "playing school" in my basement, I can imagine that being Student Teacher would have been the highlight of my second grade experience.

 The Practical Pointer:
Not every school has an extra teacher's desk. You may be thinking that some teachers in your building are lacking a desk of their own! It is easy to improvise with a card table or even a student desk turned around to face the group.

A Sneak Peek

Grades 4–8

At the opening of the school year, one quick strategy that I used with middle school students was to give each student a piece of letter-sized construction paper. We folded it in half. At home, students put a photograph on the top and made two lists. On the left, students listed, "Five Fast Things About Me." On the right, the task was to list "Five Things I Like To Do."

I gave students a specific number for each list to help them create a capsule view of themselves, a **Sneak Peek** as opposed to the whole autobiography. I also did not want students to belabor the first assignment of the school year.

"Have fun with this," I told students, "Don't make a career out of it! What are five things that immediately come to mind when you think about yourself? Then name five things that you enjoy doing."

I posted the **Sneak Peeks** from all of my students throughout the room. It quickly personalized our classroom and created a sense of belonging to our new learning community.

Morning Music

Grades 4–12

This is a quick idea for building self-confidence and making the first few minutes of the day especially enjoyable. Plan a short concert in the school entryway on a monthly basis to give musicians and the choir an opportunity to shine in front of their peers. The performances highlight small groups of students who volunteer for the 20-minute event.

At the elementary level, students gain practical experience performing for an audience. Middle and high school students are treated to a wide range of music from rock bands to a cappella.

PHONE HOME

A Good Call!

Grades K–12

One of the most effective ways to build a strong partnership between school and home is the positive phone call. Parents usually hear from the school immediately when there is a problem, but any parent will tell you that they also need to hear from the school when there is good news.

I was talking about this during a middle school staff development session just before the opening of the school year. A new teacher raised his hand. His name was Patrick Weingartner and he had just been hired, he told me, to teach seventh grade science. There would be approximately 150 students in his five classes. His goal, he said, was make one **Good Call** each school night so that by the end of the year he would have called every parent to say something positive. In fact, he told the staff that setting his goal *publicly* would help him follow through.

I asked if I could call him in June to see how it went. Sure enough, he met his goal of 150 positive phone calls! It turns out that it was a "good news, bad news" experience. The *good news* was how much *he* got out of it. He received appreciative notes, the principal received notes . . .

It took about five minutes per call. "Sometimes," Mr. Weingartner said, "I felt so good that I made two or three calls! It reminded me of why I went into teaching in the first place! I really made an effort to get to know my students because I needed something positive to talk about."

The *bad news* was that many parents expected the worst as soon as he identified himself as a teacher. Even after he explained why he had called, it was as though many parents were waiting for the other shoe to drop. Only when they fully realized that the teacher was calling with the sole purpose of complimenting their child would parents relax and let their guard down. Of course, then they were thrilled. One parent burst into tears saying, "I'm sorry, but I could not take one more negative call from the school!"

The Positive Weekend

Grades K–3

A first grade teacher told me that she devotes one of the first fall weekends each year to calling every parent of all her students. She sends a letter home during the first week of school telling parents to expect her call and she explains that the purpose is an opportunity for parents to talk about their child. She would be calling to listen.

Since she began doing this over ten years ago, this teacher remarked that there has never been a parent with whom she did not develop a true partnership. "I have not had a conflict with a parent that could not be resolved. We took that time at the beginning of the year to establish a bond. After all, we both wanted a same thing–a great school year for the child."

Sunshine Phone

Grades K–5

One principal I know used a telephone as a tool to spread good news about her students. Linda Saukennon kept a bright yellow **Sunshine Phone** in her office that was used only by students to call parents about exceptional work or behavior. The fact that the call came from the principal's office seemed to increase the value for both students and their parents. Parents were happy to be interrupted at work with a call from the **Sunshine Phone**.

It's Your Call

Grades K–5

A teacher told me that she routinely selects a student to call a parent at the end of the day from her cell phone to celebrate excellent work. She records the names of callers in her day planner so that everyone gets a turn. She describes the two-minute event as "highly motivating and ends the day on a upbeat note for everyone in the class."

SNAIL MAIL AND E-MAIL

The Positive Postcard

Grades K–12

An alternative to the phone call is the **Positive Postcard**. It serves the same purpose as the phone call but "getting it in writing" enables parents to read the postcard over and over. They do. I can tell you that from first-hand experience.

Though teachers have said positive things about my own children over the years, I have received just one postcard. It was from a high school Spanish teacher. I was delighted. I framed it and put it with family photographs on the mantle. I have probably read it a hundred times. That this teacher took the time to write it and send it made an impact. Anything that "Professora Ellison" did that year, I supported—just ask my son!

☞ **The Practical Pointer:**
   In some schools, the Parent Teacher Association supplies stamped postcards and the school office prints address labels to encourage the use of **Positive Postcards.** Every teacher receives a stack of addressed postcards with the class list at the beginning of the year.

Keeping them available and close at hand makes sending postcards effortless. The stack of cards also serves as a reminder to send one to each parent sometime during the year.

Summer Postcard

Grades 4–12

When I mentioned the **Positive Postcard** during a seminar, a middle school English teacher shared this idea that she has used for several years. Immediately after students leave for summer vacation, she sends all of her students from the year a positive postcard with a personal touch. She mentions something special about that child and then suggests one book that the student may enjoy reading over the summer. She is careful to tailor her suggestion to the interest and reading level of each student.

In the fall, she hears from many of her former students and their parents about how much the postcard meant to the family and, in several cases, how much the student enjoyed the book. Taking the time to write a note and name a specific book carried much more weight than any general suggestion to read during summer vacation!

The Welcome Postcard

Grades K–5

Many students are apprehensive about a new school year. Some are fearful about the new social environment and others are anxious about the academic expectations. One way that many elementary teachers connect with their new students before the first day of school is to mail a personal postcard to each student a few days before school begins. The teacher greets each student, gives a very brief personal introduction, mentions one or two class activities, and tells each student how much the teacher is looking forward to their year together in Room 203. For many students, this breaks the ice, reduces stress and anxiety.

☞ **The Practical Pointer:**

For students with unusually high anxiety or for students who struggle greatly with any type of change, a tour of the school and classroom before the school year begins can make a tremendous difference in school success. For some middle school students who are very fearful about finding their classes, visiting the school a few days early and practicing the route from class to class before halls are crowded with students can do much to build confidence.

E-Mail It!

Grades K–6

Most of us get annoyed when we log onto our computers and find plenty of unwanted mail to delete. A welcome surprise is a positive e-mail from a teacher. Telling the parent about a job well done or progress made by a child can make a parent's day:

Shannon had a great day today!

Ask Toni about how well he did in math today. Wow!

Excellent essay in English! Josh is making tremendous strides in writing!

☞ **The Practical Pointer:**
E-mail can be a way to open communication between children and their parents about school. The e-mail does not *give* the good news but simply *suggests* that a parent ask a child about the day.

GOOD TICKETS

Address Labels with a Twist

Grades K–12

Most of us receive advertising flyers for address labels in the Sunday newspaper and in the mail.

Receive 450 address labels for only $4.95!

While you may actually order address labels, you can also order labels for other purposes. You do not have to write your address. You can write whatever you choose! Typically, there are three or four lines of print with room for a specified number of characters. Instead of ordering address labels, I have ordered labels that reward my students' effort:

Linda Tilton's Award

For Your Best Work

Congratulations!

Printed on gold foil, the labels were ready to go for immediate reinforcement. As I walked around the room, I quietly handed a label to a student with a simple, "Nice job today." The focus was on the effort and personal best. Shortly after I first began using the labels, one boy told me, "When you first told us about those, I never thought I'd get one . . . I've gotten two!"

The label can be an end in itself without any additional reward. For variety, I have also occasionally attached the label to a piece of hard candy or put the student's name in a drawing for a prize at the end of the week or grading period. This simple, quiet affirmation is an opportunity for the teacher to recognize the value of effort. If not overused, it is a powerful motivator at all grade levels.

☞ **The Practical Pointer:**
The message you select may be different. Adapt it to fit your needs. A middle school health teacher selected a message for her labels that was motivational and appropriate to health class:

Make healthy choices every day.

You are wonderful!

She awarded these the same way, for personal best both in academics and behavior in health class.

KEY IDEA

Personal best is our goal for students. Personal best is different from perfectionism. I have worked with students who could not finish assignments, not because the work was not completed, but because the student was never satisfied. Perfectionism created a cycle of incompletes as the student lagged further behind. The pressure to get caught up added more to the student's frustration. While we must promote high standards, we need to help our students recognize when a task is finished.

Admit One!

Grades K–12

Like the address labels, "Good Tickets" reward effort. While you probably have seen rolls of "Good Job" tickets in commercial teaching catalogs, you can also go to the local business supply store and purchase a large roll of "Admit One" tickets for a lot less money.

You may wish to keep several in a pocket and occasionally leave one on the desk of a student as you circulate in the room. Like the gold labels, receiving the ticket does not have to be connected to a tangible reward.

If you do favor the reward concept, students can earn a variety of privileges or prizes with their tickets. At the middle and secondary levels, students tear their tickets in half and drop the stub into a designated container for a drawing. If the student's stub is lost, there is no opportunity to win because only the number is called. The more tickets a student earns, the more likely are the chances of winning prizes such as a *No Homework* ticket, ten extra points, a can of soda, permission to chew gum or wear a hat in class. You may even consider including an occasional *Get Out of Detention Free* card.

☞ **The Practical Pointer:**

When students help determine the rewards, they are more likely to want to be in the drawing. When primary students earn a ticket, I have them write their name on the back and drop the whole ticket into the jar. When a ticket is drawn, the name is called instead of the winning number.

⚷ KEY IDEA

Like the address labels, the ticket itself can be the reward. It is not desirable to always connect the ticket to a tangible reward. Much of the success of any award or reward system depends on how it is presented to the class.

Terrific Tickets

Grades 2–12

These small reward tickets can be connected to a drawing or can be a simple reward. Parents have told me later that their children saved all the **Terrific Tickets** on the refrigerator or in their room. Each time they saw them, they were reminded that they had done a good job. It was a very effective motivator. (See "B.I.Y." later in the chapter.)

Worker Bee Award

Grades K–3

The **Worker Bee Award** is a thumbnail-sized bumblebee cut out of yellow construction paper. The awards go to hard workers who demonstrate independent learning skills and perseverance. There are no additional prizes involved. The goal is to provide simple acknowledgement for consistent effort. I found that each bumblebee award guarantees an ear-to-ear grin!

PUT IT IN WRITING

Written Round of Applause

Grades K–12

A very simple way of noting academic progress, reinforcing desirable behavior, affirming an act of kindness or giving a compliment for any reason is the **Written Round of**

Applause. I noticed this on a reception desk at the Mayo Clinic in Rochester, Minnesota. A small pad of paper was illustrated with hands applauding in a circle. Beneath the illustration were three lines and the words:

(Name,)

you deserve a round of applause for . . .

(Signature)

When I asked about it, I learned that every staff member had a **Written Round of Applause** pad handy to compliment a colleague who went the extra mile for a patient or another staff member. I was told that it was a stress-reducer and also a motivator. There were no drawings or prizes involved, just a written note.

I was so impressed with the idea that I made my own **Written Round of Applause** awards on my computer to use with both staff and students. I especially liked the fact that only three lines were allotted for comments. Sometimes we may hesitate to write a note because it might "take too long."

 Bringing Up Grades (BUG Award #1)

Grades K–6

Another example of a written award is the **BUG Award**, which actually has two versions. The first version focuses on grades; the second focuses on behavior. The *BUG Award* that I have used stands for *Bringing Up Grades.*

A drawing of a generic bug decorated the award. Below were places for the student's name and the note: *Congratulations for Bringing Up Grades!* It was a very simple way to affirm progress.

In any classroom, it is particularly important to recognize that student who exhibits effort and has raised a grade but is still unable to make the honor roll. In fact, some of my students with special needs worked rigorously for the **BUG Award** that for them became the equivalent of the honor roll.

 Invasion of the Ladybugs

Grades K–6

My use of the **BUG Award** did not go beyond the certificate itself. In another school district, it became part of a school wide improvement project supported by the whole community. The **BUG Award** centered on an extensive ladybug theme complete with ladybug-shaped certificates, ladybug pins, ladybug bumper stickers, and drawings for ladybug t-shirts and coupons for free ice cream and pizza. Raising grades and ladybug mania were the rage! The project generated a lot of enthusiasm among students, teachers and parents alike.

Clap! Clap! Clap! Clap! Clap! Clap!

Great

Hooray! Yeah!

You deserve a Round of Applause for _____

_____

☞ **The Practical Pointer:**

While that project was very successful and raised awareness about excellence in education, not every school district or community is in a position to turn the **BUG Award** into an extravaganza. Remember that *one* teacher in *one* school can make a difference with *one* class, *one* student at a time. The written note itself can be extremely powerful in acknowledging and recognizing personal improvement.

Being Unusually Good (BUG Award #2)

Grades K–5

A second version of the **Bug Award** stands for **Being Unusually Good.** It is given to the student who has been striving to make changes in specific behaviors and has shown improvement. It can represent positive behavior on a certain day, for a particular span of time or in a specific setting. It features the same visual as the award for improving an academic grade but describes the positive behavior that the student achieved.

(Name,)

Congratulations for . . . (raising your hand today and waiting for Mrs. Casserly to call on you . . . or keeping your hands to yourself as we walked to the cafeteria this week . . .)

☞ **The Practical Pointer:**

Reserve awards like the **BUG Award** for the *occasional* reinforcement so that the award retains its value.

Thinking of You

Grades 1–12

This is a simple but effective way that a parent can "bank" positive comments for a day when a child may need encouragement. At Fall Open House or during conferences, provide notepaper and an envelope. Request that parents write a personal note to their child and then ask them seal it in the envelope. Assure them that only their child will read it.

The note will be saved for a time when the child is having difficult day due to academic or emotional issues. In an unobtrusive way, the teacher will quietly hand the student the sealed note. It could contain a list of ten wonderful qualities that child embodies, it may be thoughts of encouragement for persevering despite difficulty, or it may be a simple letter of a parent's unconditional love.

The strategy can be used at the secondary level, as well. Most teachers have a good sense of when a student is hurting. Even though there is little time to connect individually in a school day of seven or eight class periods, any teacher can quietly call the student aside to deliver the note. This takes only seconds and creates a powerful impact.

The Practical Pointer:
For some students, there may not be an occasion during the semester or even during the school year when the note appears to be needed. For these students, the notes can be a gift presented at the end of the term.

"Caught Cha" Award

Grades 1–4

A baseball mitt forms the background for this popular award. Use brown construction paper and cut out a baseball mitt. When the teacher "catches" the student performing at an exceptionally high level for that individual, the teacher writes a quick description in the mitt and delivers it to the student with a gentle, **"I caught cha!"**

CLASS AFFIRMATIONS

Stand and Applaud

Grades K–5

While the **Written Round of Applause** can be used effectively with any age or grade level, elementary students can also *act out* the **Round of Applause** by standing and clapping their hands while moving their arms in a large circle. Use it as a quick transition tool as the class claps for an excellent performance by the entire group or conveys special recognition for a particular student.

Silent Standing Ovation

Grades K–3

Younger students also enjoy giving the entire class a **Silent Standing Ovation** by clasping their hands and pumping a giant, victorious "O" shape over their heads. Everyone stands and enthusiastically makes the boxer's winning gesture for several seconds. It is a simple way to take a quick break before changing activities.

The "Seal" of Approval

Grades K–3

The **Seal of Approval** is also a winner with the primary set. To celebrate a job well done, students stand with their arms extended rigidly in front of them, clapping and barking like seals. Save this last one for just before recess or the end of the day!

The Practical Pointer:
Involve students in creating some whole-class kinesthetic awards. Students can be very imaginative in this department!

BACKSCRATCHERS

The Crumpled Heart

Grades K–5

Part of building self-confidence comes from positive feelings about oneself and others so that there is no need to put others down. "Put-downs" reflect negative self-image. During my experience teaching in elementary, middle school and high school classrooms, I have always insisted on a climate of respect for every individual in the learning community.

The Crumpled Heart, a short but powerful activity, can be used whenever students need a reminder to focus on respect. Gather all the students together whether it is on the rug for elementary students or in their desks if the students are older.

Cut a heart shape out of construction paper. As you do so, explain that everyone is a valuable human being and that everyone belongs as a member of the learning community. State that sometimes comments are made that can hurt others and that these comments are unacceptable.

You might mention some of the typical hurtful comments made at that grade level without singling out any individuals. Then ask students to share examples of hurtful comments that they have heard on the bus, in the classroom, in the hallway, on the playground or in the cafeteria. No one is being put on the spot. The question is never, "What did you *say?*" but "What have you *heard?*" As students share their examples of negative comments, begin to crumple the heart. Continue crumpling until it becomes a wad of wrinkled paper.

Then ask students for examples of positive comments that could be made to each other instead. Let them practice. Encourage specific comments other than using the word "nice." They may offer examples such as:

"You're friendly."

"You are the first person to help someone."

"You are a good artist."

"You can really throw the ball."

As they continue to give examples, begin to smooth out the wrinkled heart. Ask the students what they notice. Even though many positive comments have been made, the heart is still crumpled and scarred. Positive comments help to ease the pain but negative words hurt long afterward. You may want to attach the crumpled heart to the wall. At another time, you may hear a negative comment. Stop and look toward it. It is not long before everyone is following your eyes as you remind them, "I am thinking of the crumpled heart." It is simple, powerful and they get it.

Inside Hurts and Outside Hurts

Grades K–2

When I shared the idea of **The Crumpled Heart,** first grade teacher Erin Branch told me that she also had a short but effective strategy to teach the same concept. During Morning Meeting one day, she explained the difference between **Inside Hurts and Outside Hurts.** She told her first-graders that if they fell down on the playground and scraped a knee, they could come inside for help. She could clean it up and put on a bandage. Soon it would heal and be as good as new. That was an *outside* hurt. Words that hurt were different. They were *inside* hurts. These could last for a long time, she told them, but she could not fix those. Her students understood.

Picture Wheel

Grades K–5

This is a wonderful tool that can be used to celebrate a student's birthday, as a way co-teachers could introduce each other, or as a self-esteem-building tool any time during the year.

HOW TO MAKE IT:

Cut two round wheels out of contrasting colors of oak tag board. Make one about an inch smaller than the other to display both colors at once. Draw lines to divide the larger wheel into pie shapes. (I enjoyed reading the children's story *The Tenth Good Thing About Barney* by Judith Viorst in conjunction with this project. For this reason, I divided the larger wheel into *ten* pies shapes. Your wheel may be divided into as many sections as you desire.)

Next, cut a pie shape out of the smaller wheel. Attach a metal brad through the middle so that the larger wheel is on the bottom and both wheels can turn. Each child then glues his or her photo to the top wheel.

After discussing the ongoing themes of acceptance, belonging and community, students are ready to pass their **Picture Wheels** around the classroom for classmates to write positive words or phrases on the bottom wheel: "Kind," "Athletic," "Happy," "Good at drawing . . ." Kindergarten and first grade teachers will need volunteers to act as scribes for many children. By the time the wheel is returned to the owner, it is filled with positive thoughts.

The Practical Pointer:

If you decide to use this idea at the end of the year, you may wish to divide the larger wheel into as many sections as there are members of the class. Receiving positive comments from classmates makes a wonderful gift to each student on the last day. Students treasure these! Laminating the **Picture Wheels** will preserve them as keepsakes.

Back Me Up!

Grades 5–9

Older students of all ages need positive reinforcement from peers. It can be more difficult for middle and high school students to *verbalize* a compliment face-to-face. This activity is based on the same concept as the **Picture Wheel** but uses a different approach. Particularly in the middle school setting, I found that it was important for me to clearly set the tone for the activity so that no one would write negative comments, crass remarks or jokes that would destroy the positive spirit.

TRUE STORY

I began by telling students a true story that is repeated periodically in newspaper advice columns and retold in popular nonfiction books. You may be familiar with it. It involves the high school teacher in the late 1960s who was discouraged by the negative way students talked to each other. The teacher, who happened to be a Roman Catholic nun, stopped her lesson one day and asked each student to take out a sheet of paper.

She instructed them to write each class member's name on the paper, skipping a line in between. Next, their task was to go back and write a positive comment on the line below each name. The teacher collected all the papers.

Before the next class meeting, she made a composite list of positive comments submitted for each student and quietly handed them out in class. There was not a sound that day as students read their positive comments.

Some years later during the Vietnam War, it was with great sadness that the teacher attended the funeral of a young soldier who had been a student in that class. Among his possessions in Vietnam was his list of positive comments. When the family shared this with the teacher, many other former students came forward telling the teacher that their lists, too, were saved. The activity that day had made a tremendous impact on their lives.

SETTING THE TONE

My students listened quietly and we talked about the need to hear positive comments in everyone's life. The serious tone made all the difference in the success of the strategy. Heavy cardstock paper was taped to each person's back and felt tip markers were provided for students to number from 1 to 5. Everyone had just five minutes to walk around the room and anonymously write sincere compliments. No talking was allowed. If someone's sheet already had five comments, a student would move on and find a blank spot on another person's sheet. I walked around and monitored the activity. Everyone left with five good thoughts. One very shy young man left smiling, saying, "I never knew anybody thought that about me . . ."

I have used this strategy as a secondary teacher, a coach, and also as a parent hosting pregame "pasta parties" for athletic teams of my own children. Even though self-esteem has to come from within, everyone needs external positive reinforcement! When other people express confidence in an individual, that belief bolsters self-confidence and confirms positive self-esteem.

Positive Garland

Grades K–4

Another tool for expressing confidence in others is the **Positive Garland.** It can be used any time of year but a teacher suggested that in schools that have Valentines parties, that time is effective. Fall leaves and spring flowers offer alternatives to hearts for the garland.

HOW TO MAKE IT:

About a week ahead of time, students receive a class list and as many small hearts or leaves or tulips as there are students in the class. At home, each student writes one name on each of the items. Then the student writes a positive comment about each person.

On the designated day, the hearts or leaves or tulips are returned to the classroom. Usually some type of celebration is planned in conjunction with the next part of the activity. Each person receives a stack of positive comments to staple to a long piece of ribbon.

The result is a wonderful garland to take home that day to hang in the kitchen or bedroom. Students and their parents love it!

⚷ KEY IDEA

Parent education is one of the goals of this activity. It is a way of reminding parents to focus on the positive with their own children and to consistently tell them how much they are valued as human beings. I mention this because I am reminded of a father who came up to me after a parent session in a middle school. We had been talking about this need for positive focus. He said, "Thank you for the reminder. I cannot remember the last time I said something good to my son."

The 21-Day Compliment

Grades K–12

*Habit is habit, and not to be kicked out the door at any time,
but coaxed down the stairs little by little.*

–Mark Twain

Just as it is difficult to eliminate a negative habit, creating a new one does not happen overnight. It takes 21 consecutive days of repeating a behavior to form a habit. The same can be said for internalizing a compliment.

Think about a particular child who is struggling with low self-esteem. Unobtrusively, state the same compliment in a variety of ways for 21 consecutive school days.

"Jason, thank you for raising your hand before speaking."

"Jason, you have done a great job today of raising your hand
before speaking."

"Jason, great job again today on hand-raising!"

At the end of the 21 days, Jason will very likely see himself as a student who raises his hand when acknowledged by the teacher. As a practical matter, targeting just one or two children in the class for the **21-Day Compliment** makes the process manageable.

Public Compliments

Grades K–12

A simple strategy for building self-confidence is the **Public Compliment** that is given *to an individual* in the presence of others so that several people hear the positive remark. Sometimes it is even more effective to speak positively *about someone* to another individual but within earshot of the person receiving the praise.

Special Person Speech

Grades 6–12

Secondary students develop strong self-confidence and a strong self-image by noticing strengths in other people. One of my favorite English teachers, Ernie Gulner, uses a very powerful assignment called the **Special Person Speech**. Each student selects an individual who has made a significant impact on that student's life. Then, without telling the Special Person about the speech, the individual to be honored is invited to class under the pretense of a "Guest Day." A note explains that students are working on speeches and the group would appreciate a larger audience.

Unknowingly, the Special Person arrives and is invited to sit down. There are actually no other guests that day. The student goes to the front of the room and begins to speak from the heart about how the guest has influenced the student's life. It is a very powerful experience.

I was fortunate enough to be the Special Person, invited by one of my own children. I was caught completely off guard and was very moved. Other students have also invited parents. Many students chose teachers, coaches, grandparents, and members of the community or religious leaders. Mr. Gulner commented that the assignment gave students a chance to express gratitude and develop poise as they stood before their peers and shared a meaningful part of their lives.

 The Practical Pointer:
Each student gives the guest a written copy of the speech to save, reread and treasure.

Compliment Monday

Grades K–5

An elementary teacher told me that a large percentage of his students come from challenging home situations. Mondays are particularly difficult days following what can be an unsettling weekend. Attendance is generally lower on Mondays than on other days. Some students come to school more agitated. This teacher instituted **Compliment Monday** as a way to improve attendance and also as a way to begin the week on a positive note.

How It Works:

Over the weekend, the teacher writes a quick compliment to each student on a sticky note. Before school begins, he places the compliment on each desk. Students run into the classroom on **Compliment Monday,** he said, eager to find the note.

Using a sticky note works well because students can place it anywhere—on the page of a book, on a study guide or on the corner of the desk.

Too many of his students receive a lot of negative feedback from the adults in their lives, he explained, but not enough of the positive. **Compliment Monday** is his simple way of making a difference.

Once Each Grading Period

Grades K–12

Secondary teachers with 150 students each day may like the concept of **Compliment Monday** and may have some students who would surely benefit from written positive feedback. The logistics of doing so on a weekly basis, though, would be unrealistic. Here is an alternative strategy that is realistic at all grade levels.

High school teacher Eva Alverez uses this simple system to make sure that every student receives a positive short statement in writing at least once each grading period. She uses a manila file folder for each of her five classes. At the beginning of each quarter, she writes the name of each student on a three-inch sticky note and arranges the notes alphabetically inside the file folder.

In addition to spontaneous verbal praise, Ms. Alverez writes positive remarks on sticky notes to place on a student's paper or leave on a desk as the she circulates throughout the room. Using the file folder approach makes it easy to jot a quick compliment and deliver it to the student.

As the weeks go by, Ms. Alverez looks in her file folder and knows at a glance who has not received a *written* compliment so far that grading period. She makes sure that by the end of the quarter, her file folder is empty. Her students like receiving the written compliments and it is her way of highlighting her students' strengths.

Through the Vent

Grades 6–12

This quick strategy will catch secondary students off guard in a positive way. Ask the office for a list of your students' lockers numbers *without combinations*. Occasionally slip a positive note through the locker vent complimenting a student on performance or effort.

☞ **The Practical Pointer:**
Use brightly colored paper to make the note easy to spot. Some students will find the note immediately. For others, the note may not surface for quite some time . . .

BOOKENDS

Two Letters

Grades K–5

To expand the bond between home and school, consider this strategy. At the beginning of the school year, ask each parent to write a letter to the teacher describing his or her child. What are the child's interests, strengths, weaknesses? What hopes and dreams does the parent have for the child this school year? Are there any current or past circumstances that the teacher should be aware of in working with the child? Does the child express any fears or other concerns about school?

The teacher will read all the letters and save them. At the end of the year, it is the teacher's turn to write back to the parent summarizing the child's growth and development. The teacher encloses the parent's letter from the beginning of the year. The two letters form a set of bookends for the school year. Not only will they become keepsakes for the family but they will also provide valuable information that the parent may choose to share with other teachers in the future.

From Students Who've Been There

Grades 3–6

As the end of one school year draws to a close, ask current students to write a letter to next year's class welcoming them to their grade level. Students can describe some of the activities as well as things they learned. They can also offer advice on everything from homework to the playground. It is a great way for older students to put closure on their own experience and act as mentors for incoming students. These letters can be placed on each desk as a welcome gift the first day of school.

WHAT GOES AROUND COMES AROUND

Random Acts of Kindness

Grades 2–12

A few years ago the concept of the **Random Act of Kindness** was very popular, not only in schools but also in many communities. Though interest has peaked in organized programs, the concept itself is still much needed in our learning communities. Because our classrooms are more diverse than ever in every possible way, acts of kindness can be especially important in promoting acceptance of all individuals for their unique gifts and differences.

HOW IT WORKS:

Creating a **Random Act of Kindness** program can be simple. One teacher may decide to incorporate the concept in one classroom, or teachers at one grade level can make it a grade-level project, or the entire staff can embrace it as a schoolwide theme.

To begin, it can involve no more than small pieces of paper to record **Acts of Kindness**. They are filled out and dropped into a special container. In some classrooms, the *recipient* of a small kindness briefly records the event; in other classrooms, *another student* witnesses an act of kindness and records it.

At the end of the week, the notes are read to the group and are added to the class scrapbook. There may not be any prizes, awards or other recognition other than applause. Some advocates of **Random Acts of Kindness** feel strongly that we should be support this behavior as the right thing to do without tangible rewards.

In other schools, rewards are a key component of the **Acts of Kindness** program. Teachers can also be involved by carrying **Act of Kindness** tickets used to "catch students being kind." When a student is observed doing something out of the ordinary for another student or adult, the student's name is entered in a monthly drawing for prizes.

☞ **The Practical Pointer:**

It should be noted that a **Random Act of Kindness** program creates the greatest impact when the entire school staff and student body endorse it.

⚷ KEY IDEA

The goal is to create an awareness of kindness. The drawings and prizes call attention to the theme. It is hoped that after awhile, students will make acts of kindness a way of life. This learned behavior becomes a wonderful habit with intrinsic rewards taking precedence over the attraction that any tangible reward might bring.

Affirmation Hall Pass

Grades K–5

I was very impressed with a simple approach teachers used in an elementary building in New York to focus on students who needed some special attention on a particular day.

As a regular procedure, all students wore a hall pass on a string every time they left the classroom. Teachers selected one hall pass, though, with a *special string* to designate this need for affirmation and attention.

It was a quiet signal among the adults to notice the student who was wearing the **Affirmation Hall Pass** and provide extra attention. A classroom teacher might ask a student to take a note to the office. There the secretary would notice the designated hall pass by the orange string, for example. The secretary would greet the student warmly, and ask the child to take a note into the principal.

The principal would also greet the student, "Jamie, I am so glad to see you! I am so happy that you are here at school today! Would do a special favor for me? I need this envelope brought to Mrs. McMahon in First Grade. Would you do that and bring it right back to me?"

In the first grade classroom, the teacher would also notice the special hall pass and greet the student before initialing the envelope. By the time the student had returned to the office and had gone back to the classroom, several different adults had provided a much needed "pat on the back." Very little class time had been missed. Teachers at that school found that the quick trip gave this student a fresh outlook and reassurance that many people cared.

Signal Ink

Grades 6–8

A group of middle school teachers liked the concept of the **Affirmation Hall Pass** but the system of passes in their school used slips of paper signed by a teacher. The teachers decided that a specific color of ink would serve the same purpose of indicating that a student needed support that day. They chose green ink as the signal.

An adult in the office, media center or other location would notice the green ink when the student presented the pass and understand the message: This student needs some support today. Spend a few extra moments with this person.

OPTIONS FOR REWARDS

Spin a Reward

Grades 1–5

If you do use a reward system, you can offer choices by creating a basic spinner. To make one that works like typical game board spinners, use a round piece of tag board, a metal brad and an arrow. Divide the circle into several sections. One option is to number the pieces of the pie so that the spinner can be a permanent tool while the rewards can change periodically. Here are ten popular rewards that I have used:

1. Extra Minutes on the Computer

2. Borrow the Teacher's (Book, Special Pen, or Marker)

3. Become the Teaching Assistant for the Day

4. One No Homework Ticket

5. A Pass to Chew Gum

6. A Pass to Wear a Hat in Class

7. Get Out of Detention Free

8. Skip a Quiz

9. Five Free Points

10. Sit Anywhere for a Day

☞ **The Practical Pointer:**
Laminating the circle and the arrow makes both last longer!

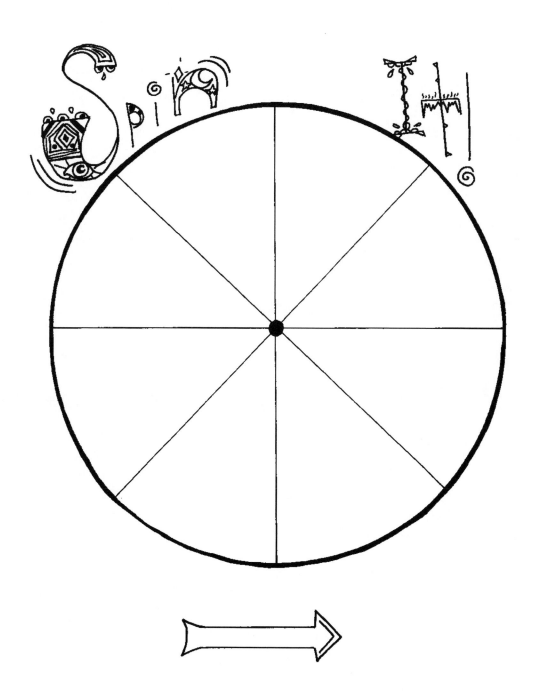

Chalkboard Jar

Grades K–4

A simple strategy to promote group goals is to draw the outline of a jar on the blackboard or white board. Whenever the class attains a goal, works well together or displays particular kindness toward each other, add another "marble" to the jar. Use colored chalk or markers to add interest.

When the jar is full, celebrate as a group with a popcorn party, games, free time or other reward. The jar is always visible and students can easily see their progress.

The Whole World!

Grades K–3

When visiting a primary classroom, I noticed a globe with a hole cut out of the top. The teacher explained that she had found the outdated globe at a garage sale and used it to hold rewards. She told her students, "You can have anything in **The Whole World!**" Students earned the opportunity to reach inside and pick a prize. There were pencils, stickers, tickets for computer time and other small inexpensive items.

To Reward or Not to Reward

Grades K–12

Second Grade was the last time you got paid when your teeth fell out.

–Erma Bombeck

Several examples of rewards were suggested in this section. It might be a good idea to share a few thoughts on the use of rewards. My own experience has been that rewards, when used intermittently, can be effective tools used to capture our students' interest and serve as a motivator for many students.

There seem to be two groups of students, though, for whom rewards carry little weight. In the first group, the motivation is already present. These students do not need a reward because they have an inner desire to succeed. In the second group, the greater challenge lies in finding something that will motivate students to excel. This last group can be extremely frustrating for a teacher because, on the surface, these students seem not to care. Rewards are like any other strategy—no single approach works for every student.

What are your feelings about tangible rewards for positive effort? Some teachers accept the use of rewards for *exceptional* work but object strongly when we reward students for doing simply what is expected of them. When we give prizes, tickets, privileges or other tangible rewards for the most basic expectations, are we preparing them for life? It is a question that is frequently raised when I visit schools. Will students be rewarded in a like manner in the workplace for simply doing what is expected? The answer can be a resounding YES!

INCENTIVES

Many companies in the private sector routinely provide incentive programs for high performance but also reward employees for doing what is merely expected. Consistent attendance is required in any job in the workplace. Should adults be rewarded for that basic expectation? Many companies apparently believe that they should.

A major airline awards eight new sport utility vehicles every six months in a drawing based on perfect attendance. As of January 2002, the number of vehicles awarded was over 100. The program continues to be extremely popular. All employees from pilots to baggage handlers who have six months of perfect attendance are eligible for the drawing. It does sound pretty enticing. I wonder what the local school board would think of the idea . . .

Through increases in pay, perks, bonuses, commissions or promotions, tangible rewards have become a major part of the workplace in the private sector. These rewards are effective because the recipients want them and see their value. They are also effective because the rewards and incentives are relatively immediate in nature.

ARE REWARDS THE ONLY ANSWER?

Rewards are less successful when they are long-term to the extent that the recipient cannot clearly see the outcome. In 2001, the Minneapolis Foundation dedicated funds for 450 kindergartners who were thought to be at high-risk for not finishing high school in 2010.

The plan was this. If the child remained in either a Minneapolis or St. Paul school and graduated from high school on time, the child would be guaranteed a $10,000 college scholarship. Tutoring, activities, mentoring and several other components were part of the program that was initiated with great optimism.

Now a year later, the Foundation is discovering that 131 children have already dropped out of the Foundation's program after kindergarten. Several students have moved more than once and no one knows where they are living. Parental commitment was less than was hoped for and the process of getting consent forms signed involved going door-to-door. The labor part of the program was vastly underrated. The biggest surprise to the Foundation was the high turnover among teachers. Many of the teachers, so critical to the success of the program, had already changed schools or left the district just a year later.

Still, the Minneapolis Foundation is not giving up. Essential changes are being made. The funding is still there. There is still great hope for the scholarship program and for the students who would benefit. It illustrates, though, that rewards—not even $10,000—can become the single solution.

LIFELONG LEARNERS

Ultimately, we hope that we are raising lifelong learners in our schools. We hope that our students will love learning because it is fulfilling, exciting, and changes our lives. We hope that we are truly preparing our students to make our world a better place through their contributions in the future.

B.I.Y. (Believe in Yourself)

Grades K–12

If we can teach students to do this, we have succeeded in helping students develop a strong self-concept. We want to help students feel confident about filling in the blanks:

"I am good at _____"

"One of my strengths is _____"

"I feel good about how well I can _____"

Sometimes it is hard for students to articulate these qualities because we, as teachers, hesitate to say these things ourselves. Many of us, when growing up, were taught not to toot our own horn. There is a difference, though, between bragging and stating strengths. Students should be able to say, "This is what I can do well."

B.I.Y. can be the basis for receiving a "Terrific Ticket." When you catch a student exhibiting self-confidence through excellent work, strong effort, or helping others, that student can receive a ticket. Like the **Address Labels with a Twist,** the tickets can be an end in themselves without a tangible reward attached or they can also become a ticket to win dropped into the weekly drawing for a prize.

Tell Them!

Grades K–12

We want our students to believe in themselves but it is also important for them to know that we, too, believe in them. Tell them. Always tell students that you believe in them. This is especially important at the end of the school year as you send them off to the next part of their journey. Don't just think it, say it.

O—🔑 KEY IDEA

When most people recall an individual who made a major impact on their lives, it is often because that individual saw potential, encouraged and nurtured them. Be that individual. Be that person. People always remember the individuals who believed in them.

SUMMARY

Helping our students develop self-confidence is a critical part of promoting lifelong learning. When our students can identify their strengths, they can build on those inner resources, believe in themselves and their ability to take on all that the world has to offer. This resilient attitude will carry them through challenges, enable them to set high goals and take the risks needed to attain those goals.

A friend sent me a humorous story recently because it reminded her of a resourceful and resilient student we shared several years ago. This little boy faced academic struggles daily but he bounced through his day with an impish grin and almost relentless energy. He always made us smile.

The story is about a parochial school at lunchtime. The children are lined up in the cafeteria, trays in hand. At the head of the long counter is a big bowl of apples. Next to the apples is a note punctuated with a large exclamation point, *"Take only one, God is watching!"*

The children move through the line and at the other end of the counter is an enormous platter of chocolate chip cookies. One little boy quickly grabs a scrap of paper and scribbles his own note, *"Take all you want, God is watching the apples!"*

I could just see our former student as that little boy, the same little boy who told me at the end of the year, *"I'm so glad someone gave me the chance to feel proud of myself."*

Let us put our minds together and see what we will make for our children.

–Chief Sitting Bull

12

WE ARE THE VILLAGE

It takes a village to raise a child . . .

It takes a village to raise a child.

We are fond of saying that in education and most of us would likely agree with the concept.

Who, though, is raising the village?

In the school community, the village is made up of every adult who comes into contact with a child from the principal to the support staff to the teachers to the volunteers. We are the village. How the village functions will have a significant impact on the success of each student.

Do we model the same cooperative spirit and respect for every individual that we are promoting among our students? Are we taking the care and time needed to build a strong, unified, nurturing village? Have we learned how to work as a team?

Only through teamwork can we combine our talent, knowledge and insight to provide the best educational opportunities possible in our schools. One of the major changes in education over the last several years is the increased inclusion of students with special needs in our schools. Our classrooms are filled with students at all ability levels who need the very best that we can offer in creating rigorous and challenging curricula for all learners.

According to the 23rd Annual Report to Congress on the Implementation of IDEA (Individuals With Disabilities Education Act) released in June 2001, the percentage of students with special needs ages 6–21 has steadily increased in regular schools and regular classrooms over the last 20 years.

For many students with special needs, the inclusion process has been extremely successful when appropriate supports and services have been provided. Graduation rates among students with special needs have continued to increase while dropout rates have continued to decline.

The most recent school year included in the 2002 report was the school year ending in 1999. At that time, 57 percent of all students with special needs, aged 14 and older, graduated from high school with a standard diploma.

To continue this trend of success in the regular classroom means that all staff members must work together with a common goal. Our unified goal must focus on the question *What is best for students? Children First* must become our mantra. It means that every student at every level must be challenged academically by differentiating or personalizing instruction for all learners. In an educational setting in which one size surely does not fit all, it means that we must celebrate differences while ensuring high expectations and high standards.

Two major strategies, collaboration and co-teaching, are highly effective in accomplishing this. *Collaboration* involves staff members planning together outside the classroom and offers tremendous opportunities to share ideas, resources and expertise. *Co-teaching* enables a team of teachers to teach together within one classroom setting using a variety of methods, tasks and groupings to teach all students. Open, honest communication underlies both. Collaboration and co-teaching bring positive results and benefit all students in the learning community from the top students to students who struggle most.

The preceding chapters in *The Teacher's Toolbox for Differentiating Instruction* have focused on working directly with students. "We Are the Village" focuses on the role of *adults working together* for student success. This chapter offers perspective as well as practical strategies, tips, and techniques for collaboration and co-teaching in several areas:

- From Isolation to Collaboration
- Quotes from the Classroom
- What's in a Name?
- Class Makeup
- Co-Teaching Formats
- 10 Keys to Successful Co-Teaching
- Tips from the Trenches
- Administrative Support
- Planning Time: 15 Strategies that Work
- Collaboration Killers

FROM ISOLATION TO COLLABORATION

ISOLATION WAS THEN . . .

I began my teaching career in 1971 in a job market overflowing with teachers. At that time, teaching was a very isolating experience. Co-teaching did not occur in my school and, generally, every staff member functioned independently.

As a new teacher, I learned on the job. Simply by chance, I shared planning time with an

English teacher who had many years of experience. Fortunately for me, we planned together and taught the same subjects. We did not differentiate our instruction. With rare exceptions, every student did every assignment in the same way.

When the bell rang, the teachers in my school went into our own classrooms and we were on our own. There were occasional staff meetings and, rarely, department meetings. My required annual review was limited to an administrator stopping in my classroom briefly, followed by an even shorter perfunctory evaluation after school. Veteran teachers in my school joked about an unspoken policy that further encouraged isolation: *Close your mouth and close your door.* That was a different era.

COLLABORATION IS NOW . . .

Now more than ever before, teams inside organizations . . . need to know how to generate divergent ideas to make things happen.

–Lisa Gundry, DePaul University

Today it is a different world indeed. Today we teach all students. We teach the top students, students with special needs, the students "falling through the cracks" and the students "in the middle." We must collaborate because we teach everyone.

We can no longer isolate ourselves from each other. Each of us has too much to offer other faculty members. Many new teachers are entering the profession. They bring with them fresh ideas, optimism and enthusiasm. At the same time, they need the wisdom and guidance that seasoned staff members can offer after years of experience.

Many schools have implemented solid mentoring programs. As educators, we have come to realize that two heads *or more* are better than one. We've learned that whether we have taught two years or 20, we can learn from each other. We've learned that collaboration helps our own professional growth and helps all of our students succeed. In fact, collaborating is no longer an option. Seeking input and help from each other is the *only way* that we can meet the needs of our diverse student population. We cannot meet this challenge alone.

Working together is often more difficult than it might seem. Many schools, and perhaps yours is one, have been collaborating and co-teaching for several years by now. In consulting with school districts across country and visiting classrooms K–12, I see many successful examples of both collaborating outside the classroom and co-teaching within our classrooms. In other school districts, staff members are moving forward but the effort is sporadic and the results are mixed. Sometimes within *one* school district, a particular school functions well as a collaborative learning community while, in another school just a few miles away, the process is only beginning.

QUOTES FROM THE CLASSROOM

While the biggest issue in collaborative planning centers on scheduling regular, consistent time to plan, the biggest issue in the co-teaching process involves interpersonal relationships and understanding how to teach together.

Let me begin by sharing several comments made to me by teachers and administrators about their experiences with co-teaching. As you will find, I have made a point of selecting a diverse representation of comments. The experiences vary tremendously and illustrate that we all have much to learn.

I'll be the first to tell you that I was apprehensive about this. I have taught for years and the idea of someone sharing my space was a concern to me. Now I just love teaching together. All of my students benefit. I don't think you could pick out which kids are in special education in this class and which teacher is which. Now I am a believer. Until I actually experienced it, though, I would never have guessed that co-teaching could be so successful.

–Middle school English teacher

As a math teacher, I have a problem when the co-teacher is "math phobic." I suddenly have an extra student and no help.

–Algebra teacher

I am the special education teacher but I started out as a general education science teacher. I have two masters' degrees. My co-teacher, the ninth grade science teacher, is 25 years younger than I am. I was teaching before he was born. Sometimes I think that he feels threatened by suggestions that I make. He treats me like an aide and expects my role to be limited to taking attendance and keeping students awake. I am not an adversary. We are supposed to be a team. I just want what is best for kids . . .

–Special education teacher

Planning time together is the key. We plan every day. It was built into our schedule last spring as we planned for this. This is our first year and both of us agree that it is going smoothly.

–Classroom teacher

That special education teacher can come into my room. Just never forget whose room this is.

–Social studies teacher

It is going beautifully for us. We finish each other's sentences. We are a team. Both of our names are on the door. We both teach. Students see us as two teachers. Neither of us has a label. How did I ever teach before?

–Fifth grade teacher

I never know what I'm walking into at the beginning of a semester. It's different in every classroom where I co-teach. First period, I might have a very active teaching role. Second hour, I function as a clerical aide. In another classroom, I am told clearly that certain students are "my students." In my afternoon class, I am directed to reinforce six vocabulary words. I've learned to be very flexible and it's getting better.

–High school special education teacher

We're really lucky, I guess. This is our first year together and we have a great working relationship. With co-teaching, I have more time to work with individual students. I wish all my classes could be co-taught.

–Middle school math teacher

The classroom teacher did not see himself as the teacher of any student with special needs. "You are the reading teacher for these students. Do whatever you want." When there is no thematic plan, it is very difficult to know what is expected and what to do.

–Middle school special education teacher

Co-teaching is fun! We have a daily planning period together. It has been going very well!

–Elementary special education teacher.

In my foreign language class, I have students at all levels. This is high school and one of my students reads at the first grade level. There is no co-teacher provided because the administration told me, "We don't put co-teachers in those classes." How could this happen?

–High school Spanish teacher

Every single teacher who was on a co-teaching team this year has asked to do it again next year. Co-teaching has been a great success!

–Elementary principal

I asked each classroom teacher for an answer key for every assignment. That was in September. I repeated my request throughout the year. It is now the end of May. No answer key was ever provided. I spend too much time looking up answers to the social studies study guide and too little time teaching students.

—High school special education teacher

I sit in the back of the classroom and take notes for a student. It is as if I am a tenth grade student instead of a licensed special education teacher with a master's degree. Wouldn't it make more sense for the teacher to provide a copy of notes and overheads at the beginning of class? Then I could help students highlight key points . . .

—Middle school special education teacher

We don't think of ourselves as a regular education teacher or a special education teacher. We are teachers. The students come to either one of us for help. No one has a label. We switch off being the lead teacher for each unit. It works.

—Earth science teacher

Co-teaching in my school is nothing like you have been describing. A special education teacher comes into my classroom and works with her students in the back of the room. We don't plan together and we don't teach together. Our content is totally different. The noise level is a problem and all the students are distracted. It seems like the resource room has just been moved into my classroom for the hour. Is this co-teaching?

—Classroom teacher

All of my students' test scores are going up! We are constantly trying new things. We are constantly stretching each other. It is energizing!

—Classroom teacher

I used to send some of my science students to the resource room to have tests read to them. Unfortunately, the special education teacher did not co-teach with me and did not have a science background. As a result, I've found that the students get higher scores staying in the classroom where I can explain some of the questions to them. This convinced me that my classroom is where they belong.

—High school science teacher

At first, very few of the regular education teachers were behind this. Now that we have been co-teaching for two years, everyone is asking when their class will have a co-teacher.

—Curriculum director

During the pilot program, all the English teachers had co-teachers in each class all day. It was wonderful! All the kids made tremendous progress. Why wouldn't everybody want to do this? We shared teaching and planning. We shared responsibility. There was so much support. We sold the concept to entire staff as the way to go.

Then the budget was cut for the following year after the whole school jumped into this. Now teachers are angry because very few teachers have any co-taught classes but their regular classes still have lots of students with special needs.

There is very little classroom support. Special education teachers only have time to pop in and check on students or leave a checklist in teachers' mailboxes. This is not how it was supposed to work. The original concept had merit. It was working so well. Now what?

—High school English department chairperson

Two things make it work for us: planning time and flexibility. We meet once a week and decide who will do what. After being together three years, we take turns teaching. At first, I had to learn the content. After three years, I have ninth grade earth science down pretty well. If the science teacher is absent, I just take over. We don't lose a day of class. The students see me as another teacher.

—Special education teacher

I think it would be a waste of my time as a special educator to co-teach in a classroom. There is already a content teacher in there who is trained in the field and was hired to do that. Why would I want to learn American history all over again and co-teach it? I would much rather work with a small group of students in a different room reading tests and helping with homework.

—High school special education teacher

I have a masters degree plus 60 graduate hours in my field teaching at the high school level. How can someone who has no training in my content area walk in and co-teach with me this semester? If someone really can do that, what does that say about the degrees, credits and experiences that I have?

—High school teacher

My co-teacher and I have a wonderful relationship. My co-teacher is the first grade classroom teacher and I am the special educator. We are having so much fun teaching together! It is her third year teaching and I have been here over 30 years. The age difference is an asset. I believe that we both have so much to offer. Our students are thriving! We also have one of the more

> *unusual co-teaching arrangements that you'll visit. My co-teacher is my daughter!*
>
> *–Special education teacher*

From the hundreds of written comments and questions that I have received over the past few years, these are typical. Understanding of what collaboration and co-teaching are all about runs the gamut. Experiences vary from excellent to poor. Some perceptions of what this should entail are accurate; others show that much work needs to be done in helping all school staff understand the scope and purpose of both collaboration and co-teaching.

☞ **The Practical Pointer:**

For more information in greater detail than is provided in this chapter, you may wish to read my book, *Inclusion: A Fresh Look—Practical Strategies to Help All Students Succeed* (Covington Cove Publications 1–888-LEARN-11). It is a companion to *The Teacher's Toolbox for Differentiating Instruction* but the focuses entirely on including students with special needs in the general classroom. It includes collaboration and implementation strategies, curriculum modification, and flexible expectations, as well as practical classroom strategies to help students succeed. "We Are the Village" focuses on two key aspects of including students with special needs: co-teaching and collaborative strategies.

A common question about co-teaching is how to make it work successfully. When a teacher tells me that co-teaching did not work in a specific classroom, I want to learn more about the situation. Usually I discover a mismatch of expectations or a serious misunderstanding of what co-teaching would look like.

Many different factors affect successful co-teaching. The number of students with special needs in a classroom, the number of special education staff available to co-teach and the number of co-taught classes all have a tremendous impact on the situation. There are several additional factors that have an impact on success. These include the amount of time invested in planning ahead, a clear description of how co-teaching will work, and an understanding of whether the commitment will be a one-year pilot project or whether the plan will remain in place over time. Co-teaching encompasses many different considerations and has many different meanings in practice. The word *co-teaching* is bantered about but what it looks like in one school may bear little resemblance to what is called *co-teaching* somewhere else.

WHAT'S IN A NAME?

> *But mom, how did you know I wanted to be called "Seamus" before I was even born?*
>
> *–Seamus McMahon-McKenna, age 6*

There is a lot in a name. In discussing co-teaching, many teachers begin their comments to me with a common phrase, "In my school, co-teaching is . . ." Then I will hear a wide range of descriptions, programs and approaches all in the name of co-teaching. It is important to differentiate among different meanings that individuals attach to this same term.

Sometimes within one school district and within one school, what people are calling co-teaching can look very different from each other. Sometimes what is called *co-teaching* in a school is anything but that. Know the real situation. To avoid frustration for everyone involved, expectations need to fit what is actually in place or what actually will occur.

I often see seven different scenarios that are referred to as co-teaching. These are described next. Of the seven that I describe, only the last one fits the real intent of co-teaching as an effective classroom strategy.

CAMEO APPEARANCES

In some schools the term co-teaching is used when what is actually occurring could better be described as cameo appearances by special education staff. There are sporadic visits to the classroom to check on students or to occasionally assist with an activity or read a test aloud. Classroom teachers often receive a checklist in their mailboxes to fill out regarding performance by targeted students.

Usually these special education teachers are responsible for so many students in different classrooms and grade levels that scheduling regular time to co-teach is not feasible. A sensible solution would be to start by assigning special education teachers to certain grades levels or departments so that each teacher is not attempting to work with students throughout the school at all grade levels and in every department. Next, they might consider scheduling small clusters of students with special needs in one or two classes that will allow for limited co-teaching.

COLLABORATION ONLY

In some schools, co-teaching is actually limited to collaboration outside the classroom. Teachers consult together during a planning session and may direct the work of paraprofessionals who then go into the classroom to assist students.

Collaboration alone can be an effective tool. Sometimes it is impossible to schedule a special education to co-teach in any classroom. This is true in schools in which one special educator is responsible for every student with special needs in the school.

Schools facing this situation might involve other special education personnel, such as a speech language pathologist, in co-teaching. What better environment could be found for assisting with language development than in the classroom itself? Too often the perception is that speech pathology focuses only on articulation. In actuality, speech pathologists spend more time with students on language skills. They are excellent resources for teaching vocabulary, developing language skills in general and providing activities for review of language-related skills.

Another option for schools with a single special education teacher is to consider the benefits of adding another teacher. Many schools have made this commitment when they have analyzed the contributions to all students by this resource.

SHARING SPACE

I see this situation frequently. There are simply two teachers teaching different content and different students while sharing a common classroom. They do not plan together and they do not teach together. The space is often too small and the noise level is too high. Basically, the special education teacher teaches "included" students at a small table in the back of the classroom. A resource room has been created within the general classroom.

Both teachers are quite sure that what is happening is not true co-teaching. The situation is not satisfactory for anyone involved. They are in an ideal position to move toward co-teaching by planning some activities for the whole group. The teachers can bring all of the students together at times and share teaching responsibilities rather than competing for space and noise levels. These teachers can continue the process by exploring a variety of co-teaching options that will mix students in large groups and small groups allowing both teachers to interact with all students.

ONE-ON-ONE ASSISTANCE

Another common scenario that I see during my consulting is also called co-teaching. It looks like this. The content teacher is doing all the teaching while a special education teacher sits next to a student, takes notes, and primarily helps a student who has little contact with other members of the class. Except for the role with the specific student, the special education teacher assumes a very passive role in the classroom.

To create a real co-teaching situation, the content area teacher can encourage the special education staff member to move away from one student and take a more active role in the class. Providing a set of class notes or copies of the overheads before class begins will free the special education teacher from copying tasks and allow time for that individual to assist other students.

When the special education teacher sits next to a specific student, the result is increased dependency on the teacher. The goal of co-teaching and including the student in the classroom is not dependence but independence. Encouraging the student to interact with classmates benefits that student and helps that individual become more independent. This shift in focus enables the special education teacher to utilize skills for the benefit of all students by taking a much more active role in co-teaching.

CROWD CONTROL

Finally, another common situation occurs in the name of co-teaching that would be better described as "crowd control." The special education teacher takes attendance, walks around checking on students, deals with discipline and functions primarily as an assistant.

As in the one-on-one example, the special education staff member is being underutilized. The purpose of co-teaching is to use the skills of both teachers in a variety of ways. I always encourage teams who are operating this way to reassess how both teachers can share responsibility for the class by planning together and deciding how the special education teacher can participate more effectively.

CLASSROOM AIDE SUPPORT

A different situation occurs when a general education teacher is assisted by a *paraprofessional*. It is not co-teaching. The paraprofessional or teaching assistant or aide acts as *support* for the classroom teacher. This support role is critical, but the responsibility of co-teaching new content does not lie with support staff. This is an important distinction. Too often individuals who have been hired in the capacity of a paraprofessional are assigned teaching responsibilities for which they have not been trained or paid.

Paraprofessionals can work effectively under the guidance of either a special educator or a general educator to review content and assist students. Many paraprofessionals are superb and their work with students is outstanding. In fact, many students will seek out a paraprofessional before going to the teacher because of the relationship that has been developed.

To expect paraprofessionals to teach new content, design materials and assume full responsibility for students, especially students with special needs, is not in their best interest or in the best interest of the students they serve. See the chapter, "Tapping the Talent of Paraprofessionals," in *Inclusion: A Fresh Look*, for more information on working effectively with paraprofessionals. For purposes of discussing co-teaching, the assumption is that two licensed teachers form the team.

PURPOSEFUL CO-TEACHING

The good news is that co-teaching, as it was intended, is alive and well and succeeding in many, many classrooms. In purposeful co-teaching, two *licensed* teachers share responsibility for students within a given class or classroom for part, or very occasionally, all of the day. Typically, one teacher is a licensed special education teacher and the other is a licensed general education teacher. In a co-teaching team made up of two teachers, everything must be shared. The two teachers share responsibility for all aspects of planning, teaching and evaluating student performance. Teachers also share responsibility for parent communication.

There are dangers in any co-teaching situation of one person being solely in charge and assuming all responsibilities. A number of problems can surface. For example, "turfism" enters in when co-teachers compete for ownership of space, students and content. Students can sense the competition between the co-teachers and will use that to manipulate the situation, playing one person against the other.

The opposite can also occur. When neither person takes ownership nor has a passion for making it work, the situation deteriorates into a lose-lose situation for both students and co-teachers. Effective co-teaching results when all individuals involved have equal ownership and a stake in the outcome.

To make co-teaching work, regular attendance is expected. Ideally, but not always, a common planning time is scheduled at least weekly. The greatest benefit for both the teachers and students is the sharing of expertise. Truly two heads are better than one.

Students recognize that both individuals are teachers and can go to either person for help. Teacher-student ratio is reduced by half allowing much more individual attention for every student in the classroom.

CLASS MAKEUP

Most often the co-taught classroom is heterogeneous in makeup including some students who have identified special needs. It is critical to avoid placing too many high-need students in a class or too many students who are "falling through the cracks" because the situation can become unmanageable even for two master teachers.

I mention this as a cautionary note after consulting in many situations where the numbers of students with special needs have been too high. It is critical to consider not only the students in the class who have identified special needs but also any other students who are struggling.

Sometimes the perception is that because "there are two teachers" a much higher percentage of high-need students will be manageable. It does not work. It also does not work when several students in the same classroom have behavior issues.

It is impossible to suggest an optimal ratio or a specific percentage of students at each level within a class for successful co-teaching. All students are different. Only those individuals who have a clear understanding of the needs of specific students can plan for the co-taught class. Other important factors such as gender, size of school, grade level, native language of students and poverty also affect the optimal makeup and size of a particular co-taught class.

CO-TEACHING FORMATS

I have two teachers this year and I love them both!

–*Fifth grade student*

There is not just one way to co-teach in a classroom. Teachers often ask me what co-teaching looks like. The format will vary from one day to the next depending on the purpose and content. Even within one class period, co-teaching may include a variety of approaches. Teams discover that initially, the special education teacher may elect to observe both the teacher and students. Gradually the special education teacher will increase the level of participation in the teaching process.

One day, for example, the two teachers may decide to divide the class in half, each working on a different topic and then rotating groups. On another occasion, the special education teacher may lead a large group activity such as a review skill while the classroom teacher works with a small group.

The small group may include students who are struggling with the content or, on another day, the small group may include high potential students who are ready for an activity beyond the scope of the curriculum. Teachers may plan to reverse the large group and small format on another occasion so that both teachers have opportunities to work with both sized groups.

Still another day, one teacher may function as lead teacher during the lesson and both teachers may assist all students later during a group activity or individual work time. On yet another occasion, students may be working on individual projects and both teachers serve as resources for students.

The classroom teacher may always be the primary teacher during the first year that the team co-teaches. The following year, the team may elect to divide content units, rotating the role of lead teacher.

The needs of the students, the subject content, students' background knowledge, the teaching strengths of the teachers—all are factors in planning the co-teaching format that will be used at a particular time. One teacher described co-teaching as *cooperative learning for adults*. Working together is a learned skill and does not come easily for all of us. Co-teaching is fluid. When it works at its very best, both teachers teach together, each supplying expertise in different ways.

From the students' perspective, both teachers are available to help them succeed. In a successful co-taught classroom, students do not differentiate between the "classroom" teacher and the "special education" teacher. They are two teachers and students know that they can approach either one.

LIMITED CO-TEACHING

In an ideal world, every classroom in the future would be co-taught by two talented, licensed teachers. This is the most desirable vision but it is not the reality for most school districts. Co-teaching on a broad scale is labor intensive to a degree that many schools simply cannot afford.

What is realistic is *limited co-teaching* both today and in the future in most schools. That is possible. Many school districts have had successful co-teaching teams for several years. The challenge for these schools is to keep teams together who share a long history while finding a way to expand and develop new teams of co-teachers within the confines of budget constraints.

ELEMENTARY AND SECONDARY CO-TEACHING

All levels including elementary, middle school and high school bring certain challenges and concerns with respect to co-teaching. Currently, co-teaching occurs more often at the elementary level than at the secondary level. In fact, it is not unusual to find elementary co-teaching teams who have been together so long that teachers can finish each other's sentences.

This is less common at the middle school and high school level although there are many, many successful teams of co-teachers. Co-teaching has increased dramatically in middle schools during the last few years and the results have been positive. Compared to both elementary and middle schools, high schools offer fewer co-taught classes, in general, and there is less collaboration outside the classroom.

This is not surprising considering the sheer numbers of staff members and classes taught at the high school level. Though not as widespread, many examples of successful co-teaching can be found. The key is to pair co-teaching with adequate planning time and administrative support.

10 KEYS TO SUCCESSFUL CO-TEACHING

Across the grade levels and content areas, co-teaching can be more successful when these ten keys are evident.

1. *Both teachers teach.*

   It may not be every day during every class but it is critical that students see both teachers in a teaching role. As a former English and reading teacher, I could step into that role again easily in classes that focused on literature, writing, reading skills and grammar.

   My own experience in teaching science and math came as a special education teacher at all grade levels and also in adult education programs. Despite years of teaching, my background in those specific fields is limited. Teachers with a similar background often ask: What and how can I teach in a classroom that is outside of my general education background and licensure?

   There are many general learning skills that a special education teacher can bring to any content area. For example, special educators often have extensive experience in teaching students how to review material, how to use a textbook effectively, how to improve study skills and how to break an assignment or task into smaller segments. Special education teachers can offer multiple strategies for content area reading and comprehension skills, as well as strategies to learn vocabulary words effectively.

In my own experience, I used all of those skills in a variety of content areas. The special education teacher might also lead one of the review activities suggested in "High-Impact Review." In the role of co-teacher, the special educator is not attempting to supplant the content teacher but to bring *different* skills. Over time, a co-teacher learns the class content well and can take a very active teaching role. It is important to note that credibility with students develops when students see both teachers teach in the classroom.

2. *Both teachers are in the room.*

   Both teachers are there together as members of the same team to help all students succeed. One of the immediate benefits of the co-teaching strategy is reducing the class ratio. Students receive twice as much attention with two teachers. I asked middle school students who had been in a co-taught social studies class during eighth grade to evaluate their experiences at the end of the year. Two themes emerged again and again from the students who would be considered typical eighth-graders.

   > You didn't have to wait so long for help; and
   > the behavior of everybody was so much better.

   Students want an atmosphere that is conducive to learning. They want to receive help when they need it and like the options that having two teachers provide.

3. *Both names are on the class list.*

   From the beginning, it is clear that both teachers have authority and responsibility for the class. Many co-teachers have commented that when the co-teacher's name was not included on the class list from the beginning, it took several weeks to establish credibility with students.

4. *Both teachers attend Open House.*

   Co-teachers introduce each other as a team to parents and students. Because both students and parents may recognize one of the co-teachers as a "special education teacher" in the school, there may be a fear that the class is, indeed, a special education class.

   There may misperceptions that standards will be lower and content will be reduced. Parents of some students may also express concerns about the qualifications of the special education teacher to participate in that class. Parents of students with special needs may have concerns about the acceptance of their children by both teachers and students. Parents may also feel some fear about their child's success in this setting.

All parents may express concern about which teacher to contact with questions or which teacher will return phone calls. The team can explain that parents can contact either teacher or that, if the need arises, either teacher may contact the parent.

It is critical that parents understand that the purpose of co-teaching is to increase opportunities to differentiate instruction for all learners by providing additional resources and increasing student-teacher contact time.

High standards and high expectations should be emphasized. Both parents and students will want to know that both teachers are licensed teachers. They will also want to be assured that the content area teacher will remain the primary source for determining what content will be taught. It can be very helpful to describe how a typical class might look focusing on the benefits of involving two teachers. When the team concept is presented clearly from the beginning to parents and students, there is increased support and understanding.

5. *Both teachers volunteered.*

   Co-teaching works best when teachers involved have volunteered to become team members. Co-teaching is not about "fixing" anyone or forcing one person to "accept" the other. I have seen both unfortunate situations. Neither will work and students are quick to see that. The focus of co-teaching is creating a positive learning environment for students through a team effort of two excellent teachers who are eager to share their skills and strengths. When teachers learn from each other, students benefit.

6. *Both teachers have equal status.*

   Co-teaching works when the team members see each other as licensed teachers who have equal status. They view each other as the professionals that they are and treat each other with respect. Both accept and share responsibility for all learners.

7. *Both teachers invest time in the process.*

   They recognize that co-teaching and collaboration are processes that take time. Even teachers who have known each other for years will not become a "team" the first day. It takes time to build trust and open communication. Learning to plan together collaboratively and teach together effectively will be a gradual process. They need realistic expectations and need to recognize that they will be learning together.

8. *Both teachers are flexible.*

   Co-teaching requires flexibility and compromise on the part of both team members. It requires that one teacher who likes to be very spontaneous and teaches "on the fly," for example, may need to commit to more concrete plans ahead of time. At the elementary level, it means that a classroom teacher may need to adhere to a set time for reading because that is when the co-teacher is scheduled to be there.

The co-teacher who moves from classroom to classroom needs to adapt to different teaching styles on a daily basis. Roles, level of involvement and expectations of classroom teachers will change from class to class.

Both teachers will need to be willing to learn new approaches and strategies. It cannot be "my way or the highway." When co-teaching works at its very best, it is like ongoing mutual staff development. The number one benefit of co-teaching cited by teachers across the country is sharing new ideas. "I have learned so much!" is a comment that I hear again and again.

9. *Both teachers commit to planning collaboratively.*

   Teachers can collaborate outside the classroom to share ideas and strategies when co-teaching is not an option. That can work extremely well. However, when co-teaching is the focus, collaborative planning is critical. Collaboration and co-teaching go hand-in-hand.

   Sometimes planning is limited to five minutes over lunch, walking down the hall or while students are getting out materials. Teachers are making it work but not at the level made possible by regular planning time. See the section in this chapter on finding ways to schedule common planning time. It is essential.

10. *Both teachers focus on the positive.*

Expect that co-teaching is both feasible and beneficial for the team and, even more important, it benefits all students. Over and over again, teachers will say to me, "How did I ever teach before?"

Know that there will be the inevitable "bumps in the road." The learning curve is steep. It helps to have agreed on a problem-solving format and to use it as needed. Rarely are there team conflicts that can be resolved only by dissolving the team. More often issues can be addressed to the satisfaction of both team members. Expect a positive outcome. Expect co-teaching to work. Most teams would agree that keeping a sense of humor makes a world of difference.

The pessimist sees the difficulty in every opportunity; the optimist sees the opportunity in every difficulty.

–Winston Churchill

TIPS FROM THE TRENCHES

Teamwork: A collection of diverse individuals who are responsible for a specific outcome, who are committed to each other and to each other's success.

–Harvey Mackay

What follows is a compilation of 45 thumbnail tips that come from my observations of co-teaching teams and my own experience in teaching together effectively.

1. First build trust.
2. Take time to get to know each other.
3. Take ownership of all students as opposed to "yours" and "mine."
4. Approach planning and teaching from the child-focused perspective.
5. Delineate shared and separate roles and responsibilities.
6. Determine the extent of the co-teaching commitment, whether it will be daily, every other day, for one grading period or for the school year.
7. Make a commitment to sharing information with each other.
8. Make sure that all adults involved, including parents, have the same information.
9. Commit to following through as agreed.
10. Maintain honest communication.
11. Respect each other.
12. Recognize that sharing the same philosophy is essential.
13. See personality differences as a benefit to students.
14. Treat each other as equals who have different strengths.
15. Recognize that expectations must be high but flexible for certain students.
16. Agree to differentiate instruction for all learners at all levels.
17. Ask for planning time and make it a priority.
18. Keep a written record of collaborative sessions.
19. Examine samples of student work during collaborative sessions.
20. Share collaborative notes with other staff members who would benefit, especially teachers of related arts classes and elective courses.
21. Define collaboration and co-teaching as it relates to the specific setting.
22. Agree on discipline and put rules in writing.

23. Know the goals and objectives stated on an IEP.

24. Determine the type of assistance needed by specific students.

25. Understand accommodations and modifications needed by specific students.

26. Do not provide more help than students need.

27. Provide the fewest modifications that will enable the student to meet the challenge.

28. Recognize that not all students with special needs are "low ability."

29. Share responsibility to modify materials ahead of time.

30. Both teachers need answer keys.

31. Discuss each teacher's tolerance for noise level.

32. Provide a space for the co-teacher to store materials and personal items.

33. Set a typical daily routine.

34. Adhere to the schedule.

35. Promote the use of charts, graphs, grids and notes for students who need them.

36. Agree on grading scales, rubrics, extra credit and late assignments.

37. Determine how homework will be assigned and graded.

38. Order two Teacher's Editions for a new text.

39. Plan for continuity when a substitute teacher is needed.

40. Share parent contact of all students.

41. Document classroom results.

42. Verbalize "bottom-line" issues that each teacher feels strongly about.

43. Flexibility, forgiveness and the willingness to compromise are essential.

44. Agree on a problem-solving format to deal with the inevitable concerns.

45. Maintain a sense of humor and laugh often.

Don't bury the hatchet if you are going to put up a marker on the site.

–Sydney Harris

ADMINISTRATIVE SUPPORT

HOW ADMINISTRATORS CAN HELP

Successful collaboration and co-teaching depend on administrative support in facilitating the process. In the same thumbnail format as in the previous section, what follows are 31 specific tips for administrators.

1. Ask co-teachers what they need in terms of administrative support.

2. Involve the co-teachers in planning for the co-teaching process.

3. Solicit the input of co-teachers in determining class makeup and schedules.

4. Support the need for additional staff needed for co-teaching.

5. Limit the number of students with special needs and in one class to maintain a heterogeneous class makeup.

6. Limit the number of additional students who are "falling through the cracks" in a co-taught class.

7. Avoid overloading a co-taught class *because there are two teachers* . . . Doing so defeats the purpose of co-teaching.

8. Avoid teacher burnout by varying which teachers work with the most challenging students year after year.

9. Eliminate classroom interruptions by P.A. announcements except for emergencies.

10. Increase the focus on learning by reducing the amount of time students leave for "pull-out" programs.

11. Keep successful teams of co-teachers together more than one semester or school year.

12. Provide one or two paid days during the summer when co-teachers can plan for the next year.

13. Respect the value of the team by refraining from using one teacher as a substitute in another classroom.

14. Ask for volunteers to co-teach together rather than arbitrarily creating teams.

15. Match areas of expertise whenever possible to content and grade level within a team.

16. Provide class lists several weeks before the term begins to enable effective planning.

17. Recognize that co-teachers can only co-teach during a specific class period; testing new students and dealing with other issues cannot be accomplished at that time.

18. Provide collaborative support for elective courses and related arts classes.

19. Provide time for ongoing evaluation by co-teaching teams and encourage change as needed.

20. Facilitate communication among schools within the district in regard to planning for new students.

21. Eliminate the name "special education teacher" in favor of a name that better describes the role: "collaborative teacher" or "co-teacher."

22. Consider realigning special education staff as members of other departments or grade levels rather than as a department unto itself.

23. Provide resources such as tape recorders, tapes, CDs, headphones, microphones, additional copies of the Teacher's Edition and modified textbooks to enable co-teachers to adapt for a wide range of students in one classroom.

24. Communicate with parents so that they understand the purpose and benefits of co-teaching for students.

25. Provide staff development opportunities for co-teachers and all staff.

26. Schedule common planning time at least weekly.

27. Visit co-taught classes regularly.

28. Get to know students in co-taught classes.

29. Observe collaborative planning sessions.

30. Evaluate the results on an ongoing basis.

31. Ask staff what additional support is needed.

Please note that the following chapter, "The Leadership Privilege," focuses on leadership traits and strategies for administrative support in all aspects of the educational process. The thumbnail suggestions here highlight practical ways that administrators can support collaboration and co-teaching in their schools.

PLANNING TIME: 15 STRATEGIES THAT WORK

One of the most difficult challenges in successful co-teaching is providing adequate, face-to-face planning time. Planning time is essential. When I ask co-teachers what they need most to make this work effectively, the single answer cited most often is time to plan. Regular, structured planning time needs to be an integral part of the co-teaching process. While scheduling it is challenging, it can be done.

The key is to "plan for planning time" before the master schedule is created. Too often this critical element is left to the end when truly there is no realistic time frame in the schedule. Co-teachers need common planning periods during the school day or before or after school within contract time.

The strategies listed below are currently being used in schools. Some can be implemented immediately while others require community input and support.

1. Consider hiring a substitute to rotate through co-taught classes one class period each week or every other week to allow teachers time to plan.

2. "Bank" time by extending the school day by ten minutes 4 days a week to provide 40 minutes of early release time one day each week. At the secondary level, planning time works best as a late-start weekly; most elementary schools prefer the early dismissal.

CO-TEACHING COLLABORATIVE PLANNING

Date: **Next Meeting:**

Attending: **Facilitator:**

Agenda Attached: Y / N   **Agenda Due:**

Copies to:
_____

Class _____

What needs to be done?

M

T

W

TH

F
_____

How will each teacher participate?

_____

Format: (parallel, stations, large group, small group, tag team)

M

T

W

TH

F
_____

What were the results?   **Today's date:** _____

3. Ask the principal to covers classes occasionally to release teachers for occasional planning sessions.

4. Schedule regular planning meetings before or after school.

5. Schedule related arts classes back-to-back one day a week at the elementary level to allow extended planning.

6. Plan during a "working lunch" one day a week.

7. Schedule common grade level planning and collaboration time weekly in conjunction with related arts classes.

8. Designate one day a week for collaborative planning with a special education teacher who meets with content teachers during their preparation periods.

9. Designate one collaborative planning period each week in middle schools that already have a team-planning period.

10. At the elementary level, shorten related arts classes by five minutes to create additional related arts sections designated as planning time for collaborating teachers.

11. Eliminate "duties" such as bus, detention or cafeteria responsibilities to provide planning time for co-teachers.

12. Divide two staff development days into eight 2-hour monthly segments of early dismissals and late starts to allow monthly planning time.

13. Allocate staff development funding to pay co-teachers who are willing to meet to plan before or after the scheduled duty day.

14. Two teachers who teach the same subject or grade level schedule one double class period each week allowing one teacher time to plan with the special education teacher. The following week, the other teacher uses the time to plan.

15. Use "cross-age buddies" as a way to create planning time weekly. One week first-graders visit their third grade buddies allowing the first grade teacher collaborative planning time; the next week third-graders visit their first grade buddies while the third grade teacher plans with a co-teacher.

COLLABORATION KILLERS

In my school, the kids aren't the biggest problem, it's the adults.

–Teacher

It can be very difficult for adults to work together. Not everyone wants to eliminate the isolation of teaching as it used to be. When I suggest the joint concepts of collaboration and co-teaching, I often hear the "Yabuts" explaining how and why this could never be

20 COLLABORATION KILLERS

1. It will never work.

2. Let's form a focus group and do a survey.

3. It's too early in the year.

4. That's not my job.

5. We tried that before.

6. There's no money in the budget.

7. Let's just think about it . . .

8. It's too close to the holidays.

9. Let's not rush into anything.

10. Maybe we should form a committee.

11. It's really too late in the year.

12. Let's wait until next year.

13. We'll never have administrative support.

14. No one else does it that way.

15. We've never done it that way.

16. We already tried it in my old school.

17. My old school didn't do it that way.

18. It would never work here.

19. It can't be done.

20. Everyone would hate it.

successful in their school. Copy the list of **20 Collaboration Killers** on the reproducible page. See if any sound familiar to staff members in your school.

Henry Ford said it best,

> *Coming together is a beginning,*
>
> *Keeping together is progress,*
>
> *Working together is success.*

A positive attitude goes a long way in making all of this work for the benefit of our students. I am reminded of a sign over the scale in the locker room at the gym:

> *Pretend it's your I.Q.*

So much is in how we approach any new concept. There will always be those who believe that it will never work and sure enough, for them it won't. And there will be just as many people who will give it a try, evaluate the results and make the needed adjustments. In education, often these teachers are the "cream of the crop" who are constantly searching for excellence and working hard to help every student succeed.

SUMMARY

There is much that adults can do to create a village that is a positive environment for children. Collaboration and co-teaching have become powerful additions to the traditional classroom. Ideally every classroom would be co-taught by two talented, licensed teachers. Unfortunately, that is not the real world. However, there are many realistic aspects of collaboration and co-teaching that can be accomplished in any school.

We can use collaborative planning effectively outside the classroom and co-teach when scheduling makes it feasible. It is also realistic to better utilize the dual skills of co-teachers in the classroom when we are co-teaching. It is realistic to address some of the common problems faced by teachers planning and teaching together. There can be workable solutions. Communication, openness to new ideas and flexibility go a long way toward a positive relationship for every adult "in the village."

Start with volunteers, ask for administrative support, and make planning a priority. Take time to evaluate, make changes as needed and celebrate success. The result is a win-win situation for both teachers and their students. Once the adults are the same page with the same goals, we can truly focus on what is best for every child.

It is good to have an end to journey towards;
but it is the journey that matters in the end.

–*Ursula K. LeGuin*

13

THE LEADERSHIP PRIVILEGE

Where goes the head, so goes the body.

–an old saying

"The Leadership Privilege" is included in *The Teacher's Toolbox for Differentiating Instruction* because it is through effective leadership that standards of excellence and high expectations are set. Today more than ever, the role of the administrator is that of the school leader. Our student population has changed dramatically and now includes students at all levels with a variety of needs. To help all of our students succeed, administrators play a critical role in encouraging staff members to implement a variety of effective teaching practices.

This chapter focuses on three areas with the greatest emphasis on the third section:

- The School Leader
- Principal for a Day
- 10 Leadership Traits, Roles, and Responsibilities

THE SCHOOL LEADER

Not only is the student population changing, the teaching staff itself is changing. In many schools, a large segment of the staff is nearing retirement age and many new teachers are entering the field. The new teachers need mentoring from the principal and from experienced staff members. At the same time, veteran teachers benefit from the fresh ideas new teachers bring. The school leader is in a position to bring out the best in every teacher.

When anyone thinks of schools, though, teachers and students come to mind immediately. Everyone assumes that a principal acts behind the scenes, but not everyone realizes the enormous impact and influence of that individual on every aspect of education within a school.

The principal's responsibilities are multiple from creating the "vision," establishing school-wide goals, providing staff development, encouraging community involvement, improving student performance, and addressing the day-to-day responsibilities for the physical plant.

The greatest responsibility of an administrator is an awesome one in the fullest sense of the word. Administrators truly have an opportunity to make a positive difference in the lives of children. They have the privilege of leading the learning community in which they work toward excellence for all.

PRINCIPAL FOR A DAY

There is no question that the role of the principal is a demanding one. Some school principals are putting in 80-hour workweeks and still feel that the job demands more. One principal told me that she routinely works on Sundays just to stay on top of the workload.

It is not surprising that, nationally, there is an acute shortage of school administrators. Recently efforts have been made to increase the number of candidates for administrative positions by a variety of public campaigns. In my home state of Minnesota, "Becoming Principal for a Day" was a highly publicized event involving business leaders, the news media, politicians and other well-known individuals. Each person shadowed a principal in a local school for a day. The goal was to bring the critical but sometimes overlooked role of the principal to the foreground.

Interestingly enough, not only did the project highlight school administration, it also called attention to very serious needs in many schools. Several business leaders were surprised to find classrooms today without a single computer. In response, they pledged financial support for technology. That was an unexpected but positive result.

All of the individuals who participated expressed tremendous admiration for the principals whom they shadowed. However, not a single politician, news anchor nor CEO opted to change careers and join the ranks of school administrators. That was not the intention. The focus was on publicizing the administrative role and garnering public support. To a person, the visitors recognized the power of an excellent leader to make a difference in a school.

While I have not had the opportunity to shadow a principal for a day, I have had the opportunity to meet many, many dedicated principals in elementary schools, middle schools and high schools. I have also taught under the leadership of eight different principals in my experience at all three levels. The influence of the principal in every aspect of the school and the learning community cannot be underestimated. The old saying is true: *Where goes the head, so goes the body.*

There are also times when the leader has to take a step back and change places with the followers as well, because a strong leader also knows when to follow. It is an extremely complex role that carries with it tremendous responsibilities. The principal sets the tone for the educational process and is responsible for the results. Students, parents, and staff invest their trust in this individual to set high expectations and high standards for all. Truly, leadership is a privilege.

10 LEADERSHIP TRAITS, ROLES AND RESPONSIBILITIES

As I consult in classrooms, converse with teachers all over the country, consider best practices, and think back over 30 years in the field of education, I have learned that many traits are crucial in a strong academic leader. While effective leaders stand out in many ways, **10 Leadership Traits, Roles and Responsibilities** are critical for leadership at the school level.

1. Vision
2. Mission Statement

3. Visibility

4. Visitation

5. Goals and Accountability

6. Planning for Change

7. Communication

8. Empowerment of Staff

9. Recognition of Others

10. Celebrating Success

VISION

Leaders must continually look within to decide what they want, what they value, and what they are willing to be courageous about.

–Richard Leider

To lead by creating the vision means that the leader must first look inside and lead from the heart. A common vision must begin with the administration and be valued by everyone in the learning community. The same clear vision must be held throughout by members of the school board, administrative staff, faculty, office support staff, and the bus drivers and custodians. When the school leader is passionate about a vision, everyone else will be more likely to embrace it. There cannot be any hesitation or the vision will only be rhetoric.

The vision in education today must encompass a single purpose: excellence focusing on high standards for all students. Today's vision must be based on the belief that all children can learn in one system of education where each child's strengths are recognized and developed by differentiating instruction. Seeing individual differences as strengths is a key part of creating a powerful vision.

Once formed, the vision becomes the theme for the learning community. When asked what could be worse that not being able to see, Helen Keller responded, "Being able to see and having no vision."

MISSION STATEMENT

The leader's vision forms the basis for the **Mission Statement**, the purpose of the school. Many schools districts already have one, of course. Is it prominently displayed? Does everyone know what it is? Does the mission statement reflect a common purpose? Does it reflect a belief in educating all students?

Sometimes individuals who are no longer present may have composed a mission statement that is still in place. If the vision has changed, it may be time to revise or create a new mission statement, one that reflects today's vision.

People will support that which they help to create.

–Mary Kay Ash

Creating a new mission statement can involve a process of putting the vision into words by a group representing all aspects of the community. It can involve teachers, parents, students, support staff, community members at large, as well as the administration.

Those who create the mission statement will have a higher stake in making it come to life on a daily basis. When the mission statement comes from the top down, the "buy in" can be difficult at best. Instead, time spent together on the task builds camaraderie and teamwork. It puts everyone on the same page, quite literally.

Displaying the mission statement in a prominent location in the school, including it in all handbooks, asking students to learn it and discuss it will ensure that the mission statement moves beyond rhetoric. It becomes the framework for the decision-making process in the school.

VISIBILITY

"Face time" is a popular phrase today in our technical world. An administrator's physical presence in classrooms, in hallways and at school events provides support and leadership for the entire learning community. This presence also gives the administrator a clear understanding of what it takes to teach in today's classroom, and gives the administrator closer contact with the student body.

5-ON-5

A middle school principal described an excellent and highly practical strategy to increase visibility and help administrators visit classrooms on a regular basis. It is called **5-on-5**. Here is how it works. Every day, the principal commits to visiting *five* classrooms for *five* minutes each. The purpose is never to evaluate staff; it is simply to get a snapshot view of what is happening in the school on a daily basis. Those five minutes on a given day may represent the best five minutes or the worst five minutes in those five classrooms. That is reality. Over time, a composite picture emerges.

This principal told me this commitment is extremely important to her.

I will excuse myself from a meeting if it conflicts with 5-on-5. When I walk into the classroom, I participate. I never sit in the back. If students are working, I walk around and see what they are doing. I might sit in on a cooperative group and join the discussion. I may just stand off to the side and listen. I'm in each room for just five minutes. By now, everyone is used to seeing me and I feel much more a part of our school. 5-on-5 has helped me get to know the students, my staff and the curriculum.

THE RED JACKET

Visibility differs from *visitation* in that it is not about mentoring and more about being seen. *Visibility* is about being a presence throughout the school and not a fixture in the office. It is about ease and comfort level on the parts of the principal, staff and students.

A principal in one high school chose a way to increase his visibility and promote school spirit at the same time.

The school colors were red and white. The principal, James Ruth, was famous for his red blazer, white shirt and striped tie. It became his daily uniform. He cruised the halls every morning before school, smiling and greeting students by name. He could be spotted at school events in his signature red sweater or red jacket. The first question alumni asked was always the same, "Does he still wear the red blazer?" The second question was, "Does he still call everyone by name?" The answer to both was yes. He was highly visible for all 17 years in his role as leader of the school.

PEOPLE FIRST

A principal told me recently that his predecessor was a computer wizard. That individual moved the school forward technologically, but never left the office. The new principal, Ev Nicholson, now leads from a people-centered perspective and is a master of public relations. Currently in his fourth year as principal, he knows all of the students and their families. Every morning he walks the halls as students arrive. Students and staff welcome his frequent classroom visits. His visibility has made a positive difference. This principal truly knows his staff and understands the community.

"I also know my place," he said, "First of all, the secretary really runs the school and is the most important person in the school. The custodian is next in importance. I fit in there somewhere but I'm in at least third place!"

VISITATION

Visitation centers on mentoring staff while taking an active role in the teaching and learning processes in the school.

STAFF DEVELOPMENT

When it comes to staff development, attendance and active participation send an important message to teachers. Too often a principal will arrange an opportunity for staff development but attend the session only briefly.

Afterward, when teachers want to implement strategies and ideas from the session, they cite lack of administrative support. The problem is not actually lack of support as much as lack of understanding because the administrator did not attend the session. A principal who attends every staff development session from start to finish commented, "How can I expect my staff to make changes if I am not aware of what the changes are and what it takes to make the change?"

When administrators and staff members participate in staff development training together, the end result is teamwork. Everyone has a clear understanding of what is required to turn ideas into practice.

REALLOCATING TIME

Many administrators comment that, indeed, they wish that they could participate in staff development but they cannot afford the time. I encourage building principals to make the time a priority. If a topic is valuable enough to *require attendance* by staff members, it should also be of enough value for an administrator to schedule it on a calendar as well.

A staff development chairperson in one school district agreed to take the position only if the principal agreed to attend every session that would be mandatory for staff. His comment to the principal was, "As long as you are there, I will be there. The minute you leave the room, I will follow and that includes times when I am the presenter."

The principal agreed. The message sent to staff was clear: We are a team and this is important to all of us.

KEY MEETINGS

Just as it is critical for administrators to attend staff development, it is also important for the school principal to attend and participate in meetings where decisions need to be made that require administrative support. For example, while most principals cannot and need not attend *every* special education I.E.P. (Individualized Educational Plan) meeting or review, some meetings are particularly challenging.

During these meetings, it would be beneficial for all concerned to have the principal in attendance. Teachers often express a common concern that having the principal there would substantially reduce the time required to make difficult placement decisions and implement the plan for a student with special needs. Without that input, these decisions can span months of the school year resulting in a child lagging further and further behind.

COLLABORATIVE PLANNING SESSIONS

Attending collaborative planning sessions occasionally enables an administrator to experience a crucial aspect of successful inclusion of students with special needs in the classroom. While not every class will be co-taught today, almost every teacher today has students at all ability levels. Through collaborative planning, teachers put their heads together outside the classroom to determine how best to meet the needs of diverse learners inside the classroom. Administrative support is essential in creating this planning time.

MENTORING

Leadership means not giving orders to others but giving of yourself.

–East African proverb

Many of our new teachers are not staying in the field of education. Two-thirds leave within three years. In fact, many of the young teachers whom I meet tell me that teaching is something they plan to do "for a few years." If we are going to attract and retain high-quality teachers, we have to do much in terms of mentoring them, noticing what they do well and encouraging them to make teaching their career.

Administrators can assist by pairing a new teacher with a veteran teacher who will act as a mentor and also take a personal interest in that individual. Visitation by the administrator provides an additional opportunity for mentoring assistance.

A case in point occurred when I visited a middle school and observed a general music class. There were 60 students listed on the roster, which is not uncommon for a required general music course at this level.

All of the students sat in plastic molded chairs on tiers. Lapboards were provided for taking notes. These lapboards were formerly *clipboards* but the metal clips had been removed after students repeatedly snapped them throughout class. What made this situation particularly challenging, though, were the eight students in the class with severe behavior problems.

Classroom management was a major issue. The teacher was new to the school and felt extremely frustrated. No co-teacher had been provided to assist with teaching and behavior management. When I asked whether the principal had observed the class, the teacher responded that an administrator had come once at her request, stayed briefly, and suggested, "Make class more fun."

Visitation, when used correctly, can be the beginning of a problem-solving process. This situation required major changes and several visitation sessions. Unfortunately, neither happened. Had the principal elected to make changes and provide much needed help, the situation could have changed dramatically.

Instead, this young teacher was left to mange on her own. By the time I visited several weeks into the semester, the situation was extremely difficult. My suggestions were the same ones that the principal could have concluded by spending more time in that classroom: address the class makeup, and provide mentoring and technical assistance. But by then, the teacher was seriously questioning whether she would return to teaching the following year. The administrator missed an opportunity to lead when it was needed most.

GOAL SETTING AND ACCOUNTABILITY

He who stops completely before taking the next step
will spend a lifetime standing on one leg.

–Chinese proverb

Just as we encourage students to put their goals in writing, we as adults find it helpful when we formulate and write our goals on paper. One of the roles of the school leader, in conjunction with staff members, is to develop schoolwide goals. These goals are often based on themes for a particular school year and emerge from the needs of students, staff and parents in that community.

In an elementary school, for example, a theme may focus on preventing school failure by targeting the areas of reading and writing skills. The principal and staff may examine examples of students' work and current reading levels, evaluate the lists of sequential competencies in the reading and writing curricula and analyze assessment scores as well as other pertinent data to determine which students need intervention.

The principal and staff together commit to specific attainable goals for students that can be evaluated in a specified amount of time. Everyone is accountable. The focus is on results.

At the secondary level, one of the themes may center on increasing parental involvement in their children's education. Low attendance numbers generated from Open Houses, conferences, postsecondary information sessions and other opportunities for involvement may demonstrate this need.

Many parents of middle and high school students participate in school events less frequently than their elementary counterparts and may assume that their input is neither encouraged nor needed.

One goal may focus on helping parents understand that the school does indeed want and value their input. Soliciting ideas from parents on specific topics through surveys, round-table discussion and focus groups may become an objective of that goal for the year.

Another goal may target increased attendance of parents at student-led conferences, Open

Houses and school functions. A third goal may center on improving communication with parents through monthly newsletters or school Internet sites.

The focus of all goals generated is on results that are measurable and can be sustained in the future.

A goal is a dream with a deadline . . .

PLANNING FOR CHANGE

Disturbers are never popular. Nobody ever really loves an alarm clock in action, no matter how grateful he may have been afterward for its kind services!

–Nellie McClung

Every principal has to build trust with staff members. Developing and maintaining that trust while facilitating a major change can be a challenge. Change is inevitable. We all know it. Still change is difficult and involves many different facets and implications.

In facilitating change, the leader is expecting individuals to function in a way that is different from how they have been functioning over time, perhaps even years. What makes this even more challenging is that several different changes frequently occur in rapid order or simultaneously. The sheer number of changes facing educators today can be daunting.

Adaptable as human beings are and have to be, I sometimes sympathize with the chameleon who had a nervous breakdown on a patchwork quilt.

–John Stephen Strange

I can identify with that chameleon, can you? I included it in *Choosing to Change*, a short video dealing with change, because it is strikes a nerve for many of us. One school district administrator connected with the idea so intensely that she gave each staff member a small, framed picture of a patchwork quilt. Coping with change became the theme for the year.

Two of the major changes in our schools were discussed in "We Are the Village": collaboration and co-teaching. Both represent a significant change in how many of us teach. Planning together and working together as teams offer tremendous opportunities to help our students succeed. Through the sharing of ideas and strategies, teachers and students benefit from the input of other staff members. To make this happen successfully, though, requires strong administrative support.

SCHOOL LEADER AS CHANGE AGENT

The role as change agent is not an easy one for every school principal. In all of the different schools where I have taught, all eight of the principals demonstrated different styles of leadership. All had numerous positive qualities and every one of those principals did a number of things very well. They were all excellent managers who were adept at keeping each school running smoothly.

They were also very different from each other. Because my classroom experience spanned 20 years, I found that some of the differences reflected changes in thinking about leadership over that period of time and, of course, changes in education.

In retrospect, though, one principal stood out from all of the others in a significant way. Only one of the eight principals tackled significant change.

That individual was the least popular with the staff. The other principals relied on maintaining the status quo but this individual came in and "shook things up." Everyone was used to doing things in a certain way. That this individual suddenly made major changes did not sit well. Looking back, she moved the staff forward in a direction that was needed. Unfortunately, she left after three years.

This is not unusual. On a national basis, the current length of time that an administrator stays in one position is just three years. As you are aware, significant change often requires five to seven years.

INVOLVING STAKEHOLDERS IN CHANGE

When people understand the rationale, they can apply a decision and carry it out.

–*Rudolph Giuliani in* Leadership

That principal would have been more effective as a change agent had she enlisted the support of staff by involving those who be directly affected by the change process. She instituted change from a "top-down" approach. People almost always resist change when it is thrust upon them and are often afraid of what is different. Change may be needed but "ownership" is also a key element in the process.

Too often those who will be most affected by the change are not brought along as part of the planning process. Resistance that results is sometimes more a factor of *not knowing* and *not owning* versus real opposition to the change itself. When an ownership approach is used, change can often go much more smoothly.

Let me share an example. Earlier this spring I had a situation in my neighborhood that demonstrates how involving the stakeholders in planning for change can bring about a positive outcome.

I live across the street from a cemetery. It is a large parcel of land, heavily wooded, and only a portion comprises the cemetery. The rest is undeveloped. The woods and wetlands form a natural habitat for area wildlife.

The cemetery has been there since the 1930s and neighbors have always been welcome to enjoy its peace and tranquility. People often walk their dogs or ride their bikes on the small asphalt road that winds around this quiet and beautiful setting.

Imagine the surprise in the neighborhood when every household received a letter from the cemetery committee inviting input before the *New Plan for Development* was submitted to the local city planning commission.

Development! The word sent shock waves through the neighborhood. Phones started ringing. Assumptions were made. Rumors circulated. Neighbors imagined increased traffic, noise and construction. Would every tree be cut? Would the wetlands be filled in for high-density housing? Would the beauty of our neighborhood, as we had known it, disappear? There was a high level of concern as the meeting room filled with neighbors on the designated evening.

The "development," it turned out, was a long-range plan to add a limited number of gravesites and a small mausoleum. The only increased traffic would be for the occasional funeral. The committee wanted neighborhood input on locating future gravesites. No trees would be cut. In fact, a landscaping plan was unveiled to *increase* the woods and *ensure protection* of the wetlands for the future.

The committee asked neighbors where more trees were needed. The architect explained that just as neighbors liked seeing woods from *outside* the cemetery, there was equal concern that the view from the *inside* for visitors and for individuals attending services would also be of trees, not of neighborhood houses.

The meeting quickly became a joint effort on the part of both neighbors and cemetery committee members to plan together for the future. The result was a plan that was submitted to the city without one dissenting comment from a neighbor.

If the cemetery committee had decided to skip the initial meeting inviting neighborhood input, it is likely that there would have been immediate resistance. Many neighbors would have arrived at City Hall resisting any change before knowing what was entailed. At the very least, community relations would have suffered and the procedure would have been lengthened.

PLANNING IS CRITICAL

Two key factors made a difference in that situation that are equally important in the school setting. *Complete information* was provided and it was provided *early.* Any change will go more smoothly when all the necessary information has been provided early enough to enable everyone affected to think it through and make adequate plans.

In co-teaching situations, for example, teachers need class lists and informal planning time several weeks before school begins. Planning adequately for the co-taught classroom requires both time and information. This takes strong administrative support to occur. Too often this information comes only days before students arrive. In fact, one of the biggest concerns teachers express about co-teaching is lack of complete information provided early enough so that the team can plan for students. The result is high frustration, a low level of trust, and a feeling that co-teaching will not work successfully.

KEY QUESTIONS

> *The problem is not to suppress change, which cannot be done,*
> *but to manage it.*
>
> *–Alvin Toffler*

Change goes more smoothly when three critical issues have been addressed.

1. *Can it be accomplished?*

    In some schools where I visit, I discover that an enormous change is being undertaken "in one fell swoop." The entire school, for example, is going to try co-teaching, starting in September. The personnel required to do so on the large scale planned simply is not in place. Obstacles are inevitable because the magnitude of the change does not fit with reality. Any situation similar to this one is set up for failure.

    The administrator's role is to determine what is possible. In the co-teaching example, it may best to "start small" beginning with just one or two co-taught classes and increasing the schedule only after determining that more would be feasible.

2. *Write your goals in pencil.*

    Several key questions center on evaluation and results. Is the change successful? Does it accomplish what was intended? What are the results? Are they positive? Should more changes be made? How and what? The administrator is crucial to evaluating the success of any major change that has been made.

    The old saying, "Write your goals in pencil" certainly applies here. Mid-year, mid-semester, mid-quarter, or mid-week, it may be necessary to take a good look and make some revisions. Only if the results are successful does it make sense to continue in the future.

3. *Can the change be continued?*

    Some changes are part of a pilot program. Just when the system is running smoothly, it ends for any number of reasons. Funding ends. A grant is denied. Key people leave, are transferred or take on other roles. It cannot be continued on a larger scale.

Returning to the example of co-teaching, this is a frequent occurrence. Two teachers co-teach all day long for a year on a pilot program. They see tremendous gains in their students' performance. Students experience success. Parents are elated. Teachers are eager to move forward. Those involved expect that it will continue as it is.

The program expands the following year despite a lack of adequate funding and without additional staff. The original team that was successful in attaining excellent results is now able to co-teach just one class together or perhaps none at all. Several additional classes were added to the co-teacher's schedule. Arranging planning time now with five other teachers becomes challenging and complex. With some of the teachers involved, no collaborative planning time is available.

Teachers involved express much less satisfaction with the change that has been made. One program was promised and something altogether different was delivered. From the outset, the impact of program expansion was not adequately explained and planning for it was non-existent.

O—x KEY IDEA

The administrator is a key player in the success of this change and in any change of this magnitude. The change process can be summarized in six components:

1. Involve those who will be affected from the beginning.

2. Plan ahead.

3. Start early.

4. Inform completely.

5. Set realistic expectations.

6. Evaluate the results.

COMMUNICATION

One of the strongest traits of an effective leader is the ability to communicate. Sometimes the best way to communicate is not to speak but to listen. However, there is an enormous difference between giving the *appearance of listening* and *truly hearing* the essence of what a speaker is trying to communicate.

A common concern expressed by staff members is that an administrator "does not listen." The message sent by teachers was going nowhere.

LISTEN = SILENT

Two words, *listen* and *silent*, have identical letters, just in a different order. They can be worlds apart when it comes to hearing a message. Listening is, after all, a two-way street. Real listening involves an inner silence that enables the message to be assimilated and processed. This is what the staff members wanted. They wanted the administrator to be silent inside and out so that the individual could truly listen to the message. Instead, the listener appeared to be listening but was actually thinking through what to say next.

RESPONSIVENESS AND CONVERSATION

"We never hear back" is a frequent concern expressed by staff members. An effective leader responds to the actual question promptly and in a way that is appropriate. Beyond basic responding is real dialogue. Communication occurs when a conversation takes place in the form of a true exchange of thoughts and ideas. Just as collaboration between teachers works so effectively as a planning tool because it involves conversation and sharing expertise, ongoing conversation must occur between administration and staff to exchange ideas.

TOO MUCH INFORMATION

> *We are drowning in information, but starved for knowledge.*
>
> –John Naisbitt

While responsiveness in communication is a concern, too much communication has also become an issue in many schools. A tool that most of us use today is e-mail. It has tremendous strengths but it also has limitations, including overuse. One teacher noted, "We want good communication but we receive several e-mails a day from the office. Because e-mail is so easy to send, we are getting too many that are too long with too many attachments. Dealing with the volume is time-consuming and inefficient."

It can be too much of a good thing when inundated with information that is neither critical nor pertinent. The same can be said of memos. However, when information can be abbreviated, does not require discussion and can be disseminated by e-mail instead of a staff meeting, teachers view it as an effective tool. Sometimes there is no substitute for *face-to-face* discussion and no form of written communication can replace that.

EMPOWERMENT OF STAFF

You can accomplish a lot in the world if you don't care who gets the credit.

–Myles Horton

When I am consulting, I am sometimes asked by administrators in a school to find out what teachers' strengths and weaknesses are. My response is always the same. "Ask them. They know. Empower them."

A strong leader can also follow. Teachers have excellent ideas. They spend every day in classrooms with students. Often they are in the best position to suggest ideas. Confident leaders know that *ideas can lead*. When we put ideas first and keep adult egos out of the way, we move toward excellence.

THE IDEA BOX

The concept of an **Idea Box** is not a new one. **Idea Boxes** are everywhere from the local bank to the counter at the drycleaners. An excellent location for an **Idea Box** in school is the main office. Encouraging its use and seriously considering suggestions made is another way of empowering teachers. Change can be initiated at any level. The **Idea Box** is a concrete strategy for inviting the exchange of thoughts, ideas and solutions. The solutions generated create opportunities for the leader to become the follower and the followers to become leaders.

To stimulate suggestions, consider posting questions near the **Idea Box**:

> How can we decrease the interruptions during the school day by announcements?
>
> How can we have fewer but better staff meetings?
>
> What ideas do you have for staff development?
>
> How can we encourage more parent participation?
>
> How can we empower parents in the education of their children?
>
> What changes in the school calendar or school day would create a better learning environment for students?

THE LEADERSHIP TEAM

Learn from the mistakes of others; you can't live long enough to make them all yourself.

–Eleanor Roosevelt

We can learn so much from each other provided we give others the chance to teach us. In the last few years, I have had an opportunity to meet several teachers for whom teaching is now a second career. These are often people aged 40 to mid-50s who have worked in the private sector for many years and are new to the field of education.

I always ask about their new experiences and perceptions of education. A comment that I hear frequently has to do with empowerment. A former businessman said, "I have a lot of experience that could be tapped. There was a hierarchy in business but we did a lot of work in groups and teams. The amount of red tape and the rigid hierarchy in education has been a big surprise to me."

Teachers want administrative support but they also want to be empowered and to act as part of the leadership team. Recently I was consulting with a school district that was working on a school improvement plan. My first suggestion to the leadership committee on school improvement was to add teachers to the team. The idea of focusing on long-term goals for the district without input from the teaching staff meant missing out on critical expertise and an opportunity to empower staff members.

RECOGNITION OF OTHERS

The credit goes to those who are actually in the arena . . .

–Theodore Roosevelt

A significant role of an effective leader is recognizing the valuable contributions made by others on a daily basis. Let me share an example of a leader in the private sector whose recognition of others is remarkable in its simplicity but almost incredible in its impact.

I have a friend who owns several local hair salons that are part of a national chain. For the last seven years, Mary Lou has always had the top four producing salons out of a total of over 1,800 salons. That represents a lot of haircuts!

You might wonder how she does it. I don't think that hair grows any faster near her salons. Other salons are located in areas of greater density, so population has nothing to with her success. Location is important but it is unlikely that Mary Lou has the four best locations in the country.

The critical difference is her focus on personal recognition. Mary Lou is both a tremendous motivator and a strong leader. She understands the needs of her staff and operates from the premise that people want to do their best.

I have noticed four strategies that she uses on an ongoing basis that focus on personal recognition.

1. Creating a Relationship
2. Showing Appreciation
3. Consistency
4. Involving Staff in Decision-Making

CREATING A RELATIONSHIP

Mary Lou creates a relationship with her staff members. She takes the time to get to know everyone. If you looked in her briefcase, you would always find a box of greeting cards because remembering birthdays, sending a card when someone is ill and providing written encouragement are extremely important to her. She cares deeply about her staff and her actions show it. In an industry where turnover is high, hers is low.

SHOWING APPRECIATION

This leader is quick to notice excellent work and makes a point of immediately giving positive feedback. She is known for the personal notes that she writes thanking staff members for exceptional work. Occasionally, Mary Lou provides tangible rewards such as movie passes or gift certificates to local stores and restaurants. She continuously tells her staff how much she appreciates them and gives credit for success to the people who are "in the arena." During the holidays, she has never missed a party for staff at each of her salons.

CONSISTENCY

Consistency is an essential aspect of recognition. There are no surprises. Mary Lou's employees would tell you two things. First, she is predictable and consistent in her expectations. Second, she is equally predictable and consistent in her praise and recognition. Consistency makes an enormous difference in creating a positive work environment.

INVOLVING STAFF IN DECISION-MAKING AND TRAINING

A final aspect of personal recognition comes from valuing the talents of staff members by involving them directly in the decision-making process. Mary Lou's employees play an integral role in planning for store promotions and quarterly competitions with other hair salons. Staff input counts.

Providing ongoing training to develop personal skills is another way that she empowers staff members. When Mary Lou hires someone, it is because she sees that person's potential. Her goals are to help that individual grow professionally and provide an opportunity for advancement. She has even helped some of her employees become salon owners themselves.

There is no question that Mary Lou is a good businessperson. There is no question that she delivers a good product because the same customers come back again and again. What makes the critical difference is Mary Lou's ability to connect with her staff and lead them to their personal best.

School leaders and business leaders can learn much from each other. Education is different from the private sector in many ways but the leadership privilege is the same. Leaders in both arenas are dealing with people who share the same need to be recognized and treated with respect.

It is not magic. It is based on celebrating the value of each person and encouraging each individual to strive for excellence. It creates the same atmosphere we want to create for our students—an atmosphere of excellence in which everyone is valued, everyone is respected and everyone belongs.

7 STRATEGIES FOR CELEBRATING SUCCESS

Celebrating success fosters more success. It encourages optimism and hope. Despite the inevitable setbacks, administrators and staff members must focus on the positive and maintain an upbeat perspective.

60 SECONDS OF SUCCESS

A staff meeting can provide an opportunity for a principal to focus on **60 Seconds of Success**. As the meeting begins, one minute is devoted to celebrating any of a myriad of daily success stories in a school. What is going right in that school? The focus may be on improved assessment results, successful collaborative efforts by a team, a positive anecdote involving a student, excellent work of a teacher or gratitude expressed to a volunteer.

The short celebration is not contrived or artificial. It is simply a way of reminding everyone to focus on the positive. Budget cuts and other factors that seem beyond control can leave staff members feeling overwhelmed and not able to see the proverbial light at the end of the tunnel. It is easy for everyone shift into a negative mode that is so destructive to morale.

Despite the difficulties faced by every staff and administration, obviously many good things are happening in every school. Taking just one minute to highlight **60 Seconds of Success** can have a tremendous impact on the tone of the agenda and the ensuing discussion during the meeting.

WHO HAS SOMETHING TO CELEBRATE?

One principal I know uses a different approach. He begins each staff meeting or staff development session with this question, "Who has something to celebrate?" Sometimes someone has major personal news to share such as a wedding engagement. More often, it might be day-to-day good news from suggesting a good movie to sharing plans for a summer trip.

There is always applause and often laughter as faculty members call out a few news items to celebrate. The day that I was there for staff development, someone mentioned that a student finally turned in a paper on time and everyone cheered.

PRICKLES AND PEACHES

Here is one more idea with a slightly different twist for revitalizing staff meetings. A teacher mentioned that in her elementary school, people arrived at mandatory staff meetings with a negative attitude. "Gripe sessions" rather than conversation and sharing of ideas had become the norm. Morale was low.

In an effort to change this, the principal tried a different approach as a new school year began. It was called **Prickles and Peaches**. The strategy was simple. The first two minutes of the meeting were open for anyone who wanted to vent briefly about a frustrating situation, a *prickle*. Then anyone who wanted to celebrate a success, a *peach*, had a chance to do so.

At first, the teacher who described the concept admitted rolling her eyes thinking, "This will never work!"

It did. **Prickles and Peaches** changed the tone of the staff meetings. By the time I met the teacher in January, she said, "Now everyone actually looks forward to staff meetings. People save funny stories and somehow, talking about the Prickles puts those situations in perspective. Some helpful ideas have also come out of this. Somebody will describe a Prickle and someone else will suggest a solution. It's been great!"

THE 6-SECOND COMPLIMENT

Any parent of a teenage daughter can appreciate the "compliment" a friend of mine received recently from her 14-year-old. The mother was in the car on one of countless trips chauffeuring her daughter to or from school, a friend's house, an activity or sport when her daughter said, "Mom, I just have to tell you. All my friends think you are SO AWESOME! All my friends think you are THE BEST!"

My friend nearly drove off the road she was so pleased—until a few moments later when her daughter added, "But frankly, Mom, I just don't see it."

Thud! The child giveth and the child taketh away . . . As the parent lamented, "If only she had quit while we were all ahead . . ." That explains why parents of teenagers need an occasional kind word from other people. Research on giving compliments shows that the average compliment takes just six seconds. So often we *think it,* but we do not *give it.*

I have had the privilege of meeting so many master teachers, teachers who truly are superb, who are making a positive difference in the lives of the children they teach. These same teachers will tell me that they do not receive compliments or positive feedback from administrators.

Yet when I sit down with their principals, I hear glowing comments about the staff, "My teachers are excellent! I am so fortunate to have such a wonderful staff! I am very proud of them!"

If you are an administrator, tell your staff. Tell them what a great job they are doing. Tell them often. Tell students. Tell others. Tell the community. Everyone needs compliments, praise, recognition and rewards. When you look at stress scales and what produces the most stress, "lack of recognition" is often cited at the top of the list just behind "death of a spouse" and "fear of public speaking."

To bring out the best in people, any leader can focus on this need for positive feedback. It instills confidence by believing in others and helping them believe in themselves. Through honest, positive feedback, each of us will exceed expectations and achieve more than we dreamed possible.

The fragrance always remains in the hand that gives the rose.

–Gandhi

THE GRATITUDE BOOK

The staff at one middle school found that the teachers' lounge had become a place not to relax and unwind for a few minutes but a location where too many people talked about what wasn't going right. As one teacher said, "If you were in a good mood going into the lounge, it was a sure bet that you wouldn't be by the time you left!"

Someone proposed the idea of a **Gratitude Book**. The concept was simple. A blank journal would be placed on one of the tables. The purpose was to create a place to write about what was going well in education, in that school, in a specific teacher's classroom. The **Gratitude Book**, combined with a commitment to make the teachers' lounge a gripe free zone, made a significant difference in morale. Any administrator can implement this simple strategy in any elementary school, middle school or high school.

CELEBRATE THE WORKER BEES

The New York Times newspaper featured a study in July 2002 in which a researcher found that front-desk staff at luxury hotels valued and wanted compliments from top management more than $20 tips from customers. They were the hard workers who were doing their jobs consistently and well.

In schools, the $20 tip is certainly not an option but the principal can do much to celebrate the day-to-day dedication of staff members. One of the privileges of leadership is to recognize ability and reward it. The individual who is quietly doing an excellent job, the dependable hard worker needs support and recognition as much as the person who is always out in front, always noticed, and always rewarded.

WRITTEN ROUND OF APPLAUSE

In "Inner Strength, Outer Confidence," a simple strategy for affirming students is called the **Written Round of Applause**. Not only is this brief written compliment beneficial for children, the same format can be used with adults. The nice thing about a sincere compliment *in writing* is that it can be saved to read over and over. Copy the reproducible form provided in the **Backscratchers** section of "Inner Strength, Outer Confidence" to make sending a **Written Round of Applause** immediate and effortless.

SUMMARY

The leadership privilege is all about learning to lead and learning to follow. There is a place for both in our schools today. Leadership is a two-way street. Administrators are in a position to energize the staff by creating and believing in a vision of what teaching and learning mean in that community.

Ten leadership traits, roles and responsibilities were suggested in "The Leadership Privilege." Many administrators would say that their role encompasses all of these and more. I would agree. These represent some of the most critical attributes needed for effective school leadership.

They are not intended to increase the workload or increase the number of hours an administrator works. Instead, these traits, roles and responsibilities are intended to encourage administrators to readjust to some degree how time is spent and how priorities are determined. Rethinking these areas may allow a principal to delegate some tasks creating more time for crucial aspects of the leadership role rather than less.

The leader of the future will be a person who can lead and follow . . .
be individualistic and a team player, and above all,
be a perpetual learner.

–Edgar Schein

*"We are now at a point where we must educate
our children in what no one knew yesterday
and prepare our schools for what
no one knows yet."*

–Margaret Mead

Announcing Linda Tilton's new book

THE TEACHER'S TOOLBOX FOR DIFFERENTIATING INSTRUCTION

700 Strategies, Tips, Tools and Techniques

You'll find over 700 highly practical "take back and use" ideas **All in One Place!**

Enhance your curriculum and help every student succeed as you differentiate instruction for all learners.

- For Educators K–12
- Includes 40 reproducible pages

"Linda Tilton is the Merlin of Motivation. She goes right for your head and gets right to your heart. Fasten your seatbelt!"
    –Harvey Mackay, author of
        The New York Times Best Sellers,
        Swim With the Sharks and *Pushing the Envelope*

"If my students had learned these organizational strategies before beginning middle school, seventh grade would have gone much more smoothly."
    –Lisa Duncan, English Teacher

"Teachers will love this! There are so many practical ideas that I can use with my students right away!"
    –Eric Cavanaugh, Fourth Grade Teacher

"Every single strategy is one that I have used successfully or is one that another teacher has enthusiastically endorsed!"
    –Linda Tilton, Author

How to Help All Students:

- Get Organized
- Be Accountable for Results
- Compensate for Difficulties
- Review Content
- Study Effectively
- Improve Reading and Writing
- Increase Math Skills
- Work in a Group
- Focus on Positive Behavior
- Build Self-Confidence

PLUS

- Tips and Tools For Effective Co-Teaching
- Strategies for Administrative Support

About the Author:

Linda Tilton has over 30 years of experience in the field of education. She has taught at the elementary, middle and high school levels. Currently she consults in classrooms and provides staff development nationally.

see reverse for ordering information

The Teacher's Toolbox for Differentiating Instruction:
700 Strategies, Tips, Tools and Techniques

448 Pages of Practical Ideas!

8.5 x 11 inches   448 pages   paperback
ISBN 0-9653529-7-8
$39.95 U.S. plus shipping
quantity discounts available

Order Toll Free: 1-888-LEARN-11

Also available from Covington Cove Publications:

Inclusion: A Fresh Look
Practical Strategies to Help
All Students Succeed

by Linda Tilton

224 pages of practical, proven ideas
to use immediately. For all school staff
working with students who struggle.

8.5 x 11 inches paperback
$29.95   ISBN 0-9653529-5-1

Covington Cove Publications
5620 Covington Road
Shorewood, MN 55331

Questions? Please call: 952-470-0297
FAX: 952-470-8768
Order Toll Free: 1-888-LEARN-11
E-mail: lindtilton@AOL.com
Web: www.LindaTilton.com

Choosing to Change Video:
Quotations to Inspire Action

by Linda Tilton

Quotes, photographs, music to
motivate, inspire, energize.

VHS Approx. 6 minutes
$29.95   ISBN 0-9653529-6-X

To contact Linda Tilton for Staff Development, call 1-888-LEARN-11

- -

Order Form (mail or fax)

Name _____

School _____

Address _____

City _____ State ____ Zip _____

Check # or P.O. # _____

to Covington Cove Publications
5620 Covington Road
Shorewood, MN 55331
FAX: 952-470-8768

Shipping charges:

First Item $6.00
Each additional item $2.00
Call for discounted shipping on large orders

Title	Price	Qty.	Amount
The Teacher's Toolbox for Differentiating Instruction	$39.95		
Inclusion: A Fresh Look	$29.95		
Choosing to Change Video	$29.95		
Subtotal			
MN Residents add 6.5% tax			
Shipping/Handling			
TOTAL			